Spiral Breath

Activating Higher Consciousness, Healing and the Glia Brain

GAYLE MACK, NMD, DBE, Rev

Spiral Breath:
Activating Higher Consciousness, Healing and the Glia Brain

© 2020 Gayle Mack. All rights reserved.

No part of this book may be reproduced or transmitted in any form or by any means, electronic or mechanical, including but not limited to: photocopying, recording, or by any information storage retrieval system without the written permission of the publisher, except for the inclusion of brief quotations in a review.

Cover and Interior Layout: Kendra Cagle (www.5LakesDesign.com)

ISBN: 978-0-578-63946-8

Gayle Mack, NMD, DBE, Rev
www.keystoascension.com

Disclaimer:
The information in this book is for personal enlightenment. It is not meant to treat, diagnose or be a substitute for professional medical advise. Though it is presented in good faith, neither the author nor the publisher can assume responsibility or liability for any results, direct or consequential, from the experiment or practical application of this information.

Dedication:

This book is dedicated to my mother and best friend, Theresa "Terri" Mack, who taught me through example to be strong, yet loving, generous and compassionate, to speak my truth and persevere through times of difficulty. She always believes in me and what I do—even when she does not understand it.

Thank you for being my Mom!

Also, to my grandparents, Frank and Mary Kuncz, who recognized my "openness" and schooled me in the ways of nature and family traditions.

Acknowledgements:

With Deepest Love and Gratitude...

I have been blessed with extraordinary friendships, teachers and role models, whose participation in my life helped culminate an amazing life journey and this book. I would be remiss if I did not acknowledge them, as well.

A very special *Thank You* goes to Mary Hardy for being an excellent example of "Trust" in God and the Elders of the Planet. Thank you for teaching me the Holy Grail Vortex and standing with me through our many profound journey's of shifting energy for the Greatest and Highest Good. Thank you for the Temple of Sakkara, the Sisterhood of the Emerald Fire, introducing me to Young Living Essential Oils and for sharing your wisdom, generosity and love. To Dean Hardy, Thank You for pseudo-adopting me as your daughter.

Thank you, Gandalf for introducing me to the Glia Brain. Great appreciation goes to R. Douglas Fields, Ph.D. for your very comprehensive book *The Other Brain: The Scientific Breakthroughs That Will Heal Our Brains and Revolutionize Our Health*. Gratitude also, to the trail blazers of science, spirituality and the glia brain - Thank you all!

Thank you, Gerda and Tobi Dobler, for opening your hearts, friendship and your hospitality to me. And for sharing your beautiful piece of Rennes le Chateau.

Blessings and tremendous Gratitude to D. Gary Young, David Stewart, Ph.D., D.N.M, Lady Olivia Robertson, founder of the Fellowship of Isis, Marsharee Chastain, Deena Buta, Jennifer (Jenni) Priestly, Margaret Starbird, Dr. Zenia Richler, Molly Robe, Pat Wheeler, Mel Motley, Jeffrey Kenney, L. Ac., Glenn Kaplan, PA-C., Dr. George Coroneos, D.C., Dr. Rick Bloom, D.C., Dr. Chad Edward, ND/NMD and to Steve Valdeck for helping with my illustrations.

Everyone I meet is a blessing and adds to my journey. For each of you,
I am sincerely Grateful!

Table of Contents:

Acknowledgments...i
List of Figures..vii
Note from the Author..ix

Chapter One: Receiving the Gift of the Spiral Breath 1
Chapter Two: The Full Experience of the Spiral Breath 11
Chapter Three: Complete and Purposeful Breathing 17
Chapter Four: Cellular Memory Flush 25
Chapter Five: The Limbic System 35
    1. Amygdala...38
    2. Olfactory Bulbs..42
    3. Hippocampus...45
    4. Thalamus..48
    5. Hypothalamus..49
    6. Pituitary...53
    7. Pineal..57
        a. *Spiritual Aspects*.................................63
        b. *Harmful EMF Fields and our Pineal* 68
        c. *Fluoride*...72
        d. *Frequency Activation and Decalcification*.........75
        e. *Pineal - The Place of God's Light* 77
        a. *Pineal Symbology in the Arts*.....................80
    8. Brainstem...83
        a. *Sistine Chapel*...................................90
    9. The Eye of Horus 93
    10. Vesica Piscis..94
        a. *Flower of Life* 97
        b. *Torus / Toroidal Field* 100
Chapter Six: The Glia Brain 113
    1. Schwann Cells..118
    2. Microglia 119
    3. Oligodendrocytes.......................................119
    4. Astrocytes...120
    5. Fractals, DNA and Glia Connection to Body, Mind and Spirit 125

Chapter Seven: Emotions 135
1. Thoughts are Energy 141
2. Changing Our Perception..143
3. Courage...149
4. Forgiveness..154
   a. Forgive as IF You Have Forgotten..........................154
5. Gratitude..157
6. Inner Peace..163
7. Be Vigilant 167

Chapter Eight: Chakras and Associated Energies...................................171
1. Ida, Pingala, Sushumna, Prana Tube and Kundalini................176
2. Thousand Petal Lotus..180
3. The Tailbone, Sacrum and Cerebrospinal Fluid....................183
4. Root Lock and the Thousand Petal Lotus 184
5. The Chakras - Attributes and Harmonizers 186
6. Dowsing and Chakras 194
7. Creating Sacred Space 198

Chapter Nine: Color / Sound / Frequency / Sacred Geometry 207
1. Color 207
2. Sound 211
3. 432 and Gematria..217
4. The Number 153...218
5. Solfeggio Tone..220
6. Iso-Principle...225
7. Entrainment..225
8. Brain Waves and Binaural Beats 229
   a. Beta Brain Waves..232
   b. Alpha Brain Waves 233
   c. Theta Brain Waves 235
   d. Delta Brain Waves...240
   e. Gamma Brain Waves 241
   f. Binaural Beats 243

Chapter Ten: Tachyon and Energy 249
1. Subtle Organizing Energy Fields...............................249
2. Zero-Point-Energy..249
3. Absolute Zero 250
4. Tachyon Energy 250
5. 7 Principles of Hermetic Laws................................251

Chapter Eleven: Incorporating Pure Essential Oils 263
    1. Essential Oils for Higher Consciousness.........................275
    2. Anointing..277
    3. Therapeutae..279

Chapter Twelve: Spiral Breath Technique Instructional...........................283

Chapter Thirteen: Spiral Breath (Expanded Versions) 291
    1. Adding the Root Lock...291
    2. Emotional Balance and Harmony................................293
    3. Spinning Your Merkaba 294
        a. *Guided Instructions to Empower Your Merkaba*...............298

Chapter Fourteen: There Where Is The 'Nous'....................................307

Summary..313
GRAS List for Pure Essential Oils 315
Glossary...317
Resources..329
About the Author...331
Index..337

List of Figures:

1.1 *Spiral Breath* Original Illustration by Gayle Mack
2.1 *Spiral Breath* Illustration by Gayle Mack
4.1 *Spiral Breath* Illustration by Gayle Mack
5.1 The Limbic System Blausen.com staff (2014). "Medical gallery of Blausen Medical 2014". WikiJournal of Medicine 1
5.2 *Amygdala* Images generated by Life Science Databases
5.3 *Olfactory Bulb* by Patrick J. Lynch, medical illustrator
5.4 *Hippocampus and Seahorse* by Professor Laszlo Seress derivative work: Anthonyhcole
5.5 *Thalamus* Images by Life Science Databases
5.6 *Hypothalamus* Images by Life Science Databases
5.7 *Pituitary* Images by Life Science Databases
5.8 *Pineal* Images by Life Science Databases
5.9 *Pigna sculpture in the Court of the Pine Cone*, Vatican courtyard photo by Lalupa
5.10 *The Temple of Angkor Wat, Cambodia* photo by Diego Delso
5.11 Kizhi Pogost, Russia Church of Transfiguration of Our Saviour photo by Elena Yurova
5.12 *Brain Stem* Illustration y Patrick J. Lynch
5.13 *Michelangelo's Separation of Light From Darkness in the Sistine Chapel* The Yorck Project
5.14 *Michelangelo Neuroanatomy* by Ian Suk and Rafael Tamargo
5.15 *Limbic System and Eye of Horus* graphic by Steve Valdeck (Limbic System of human brain by John A. Beal)
5.16 By Jon Bodsworth - http://www.egyptarchive.co.uk/html/cairo_museum_47.html, Copyrighted free use, https://commons.wikimedia.org/w/index.php?curid=4422291
5.17 *Vesica Piscis* graphic by Steve Valdeck
5.18 *Vesica Piscis with Equilateral Triangles* graphic by Steve Valdeck
5.19 *Vesica Piscis Fish* graphic by Steve Valdeck
5.20 *Seed of Life* graphic by Steve Valdeck
5.21 *Flower of Life* graphic by Steve Valdeck
5.22 *Metatron's Cube within the Seed of Life* graphic by Steve Valdeck
5.23 Weisstein, Eric W. "Spindle Torus." From MathWorld-A Wolfram Web Resource. http://mathworld.wolfram.com/SpindleTorus.html
6.1 *Glia Cells* drawing by Santiago Ramón y Cajal using the Golgi stain
6.2 *Glial Cells* Creating Connections and Protection illustration by Gayle Mack
8.1 *Chakras* CGI by Pan Czakry.png

8.2	Tube Torus - Seed of Life By Daniel M. Short (Own work (Original text: Self-made)) [CC BY-SA 3.0 (http://creativecommons.org/licenses/by-sa/3.0)], via Wikimedia Commons
9.1	*Sir Isaac Newton's Circle Color Chart from Opticks*[1]
9.2	*Triangle of Numbers graphic* by Steve Valdeck
9.3	Temple of Sakkara Egypt[2]
9.4	Tuning dimensions in Sakkara Pyramid chamber courtesy of Mary Hardy
9:5	In Phase - Out of Phase wave forms graphic by Steve Valdeck
12.1	*Spiral Breath* Illustration by Gayle Mack
13.1	*Merkaba Body* Illustration by Gayle Mack
13.2	*Orbs in the Unified Field of Love* - ASD 2014 (American Society of Dowsers) Gayle Mack (center) with Jeffery & Kris Gregory. Picture by Gary Allen
13.3	Merkaba graphic by Steve Valdeck

Glossary 1 By 克劳棣 - Own work, CC BY-SA 4.0, https://commons.wikimedia.org/w/index.php?curid=38708516

---

[1] *Opticks - A Treatise of the Reflections, Refractions, Inflections and Colours of Light* written by Sir Isaac Newton http://www.gutenberg.org/files/33504/33504-h/33504-h.htm[7/9/12 9:44:47 AM] The Project Gutenberg eBook of Op-ticks:, by Sir Isaac Newton, Knt.

[2] http://www.francescoraffaele.com/egypt/hesyra/new/ntrykht1.jpg

Note from the Author:

To my joyful surprise, in my search to heal my head injury, I discovered a way to reactive my Light Body and increase my overall vibrational frequency.

Having experienced becoming my Light Body on multiple occasions, I have searched for ways to access that 'State of Being' at will and not just when I am at a sacred site or in High Ceremony.

I believe that our 'Light Body' IS our '*original*' State of Being and we are remembering how to return to it and access it fully.

My third dimensional self had to understand how I became light, so I could explain it. Once I could explain it, then I could share the ability; enabling others to experience this magnificent state of being 'Light.' Just saying that I moved into a state of Unconditional Love isn't enough. Through my channeled wisdom, research and life's experiences, the pieces have come together. Receiving the Spiral Breath technique gave me a way to heal my injury, as well as, achieve that higher State of Being and explain it.

As a spiritual channeler, the majority of the channeled messages that I receive from Divine, Divine Mother and the Mary's are guidance to help us transition into Divine Unconditional Love and Ascension through our spiritual, physical, mental and emotional bodies. They (collectively) teach that achieving our Light Body can be done by holding the resonance of Unconditional Love with every thought, every action, every step and every breath. It sounds so simple.

Several years ago, I heard about the Glia Brain from my friend Gandalf. To my core of being, I know that the Glia Brain and Glia cells are a major key in achieving multidimensionality and ascension. It was difficult to research the Glia Brain because there was not much in print about it. Then information began to surface. R. Douglas Fields, Ph.D. released his very comprehensive book *The Other Brain: The Scientific Breakthroughs That Will Heal Our Brains and Revolutionize Our Health*. Now I had science and wording to back up what I intuitively knew.

During a meditation, I received a breathing technique to assist in healing my brain injury. It turned out that it also activated my glia brain and limbic system. I had put together a presentation on activating the Glia Brain for Higher Consciousness using the techniques that I received during my channeled messages from Divine and the Mary's, along with Gandalf's teachings and the technical information from *The Other Brain* and various research documents.

Shortly after completing this presentation, I was asked to speak on Mary Magdalene and the Glia Brain at the American Society of Dowsers.

In sacred space I asked the Magdalene for guidance as to the direction of my presentation. She guided me to re-read her Gospel. As I read through the pages, my Glia Brain presentation and my Spiral Breath technique overlaid the teachings within the Magdalene's gospels.

GOSPEL OF MARY MAGDALENE PAGE 10:

> "There where is the nous, lies the treasure."
>
> Then I said to him: "Lord, when someone meets you in a Moment of vision, is it through the soul [psyche] that they see, or is it through the Spirit [Pneuma]?"
>
> The Teacher answered: "It is neither through the soul nor the spirit, but through the nous between the two which sees the vision…"

The "nous" (pronounced noose) is important and it is the foundation of the teachings in this book. Mary Magdalene began to guide my thoughts and connect the dots. Divine wisdom, knowledge and comprehension came together for me in a swirl of light and spoken words. The hair stood up on my arms and there I sat grinning.

Then the Magdalene said, "Well my dear… write it down."

✡ ✡ ✡

I realized that I was receiving the answers to accessing our Light Body at will.

Now, I could share these teachings with others and they could experience their Light Bodies and Ascension. It came to me, that the information on the glia brain, limbic system, frontal lobes and the Spiral Breath could be part of the missing information in the Magdalene Gospels and that which has been hidden in order to suppress the achievement of enlightenment.

In the pages that follow, I will weave science together with channeled wisdom, my interpretation of the Gospels of Mary Magdalene, sacred geometry, numerology, modalities, the use of pure essential oils and the Spiral Breath technique.

I can be technical at times. I like to know how and why things work. I believe that by giving you the basics and the connections that I have made, it will help you lay a stronger foundation to support your healing and spiritual growth. It is amazing to me, that God created such intricate masterpieces with our body, mind and spirit. Mostly, I share in this book heart felt wisdom, Divine guidance, the Spiral Breath, healing modalities and my insight into Grace that can help you return to balance and reconnect spiritually.

The threads of my personal experiences will be woven throughout the fabric of these pages, especially those while in Egypt in 1993 and my trips to France. Knowing that someone really did have these experiences makes them more believable and achievable.

I bridge spirituality and science to help maximize the quality of our wellbeing and to achieve higher consciousness and our multidimensional Divine I AM – "Fully Realized Human Being-ness."

Many Blessings!

Gayle Mack

NMD, DBE, Rev.

1.1 Spiral Breath Original Illustration by Gayle Mack

Chapter 1:
Receiving the Gift of the Spiral Breath

The Spiral Breath was given to me during one of my "self healing" prayer and meditations. I asked God - *Divine All That Is* to show me how to heal the injury that I had recently experienced to my brain-stem, cerebellum, head and neck. After several moments of stillness, an emerald green Fibonacci spiral of Light appeared before me. It was a brilliant, shimmery Light that flowed and pulsed with movement. I recall waving my hand through the shimmering spiral of Light to verify that it was actually there. The Light dispersed a bit, then quickly reformed the spiral formation. I was divinely guided to 'breathe' it in.

I followed the guidance and began a slow inhalation. As I inhaled, the emerald green Light began to flow into my heart and continued up to the base of my skull, spiraling around my brain, limbic system and head, until it made its exit with my exhalation, seemingly through my amygdalae that sit on either side of my Third Eye.

The spiral action was in slow motion at the beginning. I believe that Divine All That Is slowed down time so I could grasp what was happening and for me to remember the process. My breath had blended with the emerald green Light, as it entered my heart and spiraled up around my head into my Limbic system on the inhalations.

As I exhaled, the emerald green Light shifted into a glistening golden Light as it passed through my amygdalae. My breath and the golden Light flowed out of both my amygdala like lasers and mingled with the shimmery iridescent Mother of Pearl color that surrounded my entire body. The Mother of Pearl color was several inches deep and in constant motion. Then the multi-colored iridescent Light re-entered my heart on my inhalations as a vivid emerald green Light, which continued to spiral up around my head and brain.

I continued this process of breathing in the Light and had an amazing result. I named this process the Spiral Breath Technique and began sharing it with others.

Prior to receiving the Spiral Breath Technique, I experienced a severe hit to the base of my skull. As a result of the impact and struggle, the plates of my skull shifted with the blow, as did my occiput, atlas and the vertebrae in my neck. Ligaments, attachments and muscles were torn and strained during this incident. My jaw was dislocated and it locked down, causing four teeth to fracture under the pressure, two of which I lost. My photographic memory, my short term memory and my perfect recall were deeply affected. I could not remember two sentences back to back, even if I wrote them myself and I could not write my name for three weeks. The injury also left me emotionally sensitive and I cried at the drop of a hat.

Although I was clearly aware of the physical damage that I sustained, I had not really comprehended the extent of the damage to my brain and brainstem. I just 'powered' through the emotional roller coaster, the pain and discomfort within my body, the intense pressure in my head, my forgetfulness, the moments of "spacing out" and my need to sleep.

Being a five to six hour a night sleeper most of my life, the need for frequent naps throughout the day, the constant exhaustion and inability to function normally was causing me concern.

Frustrated with feeling illiterate, I asked my doctor, "What is wrong with me?" He looked at me, a bit puzzled and reminded me that I had sustained a severe injury to my brainstem. He said that it was only by God's Grace that I was not paralyzed, brain dead or dead. According to my x-rays, I should not be walking, talking, thinking or breathing. He also commented that this type of injury generally takes upwards of eight years or more to heal and often-times, people do not make a full recovery. Because of the healing and energy work that I do, I was, in his opinion recovering faster than most.

Although, in some areas I was healing faster than normal, I was still so discombobulated. My short term memory was non-existent. I had to write everything down and that did not always work, for I would read my list and then forget what I was going to do in the time that it took to stand up. It was not just forgetting what I was going to do and needing to walk back into the room to remember. The thought was gone like it never happened!

I had been great at multitasking and was always, acutely aware of my surroundings. The 'me' I had been before the incident was no longer. I felt void and lost. I was wrapped in pain and the uncertainty of my quality of life in the future.

As I sat at home with the new realization of my situation, I ran the gamut of emotions. I was numb, fearful and angry. Then my Faith kicked in and I started praying and talking with God Divine. I asked God to show me how to heal my injury and be better than I was before the incident. I applied one of my favorite oil blends, "Highest Potential™" to the inside of my wrist, my heart, third eye and crown chakra. I inhaled the scent and began my prayerful meditation. I asked for guidance and a 'way through' this ordeal.

After I became 'still in mind', the Aramaic translation of my favorite Bible verse John 16:23-24 popped into my thoughts. I heard it as if God was speaking to me directly. It is from the *Prayers of the Cosmos: Meditations on the Aramaic Words of Jesus* by Neil Douglas-Klotz. This is a wonderful book on the Aramaic translation of the Lord's Prayer, the Beatitudes and three chosen sayings of Jesus from the Bible. The translations from the Aramaic texts are much more in-depth and exquisitely stated than what is normally presented in the Bible. This translation of John 16:23-24 is the 'third saying' in the book.[3]

"All things that you ask straightly, directly,

that you desire – like an arrow to its mark,

from the Breathing Life of All, Father-Mother of the Cosmos,

with my Shem – my Experience, my Light and Sound,

my Atmosphere, my Word from inside my Name –

> *you will be given.*
> *So far you have not done this.*
> *So ask without hidden motive and Be Surrounded by Your Answer –*
> *Be Enveloped by what you desire that your Gladness be full –*
> *That the Joy of goals MET here, may continue its story to perfection in Unity."*
>
> —*PRAYERS OF THE COSMOS: MEDITATIONS ON THE ARAMAIC WORDS OF JESUS* BY NEIL DOUGLAS-KLOTZ

My Faith rose within me in strong determination. I proclaimed that I was not going to be a victim of malice or circumstance and I refused to surrender to the injuries. I declared that I would return to the 'me' I was before the injury and surpass the greatness that I had already become. It was a bold statement, but Divine has always stated to reach for greater - my Greatest Good.

I was immediately *Surrounded by My Answer and Enveloped by what I Desired* - a way through. I was blessed with the beautiful and powerful Spiral Breath technique and *my Gladness was Full of Goals MET!*

When I first did this Spiral Breath, a buzzy, vibrating sensation started on both sides of my third eye (my amygdala). I continued to breathe and visualize my breath spiraling through my heart and up around my head, as Divinely guided. The vibrating sensation intensified and soon encompassed my third eye and forehead. Then my brainstem started to vibrate. I felt a slight buzzy, pressure incorporate into the vibration at the base of my skull and occipital region. This was the initial point of impact with my injury. The new vibrating sensation blended with the extreme pressure that already existed in my head from the time of the incident. With all the therapy modalities that I had tried, nothing diminished that excessive pressure in my head.

The blended vibrating pressure was increasing to the point of being rather uncomfortable. I was tempted to stop, but my inner voice kept urging me to complete the process. I continued breathing; spiraling my breath up and around my head; through my limbic system and out my third eye and amygdala.

Then, on one of my exhales, I heard a muffled "click - click" inside my skull as my amygdala moved from the posterior (back part) of the gland to the anterior (front part) of the gland. Immediately following the double click, the pressure released through my amygdala and was gone. I continued with the Spiral Breath and after a short time, I only had a pleasant vibration inside my head. As I continued breathing, the pleasant vibration amplified and began to move down my spine. Once the vibrating sensation reached the base of my spine, it shot back up my spinal column sending waves of warm vibrations throughout my entire body.

As the vibrating sensation reached the top of my head and crown chakra, the warm sensation became a cool, whirling breeze. I felt like I had a fan gently blowing on my brain and I drifted into 'Bliss.'

Shortly thereafter, I 'blipped out' as I call it. I was conscious and in a state of Bliss. I was not aware of my physical body, although I knew that I was still sitting up.

I not only activated the anterior of my amygdala, I had also re-activated my entire limbic system, glia brain, frontal lobes and my Thousand Petal Lotus, as well. The lobes in my brain were engaging and communicating with each other at the same time. My glia brain sent the signal vibrations down through my body; along my nervous system to re-connect the communication between my brain and my body. In turn, it re-connected my heart and mind and increased the flow of Vital Life Force.

You see, the injury and the excruciating pain, along with the anger that arose from receiving a brain injury at the hands of someone I knew and loved, topped with the fear of possibly enduring permanent damage, locked me into the posterior part of my amygdala.

Having the prior knowledge of the limbic system and glia brain, I was able to understand what had shifted in me. Being in the trauma of the injury, I was unable to 'see' what was happening to me. I was in the 'muckity-muck.' After my 'awakening' and re-connection from the Spiral Breath Blessing, I had a clearer vision and direction for my return to wellness.

The Spiral Breath technique enabled me to make the shift from the negative fueling posterior amygdala to the positive influencing anterior amygdala. The Spiral Breath was facilitating a re-connection *within* me, which allowed the multi-level healing and transformation to begin to take place.

I will go into more detail with my experience of the Spiral Breath and my journey, as well as, the glia brain, limbic system, amygdala and the Thousand Petal Lotus further on in the book, as I feel it is important to also understand the mechanics of the process.

I began to implement the Spiral Breath on a daily basis. I do the Spiral Breath every morning upon rising and before I go to sleep. My morning breath work sets the course of my day. As I breathe, I hold positive intentions of healing and give thanks for another day to share and to receive the blessings that will unfold throughout my day.

At night, I set the intention that my breath work clears away any negative residue that I have acquired during my day. I forgive what requires forgiving and give Grace to whatever is beyond my control and that which requires being Graced. I visualize my breath dissolving and moving the negative residue out of my cells, body and energy field.

In the effort to be consciously responsible, I set my intention that the disharmony leaving my energy field, is immediately transformed into Unconditional Love. This way, no one (including myself) picks up anything that I am releasing but Love.

After a couple of weeks of implementing the Spiral Breath, I noticed that my life had taken on an 'easy flow' again and my short term memory and recall had begun to improve.

Each time I do the Spiral Breath, I have a pleasant experience and each time that I achieve the bliss, I do so a little bit faster. With the continuation of the Spiral Breath technique, my memory, recall, retention and brain fog consistently improved and my physical pain continued to lessen. I now feel, for the most part, that I am back to normal. Well… that is, what's normal for me.

The Spiral Breath set into motion a healing process that spanned the physical, mental, emotional and spiritual bodies. It allowed me to activate my amygdala, pineal, pituitary, limbic system and glia brain. I was able to move through my emotional wounds with greater ease, speed up the healing time of my physical wounds, reconnect the communication between my brain and nervous system, while increasing my awareness and spiritual abilities.

Coming through this seemingly unfortunate ordeal, strengthened my faith in Divine and a 'Greater Power.' It showed me yet again, that something good can come out of something 'not so good' and that I have the courage, the tenacity and the ability through our 'God Given' - 'Divinely Given' Gifts to facilitate the healing I desire.

I began to share the Spiral Breath technique with friends and acquaintances. Soon, I was sharing it with large numbers of people. Various degrees of healing have been experienced from sensations within the body or brain, being peacefully relaxed to life changing transformations. Some participants would place their focus on an injury or a specific part of their body. Others used the Spiral Breath to transmute emotional wounds or mental blocks that were keeping them from achieving and receiving what they desired in their lives. Even those who did not have a focused intention going into the Spiral Breath process had profound experiences, as the Spiral Breath seems to know what requires healing.

During a group session, one gentleman had a diamond shape raise up on his forehead, right over his third eye. The points to the left and right of the diamond rested at his amygdalae. The skin of the raised diamond was very white and visually stood out on his tanned skin. It stayed that way for approximately 10 minutes after he stopped the breathing process. We took it as a sign of an initiation and confirmation that he had activated his crown chakra, third eye and frontal lobe during the Spiral Breath process. He had been a bit skeptical going into the class. The physical sign, as well as the bliss that he experienced, was his way of showing himself that he can achieve a state of higher consciousness and that the Spiral Breath works.

One young man, who entered into the Spiral Breath process without an intention, had a blocked memory surface. Tears began to stream down his face. I softly asked if he was alright. He smiled gently; nodded yes and continued breathing without opening his eyes. He shared later that a memory, which his emotional body had hidden from him, no longer needed protecting. He was able to address the emotional wound without fear, guilt or shame. He was able to move the resonance of that memory out of his personal energy with ease, give forgiveness and experience Grace. He left the workshop with greater understanding, greater self-worth and a much lighter heart.

A young woman that I worked with was experiencing uneasiness and apprehension. She began doing the Spiral Breath and was able to calm the feelings of uneasiness before they escalated. With regular practice, it only took a couple of breaths to bring herself back to center.

Many people hear the muffled, double clicks, as their amygdala move forward to the anterior part of their gland. Some people have achieved a multidimensionality that they had been working to access for years, while others, simply experienced a wonderful sense of peace.

The Spiral Breath technique is simple, yet powerful. It can enhance your inner peace and transform your life, as it has mine.

In the following chapter, I will share the full experience of receiving the Spiral Breath. In Chapter Twelve, I will take you step by step through the Spiral Breath technique. In Chapter Thirteen, I will share modified versions with various modalities that I sometimes incorporate into the Spiral Breath process.

In between now and Chapter Thirteen, I will cover the importance of breathing correctly, cellular memory flush, more indepth explanations of the amygdala, limbic system and Glia brain and why they hold so much importance. I will also address emotions, chakras and the Thousand Petal Lotus. Color, sound, frequency, sacred geometry and energy will be lightly addressed, as will, the benefits of incorporating the blessings of pure therapeutic grade essential oils. I address these topics, as they were the most asked about topics during my Spiral Breath presentations.

I have provided a glossary for your convenience, as some of my wordage and terminology may be new to you. First, I will begin with a complete description of how I originally experienced the Spiral Breath.

---

[3] *Prayers of the Cosmos:Meditations on the Aramaic Words of Jesus* by Neil Douglas-Klotz pages 86-87

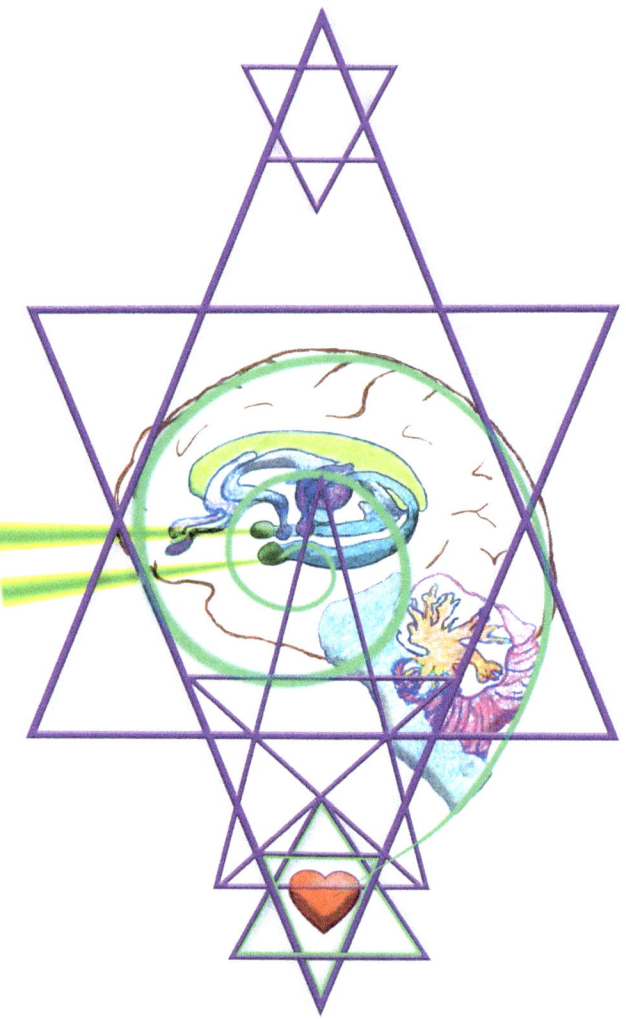

2.1 Spiral Breath Illustration by Gayle Mack

Chapter 2:

The Full Experience of the Spiral Breath

As I mentioned earlier, I asked straightly and directly for an answer to assist in the healing of my injury and I was *immediately* 'Surrounded by my Answer.' It came in the form of a brilliant emerald green Fibonacci Spiral of Light. It was tangible and perceptible by touch. I could physically see the spiraling Light with my open eyes. In disbelief, I reached out to touch it. The Light dispersed, ever so slightly, as my fingertips passed through the illuminated emerald Light before me. Then it quickly resumed the spiral form.

I was Divinely guided to 'breathe' the Light in. I followed the guidance and began a slow inhalation. As I inhaled, the tail of the emerald green Light appeared to flow into my heart. The emerald Light swirled from the left to the right, from right to left, up and over; and down and around, all at the same time. The brilliant emerald Light continued to swirl until it had completely filled the space of my physical heart and the area of my heart chakra.

When my heart was full, the emerald green Light moved up to the base of my skull. In my mind's eye, I could see the brilliant green Light completely illuminate my brainstem and cerebellum. The entire base of my skull was now glowing with this beautiful emerald green Light. Once again, the Light swirled from the left to the right, from right to left, up and over and down and around, all at the same time.

After a few moments, the emerald Light moved up to my occipital ridge, which is the protruding part of the back of the skull. Once the emerald Light had saturated this area, it moved up to my crown chakra. As before, the bright green Light swirled in several directions at the same time until my crown chakra was saturated. The spiraling emerald Light moved down to the front of my forehead, encompassing my third eye and frontal lobes.

Again, the emerald green Light swirled in several directions until my third eye area was full of Light. The Light continued to move down the front of my face into my nostrils and up past my teeth; through the roof of my mouth into the center of my brain. This is where the limbic system is located. The emerald green Light continued swirling through my limbic system, awakening and illuminating every part of this complex part of the brain.

As the bright emerald green Light passed through my amygdala that sit on both sides of my third eye, I noticed that it had changed color and was now shimmering with a golden hue. The golden Light left my amygdalae like two lasers coming out of my forehead and extended out approximately six inches from my body into my personal energy field, also known as an aura. The golden Light then blended with the All Encompassing Divine Light that shimmered an iridescent Mother of Pearl all around me and then re-entered my heart as emerald green on my inhalation.

When I first started the breathing process, it proceeded in slow motion. I believe the slow motion was to afford me time to comprehend the process and to remember all the stages of its progression. As the spiraling emerald Light continued to transition through its stages, it began to pick up speed until the flow was synchronized with my inhalations and exhalations.

I sensed that the energy of the Light and my breath was charging up as it passed through the Mother of Pearl Light that was around me. With each breath, the Light increased its frequency and resonance.

I was Divinely guided to use an audible breath. This is where you allow your breath to brush the back of your throat on your inhalations, while intentionally making the sound of your inhalations and exhalations audible. It sounds like Darth Vader from the Star Wars movie.

As I spiraled my audible breath, I began to feel a slight vibrating sensation. On my inhalations, the vibrating sensation was first felt in my heart. I continued to breathe and visualize my breath spiraling through my heart and upward around my head, as Divinely guided. The sensation moved up to the base of my skull, where my brainstem started to vibrate. With continued breathing, the sensation slowly moved up to my occipital region, to the top of my head, where the crown chakra is located and then around to my third eye area.

Now with my inhalations, I felt the vibrating sensation along the entire length of the spiraling Light from my heart around to my forehead. As I exhaled, the vibration started to feel more prominent and 'buzzy' on both sides of my third eye, where my amygdala are located.

The vibrating sensation intensified with each breath. I felt a slight pressure begin to incorporate into the vibration at the base of my skull and occipital region. This was the initial point of impact with my injury. This new vibrating sensation blended with the extreme pressure that already existed in my head since the incident.

The blended pressure was increasing to the point of being uncomfortable. I was tempted to stop the Spiral Breath, but my 'inner voice' kept telling me to carry on, trust and complete the process. I continued breathing, spiraling my breath up and around my head; through my limbic system and out my third eye and amygdala.

On one of my exhales, I heard a muffled double click and the pressure released through my amygdala and was gone. I continued with the Spiral Breath and after a few moments, I only had a pleasant vibration inside my head.

My breathing had settled into a comfortable rhythm. After a while, an emerald green merkaba appeared at my heart chakra. My heart was in the center of the two interlocking triangles that made the formation of the merkaba. These triangles resemble the Star of David and the Seal of Solomon. One triangle pointing up and one pointing downwards. Each triangle spun clockwise and counter-clockwise at the same time, while rotating up and over, as well as, down and around. The movement resembled the energy of a toroidal vortex and mirrored the movement of the emerald green Light that swirled through the various stages between my heart and brain.

Shortly after the emerald green merkaba appeared, another merkaba that was larger in size, appeared at my head. This merkaba was a deep violet color. My limbic system and third eye were in the center of this merkaba. My heart was nestled in the center of the first emerald green merkaba and the downward point of that merkaba overlaid the downward point of the violet merkaba.

I continued to spiral my breath from my heart through my brainstem, to my crown chakra, around to my third eye and down-around into my limbic system. With my exhalations, I directed the energy out through my amygdala.

Eventually, with the constant flow of the Light, energy and breath passing through my limbic system and crown chakra, my Thousand Petal Lotus was triggered and began to unfold its many folds and petals. The warm sensation became a cool, whirling breeze. I felt like I had a fan gently blowing on my brain.

A third merkaba (deep violet in color) appeared above my head, which I sensed was the Eighth Gate and a doorway to the multidimensional realm.

All the while, the emerald green Light spiraled into my heart, up and around my brain, expanding the flow of energy and the intensity of the Light.

A five pointed star completed this amazing sacred geometry matrix that encompassed me. I believe that the five points of this star represent my head, arms and legs, like Leonardo da Vinci's drawing of Vitruvian Man. For me, I interpreted this to mean that my body was communicating with my higher consciousness, which was connected to and accessing the Higher Realms of Consciousness.

My Spiral Breath seemed to be on autopilot and I was enjoying the multi-dimensional matrix of the rotating energies, shapes and color. Once again, the vibrations stepped up their frequency. The sensation in the center of my forehead had heightened its intensity to a strong whirl.

A few breaths later, the increased sensation in my forehead drifted back to my brainstem. This triggered a rush of energy waves that ran from my brainstem to my forehead and back to the brainstem in a remarkably, rapid succession. I could hear the 'woosh' as the accelerated energy waves pulsated back and forth through my brain. My entire brain was completely engaged, pulsating and vibrating.

With a couple more breaths, I drifted into 'Bliss.' I was fully conscious *and* in a state of Bliss. I was not aware of my physical body, although I knew that I was still sitting up.

Upon reaching this state of bliss, my personal merkaba activated around my body. All I saw was Light. Shortly thereafter, I 'blipped out' as I call it. I remained in this state for nearly an hour.

It truly was an amazing feeling and an experience that supercharged my healing process!

I not only moved into the anterior region of my amygdala, I had also re-activated my entire limbic system, glia brain, frontal lobes and my Thousand Petal Lotus. I had switched on the communication between my heart and brain, as well. The lobes in my brain were engaging and communicating with each other at the same time and I had reached the Gamma brain wave state. My Kundalini was activated, which increased the flow of Vital Life Force along my spinal column and bathed the spinal nerves and plexuses. In turn, the Vital Life Force sent signal vibrations through my body and nervous system to reconnect the communication between my brain and my body.

I was 'Enveloped by my Answer and the Gladness was full and the Joy of goals MET continued my story in perfection of Unity.'

I named this breathing process the 'Spiral Breath.' The Spiral Breath is a very powerful, yet simple breathing pattern with visualization. I have used the Spiral Breath technique, not only to assist the healing of my brain injury, but also in shifting emotional imbalances, easing tension, stiffness or discomfort in my body, preparing for sleep and to enhance my prayer intentions.

I have experimented with the Spiral Breath by incorporating pure essential oils and a variety of different modalities such as toning, extended visualization, color, listening to binaural beats or Solfeggio tones; adding crystals and holding acupressure points during the breathing process. Each modality enhanced the process in a unique and special way. Most of these modalities are in the comprehensive booklet, Spiral Breath - Complimentary Modalities.

I sketched out what I saw as best as I could. The complexity of the multidimensional aspects were not captured in the drawing. Fortunately, the mind is capable of imagining multidimensionally when it is guided. Picture 1.1 is presented above to give you an idea of its brilliance.

A friend of mine animated the breathing process for me. It shows the flow of the emerald green Light spiraling up from the heart; around the head and through the limbic system. Watching the animated video is great for use as a daily meditation and for those who have trouble visualizing. With the e-books, the link is provided at the end of the book. The soft cover can be purchased with or without the DVD attached to the inside of the back cover. You can also purchase the DVD on its own. See the re-source page.

Chapter 3:
Complete and Purposeful Breathing

I will take a moment to discuss the value of proper and purposeful breathing. I reference the Hindu-Yogi traditions, as they have known the importance of proper breathing for centuries and took care to record and perfect the sacredness of breath. Breathing not only keeps our bodies alive and functioning, it can also increase our clarity, our mental and higher potential, activate our higher consciousness and increase the 'Vital Life Force' that effects every organ, body system, tissue and cell of our body.[4] Breath is the language of health and harmony.[5] Breath is our 'soul' companion.[6]

Vital Life Force Energy is also known as 'Prana.' In Sanskrit, the meaning of Prana is 'Absolute Energy.' The Hindus define Prana as the universal principle of energy or force exhibited in all forms of life and matter, yet is not matter. Prana is the essence of all motion, force or energy; whether manifested in gravity, electricity, magnetism or the revolution of planets. *All energy or force is derived from this principle.* Prana is everywhere. It is all pervading and is referred to in Genesis by the Hebrew author as 'the Breath of the Spirit.'[7]

> "The breath is one's own mind; one's own mind does the breathing. Once mind stirs, then there is energy. Energy is basically an emanation of mind."
> THE SECRET OF THE GOLDEN FLOWER:
> THE CHINESE BOOK OF LIFE (IV:3) TRANSLATED BY THOMAS CLEARY

Although our breath is mostly an unconscious action, it can be consciously directed to heighten our enlightenment and healing, as with the Spiral Breath. On the reverse of that thought, the unconscious action of our breathing can reveal emotional energy that is present within our body. For instance, when we are sad, we have a tendency to sigh frequently. When we are angry, we tend to breathe more rapidly. When we are functioning out of fear or attempting to prevent certain feelings and emotions from overwhelming us, we tend to hold our breath or our breathing becomes shallow and comes from the top part of the lungs.[8]

Complete and purposeful breath can be very beneficial for emotions. Breathing is like a heart beat, it establishes the body's rhythm and flow.[9] Deep, continual and measured breathing through both nostrils at the same time can quickly defuse 'out of balance' emotions. Incorporating the practice of focused breath work, like the Spiral Breath, into your daily routine can have exponential transformation in your lifestyle and wellbeing.

Most people are also unaware that we breath through one nostril or the other. One nostril is dominant for 60 to 80 minutes and then it switches to the opposite nostril. For a few moments, we will naturally breathe from both nostrils, as our breath is shifting to the opposite nostril.[10]

This switching back and forth sets up a rhythm that effects the bio-rhythm of our body, as well as, our nervous system and the hemispheres of our brain. Each breath and directional flow will activate a specific vital energetic quality, either mental, emotional, physical or spiritual. Swami Muktibodhananda Saraswati, in his book, *The Tantric Science of Brain Breathing* refers to the three flows of breath as a trinity.[11]

The left nostril represents the mind and supports the sensory nerves, along with our eyes, nose, tongue, ears and skin. Our left nostril will be dominant when we are studying, thinking, worrying, experiencing repetitive or excessive thoughts, designing something; planning a project or a course of action.[12] I noticed that when I am writing, my left nostril is dominant with my breathing.

The right nostril represents life force and supports our bodily functions, organs of action, such as, our reproductive organs, our urinary and excretory organs, as well as, our hands, feet and speech. Our right nostril will be dominant when we are in action and physical activity, as with exercising, playing, talking, singing, etc.[13]

When both nostrils are active at the same time, we are activating our spiritual energy. Using both nostrils is extremely beneficial when meditating, in prayer and using your healing arts.[14] I find when implementing or teaching the Spiral Breath technique, that using an audible breath that brushes the back of your throat like Darth Vader from Star Wars, will activate both nostrils. It also gives your conscious mind something to focus on. Eventually, you will settle into a more refined and effortless pattern of breathing.

The more you relax into your breathing, the more subtle it will become. The more subtle your breath becomes, the deeper the 'quietude' you can achieve. The greater the 'quietude,' the faster you will move into 'true breathing' and single-mindedness.

> *"True breathing will appear, whereupon the substance of the mind will become perceptible. This is because when the mind is subtle, breath is subtle; when mind is unified, it moves energy.*
>
> *When breath is subtle, mind is subtle;*
>
> *When energy is unified, it moves mind…*
>
> *This is what is called the preservation of pure energy."*
>
> THE SECRET OF THE GOLDEN FLOWER: THE CHINESE BOOK OF LIFE (IV:8-10)

With each thought that passes through our mind, an inhalation and an exhalation accompanies it. *The Secret of the Golden Flower: The Chinese Book of Life* describes the breathing process as *"inward breathing and outward breathing accompany each other like sound and echo."*

There is a difference between basic respiration and 'true breathing' or focused breath. Focused breathing will help you quiet the mind. When you unify your energy with focused breath, you will become aware that your mind is not bouncing from one thought to another. Your eyes are not distracted by the movement of things around you and your ears will be aware of sounds happening around you, though you will not be moved from your center of quietude. Your focus is inward. You are not distracted, but alert and aware.

With continued practice, you may notice that your 'listening' skills will include that which is soundless and 'seeing' that which is formless. I noticed that I would sense or feel people coming into my space before I could hear or see them. I will often go to the door just as my client or friend's car comes comes into view. I felt them coming.

Consciously disciplining your refined, focused 'true breathing' and utilizing both nostrils simultaneously, will increase the benefits of the Spiral Breath, which in turn, stimulates the limbic system, frontal lobes and your extra sensory gifts.

I used to have trouble meditating until I was introduced to the teachings within the *The Tantric Science of Brain Breathing*. The mystery was solved. It had to do with how I was breathing. If my left nostril was dominant, then my mind wandered. If my right nostril was dominant, I was fidgety. When I intentionally breathed with both nostrils, my mind and thoughts were still, which allowed me to soar through the higher realms and superconsciousness with greater ease.

As previously mentioned, breathing with the left nostril presides over mental actions, the right presides over physical actions and both nostrils dominant presides over spiritual actions.[15]

I was in the band and chorus in school. We were taught how to breathe in order to maximize our tones and to use our diaphragms to control the release of sound and breath. Proper breath support was a *must* for clear, sustained and pitch perfect tones.

The basic breathing techniques that we used while playing an instrument in the band and for singing were similar to the breathing techniques of Swara Yoga. In band and chorus, we took quick deep breaths, but the inhalation action was the same. Swara means 'the sound of ones own breath.' Yoga means 'union.' Swara Yoga empowers us to achieve a state of union through our own breath.[16] 'The Yogi's call it 'Complete Breathing.' Proper breathing increases our oxygen, which in turn, increases our Vital Life Force energy.[17]

Babies innately breathe correctly. Watch the rolling action of a baby's lungs and belly as they expand and contract while breathing. As we experience life, we have a tendency to alter our natural breathing pattern during stressful situations, the rush of our daily lives or from inactivity.

We tend to hold our breath, creating a longer than normal time between inhalations. Some inhale using only the upper portion of their lungs causing their shoulders to rise with each breath. The Yogi's call this 'high' breathing.[18]

Others quicken their breath, while taking short, shallow breaths from the chest. Their chest expands at various degrees depending on their stress level. The Yogi's call this "mid" breathing. And then others fill their abdomen with air, expanding their belly. This is referred to as "low" breathing.[19]

As we alter our natural breathing process, we deprive our body and brain from rejuvenating oxygen. Complete Breathing is a combination of low, mid and high breathing, succeeding each other rapidly in the order given; in a uniform, supportive succession.

Your intention for the use of your breath will determine the implementation of your breath. For instance, when you are running, your focus is more metered. Oxygen in - carbon dioxide out. When singing or playing an instrument, we use breath support and breath control. We take in a quick complete breath, then use our abdominal muscles and diaphragm to regulate the amount of breath required to deliver the quality of tone and style of musicality required. With meditation, the inhalation is longer and calming. When using healing breath to move stored or blocked energy and/or increase our vitality and vibration, the addition of contracting the perineum (pelvic floor muscle) and abdominal muscles into your complete breathing increases the movement of cerebrospinal fluid and Vital Life Force energy.[20]

Whatever your focused breath intention is, the basic foundation of proper breathing remains the same. The simple act of retraining yourself to breathe correctly can improve your level of wellness; increase your stamina, creativity, productivity and acuity.

Yogi Ramacharaka, in his book, *The Hindu-Yogi Science of Breath*, instructs the readers on the proper way to breath. This little book is beneficial and a quick read. Although it is out of print, you can find an online link if you do a search of the book title or reference the footnote. I also included the link in the Reference Page at he back of the book.

The best way to practice proper breathing is to sit erect or stand. You can also lie flat on your yoga mat or bed, though you may not feel the full expansion as you would if you were to sit or stand.

There are four parts to your inhalation. Although breathing this way may feel awkward at first, with a little practice, it will soon develop into second nature and become a smooth, seamless movement.

- *Inhale through your nostrils with a smooth, steady breath. Allow the lower part of your lungs to fill first. This is the area of your lower ribs and diaphragm. If you place your palms on your lower ribs, you will be able to feel your diaphragm engage with your inhalation.*

- *As you continue your inhalation, fill the middle part of your lungs. You will feel your lower ribs, breastbone and chest inflate.*

- *Maintain your inhalation as you fill the top part of your lungs. You will notice your upper ribs (closest to your armpits), expanding. Your chest will lift up, as if being raised by a string, though your shoulders will stay down.*

- *Finish your inhalation by slightly drawing in your diaphragm and the lower part of your abdomen to support the lungs and move your breath into your upper lungs.*

- *After your inhalation is complete; hold your breath for a moment. This allows the oxygen to permeate your cells and increases the concentration of oxygen to your body.*

- *As you exhale, allow your chest to remain lifted and use your diaphragm to push the air gently out of your lungs.*

As you gently tighten and lift up with your diaphragm, your exhaled breath will remain smooth, strong and consistent. As we breathe, our diaphragm gently massages our abdominal organs and replenishes precious, restorative oxygen through our body.[21]

As you practice breathing, you can place your palms on your lower rib cage. This will help you feel the movement in the mechanics of breathing. Watching yourself breathe in a full length mirror can also be beneficial, as it allows your eyes to see the progression, as well as feel it.

Breathing through your nostrils is the proper way to breathe. Breathing with your mouth open, bypasses our built-in filtration system and allows more foreign debris to enter our body. Studies have shown that mouth breathers contract more illnesses than those who breathe through their nose.[22]

Incorporating the science of proper and purposeful breathing, along with the understanding of the limbic system and glia brain, will enhance the benefits of the Spiral Breath technique and increase your vibration and consciousness.

---

[4] *Hindu-Yogi Science of Breath* by Yogi Ramacharaka https://holybooks-lichtenbergpress.netdna-ssl.com/wp-content/uploads/The-Science-of-Breath.pdf page 7-13

[5] *Breath is a Language* by Joy Manne', PhD http://www.catherinedowling.com/breathwork/ page 10

[6] *Swara Yoga: The Tantric Science of Brain Breathing* by Swami Mukti-bodhananda Saraswati page 6

[7] *Hindu-Yogi Science of Breath* by Yogi Ramacharaka https://holybooks-lichtenbergpress.netdna-ssl.com/wp-content/uploads/The-Science-of-Breath.pdf page 14-15

[8] *Breath is a Language* by Joy Manne', PhD http://www.catherinedowling.com/breathwork/ pages 5-14

[9] Conger, John P. (1988), Jung & Reich: *The Body as Shadow*. Berkeley, California: North Atlantic Books. page 45

[10] *Swara Yoga: The Tantric Science of Brain Breathing* by Swami Mukti-bodhananda Saraswati page 8

[11] *Swara Yoga: The Tantric Science of Brain Breathing* by Swami Mukti-bodhananda Saraswati page 8

[12] *Swara Yoga: The Tantric Science of Brain Breathing* by Swami Mukti-bodhananda Saraswati page 9

[13] *Swara Yoga: The Tantric Science of Brain Breathing* by Swami Mukti-bodhananda Saraswati page 9

[14] *Swara Yoga: The Tantric Science of Brain Breathing* by Swami Mukti-bodhananda Saraswati page 9

[15] *Swara Yoga: The Tantric Science of Brain Breathing* by Swami Mukti-bodhananda Saraswati pages 8-10

[16] *Swara Yoga: The Tantric Science of Brain Breathing* by Swami Mukti-bodhananda Saraswati page 4

[17] *Hindu-Yogi Science of Breath* by Yogi Ramacharaka https://holybooks-lichtenbergpress.netdna-ssl.com/wp-content/uploads/The-Science-of-Breath.pdf pages 29-35

[18] *Hindu-Yogi Science of Breath* by Yogi Ramacharaka https://holybooks-lichtenbergpress.netdna-ssl.com/wp-content/uploads/The-Science-of-Breath.pdf page 24

[19] *Hindu-Yogi Science of Breath* by Yogi Ramacharaka https://holybooks-lichtenbergpress.netdna-ssl.com/wp-content/uploads/The-Science-of-Breath.pdf pages 24-27

[20] *Becoming Supernatural: How common People Are Doing the Uncommon* by Dr. Joe Dispenza page 126-130

[21] *Hindu-Yogi Science of Breath* by Yogi Ramacharaka https://holybooks-lichtenbergpress.netdna-ssl.com/wp-content/uploads/The-Science-of-Breath.pdf pages 29-35

[22] *Hindu-Yogi Science of Breath* by Yogi Ramacharaka https://holybooks-lichtenbergpress.netdna-ssl.com/wp-content/uploads/The-Science-of-Breath.pdf page 20

Chapter 4:
Cellular Memory Flush

Did you know that there is science, chemistry and biology behind your emotions and memories? In the next couple of chapters, I will present brief explanations of the science behind 'why' and 'how' emotions, thoughts and memories become stored, locked and released. I believe that having this understanding can help you facilitate a greater change with your emotional balancing and do so with greater ease.

When you first begin the Spiral Breath, you can sometimes experience a flood of past memories popping into your conscious thoughts. This is actually a good thing. You are simply clearing locked in emotions, beliefs and experiences from your cellular structure and stored memory. I found that the more stored emotions that I cleared and released, the faster the old memories would come and go.

I have consistently found with myself and others, that we begin to release stored emotions, when we engaged in the Spiral Breath. As we breathe, memories would drop into our conscious mind and we would say, "Wow, I haven't thought about that in a long time." Soon the memories would become a fleeting flash that would dissipate as fast as they came up. We would find ourselves saying, "I haven't thought about that in… What was I just thinking about?"

It is not that our memories are disappearing. It is the energy behind those memories, which had been stored within our cells, muscles and nervous system that are being diffused and dissolved. The memories stay, but we either have a diminished response to them or we are no longer energetically or emotionally affected by them. When you focus on clearing uncomfortable memories or unhealthy thought patterns, you will make it easier to repattern or retrain your thoughts, actions and feelings. As you continue the process of breathing and releasing 'that' which no longer serves your greatest good, you will find that the memories, thoughts and emotions, which have tripped you up in life will begin to subside.

I realize that some of the upcoming words, terms and processes may not be familiar to you, but stay with me. I have provided a Glossary for quick reference and have devoted sections and chapters to help you understand the wording and technical terms. Personally, I found that having this basic understanding of 'how' emotions work helped me to understand 'why' things are as they are, which in turn helped me to understand 'what' could be done differently and why previous modalities did not create a lasting change 'when' I tried them.

As I shared my experiences of life and the Spiral Breath Technique, I found that others who had similar uncomfortable experiences were also able to receive beneficial growth and healing. This led me to write this book and share the powerful, yet simple technique with many. The chapters and subchapters were chosen from the questions and topics that I was asked to explain in more detail during my presentations and workshops. The chapters give a full circle view and understanding of breath, energy, emotions and spirituality. Now back to bio-chemical memory…

Emotions are designed to chemically reinforce and transfer an experience into long term memory. The Hypothalamus within our Limbic system produces chemical neurotransmitters to match every emotion that we experience. Every experience we have is bio-chemically backed up to create a feeling or emotion. Therefore, feelings and emotions are chemical memory.[23]

Because our five senses are involved when we have an experience, the stored chemical memory becomes multi-layered triggers within our body and our mind.[24] When we recall an experience or memory, we reproduce the same neurochemicals that were generated at the time of the original event, including the same feelings, thoughts, actions or reactions, whether we are consciously or unconsciously aware of it.[25]

These neurotransmitters enter into the synaptic space between neurons to support an existing neural network connection or to form a new one, which then 'chemically' transforms into a long term memory.[26]

The chemical neuropeptides and neurotransmitters become bio-chemical memory that store the thought processes and the memory of the experience.[27] Every time we recall or relive the memory, we generate more bio-chemical memory and strengthen the neural network connections. When the synapse discharges the chemical memory, the emotional energy that is attached to that particular memory can be released. The experience stays in long term memory, however, the energy behind it dissipates.

Sometimes when we are overwhelmed or over-loaded, the synapse does not 'fire" and the bio-chemical memory becomes locked between the synapse and the cell. This bio-chemical memory is imprinted with the thought process and the emotion. It can continue to run like a CD on continuous play until it is discharged. If the biochemical memory is not discharged, it will eventually create an automatic program or response that becomes a hardwired quick response.[28]

Once these automatic programs are switched on, they run unconsciously with little effort. When we continually recall and relive certain thoughts and/or actions, the response connections strengthen to a point of rapid firing, even if the thought is only similar to the original experience in its nature. Unfortunately, it does takes a bit of effort and commitment to re-direct our thoughts and actions, in order to create a new healthy program to replace the old programming.[29] With commitment, consistency and the right tools (like the Spiral Breath), it can be done!

Stored bio-chemical memory can be passed down generation to generation through the DNA structure if not released. Thus, one can actually inherit thought processes and emotional patterns, both beneficial and destructive.[30] The brain strengthens frequently used signals between cells and weakens the signals that are less used. This is known as synaptic plasticity, also referred to as synaptic long-term potentiation (LTP).[31] Destructive patterns, such as anger, abandonment, distrust, lack of self worth, emotional disconnection, survival issues, etc., can affect us on a subconscious or unconscious level.[32]

These thoughts and patterns can then unconsciously direct our lives. Repeated actions become hardwired programs that direct our body, mind and emotions freely without hesitation.[33] Destructive patterns can interfere with our ability to live our lives the way we *would like* it to be.

When we experience a similar situation to one that negatively affects us, the stored chemical memory is switched on in the limbic system and more bio-chemical memory is produced, as well. Soon, the bio-chemical memory is directing us and we begin reacting out of habit, as if we are on auto-pilot. Our body, thoughts and emotions follow the chemical command of the brain, because it was trained from our repetitive actions to do so.[34]

Stored chemical memory uses the same neural networks and synapses as it does when you are creating similar new chemical memory in a present moment. It does not differentiate between experiences from our past or in recent events. If the neural networks recognize a similarity, it can produce more bio-chemical memory.[35]

Catherine Dowling, author of *The Breath of Feeling: How our Breathing Affects our Emotions* says, "…in breathwork, a memory is more than an intellectual recalling of events. It's a whole package – event, emotion, belief system – all together in a multi-dimensional experience grounded in the body."[36]

On a positive note, if the stored chemical memory that is being activated and reproduced is beneficial, then you create more joy and happiness in your life. This is the premise of emotional clearing, to reprogram your emotions, thoughts and actions in order to generate positive chemical memory. Can you imagine your autopilot being one of gratitude, fulfillment and triumph? If you can imagine it, then you can manifest it!

On occasion, one will experience sensations or emotions that are uncomfortable before they move into peace or bliss. It is a natural reaction to want to tamp the emotion or memory back down and hide it. Catherine Dowling also shares that through breath-work, "the breather can re-experience the event fully instead of pushing it away. This is when the past loses its' grip on our life."[37]

If you should experience any uncomfortable emotions, continue breathing until the emotion has passed. Allow yourself the time to finish the process of clearing. If you stop the cellular memory flush, the emotions that have not energetically cleared from the cells are still activated and present. If you cannot finish clearing within the session, be gentle with yourself and return to the Spiral Breath as soon as you can. Continue your Spiral Breath until you achieve a sense of peace. Consider adding an appropriate pure essential oil blend to help shift the energy, such as Forgiveness™, SARA™, Stress Away™, Release™, Valor™ or Peace & Calming™. I will address pure essential oils in more detail later on in the book.

Through sharing the Spiral Breath, I have found that the breathing process helps with gently and effectively releasing the burden of the uncomfortable emotional memory held within the cellular structure. Less burden allows you to restructure your thoughts and choose positive ones to replace the old ones that no longer serve your greatest good.

When you are finished with your Spiral Breath session, complete the process by infusing sincere feelings of Gratitude into your Loving, Joyful, Inner Peace. Connect to a positive feeling, hold it in your heart and allow your breath to infuse the feeling throughout your body and mind.

Many years ago, I was doing a 'rebirthing' breath session (also known as Conscious Energy Breathing), which is based on the premise that all humans carry with them the trauma of their birth experience.[38, 39] During the session, I had an unexpected experience arise. Ten to fifteen minutes into my breath work, I started to stiffen up as snippets of memories came up, where people were calling me selfish in an attempt to manipulate me into doing something for them. I thought it odd that this was what was coming up for me emotionally.

However, through my entire life until then, I always went above and beyond in the 'giving department' to avoid being called selfish. You could call me anything and it would not phase me. But if you called me selfish, I would crumble. I did not know why I was so effected like that, but I was.

About thirty minutes into the breath work session, I was experiencing a memory of being in the womb with my twin brother. I recalled the sweetness of that moment. Then, I heard my twin brother say, "You did not take all the life force. I chose not to come in when you did. You were not selfish. I *chose* not to be born. It was not my time. It was yours."

Then the tears started to roll down my cheeks as the memory dissipated. I continued to breath through it and eventually, came into a calm, peaceful feeling. That day I laid down the fear of being called selfish and stopped being emotionally tripped up by being called that.

A few days later, a pushy co-worker tried to manipulate me into giving up my family reunion weekend that I had requested 3 months in advance. She called me selfish and attempted to intimidate me by making a scene. Then she said, "When I come back from my break I will expect an answer." "Hhmmm," I thought with a new awareness, "Those words and actions are similar to my step-father's words."

When she came back from her break, she says, "Well? I'm waiting." Again, my step-father's words. I smiled at her and very calmly replied, "If it was so important to you, then you would have requested the time off like I did. The answer is still no." She looked shocked that I refused her demands and called me a B _ _ _ _. I smiled again and to my surprise, words rolled out of mouth so unfamiliar for me. "Thank you so very much! I worked hard for that title." She stood looking at me with a hint of a smile on her face. Then she laughed and replied, "Well done! I was wondering how long you were going to take my sh _ _! Enjoy your weekend."

As she went on her way, I realized that I had broken the pattern of being intimidated. Being called selfish did not have the impact on me that it had before. There is a big difference between being 'Self-loving' and being selfish. I exercised self love, which empowered me. The emotional chemical memory that I had cleared a few days before was no longer driving my response. For the knowing, we became and remain very good friends.

As a side note to this example, I did not know that I was a twin until I was fifteen years old. I was driving a car that I had won in a dollar raffle on the dirt roads around my neighborhood. (For obvious reasons, I was not on a paved road. Thank God.) Several of my neighborhood girlfriends were in the car with me. We were talking about babies. I said that I hoped to have twins when that day came. Two babies at one time and be done with it. My sister responded, "You can't have twins because you are one. They run every other generation…" and the car came to an abrupt stop. Everyone in the back seat was either on the floor or in the front seat.

I looked at her completely stunned. "What did you say?" She replied, "You didn't know? I'm sorry, I thought you knew that." As far back as I could remember, I had a dream of a nurse holding two babies wrapped in blankets. One in each arm. As she handed them to my mom there was only me in her arms. I would cry out and wake up. After that day, I never had that dream again.

Emotions and memories are powerful. Your life experiences are yours to build on and if necessary, to show where you require some attention and healing. Clearing out the energy of negative affecting emotions affords you the opportunity to live a more joyful and purposeful life.

One time, I was working with a client and his anger surfaced during the session. The emotional flood gates were open! His synapses had flooded his body with chemical-memory of accumulated anger. I knew this was a good thing, for he was flushing these chemical triggers out of his cells and neural networks that had been created, reinforced and stored for years.

He stood up with fists clenched and expressed loudly, "This isn't what I came here for! I feel like this all the time. I want to feel happy!" I asked him to trust the process and continue breathing. I placed a couple drops of Surrender (a pure essential oil blend) into the palms of his hands and had him rub his palms together, then inhale the scent. I repeated the process with Transformation™ (another pure essential oil blend). He resumed breathing the Spiral Breath and after a short time, the anger started to dissipate. With each full breath, the huffing ceased and he became calmer.

When the session was finished, he sat still for a few moments in a blank stare and then he smiled. He could not remember ever feeling that peaceful in his entire life. We finished the session by placing a few drops of Joy™ (another pure essential oils blend) into his palms and repeated the process above. His life changed that day for the better. Equipped with a tool to quickly shift his energy, the relationships with his family changed and he received a promotion at his work.

As you continue to breathe with focused breath work, you build up healing energy or Chi. The more you breathe, the greater the energy you have available to work with. Continuing to breathe when emotions surface, prepares you to eventually reach a point of acceptance. It is then, that you can begin to release the emotion and let it go. When you surrender into a focused breath, unconscious energy can surrender into a conscious change.[40, 41]

At times, the process of shifting energy comes with physical sensations. Sometimes when I flush chemical memory, it feels like ice water is running through my body from the top of my head down to my feet. The rapid wave of cold static electricity crackles inside me as the chemical memory is discharged from my cells. When it leaves the soles of my feet, my body temperature evens out and I am peaceful.

Other sensations that I have experienced or witnessed during an emotional release, have been a rising of body temperature like a heat flush; a sensation of crawling skin; a need to physically move and 'shake off' the energy or have a release of previously unshed tears. I had one young client who would break into singing old Bible hymns when she had cleared the emotion that we were focusing on. She had been adopted and her family thought it was amusing. When asked where she learned those hymns, she simply replied, "I don't know. They just come out."

After a couple sessions, this young girl reached out to hold my hand as she processed. It started with touching her pinky finger to the side of my hand. As she continued to process, she slid her hand under mine. This was a big deal, as she was unable to cope with being touched. A few sessions later, as they were about to leave the office, she ran back to give me a long hug. Her family and I were all in tears. She also turned to hug her mom and sister. They had not before this point been able to really hug her.

*Everyone is different and each will experience,
process and heal in their own way.*

As you clear the chemical memory from your cells and neural networks, you will move into a more positive way of being. You will begin to notice that you no longer react to situations the way you have in the past. Emotional challenges will be much easier to deal with and you will move through issues more quickly and with greater ease.

Challenges will still come; but how you react to them will change. I have found that the challenges give us an opportunity to see how much we have grown.

By now, you have noticed that I enjoy the science and chemistry behind emotions. What can I say… I am an alchemist at heart. An alchemist is one who shifts energy - like emotions.

While we are on the topic of bio-chemical memory, neurotransmitters and synapses, I will continue with the limbic system and the glia brain. These two topics explain why the Spiral Breath is so powerful! Since the brilliant emerald green Light spirals through the limbic system and activates the glia brain and frontal lobes, it is only fitting that I take time to explain them.

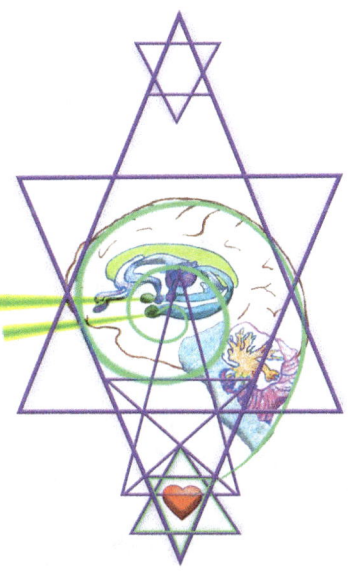

4.1 Spiral Breath Illustration by Gayle Mack

[23] *Evolve Your Brain: The Science of Changing Your Mind* by Joe Dispenza, DC page 196
[24] *Evolve Your Brain: The Science of Changing Your Mind* by Joe Dispenza, DC page 196
[25] *Evolve Your Brain: The Science of Changing Your Mind* by Joe Dispenza, DC page 197, 229
[26] *Evolve Your Brain: The Science of Changing Your Mind* by Joe Dispenza, DC page 196
[27] *Evolve Your Brain: The Science of Changing Your Mind* by Joe Dispenza, DC page 43
[28] *Evolve Your Brain: The Science of Changing Your Mind* by Joe Dispenza, DC page 197
[29] *Evolve Your Brain: The Science of Changing Your Mind* by Joe Dispenza, DC page 175
[30] *Evolve Your Brain: The Science of Changing Your Mind* by Joe Dispenza, DC page 186-187
[31] *Memories Leave their Trace FOCUS - The Flexible Brain* text by Harald Rosch Max Planck Institute of Neurobiology
[32] *The Biology of Belief: Unleashing the Power of Consciousness, Matter & Miracles* by Bruce H. Lipton, Ph. D. page 98
[33] *Evolve Your Brain: The Science of Changing Your Mind* by Joe Dispenza, DC page 434
[34] *Evolve Your Brain: The Science of Changing Your Mind* by Joe Dispenza, DC page 446
[35] *Evolve Your Brain: The Science of Changing Your Mind* by Joe Dispenza, DC page 446
[36] http://catherinedowling.com/breathwork-basics/
[37] http://catherinedowling.com/breathwork-basics/
[38] http://www.goodtherapy.org/learn-about-therapy/types/breathwork
[39] *Breath is a Language* by Joy Manne', PhD http://www.catherinedowling.com/breathwork/ page 20-21
[40] personal opinion and experience
[41] http://catherinedowling.com/breathwork-basics/

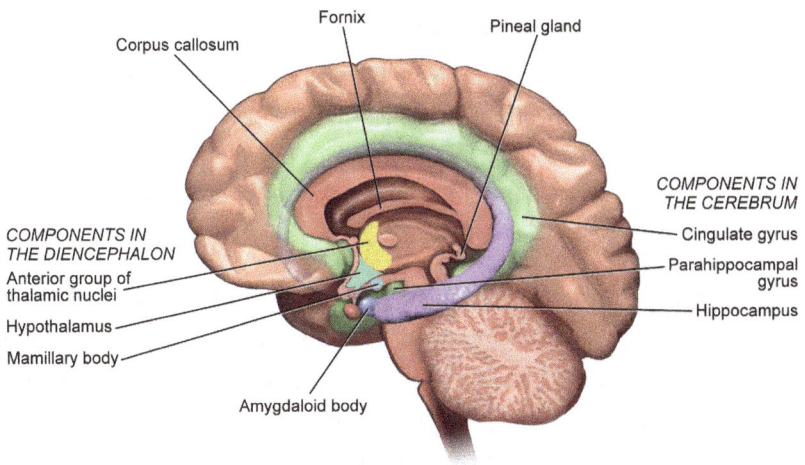

5.1 The Limbic System Blausen.com staff (2014). "Medical gallery of Blausen Medical 2014".
WikiJournal of Medicine 1

Chapter 5:

Limbic System

Even though the limbic system only occupies the lower one-fifth of the brain, the influence on behavior is exponential.[42] This tiny walnut sized, complex system of glands is one of God's masterpieces.

The limbic system (also known as the Midbrain, the chemical brain and our 'emotional brain') is the control center for our emotions, emotional responses and higher consciousness. It is directly related to our memory,[43] our sense of smell, laughter, our behavior, learning, long term memory, our motivation, ambition, creativity; our autonomic responses, our untapped intelligence and our pleasure center.[44, 45] The limbic system automatically controls body temperature, digestion, sugar levels, blood pressure, hormones and is in control of the 'Four F's': Fight, Flight (fleeing), Feeding and Fornicating.[46]

The limbic system is a repository of ancient emotional responses that are prelogical, inherited and acquired through environmental influences, which create a biological and psychobiological foundation for human behavior.[47] The evolution of the limbic system created a unique system for converting chemical communication signals into sensations that are experienced by all of our cells. Our conscious mind experiences these chemical signals as emotions. The conscious mind not only reads the signals, it can also generate the chemical signals within the limbic system that we call emotions.[48]

Candace Pert's study of the human brain brought us the realization that, through self-consciousness, the mind can use the brain to generate "molecules of emotion" and override the system. Her research and book, *Molecules of Emotion: The Science Behind Mind-Body Medicine*, has been the scientific foundation of many forward thinkers in this area of mind-body connections.

Healthy consciousness is beneficial to our wellbeing. Negative emotions that are unconsciously generated can be destructive to our mental, emotional and spiritual wellbeing.[49] Conscious and sub-conscious minds are separate aspects. However, they are also interdependent on each other.[50]

Fundamental reflex behaviors are passed down through offspring in the form of genetic-based instincts. Learned reflex behaviors are conditioned behavioral responses, which become unconscious responses and are not controlled by reason or thought.[51]

Our 'conscious' mind processes thought and information. It is the part of our mind that processes knowledge, conceptions, perceptions and realizations into learning. The conscious mind allows us to focus our attention on one thing. Our conscious mind is our self identity and our free will.[52] It operates our choices, wishes, desires, aspirations and positive thoughts.[53]

Our 'subconscious' mind is controlled by our limbic system, cerebellum and brainstem. It is basically habitual. It replays the same reflex behavioral responses when signaled by same or similar life events in a stimulus-response behavioral program.[54] The subconscious mind is our auto-pilot mode.

*The subconscious mind is more than a million times
more powerful than the conscious mind!* [55]

Programmed messages from our subconscious mind can sabotage our best efforts to change our habits, thinking and emotional response. Neuroscience has now recognized that the conscious mind is in control approximately 5% of the time, while the pre-programmed, subconscious mind influences 95% or more of our life experiences. (Szegedy-Maszak 2005)[56]

The limbic system and glia brain are also an exponential part of achieving higher consciousness. John Chang, nicknamed 'Dynamo Jack,' is living proof that we can achieve higher consciousness. He states, *"We all have undreamed of powers waiting within us, natural and life affirming abilities simply waiting to be released by focusing the innate energy of our minds and brain."* John Chang was observed for many years and worked with a physicist from Albert Einstein University, a medical expert and a scientific investigator. He agreed to be videoed for the purpose of keeping 'what is possible' alive in peoples consciousness.[57]

With the short bit of information that I have presented so far, you can see why I choose to share the techniques and knowledge that can enhance our wellbeing mentally, physically, emotionally and spiritually.

I believe that having some understanding about the functions and capabilities of the limbic system and its individual components will help you to utilize their particular aspects and achieve a greater balance in many areas of your life. Therefore, I have provided a brief overview of the main elements that make up the limbic system and the glia brain.

The amygdala, cingulate gyrus, fornix, pineal, pituitary, hippocampus, hypothalamus, thalamus and limbic cortex are the main components in the limbic system. Some people include the olfactory bulbs in the septal area and some do not. I agree with those who do, as they are important in conjunction with the glia brain.

THE AMYGDALA

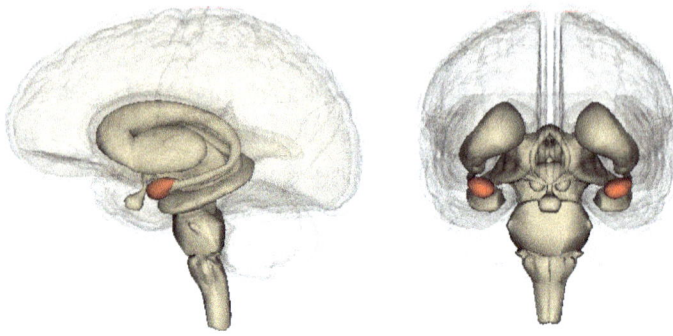

5.2 Amygdala Images generated by Life Science Databases

The amygdala gland is almond shaped and about the size of one. There are two amygdalae, one for each of the left and right hemispheres of the brain. The amygdalae work together in unison and are usually referred to by neurologists in the singular form. The amygdala glands can be found inside of the brain approximately one inch from each temple. A simple way to locate your amygdala gland is by placing your thumbs in your ears and the tips of your middle fingers on your forehead above the inside corners of your eyes. The amygdalae sit on each side of your third eye.[59]

The amygdala is found within the structures of the limbic system and is directly connected to the reptile brain and the frontal lobes. The reptile brain is part of the Triune brain, which consists of three parts, the reptile brain, the mammal brain and the primate brain. The reptile brain address basic body functions, non-thinking reactions, fight or flight and attack counter-attack responses. The mammal brain pertains to emotions and more complex social behaviors. The primate brain and frontal lobes pertain to your advanced thinking and produces, generates and calculates perception. Perception is the aspects of cooperation, imagination, creativity, intuition and logic. The acronym CICIL makes it easy to remember.[60]

The amygdala is the center for forming, retrieving and processing emotions.[61]

Emotions are neural shortcuts that allow you to quickly determine whether something would be pleasant or unpleasant. The amygdala is like an early warning system that enables you to react quickly to avoid danger or harm, even before you know what the cause is.[62]

Neil Slade describes our amygdala as, "a compass that indicates your direction - either towards happiness and survival or away from it. It is inherently a Cooperation/Conflict meter."[63]

The amygdala is associated with the storage of emotional memories, along with the perception of certain situations that are based on these memories.[64] The highly charged emotions such as anger, fear, sadness and joy are chemically encoded by the amygdala for long-term memory.[65]

Functional imaging studies found that the right amygdala and auditory cortex were activated by unpleasant words, while the left frontal pole of the amygdala was activated only by pleasant words.[66] When the amygdala is pointing down and backwards in its direction, we can get locked into negative and not-so-pleasurable emotions, such as, fear, anxiety, anger, rage, depression, feelings of being without hope, etc.[67]

Fortunately, there is an easy way to shift into the frontal pole of our amygdala to recalibrate hope, peace and joy.

Activating the anterior pole of our amygdala stimulates the frontal lobes of our brain. Once this gateway is opened, electro-consciousness energy flows into your frontal lobes and you begin to experience the phenomenon of transcendence. Transcendence automatically rebuilds self-confidence, motivation, self-love, love of life and awakens your full, God-given, genetic potential![68] The frontal lobes, in return, stimulate your amygdala creating a wonderful loop of positive brain energy.[69]

The more you stimulate the anterior amygdala and frontal lobes, the greater your ability to transmute emotional trauma and destructive emotions. Eventually, when you have fully activated your frontal lobes, you will know greater joy, creativity and peace. The beautiful part about activating your frontal lobe and glia brain is that it is easy and can be permanent!

The amygdala is a gateway to happiness, intelligence, increased problem solving skills, intuitive ability and higher consciousness. When you consciously stimulate your anterior amygdala, you produce neuro-chemicals that activate the glial cell formation in the frontal lobe of your brain. Researchers have confirmed that approximately 90% of our frontal lobe is dormant and 'untapped.'[70]

"Happiness is nothing more than self-releasing your 90% dormant brain into transcendence: into whole brain power. Unhappiness is nothing more than enduring the pain of a 10% functioning brain."[71]

Frequent amygdala stimulation turns on previously un-accessed or "hidden" brain functions, such as clairaudience, clairvoyance, pre-cognition, telekinesis, telepathy and other esoteric abilities, as well as, accessing higher dimensional realms of Being.[72]

Your frontal lobes are the most advanced part of your brain. Activating the frontal lobes of the brain can help you transcend space, time, energy, matter and cosmic consciousness. The Universe is made up of these five elements. TDA Lingo gave them the acronym STEM-C for easy recall.

"Cosmic Consciousness is universal and creates space, time, energy and matter. Cosmic consciousness creates energy, which creates sub-atomic particles, which create electrons and protons, which create atoms, which create molecules of deoxyribonucleic acid (DNA)… Cosmic consciousness enters the brain through a pinpoint of tissue at the base of the skull where the bone ends… called the reticular activating formation. This pinpoint of cells [located within the brainstem] form your consciousness click-switch."

When we re-open the circuit and allow cosmic consciousness to flow from our brainstem into our frontal lobes, we naturally generate emotions of love, thoughts of genius, activate the genetic intelligence of our DNA and create harmony between Self, Life and Universe.[73]

You can activate your amygdala and frontal lobes simply by using guided imagery, pure essential oils, sound or toning and focused breath work, like the

Spiral Breath. I explore these topics in greater detail in the next few chapters.

TDA Lingo (Theocharis Docha Anthropotis Lingo), a behavioral researcher, called the process of activating the amygdala "clicking" forward into the anterior amygdala. This "clicking" process lets you know that you have activated the frontal lobes of your brain. TDA Lingo also termed this process "popping" into your frontal lobes. As we learn to control this process, we can actually feel the sensation as we slide into the front anterior amygdalae and often times we will hear the click inside our heads.

When you can "click" or "pop" forward into the anterior portion of the amygdala and your frontal lobes, you can reach feelings and sensations of euphoria. When you are fully activated, you are in a state of bliss and euphoria!

To locate your forebrain or frontal lobes, place one hand over your forehead. Everything under your palm is your frontal lobes. Your frontal lobes are the front 1/3 of your brain.[74]

When working with clients, I will often hear the clicking inside their head. If I am holding one hand to their frontal lobe and the other hand at the base of their skull I can feel the click with my hands. When they shift into their anterior amygdalae and frontal lobes, my clients will get very relaxed and at times, giddy or euphoric. This process of moving into the anterior amygdala, also has a tendency to switch on the persons' healing and psychic abilities.

Discovering TDA Lingo's work, as well as his student, Neil Slade, who wrote *Tickle Your Amygdala* enabled me to explain scientifically what was happening when we heard this clicking sound during sessions.

TDA Lingo and his students described the awakening or activation of their amygdalae as: "feels like flying" or "being tickled with a feather."

For me, the area of my third eye begins to vibrate. As the sensation increases, my amygdala "hum." And at times, when I tone while my anterior amygdala is activated, I begin to harmonize with myself. My single tone merges into two or three tones at the same time – a harmonic chord.

Daily practice of the Spiral Breath can activate your amygdalae and frontal lobes. Within a very short period of time, you will be able to activate your frontal lobes at will and on command.

✡ ✡ ✡

OLFACTORY BULBS

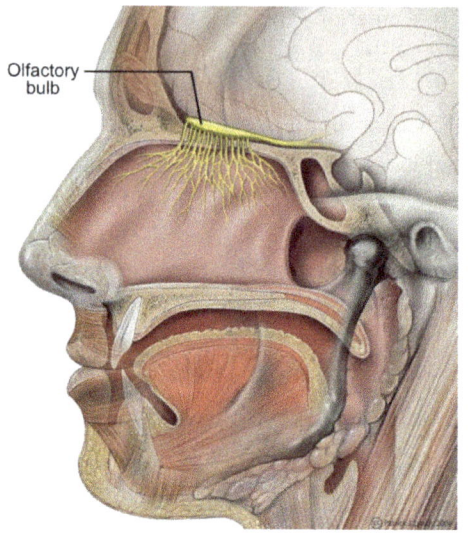

5.3 *Olfactory Bulb by Patrick J. Lynch, medical illustrator*

The olfactory bulbs are located in the forebrain on the underside of the brain, behind the eyes and are connected directly to the amygdalae. The olfactory bulbs have open access to the nasal passages and allow the frequency of a scent to have an effect on your amygdala glands, nervous system, limbic system, brain, organs, hormone balance, memories, stress levels, etc., simply by inhaling and breathing it in.[75, 76, 77, 78] With a pure essential oil for example, as you inhale, the scent enters the nasal cavity. Tiny hairs called cilia receive the frequencies of the oils and immediately transfer the frequencies through millions of tightly packed olfactory receptor cells.[79]

Olfactory and taste receptor cells are expressed primarily in the nasal olfactory epithelium and gustatory taste bud cells. These receptors act as an antenna system that receives the frequency of the scent and then transmits real-time signals within seconds, via the glomeruli, to the brain and limbic system. The gustatory system is the sensory system comprised of taste cells in the mouth that sense the five taste modalities of salty, sweet, bitter, sour and savory (umami).[80]

Signal impulses transmitted to the amygdala and other parts of the limbic system can have a psychological and physiological effect on emotions, memories, blood pressure, heart rate and stress levels. This is the science behind Aromatherapy.[81]

As a neural circuit, the glomerular layer receives direct signal input from afferent nerves, made up of the axons from approximately ten million olfactory receptor neurons in the olfactory mucosa in the nasal cavity. This glomeruli layer of the olfactory bulb is the first level of synaptic processing. The second layer contains astrocytes (glia), interneurons and mitral cells.[82] I will address astrocytes, glia, synapses, axons, etc., in the chapter on the Glia Brain.

The olfactory bulbs are the reason why smelling an apple pie can bring you back to grandma's kitchen or the scent on a shirt of someone you love brings you comfort. Just as quickly as the scent of baby powder can move you into a sweet disposition, scents can also trigger emotional wounds. The smell of Old Spice cologne used to make the hair stand up on the back of my neck and my fists would automatically clench ready to protect myself. I could be walking through a crowd and be triggered into hyperawareness within seconds of interacting with the scent.

Fortunately, from my research and my experience with techniques like the Spiral Breath and the blessings of pure therapeutic grade essential oil blends like SARA™ and Forgiveness,™ I was able to transform the bio-chemical memory that triggered uneasy emotions and gently replace them with emotions that elicit harmony.

The olfactory bulbs are not just for stimulating the amygdalae and memories. According to the BBC, in a recent experimental surgery, surgeons in Poland took nerve cell bundles from the olfactory bulbs of a paraplegic man and transferred them to the severed nerves in his spinal column.

Olfactory nerve cells are one of the few cells in our nervous system that regenerate throughout our entire life. These olfactory nerve cells were found to have regenerative potential on tissue and nerves.

One of the patient's two olfactory bulbs was removed and the olfactory ensheathing cells (OECs) were grown in a culture. Two weeks later, the surgeons placed 100 micro injections of the olfactory ensheathing cells above and below the damaged area of the spinal cord, along with four thin strips of nerve tissue taken from the man's ankle to bridge the 8 millimeter gap.

The scientists believe that the OECs acted as a pathway to stimulate the spinal cord cells causing a regeneration. Using the nerve grafts as a bridge, the olfactory cells did in fact, regenerate new cells, which reconnected the severed nerves and spinal cord.

Before the surgery, Darek Fidyka had been paralyzed for nearly two years with no sign of recovery in site, despite many months of intensive physiotherapy.

Within three months of the transplant, Mr. Fidyka noticed muscle mass improving in his left thigh. Six months after surgery, the paraplegic man from Bulgaria took his first steps with the assistance of leg braces and his physiotherapist. Two years after surgery, Mr. Fidyka can walk with the assistance of a walker and has regained lower body functions. He is reported to be the first person to walk after experiencing a total severed spinal cord.[83]

HIPPOCAMPUS

5.4 Hippocampus and Seahorse by Professor Laszlo Seress derivative work: Anthonyhcole

The hippocampus is a curved tube that connects the almond shaped amygdala to the thalamus. It is important that these three glands are properly functioning with each other, as they influence the way we find friendship, love and express our moods.

It is interesting to mention that the hippocampus is shaped like a seahorse. Venetian anatomist Julius Caesar Aranzi (1587) named it after the Greek word "hippo" which means horse and "kampos" for sea or sea monster.

The hippocampus contains two interconnecting bilateral symmetrical parts known as Ammon's horn and the dentate gyrus. These two parts of the hippocampus run along the edge of both cerebral cortex hemispheres and connects them to the limbic system. Around 1832, a Parisian surgeon, de Garengeot referenced the hippocampus as "cornu Ammonis," which means horn of Amun after the ancient Egyptian god.[84]

The hippocampus receives signal information from the thalamus and also transports signal information from serotonin, norepinepherine and dopamine along its tightly packed cell layers. Neuronal cells are neatly organized within these tightly packed layers of the hippocampus. They form a neural plasticity called long-term potentiation (LTP), which is one of the primary processes in which memory is stored in the brain.[85, 86]

The hippocampus converts information from short-term memory to long-term memory. Damage to the olfactory region can impair the hippocampal theta rhythms and affect certain types of memory. Severe damage to the hippocampus in both cortex hemispheres can cause difficulty in forming new memories.[87]

The dorsal (upper) region of the hippocampus works with our spatial navigation, memory, verbal memory and our learning of conceptual information. The ventral (lower) region of the hippocampus operates our fear conditioning.[88]

The hippocampus has two prominent patterns of energy activity, which can be measured by an electroencephalogram (EEG). An EEG can measure the neural population activity and the waves of electrical activity generated within the hippocampus.

One pattern is the theta mode, which functions while in active states, alert behavior and during REM (Rapid Eye Movement/dreaming) sleep. During an EEG, theta mode will register dominate Large Regular waves.[89]

The tightly compacted neural layers of the hippocampus can produce some of the largest EEG signals within the brain. Some signals have been recorded as reaching 3 – 10 hertz and lasting for several seconds. The spiking of neurons creates a wave pattern that travels along the length of the hippocampus. This is known as a theta rhythm.[90]

The second prominent pattern of activity generated from the hippocampus is the Large Irregular Activity (LIA). The LIA is present when in a slow-wave or non-dreaming sleep and during an inactive waking state like resting or eating. The LIA pattern registers sharp burst waves that are irregular or random in their nature.[91]

Memory is a two stage process, whereupon the memories are stored within the hippocampus during the active experience and then transferred to the neocortex for long term memory during sleep.[92]

Walking and aerobic exercising has been found to increase the size of the hippocampus, thus improving memory and spatial functions.[93]

Long term stress, depression, oxygen deprivation, infection, inflammation and excessive excitability can cause a reduction of new neurons, which in turn, can cause the hippocampus to atrophy and deteriorate.[94]

When we experience a traumatic or an emotionally stressful event, our hypothalamus, in concert with our amygdala, release stress hormones that create an encoded biochemical memory of that event. The encoded chemical memory is then transferred to the hippocampus, to be stored into long term memory. Our heightened state of awareness locks that memory into our brain.[95]

When we recall the memory or when we are triggered into remembering that memory by anything related to that experience (such as sound, smells, sight, thoughts or actions), the memory is transferred back to the hippocampus. Here it prompts **the hypothalamus and the amygdala to produce more of the same encoded chemical memory that causes the body and the mind to react as if the event were happening at that very moment. The body and the mind relive that memory with the same increased heart rate, breathing patterns or state of panic with only the power of 'thought.'** [96]

Same is true with an extremely positive experience. We are in essence, training our mind and body to respond in an auto-pilot mode.

Activating the amygdala, frontal lobes and glia brain can help support a more harmonious environment and regenerate the hippocampus.

THALAMUS

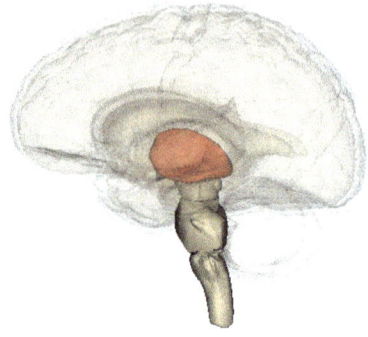 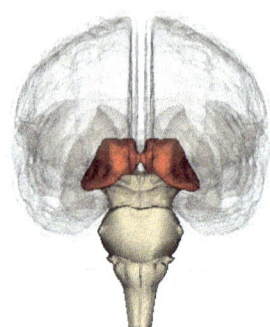

5.5 Thalamus Images by Life Science Databases

The thalamus is a complex structure that has multiple functions. It acts like a hub or relay station. Nearly all the nerves that connect one part of the brain to another; that connect the body to the brain or the brain to the body meet at the thalamus.[97] It works like a switchboard operator for the hippocampus, receiving and sending messages to their appropriate places. Tiny myelinated fibers connect the thalamus to its subparts of the cerebral cortex that address memory, attention, perception, cognition, awareness, thought, language and consciousness.[98]

Every signal from the environment goes through the thalamus. Every sensory organ (eyes, ears, skin, tongue and nose) sends messages to the thalamus, which then identifies them, sorts them and sends the signals to their intended target.[99]

The thalamus is located above the brain stem between the cerebral cortex and the mid-brain. Its name is derived from the Greek word for "inner chamber." The thalamus has two symmetrical parts that resemble the shape and the size of a walnut. These two parts are connected by a flattened gray band called the interthalamic adhesion.

The thalamus connects to the hippocampus, cerebral cortex, subcortical areas and to the spinal cord through the spinothalamic tract. The spinothalamic tract is a sensory pathway that transmits signals from all the senses to the thalamus related to pain, temperature, itch and crude touch, with the exception of the olfactory.[100, 101]

This sensory pathway has strong thalamic nucleus connections that affect our sight, sound/hearing, touch and taste. The sense of smell (the olfactory) is the only sense without a thalamic nucleus.[102]

The thalamus is important in regulating our arousal, our levels of awareness, some emotion and memory functions, as well as our activity and motor skills. The thalamus also has a large role in regulating our states of sleep, wakefulness and our consciousness.[103]

Are you beginning to see why the limbic system is so important? Let's continue.

HYPOTHALAMUS

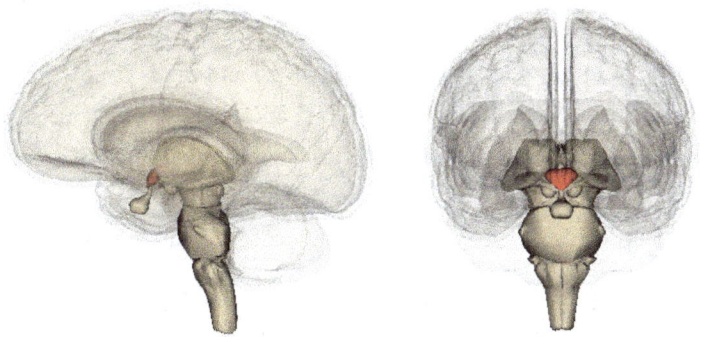

5.6 Hypothalamus Images by Life Science Databases

The hypothalamus is located above the brainstem and under the thalamus. One of the most important functions of the hypothalamus is to connect the nervous system to the endocrine system through the pituitary gland. The link between the neural and endocrine system also connects emotions and sexual activity to our higher cognitive systems. [104]

The primary function of the hypothalamus is to keep our body in homeostasis. This means that it is constantly attempting to maintain the perfect balance of the environment inside our body as it relates to the external influences of our daily and lifelong habits and experiences. Regulating our autonomic nervous system, blood pressure, body temperature, hunger, food intake, thirst, fatigue, sleep, sex drive and breathing are just a few of these functions.[105]

The hypothalamus produces chemical messengers for every organ or tissue for the entire body.[106] These messengers are known as neuropeptides, neurotransmitters and neuromodulators. They enable homeostasis to take place within the body or trigger a survival mode of 'fight or flight' response. The hypothalamus makes sure that your body is physiologically ready to run, jump or turn quickly when necessary.[107] The hypothalamus also oversees the internal state of your body so it can direct chemical messengers towards the action of flight or flight verses digestion.[108]

In a stress response, whether it is in real-time, a thought, the anticipation of the presence of stress or the memory of a past stress, the thalamus signals the hypothalamus to produce chemical messengers called peptides that signal certain body parts to switch on and produce. The hypothalamus manufactures and releases the peptide corticotrophin releasing hormone (CRH) and sends it to the pituitary. The CRH signals the pituitary to manufacture and release the chemical peptide adrenocorticotropic hormone (ACTH). This chemical messenger is received by the adrenal gland receptors and gives the signal to produce various chemicals called glucocorticoids.[109] The most common glucocorticoid is cortisol.[110, 111]

Both cortisol and adrenaline (also produced by the adrenal gland) are responsible for most of the chemicals generated during a stress response. When the hypothalamus perceives a threat, it mobilizes the sympathetic nervous system (SNS) and the hypothalamus-pituitary-adrenal gland axis (HPA axis) to create a chemical feedback loop that deliver the chemicals required to react and then to find a balance.[112]

The hypothalamus receives and recognizes environmental or emotional threats; then signals the pituitary to organize the 50 trillion cells of our body to prepare for the perceived threat, as well as, signal the adrenal glands to produce the bio-chemicals necessary to invoke the 'fight or flight' response.[113]

With chronic stress or chronic recall, the body will require more of the chemicals to achieve the same level of homeostasis. This sets us up for becoming 'emotionally addicted' to our thoughts.[114] When we are locked in this chemical feedback loop, we are no longer in control - our emotions are. We can find ourselves losing our identity to our past memories or a past trauma. Our dreams, ambitions and goals get lost in the flurry of emotions, bio-chemicals, actions and reactions.[115]

The blessing is that once we realize that we are stuck in the muckity-muck, we can begin to make change and change can be as simple as learning the Spiral Breath. The Spiral Breath can activate our frontal lobes and move us into a more centered place. Incorporating pure essential oils on a daily basis can enhance the Spiral Breath, as well as, enhance our daily lives. I will share several modalities throughout this book that can enhance the Spiral Breath and help you bring about a more harmonious change.

The hypothalamus has an innate sense to automatically make changes within our body when it detects an unfavorably change that could potentially interrupt the state of our balanced health.[116] The hypothalamus regulates the birthing process as well as, the synthesis of milk in new mothers.[117]

The hypothalamus coordinates many hormonal, behavioral and circadian rhythms, along with, complex patterns of neuroendocrine outputs and the release of neurohormones that can either stimulate or inhibit the secretion of pituitary hormones, such as oxytocin and vasopressin. [118]

The hypothalamus responds to internal generated signals, as well as, external generated signals, such as, day length for regulating the circadian rhythm, Delta brain waves and olfactory stimuli (including pheromones). Delta brain wave signaling can influence the secretion of releasing hormones, such as, GHRH (Growth Hormone Releasing Hormone).

The hypothalamus is also linked to laughter. Laughter helps to reduce the stress hormones produced in the hypothalamus and has been known to lower blood pressure. The hypothalamus is the part of the brain that is not protected by the blood brain barrier. This allows the hypothalamus to monitor what chemical messengers are going into the blood, while regulating the stress hormones and peptides being produced and released.[119]

Over stimulation of the hypothalamus can produce loud and uncontrollable laughter, while under stimulation can cause a lack of laughter.

Using an electroencephalograph (EEG), Humor researcher Peter Derks was able to measure the brain activity produced in the brain when people laughed. The largest response of activity was located in the frontal lobes of each person. The brainwave activity then spread out into the sensory processing area of the occipital lobe and stimulated physical motor responses. Interesting to note here, is that the left hemisphere of the brain analyzes the words and the structure of a joke, while the right hemisphere works to 'get' the joke.[120]

It is safe to say that a good hearty laugh on a daily basis is very healthy for our body and our brain health.

Also included in the limbic system are the pineal and pituitary glands.

Recently, there has been much talk about the pineal and pituitary. Their symbolic images show up in art, architecture and religious artifacts. Several suggestions have been circulating in the media to help clear and activate these glands. The Spiral Breath can activate the entire limbic system and the glia cells at the same time.

PITUITARY

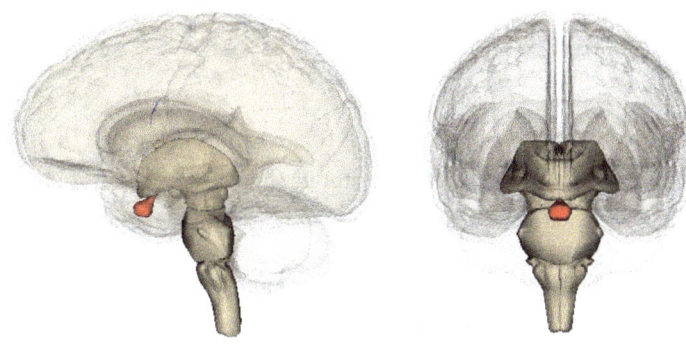

5.7 Pituitary Images by Life Science Databases

The pituitary gland is heart shaped and hangs at the end of the hypothalamus like a piece of fruit.[121] It is cradled harmoniously within the sellaturcica of the sphenoid bone.[122, 123] The pituitary gland is about the size of a pea and weighs 0.5 grams (0.018 oz) in humans,[124] yet it produces some of the most powerful hormones for our body.[125] It is an important link between the nervous system and the endocrine system. The pituitary acts like a switchboard operator, who signals the other endocrine glands to produce or stop producing hormones.[126]

The pituitary gland has three lobes: the anterior, the intermediate and the posterior. The anterior and posterior lobes secrete nine hormones that regulate homeostasis, which is our internal environment. The nine hormones from the pituitary gland influence ALL the endocrine glands and virtually every cell in the body, one way or another.[127] They are responsible for thyroid activity, regulating body temperature, blood pressure, energy management, all functions of the sex organs, ovulation and estrogen production in women, testosterone production in men, human reproduction, fluid and water retention, sleep, growth, appetite, metabolism, sexual development; plus the emotions of fear and pleasure, to name a few.[128]

The anterior pituitary lobe (adenohypophysis) is glandular tissue that develops from the primitive digestive tract.[129] The anterior pituitary lobe produces and secretes six hormones. The posterior pituitary lobe (neurohypophysis), which is neural tissue,[130] only stores and releases two hormones that are produced in the hypothalamus.[131]

The anterior pituitary lobe produces: human growth hormone (hGH), thyroid stimulating hormone (TSH), follicle-stimulating hormone (FSH), luteinizing hormone (LH), prolactin (PRL) and adrenocorticotropic hormone (ACTH).[132, 133]

Each of these hormones target specific glands and tissue in the body. The thyroid gland, ovaries, testes, mammary glands, liver, the adrenal cortex and adipose tissue are all stimulated by hormones produced in the anterior pituitary.

The two hormones that the posterior pituitary stores and releases are vasopressin antidiuretic hormone (ADH) and oxytocin. Vasopressin assists in the regulating of water and fluid retention and in high concentrations, causes constriction of blood vessels, which increases blood pressure by increasing peripheral resistance.[134, 135] Oxytocin helps regulate sexual reproduction and is a key hormone that regulates empathy, love, positive attitudes, bonding, traumatic bonding, uterine contractions, preparing fetal neurons for delivery, maternal behavior, breastfeeding and more.[136, 137, 138] Deficiencies in this hormone have been detected with attachment disorders, sociopaths, psychopaths, narcissists and lying.[139, 140]

The intermediate pituitary is a webbing of cells between the anterior and posterior pituitary lobes that secretes the hormone melanocyte-stimulating hormone (MSH), which induces melanin production in the skin's melanocytes.[141]

Although the pituitary is considered the 'master' gland, it takes its cues from the hypothalamus. The hormones produced from the hypothalamus either stimulate secretions (releasing hormones) or turn off the secretions (inhibiting hormones). The hypothalamus releases thyrotropin-releasing hormone (TRH) and gonadotropic-releasing hormone (GnRH) also known as gonadoliberin, that stimulate the anterior pituitary lobe to release TSH, FSH and LH, while growth hormone-inhibiting hormone (GHIH) prevents the secretion of hGH and TSH.[142]

The endocrine glands work in tandem with each other, so it is important to have them all functioning at their greatest potential and synchronized with each other. I mentioned the hypothalamus/pituitary/adrenal (HPA) axis in the above section on the hypothalamus. Similar to the HPA axis is the hypothalamus/pituitary/thyroid (HPT) axis, which can cause behavioral, emotional, physiological and psychological issues when they are not performing at their peak ability.

Emotionally traumatic events that are experienced in early childhood and adolescence can have an adverse affect on the HPA axis.[143, 144] If the emotional trauma is not addressed and healed, it can influence patterns of stress response within the body.

Prolonged stress can affect the HPA/HPT axis and generate feelings of inadequacy, overwhelm and burnout.[145] Check with your physician or health practitioner if you require more assistance with this. The Spiral Breath technique and other modalities that are mentioned in this book can assist in finding some calm in a hectic environment.

Now we will address the spiritual aspects of the pituitary gland.

It has been said that the pineal compares to the pituitary as "intuition is to reason."[146]

The energies of the lower 5 chakras, which are influenced by the emotional, mental and physical third dimensional issues, unite at the sixth chakra. It is here that the bridge to higher consciousness begins. The pituitary is the direct connection between the physical third dimension and the higher vibrational realms.[147] Regular stimulation of the pituitary gland activates the sixth chakra and increases theta brain waves.[148]

The sixth chakra is referred to as the "seat of the mind,"[149] whereas the pineal (seventh chakra) is known as the "seat of the soul."[150] When the pituitary and sixth chakra are activated, the frontal lobes engage to produce greater creativity, expanded awareness, as well as, increased intellectual and psychic acuity.

The pituitary and pineal work in tandem with each other to activate the frontal lobes and achieve a more spiritual, multidimensional and higher consciousness. Master M. H. Blavatsky stated that "the pituitary is the page and the light bearer of the pineal gland." [151] Dr. Krumm-Heller, professor of medicine at the University of Berlin, states that, "Between the pituitary and the pineal glands exists a small, very subtle channel or capillary. This channel or capillary is only found in living human beings." [152]

With all my research and personal experience, I realize that the pituitary is one of the keys to higher consciousness. As I was preparing this section, a quote from Nikola Tesla's drifted down into my consciousness and I saw that within the pituitary gland, aspects of the Universal Code can be found. Nikola Tesla said, "If you only knew the magnificence of the 3, 6, 9, then you would have a key to the Universe." [153]

The three lobes of the pituitary gland create a trinity, as they set up a triangle or pyramid shape and a frequency that can be found in all creation.[154] This trinity produces 9 hormones, of which six of the hormones are produced within the anterior pituitary. There within the pituitary gland lies the 3-6-9.

PINEAL

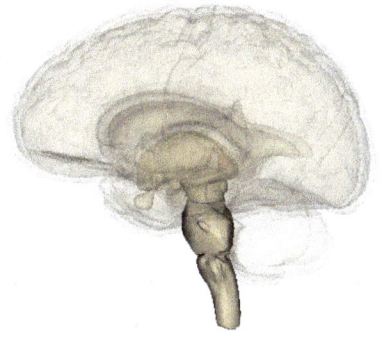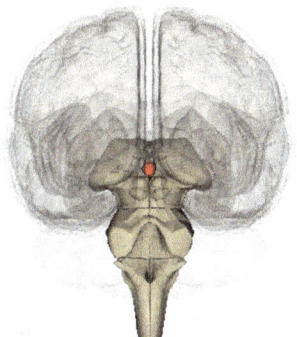

5.8 Pineal Images by Life Science Databases

"The lamp of the body is the eye; when your eye is sound, your whole body [is] bright; but when your eye is bad, your whole body is dark.

If, then, the light in you is darkness, how great is the darkness!

...The wholly luminous body's brightness is like a lamp giving light with its rays..."
Q 11:34 - 11:36 THE GOSPEL SAYINGS OF QUELLE

On the physical and scientific aspects, the pineal gland is a reddish-grey gland that is approximately 8 mm in length, 4 mm in width[155] and resembles a pine cone in its shape. When fully activated and engorged, it is about the size of a grape. However, as we age, along with lack of use, improper nutrition, electromagnetic stress and chemical toxicity, the pineal gland begins to calcify and reduce in size to that of a small pea[156] or pine nut.

The pineal gland is located near the midbrain, between the right and left hemispheres of the brain; where the two rounded thalamic bodies come together.[157] The pineal is connected to the posterior end of the third ventricle through its stalk.[158]

As tiny as it is, the pineal gland receives the highest amount of blood flow, nutrients and oxygen than any other gland or organ, with the exception of the kidneys.[159] The pineal gland can receive an extraordinary amount of oxygen, especially with pineal activation exercises and breath work like the Spiral Breath.[160, 161, 162]

The Pineal gland also receives information at lightening speeds. Fast light phenomena runs through the retina within the eye, to the optic nerve connections into the hypothalamus, through the upper ganglia on either side of the upper cervicals of the spine, to the corpus callosum and into the pineal gland. The multi-stimuli pineal gland also reacts to our physiological senses, such as sound and scent, light and dark, as well as frequency, resonance and vibrations.[163]

The pineal is an endocrine gland that produces serotonin, melatonin, pinolin, 5-MeO-DMT and DMT.[164] The pineal gland uses tryptophan to produce serotonin and is responsible for converting the pre-cursor hormone/neurotransmitter serotonin into melatonin. The ability to convert serotonin becomes compromised if the pineal is calcified or atrophied.[165] The calcification of the pineal gland accumulates calcium particles called corona arenacea or 'brain sand' that have been associated with certain types of migraines, cluster headaches, Alzheimer and aging.[166]

Serotonin is produced and circulated by the pineal gland during daylight hours and keeps us awake and alert. In our waking consciousness, serotonin helps us think clearly, be rational and interact socially. [167, 168]

Serotonin can influence our mood and emotions, such as our joy, happiness, satisfaction, optimism and a sense of well being. [169, 170] Serotonin generates the serenity, ecstasy and the lingering pleasure sensation when we feel good.[171] Studies have found a solid link between feeling good and living longer.[172]

When serotonin levels are deficient, it can impart a lack of joy.[173] Low levels of serotonin can also cause you to crave bread, flour products, candy, sweets and chocolate. Eating these foods can cause a rapid increase of serotonin levels within the brain and shift sadness into joy.[174] You have heard the phrase, "chocolate can be orgasmic." Now you know why. Naturally elevated serotonin levels can ease these cravings, while maintaining a sense of joy.

Serotonin is not only a 'feel good' hormone/neurotransmitter, it also affects and/or regulates numerous body functions, such as, digestion, blood clotting, bone density and sexual function.[175]

Melatonin is a 'super-molecule' that can penetrate every cell in our body.[176] It can also cross the Blood Brain Barrier (BBB). Melatonin has many beneficial properties and characteristics, such as, an antioxidant to decrease oxidative stress, anti-inflammatory; it is anti-apoptotic, beneficial for cardiovascular system and blood pressure, as well as, benefits pregnancy and the birth process.[177] As a neuro-protector for the Central Nervous System (CNS), melatonin is beneficial for traumatic brain injury (TBI) and spinal cord injuries (SCI).[178]

Low concentration of melatonin has been linked to depression.[179] Melatonin is an anti-aging hormone that influences our sexual development, menopause, skin and memory.[180] As an antioxidant, melatonin is five times more powerful than vitamin C and two times more powerful than vitamin E.[181]

Although melatonin is primarily produced in the pineal gland, it is also produced in some degree from our retina, intestines, liver, kidney, spleen, ovaries, bone marrow, leukocytes and lymphocytes.[182]

Melatonin also influences our wake - sleep cycle. The pineal gland begins to release melatonin as the day becomes dark and slows its production after we peak in our first REM sleep and as the day becomes light.[183] Reduction of melatonin can create disturbances in our sleep and has also been linked to certain heart complications and a lowered immune.[184]

As we fall asleep, our brainwave patterns quickly move into alpha; followed by theta and then delta, which is our deepest sleep and slowest brainwave pattern. Deep sleep initiates our biological repair process.[185] It is one of the reasons why good, deep sleep is so important for our immune and the well being of our mind.

It has been noted that women with breast cancer, men with prostate issues and autistic children were found to have less than half the normal levels of melatonin. Nightshift workers have a 50 percent greater chance of cancer due to lower melatonin levels.[186]

The pineal gland is light sensitive, thus it has a built in biological clock and regulates our biochemistry to the subtle rhythms, such as seasonal, lunar, astrological and celestial changes, as well as, time zones, daily shifts from day to night and the duration of daylight to darkness.[187]

The pineal gland only secretes melatonin at night, as we sleep and when it is dark. Each day, our body loses 2 million red blood cells per second. Our body is designed to replace those cells roughly at the same rate per second through a division of cells called cell mitosis. This process creates free radicals that attack healthy cells.[188] Melatonin is the antioxidant that neutralizes the damaging effects of free radicals.[189] Appropriate sleep in a dark room and the addition of natural pineal stimulation, like the Spiral Breath and meditation, can contribute to a healthy production of melatonin.

The pineal gland also produces the natural chemical N-dimethyl-tryptamine (DMT) that can increase altered states of higher consciousness, which brings us to the spiritual aspect. Melatonin is converted into pinolin, 5-MeO-DMT and DMT just before we move into REM (rapid eye movement) sleep or our dream state.[190]

Pinolin is a cellular repair hormone. Pinolin stimulates cell division, which regenerates and repairs cells and DNA. Pinolin, 5-MeO-DMT and DMT are able to intercalate. Intercalation means it is able to move between the base pairs (genetic coding) of DNA within our cells and alter the gene expression, the pattern of genes and copy genetic codes in the form of the messenger RNA.[191] Pinolin is also present with lucid dreaming.[192]

5-MeO-DMT (also known as 'akashon') is luminescent and emits light. After being stimulated by its light, it becomes phosphorescent. 5-MeO-DMT can initiate telepathy, the sensation of astral traveling outside of your body in a spatial hologram-like reality and invoke deep, meditative trance states.[193] 5-MeO-DMT activates the cerebral cortex 40% more than normal.[194] The cerebral cortex is the largest region and the most anterior of the brain and plays a key role in memory, attention, cognition, awareness, thought, language and consciousness.[195] The frontal lobes are part of the cerebral cortex.[196]

DMT is called the visionary hormone.[197] If enough DMT is circulated through the body, our eyesight can actually expand to infrared and ultraviolet.[198] DMT has also been referred to as the "Spirit Molecule" and a book of the same title has been written by Rick Strassman. Structurally, melatonin and DMT are very similar and serotonin is the pre-cursor for both.

Deep meditation, focused breath work, like the Spiral Breath and pineal gland stimulating modalities will allow you to release DMT naturally from within your own body and it can reduce your stress levels![199] Stress can increase cortisol and adrenaline production. The elevated cortisol and adrenaline can interfere with serotonin and melatonin levels, both of which are crucial for DMT production. Take time to relax, meditate and breathe. Listening to or achieving Theta or Delta Brain waves through meditation can also stimulate the production of natural occurring DMT from the Pineal gland.[200]

It was interesting to discover that the pineal is the first gland to form in a fetus and it can be detected at three weeks of gestation. It is fully developed forty nine days after conception, upon which it releases the first surge of DMT that brings the Vital Life Force into the fetus body.[201]

The second release of DMT is at birth. During our lifetime, DMT is naturally released when our pineal gland is activated and stimulated through deep meditation, breath work, sound and achieving shamanic states of higher consciousness.[202]

It is also worth mentioning that just before we expire our physical body, we purge the last of our DMT supply. This is known as the 'surge' or a 'rally.' It helps the physical body prepare for the transition from the physical realm into the Heavenly realms.[203]

Although DMT is naturally produced in the pineal gland and that is how I prefer to access it, I feel that I must be complete with my information. Here is my disclaimer: *The following information is presented only for the purpose to deliver facts and NOT meant to condone or as a suggestion of use.*

DMT is the active ingredient in psilocybin, which is a naturally occurring psychedelic compound produced by more than 200 species of mushrooms, collectively known as psilocybin mushrooms, hallucinogenic or 'magic' mushrooms. Archeological evidence suggests that psilocybin mushrooms have been used in spiritual and ritual ceremonies by the Mayan and Aztec cultures of Mesoamerica for over 7,000 years.

DMT is also found in the ayahuasca tea that the Amazon shamans use in spiritual ceremony to achieve altered states of consciousness or out of body experiences for those who choose not to do it on their own. However, it often comes with unfavorable bodily side effects. The chemical compounds in natural occurring DMT are similar to synthetic man-made psychedelic drugs like LSD. Swiss Chemist Albert Hoffman isolated psilocybin in his lab in 1957 and produced the synthetic compound a year later.[204]

DMT naturally produced within our own pineal gland is a biochemical process, where a hormone cascade takes place as tryptophan is converted into serotonin, which converts into melatonin, then 5-MeO-DMT and finally converts into DMT. This process creates metabolites (waste products) that inhibit the production of a continual DMT release by the pineal, in order to maintain a biochemical balance.[205]

Respectful use, like that in the shamanic traditions, may not disturb the balance. However, with frequent use of outside sources of DMT from plants or synthetic forms, the chain of conversion and balance is not accomplished. This leads to an excess of DMT metabolites, that compromise the pineal gland and stops production of natural, biological DMT.[206]

Spiritual Aspects

Enough science and biology on the pineal gland. Let's return to the spiritual aspects of the pineal gland, which is one of my favorite subjects.

The pineal gland is one of the most revered parts of our body, especially within the mystic cultures. The ancient Egyptians and esoteric societies, like the Therapeutae and Essenes protected the teachings, wisdom and the benefits pertaining to the pineal with great care.[207, 208]

The literal translation of the Biblical Hebrew word Peniel means "Face of God."[209] The pineal gland is known as the pineal body, epiphysis, epiphysis cerebri, conarium and the third eye. It is considered to be the gateway to other worldly dimensions.[210] Satyananda in 1972 stated, "…the pineal gland is the receptor and sender of the subtle vibrations which carry thoughts and psychic phenomena throughout the cosmos."[211]

Herophilus, a Greek physician three hundred years before the birth of Christ, discovered and illustrated the pineal gland. He also believed that the pineal played a major role in consciousness and was the 'gateway' to our real self.[212]

Rene` Descartes, a seventeenth century philosopher and scientist, wrote about the pineal gland in his first book, *Treatise of Man* (written before 1637, but published posthumously between 1662-1664). In his second book, *The Passions of the Soul* (1649), Descartes referred to the pineal as the "principle Seat of the Soul and the place in which thoughts are formed."[213] Plato called the pineal gland the 'Connection to the Realms of Thought' (Knowing - Gnosis) and the 'Eye of Wisdom.'[214]

Other metaphysical names for the pineal gland are the Seat of God, the Seat of Christ Consciousness,[215] the Seat of the Soul,[216] the Seat of Illumination,[217] the Solar Fire,[218] the Eye of Horus,[219] the Eye of Ra,[220] the Eye of Heru,[221] the Eye of Shiva,[222] the Cave of Isis (the Goddess),[223] the Star Chamber of Isis,[224] the Holy of Holies,[225] the Throne of the Most High,[226] the Center of Awareness, the Center of Bliss and the Heavenly Heart.

> *"The Heavenly Heart is like the dwelling place,*
> *the Light is the master…*
> *Therefore you only have to make the Light circulate:*
> *that is the deepest and most wonderful secret.*
> *The Light is easy to move, but difficult to fix.*
> *If it is allowed to go long enough in a circle,*
> *then it crystallizes itself:*
> *that is the natural spirit – body. .*
> *This crystallized spirit is formed beyond the nine Heavens.*
> *It is the condition of which it is said in the*
> *Book of the Seal of the Heart:*
> *Silently in the morning thou fliest upward.*
> *In carrying out this fundamental truth*
> *you need to seek for no other methods,*
> *but must only concentrate your thoughts on it."*
> THE SECRET OF THE GOLDEN FLOWER [227]

When you regularly stimulate your pineal gland, it naturally begins to release the bio-chemical DMT. A stimulated or activated pineal can bring about euphoria, accelerate learning, enhance intuition, as well as, multi-sensory and extrasensory perception.[228] It can allow you to access other esoteric modalities, such as, prophetic dreams and visions, Kundalini awakening and shamanic states of consciousness, tapping into Divine Wisdom, higher intelligence, Direct Knowing, Universal Knowledge and accessing the Akashic Records. It also enables you to astral project, astral travel, time travel, bi-locate, remote view, move multidimensional and quantum jump alternate realities.[229]

I know first hand that these things are possible. I have accomplished many of the above mentioned aspects, such as, astral travel, experienced higher dimensional realms and the City of Light and increased my extrasensory perception. I have accessed Akashic records, Divine Wisdom and Direct Knowing and have become my Light Body multiple times, thus far.

The pineal gland has been called a hyper-dimensional 'Star Gate' within our physical body.[230] When the pineal is activated, it can open the Thousand Petal Lotus within our brain that connects us to the highest source of Universal Energy, Wisdom and Light.[231] With our pineal, frontal lobes, limbic system and glia brain activated, we can access our God given abilities and look beyond our present third dimensional physical reality.

The pineal gland is filled with fluid and it floats in a pool of cerebrospinal fluid like an island. This fluid allows the pineal gland the freedom to move and vibrate.[232]

Within the pineal fluid are tiny molecular structures called piezoelectric calcite 'micro-clusters.' They are plutonic solid geometric forms made up of calcium, carbon and oxygen and they are similar to the calcite crystals in the inner ear.[233]

These calcite micro-clusters produce a bioluminescence light that emanates varying shades of blue to green in color. This light is a cold light and does not produce heat.[234]

Unconditional Love resonates at 528 Hz. The light frequency of the color emerald green, also vibrates at 528Hz, which happens to be the same frequency that chlorophyll vibrates. Nature, unconditional love and the piezoelectric calcite micro-crystals of our pineal gland all vibrate and resonate to various levels of green.[235] Healers have been photographed and have had brain imaging and/or EEG's (electroencephalogram) performed,[236] while in a healing mode, that has registered or captured the energy and often a green glow around their head, brain, heart and hands.

Mary Magdalene and the mystic/alchemical High Priestesses and High Priests are often depicted in paintings with green sleeves or robes. This is to imply that they have mastered the connection between the physical heart and the Heavenly Heart (pineal) and have the ability to spin their heart chakra and vibrate pure Divine Unconditional Love.[237]

The piezoelectric calcite crystals are generators, transmitters, receivers and transformers. Piezoelectricity means 'electricity resulting from pressure.'[238] Piezoelectricity (also called the piezoelectric effect) is the ability of certain materials to generate an AC (alternating current) voltage when subjected to sound, radio frequencies, vibration or mechanical stress and when subjected to an AC voltage.[239] As a transformer, the piezoelectric calcite crystals can transfer electrical energy between two or more objects. They can increase or decrease the alternating magnetic flux or electromotive force to transfer more energy/power without reaching saturation with less turns and rotation. Piezo transformers in technology are some of the most compact high voltage sources of energy.[240, 241]

Piezoelectric crystal elements, whether in the our pineal or technology, can act as both a sensor and an actuator, which is often called a transducer. In a technology capacity, piezoelectric calcite crystals can be used to detect muscle movements in medical equipment and they are used in automotive management systems and emission testing. Piezoelectric calcite crystals are used in sonar technology for detecting echo and used in the penetrometer instrument on the Huygens atmospheric entry probe that successfully landed a spacecraft on Saturn's moon Titan.[242]

Piezoelectric crystals can also be used in microphones, drum pads, speakers, atomic force and scanning tunneling microscopes, as well as, a microbalance for very sensitive chemical and biological sensors.[243] Piezoelectric plates are used to convert audio signals into sound waves.[244]

The most common piezoelectric material is the calcite micro-clusters of the pineal gland, our DNA, our inner ears and quartz. Other natural occurring piezoelectric material, to a lesser degree, are Berlinite, Topaz, Tourmaline, Macedonite, Sucrose (table sugar), Rochelle salt (Potassium Sodium Tartrate), silk, wood, enamel, dentin (the hard, dense bony tissue forming the bulk of the tooth beneath the enamel), our bone, tendons, collagen and viral proteins, including those from bacteriophage.[245, 246, 247]

As a transmitter, these piezoelectric calcite micro-clusters generate, resonate and transmit electromagnetic energy out from our pineal.[248]

As a receiver, the piezoelectric calcite crystalline micro-clusters act like antennas to receive waves of living Light and energetic frequencies from the higher realms. They also respond to electromagnetic influences outside of our body.[249] Piezoelectric crystalline micro-clusters have the ability to convert Earth's natural electromagnetic vibrations into usable energy called geomagnetic energies.[250] This is why we feel so 'charged up' at sacred sites, vortexes, when we are near or on certain Ley lines, being barefoot and being in nature.

Due to the piezoelectric effect, intense shifts in the earth's electromagnetic field could produce a surge of DMT in our body. Especially, with the cosmic and planetary alignments, eclipses and blood moons that have been taking place at this time. The surge of natural and cosmic energy could trigger a DMT release, as the energy is stepped down within the Thousand Petal Lotus and pineal, which allows us to be more intuitively active.[251]

The mechanical flexing that occurs within the quartz and calcite crystals generate standing columnar waves within the crystals' molecular structure.[252, 253] Standing columnar waves are how energy moves throughout our universe and all of creation. Standing columnar waves also resemble our DNA.

An interesting tidbit is that the blocks used to build the Great Pyramid are made up of quartz and calcite crystal similar to our pineal crystals. With appropriate focus and amplified acoustic waves, the blocks could generate a strong electromagnetic field that would allow for acoustic (sound) levitation.[254] This makes me consider the possibilities… We are not as heavy as the blocks of the pyramids and it is quite possible that they were levitated into place, therefore, I believe that we too, have the possibility to levitate.

Many of the ancient temple sites, such as the Maya, Aztec and Inca sites in the Andes, the sacred sites of Newgrange, Knowth and Dowth in Ireland, Teotihuacan in Mexico, Stonehenge in England, Machu Picchu in Peru, The Temple of Isis at Philae, especially the stepped pyramid of Sakkara (Saqqara) and the Great Pyramid in Egypt used resonating chambers, basins and platforms that incorporated advanced psychoacoustic heartbeat synchronization to activate the 'third eye' chakra and pineal.[255] The sacred geometric shapes of the micro-crystals within the pineal create individual resonating chambers that, when vibrating collectively, enable us to transcend the space/time and time/space continuum.[256]

We have the ability to vibrate ourselves into a state of Harmony, using the resonance of infrasound standing waves, along with focused breath to awaken the micro-clusters of our pineal gland and DNA. The piezoelectric effect within the crystalline structures of certain temples and sacred sites is an added bonus to help keep us attuned. Solfeggio tones, resonance frequency and the binaural beats that we use today are part of the infrasound standing waves. These could activate and connect the physical heart to the Heavenly Heart through the process of entrainment.[257]

✡ ✡ ✡

Harmful EMF Fields and Our Pineal

When we are exposed to a frequency, resonance, light vibration or electromagnetic fields (EMF), our pineal gland vibrates and sends electromagnetic signals throughout our body. Every cell of our body is constantly shifting the penetrating waves of energy to achieve a harmonic resonance between our body, the imposed energy and the electromagnetic energy signals of our earth.[258]

In a study at Ben-Gurion University, it was found that the calcite micro-crystals within the pineal have an excitable piezoelectric response to frequencies in the mobile communications range. Any energy that produces an electromagnetic response in relationship with the pineal could alter energy patterns within the physical body, including our brain, our central nervous system, sleep cycles and sleep deprivation, sexual function and hypersensitivity from long exposure to electromagnetic stimulation.[259]

Unfortunately, we are being bombarded with intense man-made electromagnetic stress every day. With excessive radio and cell phone towers, having a cell phone active and carried on our body most of the day, smart watches, sitting in front of a computer or television for hours, Wi-Fi, computerized cars and electric/Wi-Fi appliances, power substations close to our home; smart meters and power lines connected to our homes and lining our streets, we are saturated with man-made frequencies.

ELF (extremely low frequency) was originally created to communicate with submerged submarines during World War II. Shortly after implementing this technology, it was discovered that the people working around the ELF transmissions were quickly becoming very sick. Russia and America began to develop this discovery into weaponry.[260]

ELF critically affects the replication process of our DNA and causes it to unravel. In order to form a new cell, our DNA must duplicate itself. ELF interferes with the heterodyning process. Heterodyning works on an echo response that sends signals to the eight essential amino acids that determine which protein to absorb in order to complete the DNA replication. Our DNA emits a high frequency sound in the neighborhood of 1.92 megaHertz to detect through the course of the echo response which protein is missing.

ELF causes our body to assimilate proteins that it normally would excrete as toxins. The heterodyning interference results in fractured DNA and genetic issues. ELF disrupts the metabolism of liver cells, which lower our ATP metabolism and interferes with the Krebs cycle. ELF also shortens our circadian rhythm. In turn, the shortened circadian rhythm shortens the biological response time available to produce healthy cells through mitosis. This renders cells with incomplete information of genetic coding, which creates a gradual decline and destruction of our cellular integrity.[261]

Dr. Robert O. Becker states in his book, *Cross Currents: the Perils of Electropollution, the Promise of Electromedicine*, that "The exposure of living organisms to abnormal electromagnetic fields result in significant abnormalities in physiology and function." [262]

The natural electromagnetic energy fields of the Earth's frequencies range from 0 (zero) to 30 Hz (30 cycles per second). Lightening flashes produce energy fields in the frequency range of 10 - 20 kHz (KiloHertz - thousands of cycles per second) and the narrow band of visual light is in the trillions of Hertz cycles per second. Between each of these natural frequency fields are supposed to be large layers of spectrum that are basically empty of any electro-magnetic frequencies.[263]

With all the man-made electromagnetic fields, radio waves, microwaves, radar, Wi-Fi, 5G and powerful satellite transmissions, we have almost filled our once near empty spectrum with man-made frequencies that did not exist 100 years ago. These man-made frequencies are layered just above the naturally occurring frequencies.[264] It has been established that exposure to abnormal electromagnetic fields generate additional stress responses to our overall wellbeing,[265] as well as electromagnetic hypersensitivity to our pineal.[266]

Our DNA is an antenna, which is both a transmitter and a receiver. If you were to unfold one DNA, you would have a 3 foot antenna. DNA is tuned to radio frequencies between 375 to 386 megaHertz. It is tuned to a frequency that is based on the cycle of one revolution of the wave from positive current to negative current, which is the rise and the fall of the wave. If the wave is too slow, our DNA cannot absorb the energy to utilize it.[267]

Radio waves measure in the megaHertz (MHz) range, which means the wave oscillates or rotates millions of cycles per second. Radar waves measure in the gigaHertz (GHz) range, which is billions of times per second. Satellite transmissions measure in the 50 - 80 gigaHertz range[268] and microwave towers, UHF and EHF transmission operate in the 1 GHz to 100GHz range.[269] TeraHertz (THz) measure a trillion oscillations or rotations per second.[270]

Cellular and Wi-Fi networks rely on microwaves - a type of electromagnetic radiation utilizing frequencies up to 6 gigaHertz in order to transmit voice and data wirelessly. The frequency that is transmitted from 5G towers has been found to have a very negative impact on our sweat glands, pineal and cellular integrity.

Sweat ducts in humans are located in the second layer of our skin, known as the dermis. The sweat ducts are helically (coiled) shaped tubes that are filled with a conductive fluid, similar to that of the pineal. The dermis also has dielectric permittivity, which means that it can transmit and insulate energy. Our sweat glands become low Q helical antennas when exposed to extremely high sub-Terahertz frequencies. This causes the dermis to absorb the microwave radiation at excessive levels. The high level of exposure and absorption has shown to reflect critical cellular stress within the body.[271, 272]

The same 5G RF-EMF (radio frequency - electromagnetic field) technology that is connecting the world in high speed internet access is also being developed for weapons that interact directly with human skin.[273] In 2017, 180 Scientists and researchers in 35 countries sign a moratorium, attempting to prohibit the activity of 5G technology.[274]

On a grander scale of electromagnetic stress, there is EMP (electromagnetic pulse) weaponry and CERN (French Conseil Européen pour la Recherche Nucléaire or Council for European Nuclear Research). CERN uses the world's largest and most powerful particle generator called a Large Hadron Collider.[275] Its purpose is to accelerate gold and lead ions at unprecedented speeds and made to collide head-on creating a fireball of energy that melts or turns everything in its surroundings to dust.

Besides destroying objects into nothingness, it has been said that this process creates a black hole or portal to alternate realms, similar to a stargate.[276, 277] We also have HAARP (High Frequency Active Auroral Research Program) and ELF (Extremely Low Frequency) used for weather manipulation and electromagnetic warfare.[278, 279] The list goes on.

In Preston B. Nichols book series *The Montauk Project*, he writes that in the 1960's, the US government conducted secret projects, like the Sage Radar project, at Camp Hero and the decommissioned Montauk Air Force Station, for the purpose of developing psychological warfare. They discovered that they could alter the mood of the people on the base by simply increasing or decreasing the strength of the pulse duration and frequency of the radar, which used middle infrared band energy waves.[280]

These low frequency pulse waves had an adverse effect on the brain and the calcite micro-clusters in the pineal gland. Some of the effects were agitation, aggression, anxiety, crying, depression, fear/terror, grief, hopelessness, sleepiness and death.[281]

Infrared energy waves are the lower frequency waves on the light spectrum and have longer wave lengths. They can lower emotional energy, moods and can have a harmful effect on the human body. Higher light spectrum frequency waves, such as those produced in the green, blue and violet range, generate more positive emotional energy, moods and supportive effects on the body.[282]

Technology has been created that can direct an electromagnetic pulse wave to an individual who will hear words and sentences form as the wave passes through their brain. In 1961, Alan Frey provided evidence that "the perception of sound can be induced in normal and deaf humans by irradiation of the head with low power density, pulse modulated UHF. The ability to modify behavior with auditory-cortex stimuli... brain rhythm modification and many other biological applications of microwaves has been repeatedly shown since the 1950's." From declassified records on Project Pandora that was released on December 19, 1994.[283]

UHF (ultra high frequency) is designated for radio frequencies in the range between 300 mega-Hertz and 3 gigaHertz. This range is also known as the decimeter band because the wavelengths range from one meter to one tenth of a meter, which is one decimeter. Radio frequencies above the UHF band are called SHF (super high frequencies) or microwave frequencies.[284]

The U.S. Patents office now holds dozens of patents for devices that could communicate directly with an individual through their thoughts, such as, U.S. Patent 5,159,703 – SILENT SUBLIMINAL PRESENTATION SYSTEM and US PATENT 3,951,134 - APPARATUS AND METHOD FOR REMOTELY MONITORING AND ALTERING BRAIN WAVES.[285]

Taking preventative measures to shield, decrease or eliminate the harmful EMF energy that we are exposed to daily, while repairing the integrity and performance of our pineal gland would be beneficial for our body, brain, lifestyle and the environment.

Fluoride

Continuing with the things that are potentially harmful to our pineal, we will address fluoride. Great measures have been taken to shrink and calcify the pineal gland. The former Soviet Union began adding fluoride to the water of the concentration camps and the community water supply in an attempt to sedate the population and atrophy the pineal gland. The added fluoride made the population more controllable. The United States and several other governments followed suit.[286]

Fluoride was used in the mental hospitals to sedate the patients and render them docile. The pineal gland readily soaks up fluoride, more so than any other part of the body. Halides, such as fluoride, chloride and bromide coat the pineal gland with calcium crystals that inhibit the functional aspects of the pineal. This is known as 'calcify'. It appears that the higher the volume of absorbed fluoride, the higher the rate of calcification.[287] Fluoride has also been known to induce inflammation, oxidative stress and excitotoxicity effects on brain cells.[288, 289, 290]

Fortunately, studies have shown that a reversal of the toxic immuno-excitotoxicity effects of fluoride on the pineal and our body is possible with the elimination of exposure for two months, while increasing antioxidants and proper nutrition.[291]

Further steps were taken to ensure pineal atrophy when genetically modifying our food with harmful chemicals began. Excessive promotion and use of chemical scents to freshen the air, your furniture, carpets and clothes are not only carcinogenic, they calcify and atrophy the pineal gland.[292] If you wish to freshen up your environment, it would be to your advantage to use high quality pure essential oils, flowers, herbs and other scents from nature.

If not stimulated and protected, our pineal gland begins to calcify and harden in our adolescence. GM/GMO (Genetically Modified Organisms) food, excessive intake of meat and meat by-product, excessive carbohydrates and sugar, high fructose corn syrup, chemical sugar substitutes, food additives and colorings, caffeine, alcohol, soda, tobacco, fluoride toothpaste, chlorinated/fluoride tap water, as well as, party and pharmaceutical drugs can affect and contribute to accelerated atrophy and calcification of the pineal.[293, 294] Sadly, we have been conditioned to atrophy our own pineal glands instead of enhancing it.

Besides avoiding the above known toxins, implementing the rhythmic breathing[295] of the Spiral Breath, along with using any of the healthy modalities referenced in this book, can help stimulate and reactivate the pineal gland.

Alkalizing your body to a proper pH helps to detoxify the pineal. Eat non-GMO foods, alkaline foods and organic foods, such as sesame seeds, blue-green algae, spirulina, chlorella, dulse and kelp.[296] Also, raw cacao and organic dark chocolate are tasty and beneficial. The sacred herbal Neem oil extract from India has been known to decalcify and detox the pineal. Activated charcoal is also alkalizing to our body.[297, 298, 299] Boron, magnesium, calcium and iodine in moderation, have been found to be successful with inhibiting absorption and detoxifying sodium fluoride from the pineal and our body.[300]

I use a mineral and energy balancing formula made from organic minerals called DeSpark. It enhances cellular functions and promotes cellular repair. My body and pineal respond well to this formula. Check the resource page for information.

Essential fatty acids (omega's 3, 6, 7 and 9) and liposomal lecithin are extremely crucial to brain, limbic system and pineal support. Lecithin is found at higher concentrations in the brain, especially the pineal gland, more so than any other place in the body.[301] I use Young Living Essential Oil's MindWise™, OmegaGize™ and Brain Power™ on a daily basis to keep myself above the wellness line. Other essential fatty acids that have been found to be beneficial would be a good quality MCT (medium chain triglyceride) oil derived from coconut oil, Sea Buckthorn oil (Omega 7) and Black Cumin Seed oil, all of which have been shown to be exceptional for brain, limbic system and pineal support.

Herbs that are used appropriately, such as, Cilantro, can help lessen fluoride and heavy metals in the body.[302] Chamomile, Devil's Claw, Ginseng, Gota Kola, Licorice, Mugwort, Mullien, Oakmoss, Parsley, Pine Bark, Uva Ursi, Wild Indigo Bark and Wood Betany have multiple benefits that support our wellbeing. Again, in moderation and when used appropriately. Do a little research and check with your health care provider.[303]

The Master Cleanse is particularly beneficial not only for your pineal, but for your entire body. I have found Tom Woloshyn's book *The Complete Master Cleanse: A Step-by-Step Guide to Maximizing the Benefits of the Lemonade Diet* to be very thorough for at home cleansing.[304] (Contact information in References)

Sandalwood is also very supportive for pineal activation and is known to facilitate spiritual wisdom and higher resonance. There is a reason why Solomon built his temple out of Sandalwood and not just because it was fragrant. Sandalwood holds a higher frequency than other trees.[305]

And speaking of temples... it is highly beneficial on so many levels to live in a chemical-free environment in your home and office. Synthetic chemicals in household products and personal care items contain endocrine disruptors (EDCs) that can wreak havoc on our endocrine systems, which the pineal is a part of. The list of detrimental effects from synthetic chemicals is massive.[306]

Using natural cleaners, air fresheners, pesticides, etc. can improve the environment inside our body, as well as our immediate surroundings and they grace the Earth that we live on. Now, let us get back to the beneficial influences for our pineal gland.

✡ ✡ ✡

Frequency Activation and Decalcification

It has been documented that a frequency resonating at 110Hz - 111Hz can activate the frontal lobes and elevate the body, mind and spirit. Many temples and cathedrals resonate at 110Hz - 111Hz using the Pythagorean scale. These structures hold and resonate a higher frequency intended to balance our individual frequency and raise it up. Our cells and DNA remember these harmonizing frequencies upon entering these structures, even if they are only the ruins. The resonance can stimulate the limbic system, calm and balance the brain and promote access into higher consciousness through entrainment.

Solfeggio Tones were discovered in the ancient megalithic Temple of Mnajdra, located on the Island of Malta. All of the impressive stone temple rooms resonate to the frequency of 110Hz - 111Hz.[307] Simply entering the room, activates the frontal lobes, limbic system and the pineal response within the brain, which naturally encourages a positive shift in mood, healing and increased energy intake.

The 'SI' (963Hz) - Solfiggio Tone opens the pineal gland, enables a direct experience with Divine Source and a return to "Oneness." The use of Solfeggio frequencies and binaural beats can help entrain the brain waves to the theta or trance state and support the pineal.[308]

PEAR (Princeton Engineering Anomalies Research), a program that researches the acoustic behavior in ancient megalithic sites documented the above findings in 1994.[309]

Shamanic drumming with a continual structured beat of four and a half beats per second can also effect the pineal gland. We use the Shamanic drumming and chanting to prepare us for our fire walks.

The practice of yoga stimulates the pineal gland and can raise your Kundalini and Prana.

Crystals have unique energetic qualities that can assist you in your pineal awakening.[310] Here are a few that work well with the pineal to get started: Quartz, blue/green/pink Calcite, Amethyst, Ametrine (mixture of citrine and amethyst), Angel Fire, Blue Coral, Buddha Quartz, Moonstone, Purple Fluorite, Purple Lepidolite, Purple Sapphire, Rhodonite, Ruby and Platinum. You can also dowse or use kinesiology to see which stone or combination of stones works best for you at that time.[311, 312]

Sometimes, when I change things up, I will place Zervana Holograms (which is a 7th Dimensional Labyrinth) in the four corners of my room or my body as I sit or lay. I also place a Mau Gem (a 7th Dimensional Labyrinth in a shungite mold) at my brainstem. Information on Zervana Holograms are in the Reference section.

For me, the inclusion of pure essential oils was extremely beneficial to accelerate the increase of higher frequencies within my energy field and body. The Oils of Ancient Scripture are some of my favorites to use on my Third Eye and pineal. They are Sacred Sandalwood™, Cassia™, Cedarwood™, Cypress™, Frankincense, Hyssop™, Myrrh™, Myrtle™, Onycha™ and Rose of Sharon (Cistus)™. Not only are these essential oils referenced repeatedly in the Bible, they ALL pass through the protective Blood Brain Barrier and go directly to the brain to deliver support. We were given natural ways to protect and restore ourselves from harmful energy fields and toxic substances over 3,000 years ago in one of the most sacred writings on this earth. That is impressive and a true blessing!

Other custom blends that I like to use are Awaken™, Clarity™, Envision™, Highest Potential™, Inspiration™, Joy™, Magnify Your Purpose™, and Transformation™.

Of course, I use my Spiral Breath, most often, to activate my pineal.

Now let us return to more spiritual aspects of the Pineal Gland.

✡ ✡ ✡

Pineal - The Place of God's Light

The pineal is associated with the seventh crown chakra though it is energetically connected to the sixth chakra and the pituitary gland.

When the sixth chakra pituitary – 'Seat of the Mind' is open and connected to the seventh chakra pineal – 'Seat of Illumination' the two create a synergy that awakens the third eye – 'Seat of the Soul.' It becomes an energetic partnership or rather a sacred energetic Trinity.[313]

The pituitary possesses a masculine energy and a positive charge (+) and the pineal possesses a feminine energy and a negative charge (-). When both the pituitary and the pineal gland are activated and in harmony, they commune together as 'One.' In this communion, the 'Oneness' and the Mystical Marriage – Hieros Gamos takes place. It is with this Union that the doorway to multidimensionality opens and the higher dimensional - Higher Consciousness realms are accessed.[314]

Pure Life Force energy rises up from the Earth and radiates up through the chakras and spinal channel. We also receive pure Life Force through our chakras and our breath from the Life Force that surrounds us.

As we balance the emotionally charged issues that have weighed our body, mind and emotions down, we create a clearer passage for the pure Life Force to rise up through. This rising energy is referred to as Kundalini or Prana. The Prana *(which is pure energy)* flows up through the chakras; into the pituitary and merges with the pineal.[315]

At the same time, Christic and Cosmic Light flows from the higher dimensional realms down into the pineal and crown chakra. The pineal receives the Light and merges it with the incoming third dimensional Life Force from the pituitary.[316]

Dr. Krumm-Heller, professor of medicine at the University of Berlin, found the subtle channel or capillary that sets up a bio-electromagnetic interchange between the pituitary and the pineal that opens the 'cosmic gateway.'[317]

The merging of energies form a bridge that seamlessly connects the physical ego self with our Higher I AM Self, thus awakening the Third Eye, which in turn, begins to open our Thousand Petal Lotus.

This awakening generates a toroidal energy that opens the connection to the higher vibrational level of the eighth chakra or the eighth gate, creating As Above – So Below.[318]

Opening the doorway to the eighth gate (Sahasrara chakra) connects the physical self to the astral or Divine Self. This allows an increase of Christ Light and Supreme Consciousness to saturate and illumine the physical body.[319] With continued practice and focus on activating and maintaining a higher vibrational resonance in your pineal and overall wellbeing, the separation between the physical and spiritual body disappears.

> *"The pineal gland is the receptor and sender of the subtle vibrations, which carry thoughts and psychic phenomenon throughout the cosmos."*
> SATYANANDA, 1972 [320]

Remember from the amygdala section, I mentioned the reticular activating formation. When this pinpoint of tissue is opened, cosmic consciousness flows into the pineal and moves like a wave to the frontal lobes. Cosmic consciousness is the wave that brings cosmic intelligence. Cosmic intelligence enters the brain-body where it creates genetic intelligence, which is DNA.[321]

In the Bible, after Jacob wrestles with an angel, he heard God speak, *"...Thy name shall no more be called Jacob, but Israel: for as a prince hast thou power with God and with men, and has prevailed."* (Genesis 32:28).

I believe that Jacob wrestled with his higher self as he activated his peniel gland and experienced the higher vibrational Christic Realms.

Two verses later in Genesis 32:30 the Bible states, *"And Jacob called the place the Island of Peniel, for I have seen God face to face, and my life is preserved."*

Coincidentally, the contributing root for the word peniel is pana, which can mean "to look within" or "a place within you."[322]

It is also interesting that the Latin term for the pineal is 'epiphysus,' which is closely related to Ephesus. Celsus was the third largest esoteric and alchemical Library in Classical Antiquity located in Ephesus, Turkey. Here, the ancient priestesses and priests learned alchemy and the sacred esoteric wisdom. It is said that over 20,000 scrolls were once housed there.[323] From my own experience, I believe that by activating the pineal gland and frontal lobes, you can gain access to the sacred library of wisdom that was taught so many years ago.

In Genesis 32:31 Jacob continues, *"And as he passed over Peniel, the sun rose upon him, and he halted upon his thigh."*

Jacob is referencing the place 'within us' that enables us to experience the *place of God's Light* and that is the pineal gland. Remember that the pineal gland sits in the center of our brain; floating like an island in a pool of cerebrospinal fluid.

When I became *Light*, while in the sarcophagus in the King's Chamber of the Great Pyramid and at the main altar of the Temple of Isis on Philae, as well as the column of Light in Banf, Canada, it was like the sun rose upon or rather, within me.

Joshua Tilghman, put it nicely in his article *'How Wrestling God Awakened Jacob's Pineal Gland'* that Jacob was a physical man and after God awakened Jacob's pineal gland, Jacob (now Israel) transformed himself and was a spiritual man who accessed the higher realms. He had raised his vibration, activated his pineal and experienced his 'Divine Light' and his Light Body *'rose upon him.'* [324]

Our pineal gland contains light sensitive cells that are very similar to the cells found in the retina of our physical eyes. Jesus says in the Bible, "...*The light of the body is the eye. If therefore thine eye be single, thy whole body shall be full of light.*" (Matthew 6:22). Jesus is referencing our pineal and third eye.

The pineal can be activated through meditation, breath work (such as the Spiral Breath), visualization, sound and the frequencies of pure essential oils. The musical note D# resonates at 152.89924 Hz using the Pythagorean scale and is also excellent for activating the pineal, as well as the amygdala.[325] You find a mystical aspect of D# at 152.89924 Hz, if you divide the frequency numbers by Pi.

It equals the radius of the inner circle of Stonehenge. If you multiply 152.89924 by Pi, you get the height of the Great Pyramid.[326]

Toning the note of D#, while saying the word 'HU', stimulates the frontal lobes, as well. Eckankar (which means Co-worker with God) considers the singing or chanting 'HU' as a 'love song to God.' [327] The D# tone gives thought to the word 'human.' God spoke man into existence with the spoken word or was it the vibrational tone of D# that accompanied the word HU?

Pineal Symbology in the Arts

At the Walker Art Center in Minneapolis, Minnesota there is a giant cherry resting on the tip of a spoon that hovers above a small pond of water. This sculpture is called Spoonbridge and Cherry. The artists are Claes Oldenburg and his wife, Coosie van Bruggen. Whether intentional or by happenstance, this sculpture captures the image of the pineal within the limbic system. The cherry is the pineal gland, the spoon is the thalamus and the pond of water is the pool of cerebrospinal fluid that surrounds the pineal. It reflects for me without words, that when you activate your pineal gland, life becomes like a dessert with a cherry on top.

Pine cones have been a sacred symbol throughout history and represent Divine Wisdom, Illumination and Spiritual Enlightenment.[328]

The most prominent portrayal of pineal symbology is the pine cone. It is often depicted in religious, cultural and new age art, paintings and statues. The pineal symbol can be found in architecture and temples from the Egyptians, Babylonians, Indonesians, India, the Greeks, Romans, Sumerians, Hinduism, Buddhism, Taoism, Christians and secret societies like the Freemasons.

Pine cone sculptures can be readily found around the world. One of the most impressive, is the bronze Pigna sculpture in a Vatican courtyard called the Court of the Pine Cone. The bronze Pigna was originally the fountain located next to the Temple of ISIS (the Goddess) in Ancient Rome and was relocated to the Vatican's courtyard.[329]

5.9 Pigna sculpture in the Court of the Pine Cone, Vatican courtyard photo by Lalupa

5.10 The Temple of Angkor Wat, Cambodia photo by Diego Delso

The Temple of Angkor Wat in Cambodia is spectacular with it's sacred geometry architecture and pineal symbology!

The historical site of Kizhi Pogost is the home of the magnificent 22 pine cone domed Church of Transfiguration of Our Saviour and the 9 pine cone domed Church of the Intercession of the Virgin, that were built in the 17th century on Kizhi Island in Russia.[330]

5.11 *Kizhi Pogost, Russia Church of Transfiguration of Our Saviour photo by Elena Yurova*

Spiritual leaders such as Buddha, Krishna and Shiva are depicted with pine cone hair or headdresses or holding a pine cone in their hands. Statues of the Mesoamerican god Quetzalcoatl are depicted with a pine cone necklace.[331] The esoteric pine cone can also be found on the Pope's staff, the staffs of Osiris and Dionysus, as well as, the Masonic Pine Cone Caduceus on the side of the Whitehall Building in New York. The staffs and caduceus represent the feminine and masculine energies of the Kundalini rising through the alignment of the chakras and merging in the pineal gland to attain 'Divine Wisdom.'[332]

Images of pine cones have even appeared in crop circles in England.[333]

As you see, the mystique and the reverence for the sacred pineal is worldwide and is shared by many cultures.

✡ ✡ ✡

BRAINSTEM

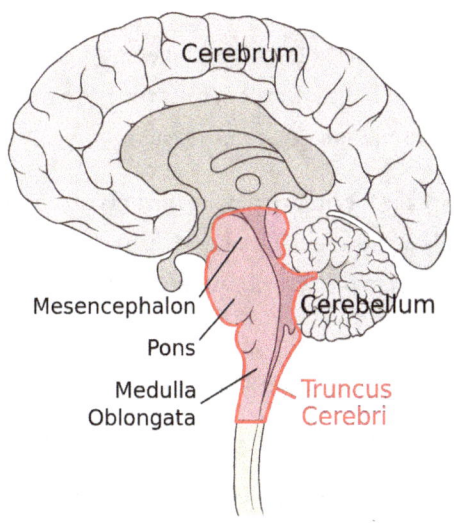

5.12 Brain Stem Illustration y Patrick J. Lynch

The brainstem (truncus cerebri) connects the spinal cord to the brain and the limbic system. It is part of the bridge that unites the physical body to our spiritual body.[334]

The brainstem is responsible for our motor and sensory responses that are stimulated from the impulses of the cranial nerves. There are twelve pairs of cranial nerves and ten of those pairs originate from the brainstem.[335]

The **Vagus Nerve**, also known as the pneumogastric nerve, is the 10th cranial nerve (CNX). It is the longest of the 12 cranial nerves and the longest nerve of the autonomic nervous system.[336] The vagus nerve is one of the most important nerves, as it is a major control center for our body.

I would like to take a few moments to address the vagus nerve before we continue on with the brainstem. Repairing my vagus nerve was another key aspect of my healing process. The Spiral Breath and proper structural alignment helped me to reestablish the integrity of my vagus nerve.

The vagus nerves interface with the parasympathetic nervous system's control of the heart, lungs and digestive tract.[337] It is responsible for signaling our brain, organs and immune system. The vagus nerve also controls the overall levels of inflammation within our body.

The vagus nerve contains both sensory (afferent) fibers and motor (efferent) fibers. It also interfaces with the sympathetic nervous system, the parasympathetic nervous system and the autonomic nervous system.

The vagus nerve exits the brain from the medulla oblongata at the brainstem. It then travels laterally across the skull, where it exits through the jugular foramen and joins the cranial root of the 11th cranial nerve, known as the accessory nerve (CN XI).

The vagus nerve then travels down behind the ears on both sides of the neck between the carotid artery and the internal jugular vein, within the carotid sheath.

At the base of the neck, the vagus nerve enters the thorax. The left vagus nerve travels to the aortic arch, behind the primary left bronchus and into the esophagus. The right vagus nerve travels behind the esophagus and into primary right bronchus.

The left and the right vagus nerves enter the abdomen through the esophageal hiatus of the diaphragm and continues individually to the stomach. Branches of the left vagus nerve form the anterior gastric plexus on the anterosuperior surface of the stomach. The right branches of the vagus nerve form the posterior gastric plexus on the posterioinferior surface of the stomach. The fibers of the anterior gastric plexus extend into the pylorus and upper part of the duodenum. The posterior vagal trunk, along with the posterior gastric branches, extend into the areas of the celiac, renal and superior mesenteric arteries.

The celiac branches of the right vagus nerve interfaces with the pancreas, kidneys, spleen, suprarenal bodies and the intestines. The hepatic branches of the left vagus nerve interface with the liver.[338]

From the brainstem to the intestines, the vagus nerve helps regulate internal organs by sending motor signals to our organs and distributing the sensory communications from the organs back to the central nervous system.[339]

When the vagus nerve is functioning properly, it sends signal messages through the body to decrease inflammation and help our body to recover from stress, anxiety and fear.[340]

An overstimulated or underactive vagus nerve can cause a multitude of issues, such as low, elevated or abnormal blood pressure; slow, unusual or irregular heart rate, nausea, fainting, obesity, anxiety, mood disorders, gastrointestinal disorders, chronic inflammation, hoarseness or loss of voice, difficulty with speaking, swallowing or with gag reflex, issues with the smooth muscle of the trachea, pharnyx or larynx, ear pain, decreased production of stomach acid or reflux, loss of appetite, feeling full shortly after beginning a meal, sudden loss of weight, bloating, fluctuations in blood sugar, nervous system issues, difficulty in breathing, low thyroid functions, malnutrition, dehydration and more.[341]

The vagus nerve communicates with the diaphragm, therefore, deep breathing, such as the Spiral Breath, can help relax and tone the vagus nerve.

Having positive social relationships, exercising compassion and positive emotions, like joy, hope and laughter can help improve the integrity of the vagus nerve. Meditation, massaging your neck along the carotid arteries on both sides, massaging your feet, as well as, regular practice of yoga and Tai-Chi are also beneficial. Singing, humming and chanting sends out vibrational waves that can relax the vagus nerve. Exercise, coughing or tensing the stomach muscles, improving gut health and eating habits, as well as, cold water exposure, like cold showers, baths and dunking the face in ice water, can contribute to a healthy vagus nerve.[342]

A strengthened and toned vagus nerve can improve health on so many levels. Now, back to the brainstem.

The brainstem is also responsible for our vital autonomic responses like our blood pressure, heart rate, perspiration, respiration/breathing, salivation, eating, wakefulness, sleep, urination; dilation and contracting of the pupils and maintaining consciousness.[343]

It also regulates our fine touch, vibrational sensation and one's own perception through the posterior column-medial lemniscus pathway, as well as, pain, itch, temperature and crude touch through the spinothalamic tract.[344]

The brainstem helps regulate our central nervous system and is responsible for our emotional reactions and our facial expressions (physiognomic) like anger, fear, joy, sadness, tenderness, etc.[345]

The brainstem includes the medulla oblongata, pons, thalamus, hypothalamus, the midbrain (mesencephalon) and the reticular activating formation.

The **medulla oblongata** is located at the bottom of the brainstem. It regulates our vital functions like blood pressure, heartbeat, breathing, digestion, sleep cycles and the reflexes of the face, neck and throat, such as, blinking coughing, sneezing and gagging. It also signals motor control and some of our senses dealing with touch.[346]

The **pons** is located between the medulla and the midbrain. It is made up of nerve fibers that connect the two cerebral hemispheres. It transfers information between the medulla oblongata and the cerebral cortex, regulates voluntary movements and relays neural, as well as, sensory impulses that address sleep.[347]

The **midbrain** or mesencephalon,[348] is part of the central nervous system and is associated with the limbic system, emotional brain and chemical brain. It regulates vision, hearing, motor control, sleep/wake, alertness and temperature regulation. The midbrain adjoins the diencephalon (thalamus, hypothalamus, etc.) and the hindbrain (pons, medulla and cerebellum).[349] It is located in the upper part of the brainstem and is approximately the size of an apricot.[350] The midbrain is constantly monitoring, adjusting and regulating many of our internal functions in response to external stimuli.[351]

I covered the limbic system, thalamus and hypothalamus in greater detail at the beginning of this chapter. The thalamus, as part of the brainstem, receives sensory impulses (with the exception of smell) and sends out motor impulses.

The hypothalamus (which sits under the thalamus) works with activities such as, drinking, eating, sleeping, sexual activity, regulating body temperature, internal organs and coordinating all the activity processing through the brainstem.[352]

The human **reticular activating formation** is composed of more than 100 complex neural networks located in the core of the brainstem that address a variety of functions. The reticular formation contains multiple interconnected projections that pass into the forebrain, brainstem and cerebellum. These complex networks extend from the upper part of the midbrain to the lower part of the medulla oblongata, into the hypothalamus, thalamus, the cortex in the ascending reticular activating system (ARAS) and the descending pathways that connect to the spinal column through the reticulospinal tract.[353]

The brainstem is the transmitter and receiver for the body to the brain and from the brain to the body. It also is involved with higher cognitive functions.[354] The brainstem connects the spinal cord to the brain, the limbic system, the glia brain, the orbitofrontal lobe and ultimately higher consciousness.[355] The pineal is directly connected to the section of the brainstem called the 'epithalamus.'[356]

Remember from the amygdala and pineal sections, that T.D.A. Lingo believes that the reticular formation is the pinpoint opening that allows the universal cosmic consciousness to usher in through the brainstem to bathe the pineal and frontal lobes with cosmic consciousness, cosmic intelligence and genetic intelligence.[357]

During a channeling session, Divine Mother shared through me that the brainstem not only stores our memories for this lifetime, but for all of our past lives and our entire souls' existence.

Using the Spiral Breath technique, vibrational energy and breath is brought up from the heart through the brainstem to clear out negative thought processes and energetic signatures that are locked in our cells and DNA. I found that as I visually brought my breath up from my heart through my brainstem, energy patterns and thoughts that were causing me to be unbalanced in life surfaced into my consciousness. Whether they were acquired in this lifetime or inherited through my DNA lineage, the issues began to dissolve in intensity with Grace and Ease.

The more I breathed, along with adding the energetic blessings of Compassion, Forgiveness and Gratitude, the faster the emotion or thought process dissipated. I add Compassion, Forgiveness and Gratitude for the issue or thought patterns that surface, for they were created and co-created to help me grow on some level, show me my strengths or to protect my mind and my heart until I had the tools, wisdom and guidance to shift the 'out of balance' energies. I address Compassion, Forgiveness and Gratitude later on in the book.

I believe that the energy connection between the heart, the limbic system and frontal lobes are essential to higher consciousness. It is when our heart and limbic system are activated through Divine Unconditional Love that we access our true Divinely Given gifts.

I also believe that the brainstem is part of the '**nous**' that Jesus and Mary Magdalene share in their teachings. In *The Gospel of Mary Magdalene* translated by Jean-Yves Leloup, page 10 lines 12 - 25, when Mary Magdalene sees Jesus at the cave, she asks,

"Lord I see you now in this vision." And he answered: "You are blessed for the sight of me does not disturb you. There where is the nous, lies the treasure."

Then I said to him "Lord, when someone meets you in a Moment of vision, is it through the soul [psyche] that they see, or is it through the Spirit [Pneuma]?"

The Teacher answered: "It is neither through the soul nor the spirit, but the nous between the two which sees the vision and it is this which..."

(The next line and page of the Gospel of Mary Magdalene are missing.)

During a channeled message from Mary Magdalene, she showed me that my Spiral Breath technique activated the 'nous.' The Spiral Breath activated the heart and the mind - the soul and the spirit. The bridge between the two is the brainstem.

Mary Magdalene presented before me, my original Spiral Breath image suspended in the middle of a multi-directional rotating Merkaba. The shimmery emerald green breath emanated from the heart and rose up through the brainstem, moving on around to the crown chakra; third eye, then illuminating the limbic system and unfolding the activated Thousand Petal Lotus. The emerald green Light of the spiral transformed into shimmery gold and Mother of Pearl as it continued to flow out through the amygdalae and third eye, and recirculated with the Light from Heaven.

Then a vision dropped into my mind's eye, as Mary Magdalene allowed me to see why people were hung with a noose or beheaded during the crusades. It was an attempt to sever the 'nous,' which is the precious energetic connection that guaranteed their salvation in the multidimensional realms of higher consciousness.

Those with the knowledge of how to activate one's 'nous' were targeted. They were Jesus, Mary Magdalene, the Apostles, High Priestess/High Priests, Alchemists, Mary's, Magi's, Cathars and those trained in the Hermetic and esoteric temple arts.

I thought it coincidental that my injury was to my brainstem. I couldn't help but wonder if the person that caused my injury was somehow (consciously or unconsciously) attempting to break my connection to Divine Spirit.

I saw in this vision that breaking the connection between the physical realm and Christic realm was paramount for the Church of Rome in order to prevent humanity from achieving ascension and their Light Body. You cannot control the masses if everyone is resonating at the frequency of Unconditional Love and moving multidimensional. What the Church of Rome did not understand is that the **'nous' is energetic and cannot be broken. It can be turned off from fear, reactivated in faith and unconditional love, but it can never be broken.**

The Greek word nous means higher mind and is revered as the *'finest point of the soul.'* It has also been referred to as the *'angel of the soul.'* The *nous* is how we enter the intermediate realm between the purely sensory and the purely spiritual. Jean-Yves Leloup refers to this as 'the imaginal' realm, where *"between the purely sensory and purely spiritual lies image and representation, which is just as real as sense and intellect."*[358]

The 'nous' is the energetic connection between the heart and the limbic system. It connects the heart and the mind; activating the frontal lobes and the

Glia Brain. The core or 'heart' of the Glia Brain is in our heart. It is activated with Unconditional Love. When the Glia Brain is fully activated, one can transcend time, space and matter.

✡ ✡ ✡

Sistine Chapel

While researching the brainstem, I came across an article written by Joshua Tilghman called *'Separation of Light and Darkness: Another Esoteric Message from Michelangelo.'*

I literally laughed out loud as his words confirmed my beliefs and the Divine teachings that I had received. Michelangelo painted the fresco, entitled *Separation of Light and Darkness,* on the ceiling in the Sistine Chapel directly above the main altar. It is one of the panels from the set of nine depicting scenes from the Book of Genesis.

There are many esoteric messages within Michelangelo's paintings, but this painting in particular, places the emphasis on the importance to activate and access our brainstem, limbic system and frontal lobes.

Michelangelo showed us that the way to move the darkness out of our physical life was to go within; raise the Light (Kundalini) up through our physical body and connect the brainstem to our higher brain in order to see God.

Painted in the neck of God is the anatomically correct brainstem with the limbic system and frontal lobes as God's chin and beard. When you enlarge the section, it is very clear to see.[359]

This was discovered by two gentlemen: Ian Suk and Rafael Tamargo. They published an article in the publication 'Neurosurgery,' entitled *'Concealed Neuroanatomy in Michelangelo's Separation of Light From Darkness in the Sistine Chapel'* Suk, Ian BSc, BMC; Tamargo, Rafael J. MD, FACS.

*5.13 Michelangelo's Separation of Light From Darkness in the Sistine Chapel
The Yorck Project*

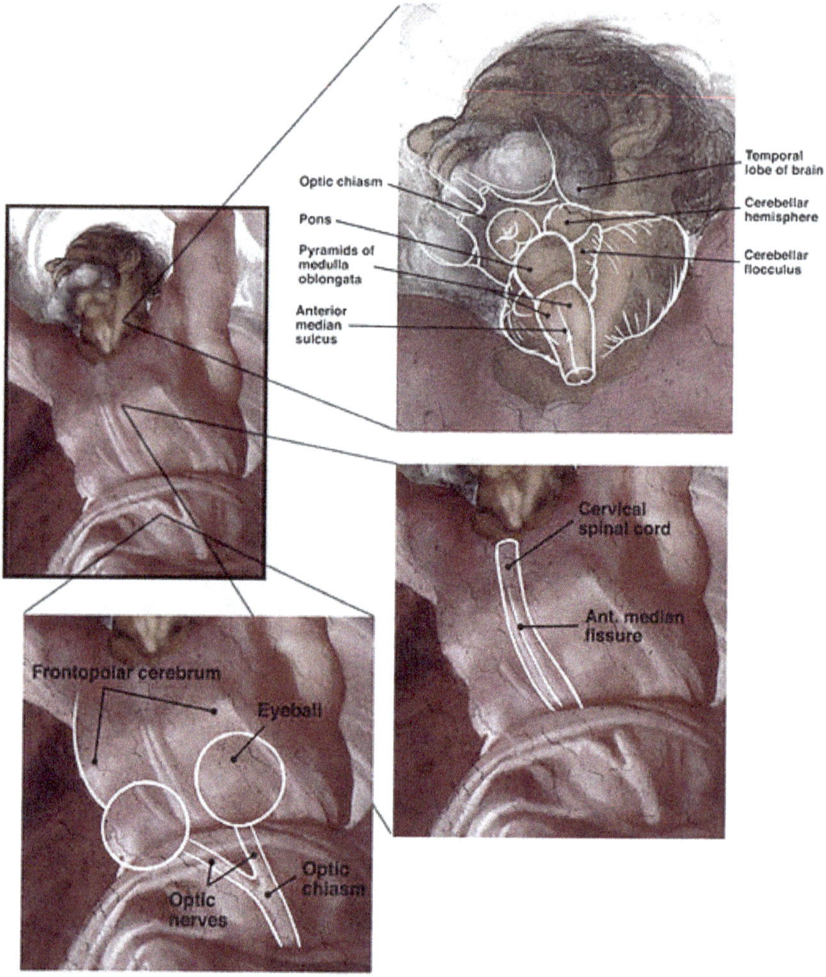

5.14 *Michelangelo Neuroanatomy by Ian Suk and Rafael Tamargo*

✡ ✡ ✡

THE EYE OF HORUS/RA/WADJET

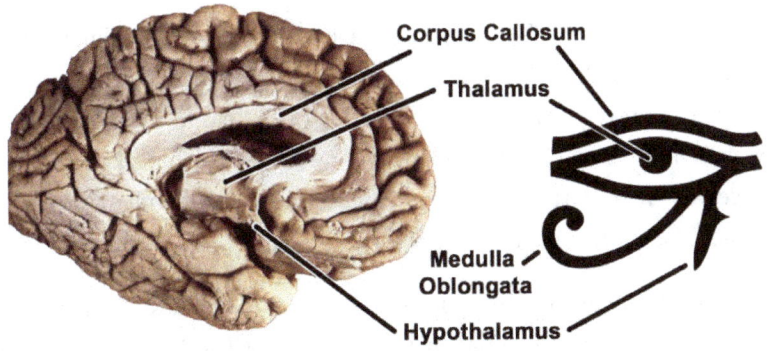

5.15 Limbic System and Eye of Horus graphic by Steve Valdeck
(Limbic System of human brain by John A. Beal)

Here is another interesting comparison. The Wadjet or Eye of Horus is uniquely similar to the limbic system. One more symbolic and subliminal reminder to help you remember to raise your Kundalini and keep your limbic system and frontal lobes activated.

If you compare the Eye of Horus to the limbic system and frontal lobe, you have all the components. The brainstem, the medulla oblongata which curls up into the cerebellum, the thalamus, pineal, pituitary, the amygdala, hypothalamus, hippocampus, corpus callosum, cingulate gyrus and the fornix. They are all represented in the Eye of Horus. The Eye of Horus necklace of Tutankhamun is more detailed with the limbic system.

5.16 By Jon Bodsworth - http://www.egyptarchive.co.uk/html/cairo_museum_47.html,
Copyrighted free use, https://commons.wikimedia.org/w/index.php?curid=4422291

Refer back to the limbic system image at the beginning of this chapter for a more complete view.

Wadjet (one of the oldest Egyptian goddesses) means 'Whole One' and 'The Green One' (remember Unconditional Love vibrates the color green). The Eye later became known as the Eye of Horus. One legend has it that during a battle between Horus and Seth, Horus lost an eye and it was torn into six pieces.[360] The six pieces are said to correspond to the six senses, as does our limbic system. They are: Touch, Taste, Thought, Hearing, Sight and Smell.[361]

The god Thoth found the original six pieces and the goddess Hathor restored Horus' sight, so he could continue his mission.[362] The 'Eye' is drawn in six parts and represents the restored senses. In gratitude, Horus gave the restored eye to his father, Osiris, so he could see clearly in the Underworld.[363]

The restored eye became the symbol of the re-establishment of order from chaos. It reflects the path that we are on as we move from our personal chaos to re-establish our enlightenment in Divine Truth. The rising cobra wearing a crown is our risen kundalini and awakened crown chakra. The Eye of Horus/Wadjet is said to protect all that is behind it, protects in the 'after life' and restores good health.[364]

The Eye of Horus is a symbolic reminder that every human being can restore order from chaos, awaken our senses and achieve our 'God given' right to attain our spiritual Divine Higher Self.

✡ ✡ ✡

THE VESICA PISCIS

As you can see from the information shared within this chapter, an active, high functioning Limbic system is important not only for our physical and emotional well being; it is essential to our spiritual well being and higher consciousness. For centuries, Master Teachers have been leaving us subtle reminders for *"Those who have eyes to see and ears to hear."*[365]

The Vesica is the almond or fish shape that is created when the intersection of two circles with the same radius are placed so that the perimeter of one lies on the center of the other.[366]

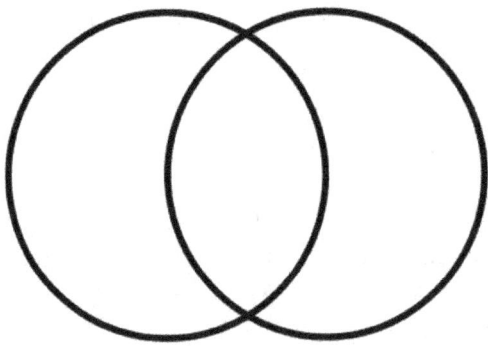

5.17 Vesica Piscis graphic by Steve Valdeck

One circle represents the spiritual realm and the other the material realm.[367] The Pythagoreans called the overlapping area the Vesica Piscis, which represents the transcendental region or realm[368] and Creator's Consciousness.[369] God is said to have created Light through the creation of the second sphere that forms the Vesica Piscis.[370] The Vesica Piscis is believed to be a geometric formula that represents the electromagnetic spectrum of Light.[371]

The Vesica Piscis is the symbol that represents the 'fusion of opposites,'[372] such as the fusion of electric and magnetic energy. The image above is also the process of cell division. One cell moves into separation as it divides itself into two and then becomes one.

The Vesica Piscis is also the symbol for the Holy Trinity, as with the Father, Son and Holy Spirit and the three realms of the Triple Goddess of the Moon and Fate: Earth, Sky and Sea.[373]

When I look at each circle as being one half of the brain, the Limbic system lies in the area of the Vesica. I see the Limbic system as the blending or "Mystical

Marriage" of the physical and spiritual realms. When the logical aspects of the left brain senses a shift into absolute unity, it starts to relax its control. The fibrous band of the corpus callosum begins to open in a way that allows the two hemispheres of the brain to share information and frequency between them. The corpus callosum activates the pineal gland and can produce a 'full' brain synchronization[374] working as one in unity. The 'Mystical Marriage' of the two hemispheres of the brain, as well as, the bridge generated between the pineal (seventh chakra) and pituitary (sixth chakra), allow us to access the eight gate chakra, which activates our higher spiritual consciousness, our Light Body and our personal Mer-Ka-Ba.[375]

The Vesica Piscis is mathematically linked to the number 153, which is considered to be a holy number.[376] John the Evangelist, Pythagorus, Euclid and Archimedes (Greek's most accomplished mathematician) believed 153 to be a sacred number. They employed mathematics and metaphor to allude to the coded reference that the number 153 related to 'All Wisdom.'[377, 378]

The ratio of the width of the Vesica Piscis to the length is 153:265 and is the nearest whole number to the square root of 3 or 1.7320508. If you draw a straight line connecting the center of each circle to the point where they meet or intersect, they form two equilateral triangles. The ratios are 265:153 = 1.732061 and 1351:780 =1.7320513.[379] The ratio of 265:153 equal to 1.732061 has also been called the 'measure of the fish.'[380]

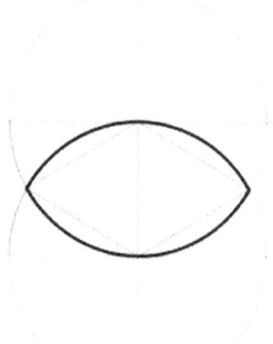

5.18 Vesica Piscis with Equilateral Triangles graphic by Steve Valdeck

Christians use this fish symbol to represent Christ. In John 21:11 "So Simon Peter... dragged the net ashore. It was full of large fish, 153, but even with so many the net was not torn." [381, 382]

5.19 *Vesica Piscis Fish graphic by Steve Valdeck*

153 and the above ratios of the Vesica Piscis are also linked to the Great Pyramid and other spiritual leaders throughout time. I'll address the sacredness of 153 in more detail later in the chapter on Color, Sound, Frequency and Sacred Geometry. Here I am making a connection between the Vesica Piscis as it relates to the Limbic System and activating Higher Consciousness.

Flower of Life

The Flower of Life is considered by many to be one of the most sacred geometric patterns of our universe. The Flower of Life is the 'Creation' pattern[383] and the blueprint of the universe.[384] It is believed to contain 'ALL Knowledge.'[385]

Cell division follows the pattern of the Vesica Piscis and the Flower of Life. With cell division, the first cell divides into two cells, then to four cells, then to eight. The continuation of this process eventually creates the human body and all things that contain Vital Life Force energy within their systems.[386]

The 'Seed of Life' is formed when seven circles of equal diameter are placed, whereupon the circumference of one circle is on the center of another in a sixfold circular symmetry. This forms the six petal 'Vesica' base of the Flower of Life's design.[387]

If you connect thirteen of the Vesica Piscis circles together within a circle, it creates the Flower of Life. The most common form of the complete Flower of Life pattern is the hexagonal pattern made up of 19 complete circles and 36 partial circular arcs that are within one outer circle.[388]

The Flower of Life holds within it every mathematical formula, every law of physics, all harmonies in music, all biological life forms, every atom and every dimensional level of reality that exists within waveform universes.[389]

This sacred pattern can be found in temples, caves and sacred sites around the world including Assyria, Austria, Bulgaria, China, Egypt, England, Greece, Hungary, India, Ireland, Israel, Italy, Japan, Mexico, Peru, Spain, Tibet and Turkey.[390, 391] The oldest Flower of Life pattern is found in the Temple of Osiris at Abydos in Egypt.[392]

The Seed of Life structure forms the basis for music. The distance between the tones and half tones of our musical scale are exactly the same distances between the circles or spheres.[393]

5.20 Seed of Life graphic by Steve Valdeck

Leonardo da Vinci studied the Flower of Life pattern and its mathematical properties.[394] Within the complete Flower of Life pattern, you will find the Kabbalah's Tree of Life, Metatron's Cube, the geometric shapes of the platonic solids (which are the building blocks of creation), as well as the 'elder futhark' runes alphabet, the Phoenician alphabet and several alchemical symbols.[395]

5.21 Flower of Life graphic by Steve Valdeck

Multiple Flower of Life symbols create the Tree of Life and Metatron's Cube.[396]

5.22 Metatron's Cube within the Seed of Life graphic by Steve Valdeck

Also, within this pattern of Life, you can find the Fibonacci Spiral.[397] The Fibonacci Spiral can be found throughout nature from our body to shells, flowers and plants.[398]

Torus / Toroidal Field

It is interesting to know that the Vesica Piscis that lies within the intersection of two equal circles forms the sacred geometry shape of the 'spindle torus.' The torus is based on the Flower of Life. It consists of a central axis with a vortex at both ends of a surrounding coherent field. Vital Life Energy flows in one vortex, along the central axis, out the other vortex, then wraps around itself and returns to the incoming vortex in a multidirectional flow.[399] Up and over, down and around, left to right and right to left all at the same time. In superstring physics, the torus is known as the "perfect" shape.[400]

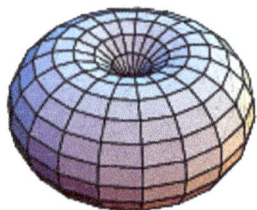

5.23 Weisstein, Eric W. "Spindle Torus." From MathWorld-A Wolfram Web Resource.
http://mathworld.wolfram.com/SpindleTorus.html

This toroidal energy flow can be found on Earth within the atmosphere and oceans, our Ecosystems, plants and trees, hurricanes, tornadoes, as well as, the magnetic fields around the planets and stars, including whole galaxies and the Milky Way.[401] The toroidal energy flow is also found in the auric or energy field around our body and within our body in our organs, cells and DNA. It is also the shape and energy flow pattern of our individual chakras.[402] Taking it into a quantum realm, the toroidal energy flow form is found in molecules, atomic and sub-atomic structures.[403]

The torus is the fundamental energy form that allows a seamless transition of fractals to occur between the micro-atomic to the macro-galactic.[404] Fractals are objects of matter or energy patterns that occur over and over in different scales and size.[405]

Another amazing aspect of a toroidal spin and configuration is found in the human heart.[406]

There are seven energetic rotational spins on the outside of the heart that correspond to the seven layers of the heart muscle. The seven spiraling layers of our heart muscles tilt exactly to the points of a tetrahedron (four sided pyramid). Also, there are five energetic rotational spins on the inside of the heart. A sonic harmonic wave is formed as our heart beats that makes up our cardiac rhythm. This sonic wave also casts a shadow that creates a Hebrew Fire letter.[407]

You can find the Hebrew letter 'Shin', if you trace the curve of the heart going under the left and right ventricles and draw a line or 'finger' going up the middle between them. This is the first letter of one of the names of God in Hebrew, which is 'Shaddai' and means 'God Almighty.' Abraham, Isaac and Jacob knew God as El Shaddai.[408] Stan Tenen has an interesting book, *The Alphabet That Changed the World: How Genesis Preserves a Science of Consciousness in Geometry and Gesture*, where he shares his research and discovery of the codes that he found within Genesis 1:1 and the hand positions that reflect the Hebrew letters.

To discover that God's signature is placed on our hearts was an exceptionally sweet gift for me! It is another confirmation that the presence of God is with us in every beat of our heart.

---

[42] *The Brain : The Last Frontier* written by Richard M. Restak, M.D. page 65
[43] http://psychology.about.com/od/lindex/g/limbic-system.htm
[44] http://www.healing-arts.org/n-r-limbic.htm
[45] *Molecules of Emotion: The Science Behind Mind-Body Medicine* written by Candace B. Pert, Ph. D page 133
[46] *Evolve your Brain: The Science of Changing Your Mind* written by Dr. Joe Dispenza page 111
[47] *The Brain : The Last Frontier* written by Richard M. Restak, M.D. pag-es 417-418
[48] *The Biology of Believe: Unleashing the Power of Consciousness, Matter & Miracles* by Bruce H. Lipton, Ph.D page 102
[49] *The Biology of Believe: Unleashing the Power of Consciousness, Matter & Miracles* by Bruce H. Lipton, Ph.D page 102-103
[50] *The Biology of Believe: Unleashing the Power of Consciousness, Matter & Miracles* by Bruce H. Lipton, Ph.D page 97
[51] *The Biology of Believe: Unleashing the Power of Consciousness, Matter & Miracles* by Bruce H. Lipton, Ph.D page 103
[52] *Evolve your Brain: The Science of Changing Your Mind* written by Dr. Joe Dispenza page 70
[53] *The Biology of Believe: Unleashing the Power of Consciousness, Matter & Miracles* by Bruce H. Lipton, Ph.D page 97
[54] *The Biology of Believe: Unleashing the Power of Consciousness, Matter & Miracles* by Bruce H. Lipton, Ph.D page 97
[55] *The Biology of Believe: Unleashing the Power of Consciousness, Matter & Miracles* by Bruce H. Lipton, Ph.D page 98
[56] *The Biology of Believe: Unleashing the Power of Consciousness, Matter & Miracles* by Bruce H. Lipton, Ph.D page 98
[57] John Chang AKA Dynamo Jack https://www.youtube.com/watch?v=Pdmz13YaO0w
[58] *Evolve your Brain: The Science of Changing Your Mind* written by Dr. Joe Dispenza page 120
[59] *Brain Self-Control* by T.D. Lingo http://www.brainselfcontrol.com/Brain_PDFs/Amygdala_Clicking.pdf page 7.1
[60] *Tickle Your Amygdala* written by Neil Slade iBook page 66
[61] *Tickle Your Amygdala* written by Neil Slade iBook page 123
[62] *Tickle Your Amygdala* written by Neil Slade iBook page 123, 125

63. *Tickle Your Amygdala* written by Neil Slade iBook page 178
64. *Evolve your Brain: The Science of Changing Your Mind* written by Dr. Joe Dispenza page 121
65. *Evolve your Brain: The Science of Changing Your Mind* written by Dr. Joe Dispenza page 121
66. *Posterior cingulate cortex activation* by emotional words: fMRI evi-dence from a valence decision task Richard J. Maddock Amy S. Garrett Michael H. Buonocore, First published: 08 November 2002 https://doi.org/10.1002/hbm.10075, *Human Brain Mapping: Volume 18: Issue 1* January 2003 pages 30-41 https://onlinelibrary.wiley.com/doi/abs/10.1002/hbm.10075
67. Tickle Your Amygdala written by Neil Slade iBook page 50
68. *Self Transcendence Workbook* by T.D.A. Ling http://www.co-bw.com/SelfTranscendenceWorkbook.pdf pages 23-24
69. *Tickle Your Amygdala* written by Neil Slade iBook page 97,
70. Click Your Amygdala ViewZone Article #1 http://www.neilslade.com/chart.html
71. *Self Transcendence Workbook* by T.D.A. Ling http://www.co-bw.com/SelfTranscendenceWorkbook.pdf page 7
72. *Tickle Your Amygdala* written by Neil Slade iBook pages 198-236
73. *Self Transcendence Workbook* by T.D.A. Ling http://www.co-bw.com/SelfTranscendenceWorkbook.pdf pages 34-36
74. *Self-Amygdala Stimulation: Popping Your Amygdala The Crazy Wisdom of TDA Lingo* http://www.neilslade.com/Papers/Library.html
75. https://en.wikipedia.org/wiki/Olfactory_bulb
76. https://www.ncbi.nlm.nih.gov/pubmedhealth/PMHT0025083/
77. https://www.britannica.com/science/olfactory-bulb
78. *Essential Oils Desk Reference Seventh Edition* by Life Science Publishing page 26
79. *The Chemistry of Essential Oils Made Simple* by Dr. David Stewart Ph.D, D.N.M. page 111
80. *Therapeutic Potential of Ectopic Olfactory and Taste Receptors* by Sung-Joon Lee, Inge Depoortere & Hanns Hatt Nature Reviews Drug Discovery Volume 18, pages 116-138 https://www.nature.com/articles/s41573-018-0002-3
81. *Essential Oils Desk Reference Seventh Edition* by Life Science Publishing pages 26-27
82. https://en.wikipedia.org/wiki/Olfactory_bulb
83. *Paralyzed man walks again after cell transplant* By Fergus Walsh: Medical correspondent http://www.bbc.com/news/health-29645760
84. https://en.wikipedia.org/wiki/Hippocampus
85. *Evolve your Brain: The Science of Changing Your Mind* written by Dr. Joe Dispenza pages 118-120
86. https://en.wikipedia.org/wiki/Hippocampus
87. https://en.wikipedia.org/wiki/Hippocampus
88. https://en.wikipedia.org/wiki/Hippocampus
89. *Theta Oscillations in the Hippocampus* Neuron, Vol. 33, 1–20, January 31, 2002, Copyright 2002 by Cell Press
90. https://en.wikipedia.org/wiki/Hippocampus
91. https://en.wikipedia.org/wiki/Hippocampus
92. *Where Are Memories Stored In The Brain - Queensland Brain Institute: The Brain - Learning & Memory* https://qbi.uq.edu.au/brain-basics/memory/where-are-memories-stored
93. https://en.wikipedia.org/wiki/Hippocampus
94. https://en.wikipedia.org/wiki/Hippocampus
95. *Evolve your Brain: The Science of Changing Your Mind* written by Dr. Joe Dispenza pages 329-330
96. *Evolve your Brain: The Science of Changing Your Mind* written by Dr. Joe Dispenza pages 329-330
97. *Evolve your Brain: The Science of Changing Your Mind* written by Dr. Joe Dispenza pages 114-115
98. https://en.wikipedia.org/wiki/Thalamus
99. *Evolve your Brain: The Science of Changing Your Mind* written by Dr. Joe Dispenza pages 114-115
100. https://en.wikipedia.org/wiki/Thalamus
101. *The Other Brain: The Scientific Breakthroughs That Will Heal Our Brains and Revolutionize Our Health* by R. Douglas Fields, Ph. D. pages 254
102. https://en.wikipedia.org/wiki/Thalamus
103. https://en.wikipedia.org/wiki/Thalamus
104. *The Other Brain: The Scientific Breakthroughs That Will Heal Our Brains and Revolutionize Our Health* by R. Douglas Fields, Ph. D. pages 255
105. *Evolve your Brain: The Science of Changing Your Mind* written by Dr. Joe Dispenza pages 114-115
106. *Evolve your Brain: The Science of Changing Your Mind* written by Dr. Joe Dispenza pages 114-115
107. *Evolve your Brain: The Science of Changing Your Mind* written by Dr. Joe Dispenza pages 115

108 *Evolve your Brain: The Science of Changing Your Mind* written by Dr. Joe Dispenza page 115
109 *Evolve your Brain: The Science of Changing Your Mind* written by Dr. Joe Dispenza pages 270
110 *Evolve your Brain: The Science of Changing Your Mind* written by Dr. Joe Dispenza page 292
111 *The Other Brain: The Scientific Breakthroughs That Will Heal Our Brains and Revolutionize Our Health* by R. Douglas Fields, Ph. D. page 118
112 *Evolve your Brain: The Science of Changing Your Mind* written by Dr. Joe Dispenza pages 291-292
113 *The Biology of Believe: Unleashing the Power of Consciousness, Matter & Miracles* by Bruce H. Lipton, Ph.D pages 117-118
114 *Evolve your Brain: The Science of Changing Your Mind* written by Dr. Joe Dispenza pages 295-296
115 *Evolve your Brain: The Science of Changing Your Mind* written by Dr. Joe Dispenza page 333
116 *Evolve your Brain: The Science of Changing Your Mind* written by Dr. Joe Dispenza pages 114-115
117 *The Other Brain: The Scientific Breakthroughs That Will Heal Our Brains and Revolutionize Our Health* by R. Douglas Fields, Ph. D. pages 188, 254-258
118 https://en.wikipedia.org/wiki/Hypothalamus
119 Why More Laughter = Less Stress = Better Health And More Energy https://www.laughteronlineuniversity.com/laughter-less-stress-better-health-energy/
120 How Laughter affects the Brain https://www.sharecare.com/health/brain/how-laughter-affect-brain
121 *Evolve your Brain: The Science of Changing Your Mind* written by Dr. Joe Dispenza page 116
122 https://gnosticteachings.org/books-by-samael-aun-weor/sexology-the-basis-of-endocrinology-and-criminology/1438-the-pituitary-gland.html
123 108 17.3 The Pituitary Gland and Hypothalamus https://opentextbc.ca/anatomyandphysiology/chapter/17-3-the-pituitary-gland-and-hypothalamus/
124 https://en.wikipedia.org/wiki/Pituitary_gland
125 *Exploring The Stress Response: HPA Axis, Nutrition, Emotions & The Limbic System* by Michael McEvoy, FDN, CNC, CMTA, https://metabolichealing.com/exploring-the-stress-response-hpa-axis-nutrition-emotions-the-limbic-system/
126 *Evolve your Brain: The Science of Changing Your Mind* written by Dr. Joe Dispenza page 291
127 https://en.wikipedia.org/wiki/Pituitary_gland
128 https://en.wikipedia.org/wiki/Pituitary_gland
129 108 17.3 The Pituitary Gland and Hypothalamus https://opentextbc.ca/anatomyandphysiology/chapter/17-3-the-pituitary-gland-and-hypothalamus/
130 108 17.3 The Pituitary Gland and Hypothalamus https://opentextbc.ca/anatomyandphysiology/chapter/17-3-the-pituitary-gland-and-hypothalamus/
131 https://opentextbc.ca/anatomyandphysiology/chapter/17-3-the-pituitary-gland-and-hypothalamus/
132 https://www.neuroscientificallychallenged.com/blog/know-your-brain-pituitary-gland
133 108 17.3 The Pituitary Gland and Hypothalamus https://opentextbc.ca/anatomyandphysiology/chapter/17-3-the-pituitary-gland-and-hypothalamus/
134 https://www.neuroscientificallychallenged.com/blog/know-your-brain-pituitary-gland
135 108 17.3 The Pituitary Gland and Hypothalamus https://opentextbc.ca/anatomyandphysiology/chapter/17-3-the-pituitary-gland-and-hypothalamus/
136 https://metabolichealing.com/exploring-the-stress-response-hpa-axis-nutrition-emotions-the-limbic-system/
137 https://en.wikipedia.org/wiki/Oxytocin
138 *The Other Brain: The Scientific Breakthroughs That Will Heal Our Brains and Revolutionize Our Health* by R. Douglas Fields, Ph. D. pages 257-259
139 http://www.thewayup.com/newsletters/041512.htm Priscilla Slagle M.D.
140 *Exploring The Stress Response: HPA Axis, Nutrition, Emotions & The Limbic System* by Michael McEvoy, FDN, CNC, CMTA - April 3, 2012 https://metabolichealing.com/exploring-the-stress-response-hpa-axis-nutrition-emotions-the-limbic-system/
141 108 17.3 The Pituitary Gland and Hypothalamus https://opentextbc.ca/anatomyandphysiology/chapter/17-3-the-pituitary-gland-and-hypothalamus/
142 https://biologydictionary.net/pituitary-gland/
143 *The Biological Effects of Childhood Trauma* by Michael D. De Bellis, MD, MPH and Abigail Risk A.B. https://www.ncbi.nlm.nih.gov/pmc/articles/PMC3968319/
144 *Exploring The Stress Response: HPA Axis, Nutrition, Emotions & The Limbic System* by Michael McEvoy, FDN, CNC, CMTA, https://metabolichealing.com/exploring-the-stress-response-hpa-axis-nutrition-emotions-the-limbic-system/
145 https://metabolichealing.com/exploring-the-stress-response-hpa-axis-nutrition-emotions-the-limbic-system/
146 *The Six Chakra and Opening The Third Eye* by Suzanne Lie, Ph.D. http://www.multidimensions.com/the-conscious/thoughts-door/the-sixth-chakra-and-opening-the-third-eye/

[147] *The Six Chakra and Opening The Third Eye* by Suzanne Lie, Ph.D. http://www.multidimensions.com/the-conscious/thoughts-door/the-sixth-chakra-and-opening-the-third-eye/
[148] *The Six Chakra and Opening The Third Eye* by Suzanne Lie, Ph.D. http://www.multidimensions.com/the-conscious/thoughts-door/the-sixth-chakra-and-opening-the-third-eye/
[149] http://www.multidimensions.com/the-conscious/thoughts-door/the-sixth-chakra-and-opening-the-third-eye/
[150] The Pineal Gland: Is It The Seat of the Soul? http://www.viewzone.com/pineal.html
[151] *Sexology: The Basis of Endocrine and Criminology* by Samuel Aunt Weor https://gnosticteachings.org/books-by-samael-aun-weor/sexology-the-basis-of-endocrinology-and-criminology/1438-the-pituitary-gland.html
[121] *Sexology: The Basis of Endocrine and Criminology* by Samuel Aunt Weor https://gnosticteachings.org/books-by-samael-aun-weor/sexology-the-basis-of-endocrinology-and-criminology/1438-the-pituitary-gland.html
[153] http://blog.world-mysteries.com/science/why-did-tesla-say-that-369-was-the-key-to-the-universe/
[154] https://gnosticteachings.org/books-by-samael-aun-weor/sexology-the-basis-of-endocrinology-and-criminology/1438-the-pituitary-gland.html
[155] *The Effects of Fluoride on the Physiology of the Pineal Gland* by Jennifer Anne Luke http://www.fluoridealert.org/wp-content/uploads/luke-1997.pdf page 19
[156] *The Pineal Gland - The Bridge to Divine Consciousness* by Scott Mowry http://www.miraclesandinspiration.com/pinealgland.html part 1
[157] https://en.wikipedia.org/wiki/Pineal_gland
[158] The Pineal and Melatonin http://www.vivo.colostate.edu/hbooks/pathphys/endocrine/otherendo/pineal.html
[159] https://en.wikipedia.org/wiki/Pineal_gland
[160] *The Pineal Gland – Biology and Consciousness* By Saskia Bosman, Ph.D. https://inspiradiance.nl/wp-content/uploads/2017/04/PinealTIGpaperupdated.pdf
[161] *The Pineal Gland: Is It the Seat of the Soul?* by Gary Vey http://www.viewzone.com/pineal.html
[162] *Exploring The Stress Response: HPA Axis, Nutrition, Emotions & The Limbic System* by Michael McEvoy, FDN, CNC, CMTA https://metabolichealing.com/exploring-the-stress-response-hpa-axis-nutrition-emotions-the-limbic-system/
[163] *The Pineal Gland – Biology and Consciousness* By Saskia Bosman, Ph.D. https://inspiradiance.nl/wp-content/uploads/2017/04/PinealTIGpaperupdated.pdf
[164] *The Pineal Gland – Biology and Consciousness* By Saskia Bosman, Ph.D. https://inspiradiance.nl/wp-content/uploads/2017/04/PinealTIGpaperupdated.pdf
[165] *The Piezoelectric Effect and the Pineal Gland in the Human Brain* by Debbie Edwards https://physics.knoji.com/the-piezoelectric-effect-and-the-pineal-gland-in-the-human-brain/
[166] https://en.wikipedia.org/wiki/Pineal_gland
[167] *The Pineal Gland – Biology and Consciousness* By Saskia Bosman, Ph.D. https://inspiradiance.nl/wp-content/uploads/2017/04/PinealTIGpaperupdated.pdf
[168] *Evolve your Brain: The Science of Changing Your Mind* by Dr. Joe Dispenza pages 116
[169] *Emotions and the Endocrine Glands* written by Dave Cowan
[170] *Happiness & Health: The Biological Factors-Systematic Review* Article by Dariush Dfarhud, Maryam Malmir, and Mohammad Khanahmadi https://www.ncbi.nlm.nih.gov/pmc/articles/PMC4449495/
[171] Sex and the Brain: How Neuroscience May Soon Change All Our Rela-tionships by Mark Turrell https://markturrell.wordpress.com/2012/03/18/sex-and-the-brain-how-neuroscience-may-soon-change-all-our-relationships-6/
[172] *How to Increase Serotonin in the Human Brain without Drugs* by Simon N. Young https://www.ncbi.nlm.nih.gov/pmc/articles/PMC2077351/
[173] *How to Increase Serotonin in the Human Brain without Drugs* by Simon N. Young https://www.ncbi.nlm.nih.gov/pmc/articles/PMC2077351/
[174] *Emotions and the Endocrine Glands* written by Dave Cowan
[175] *How Serotonin Regulates Different Body Functions* by Kristalyn Salters-Pedneault https://www.verywellmind.com/what-is-serotonin-425327
[176] *The Supermolecule the UK Government Ignores* By Roger Coghill, MA (Cantab) C Biol MI Biol MA(Environ Mgt) Director, Coghill Research Laboratories, Pontypool South Wales https://www.canceractive.com/cancer-active-page-link.aspx?n=1241&title=Melatonin--cancer-protection
[177] *Potency of Melatonin in Living Beings* by Donchan Cho https://www.ncbi.nlm.nih.gov/pmc/articles/PMC4282293/
[178] *Potency of Melatonin in Living Beings* by Donchan Cho https://www.ncbi.nlm.nih.gov/pmc/articles/PMC4282293/
[179] *Potency of Melatonin in Living Beings* by Donchan Cho https://www.ncbi.nlm.nih.gov/pmc/articles/PMC4282293/

180. *Potency of Melatonin in Living Beings* by Donchan Cho https://www.ncbi.nlm.nih.gov/pmc/articles/PMC4282293/
181. *The Supermolecule the UK Government Ignores* By Roger Coghill, MA (Cantab) C Biol MI Biol MA(Environ Mgt) Director, Coghill Research Laboratories, Pontypool South Wales https://www.canceractive.com/cancer-active-page-link.aspx?n=1241&title=Melatonin--cancer-protection
182. *Potency of Melatonin in Living Beings* by Donchan Cho https://www.ncbi.nlm.nih.gov/pmc/articles/PMC4282293/
183. *Evolve your Brain: The Science of Changing Your Mind* written by Dr. Joe Dispenza page 116
184. Pineal Gland - The Transcendental Gateway http://humanityhealing.net/wp-content/uploads/2010/08/Pineal-Gland-The-Transcendental-Gateway.pdf page 2
185. *The Pineal Gland – Biology and Consciousness* By Saskia Bosman, Ph.D. https://inspiradiance.nl/wp-content/uploads/2017/04/PinealTIGpaperupdated.pdf
186. Circulating Melatonin and the Risk of Breast and Endometrial Cancer in Women Akita N. Viswanathan and Eva S. Schemhammer https://www.ncbi.nlm.nih.gov/pmc/articles/PMC2735793/
187. *The Pineal Gland – Biology and Consciousness* By Saskia Bosman, Ph.D. https://inspiradiance.nl/wp-content/uploads/2017/04/PinealTIGpaperupdated.pdf
188. http://scienceline.ucsb.edu/getkey.php?key=4831
189. *The Pineal Gland – Biology and Consciousness* By Saskia Bosman, Ph.D. https://inspiradiance.nl/wp-content/uploads/2017/04/PinealTIGpaperupdated.pdf
190. *The Pineal Gland – Biology and Consciousness* By Saskia Bosman, Ph.D. https://inspiradiance.nl/wp-content/uploads/2017/04/PinealTIGpaperupdated.pdf
191. *The Pineal Gland – Biology and Consciousness* By Saskia Bosman, Ph.D. https://inspiradiance.nl/wp-content/uploads/2017/04/PinealTIGpaperupdated.pdf
192. *The Pineal Gland – Biology and Consciousness* By Saskia Bosman, Ph.D. https://inspiradiance.nl/wp-content/uploads/2017/04/PinealTIGpaperupdated.pdf
193. *The Pineal Gland – Biology and Consciousness* By Saskia Bosman, Ph.D. https://inspiradiance.nl/wp-content/uploads/2017/04/PinealTIGpaperupdated.pdf
194. *The Pineal Gland – Biology and Consciousness* By Saskia Bosman, Ph.D. https://inspiradiance.nl/wp-content/uploads/2017/04/PinealTIGpaperupdated.pdf
195. Cerebral Cortex, Wikipedia https://en.wikipedia.org/wiki/Cerebral_cortex
196. Frontal Lobe: Function, Structure and Damage by Zawn Villines https://www.medicalnewstoday.com/articles/318139.php
197. *The Pineal Gland – Biology and Consciousness* By Saskia Bosman, Ph.D. https://inspiradiance.nl/wp-content/uploads/2017/04/PinealTIGpaperupdated.pdf
198. *The Pineal Gland – Biology and Consciousness* By Saskia Bosman, Ph.D. https://inspiradiance.nl/wp-content/uploads/2017/04/PinealTIGpaperupdated.pdf
199. *The Pineal Gland – Biology and Consciousness* By Saskia Bosman, Ph.D. https://inspiradiance.nl/wp-content/uploads/2017/04/PinealTIGpaperupdated.pdf
200. *The Pineal Gland – Biology and Consciousness* By Saskia Bosman, Ph.D. https://inspiradiance.nl/wp-content/uploads/2017/04/PinealTIGpaperupdated.pdf
201. *The Pineal Gland – Biology and Consciousness* Pineal Gland: The Transcendental Gateway http://humanityhealing.net/wp-content/uploads/2010/08/Pineal-Gland-The-Transcendental-Gateway.pdf pages 2-3
202. *The Pineal Gland – Biology and Consciousness* Pineal Gland: The Transcendental Gateway http://humanityhealing.net/wp-content/uploads/2010/08/Pineal-Gland-The-Transcendental-Gateway.pdf pages 2-3
203. *The Pineal Gland – Biology and Consciousness* Pineal Gland: The Transcendental Gateway http://humanityhealing.net/wp-content/uploads/2010/08/Pineal-Gland-The-Transcendental-Gateway.pdf pages 2-3
204. https://en.wikipedia.org/wiki/N,N-Dimethyltryptamine
205. *The Pineal Gland – Biology and Consciousness* By Saskia Bosman, Ph.D. https://inspiradiance.nl/wp-content/uploads/2017/04/PinealTIGpaperupdated.pdf
206. *The Pineal Gland – Biology and Consciousness* By Saskia Bosman, Ph.D. https://inspiradiance.nl/wp-content/uploads/2017/04/PinealTIGpaperupdated.pdf
207. *The Secret Teachings of the Ancients of All Ages* by Manly P. Hall http://www.istitutocintamani.org/libri/The_secret_teachings_of_all_ages.pdf page 109
208. Pineal Gland: The Transcendental Gateway http://humanityhealing.net/wp-content/uploads/2010/08/Pineal-Gland-The-Transcendental-Gateway.pdf page 5
209. *The Psychedelic Rabbi* by Natalie Jacobs http://sdjewishjournal.com/sdjj/february-2014/the-psychedelic-rabbi-2/

[210] Pineal Gland: The Transcendental Gateway http://humanityhealing.net/wp-content/uploads/2010/08/Pineal-Gland-The-Transcendental-Gateway.pdf page 7
[211] *The Pineal Gland: Is It the Seat of the Soul?* by Gary Vey http://www.viewzone.com/pineal.html
[212] *The Pineal Gland: Is It the Seat of the Soul?* by Gary Vey http://www.viewzone.com/pineal.html
[213] https://en.wikipedia.org/wiki/Pineal_gland
[214] *The Pineal Gland – Your Spiritual Eye* - Margo Kirtikar Ph.D. https://www.linkedin.com/pulse/pineal-gland-your-spiritual-eye-margo-kirtikar-phd-kirtikar-ph-d-
[215] *The Pineal Gland is the Seat of Christ Consciousness* by Denize http://soundofheart.org/galacticfreepress/content/pineal-gland-seat-christ-consciousness
[216] Pineal Gland: The Transcendental Gateway http://humanityhealing.net/wp-content/uploads/2010/08/Pineal-Gland-The-Transcendental-Gateway.pdf pages 2-
[217] *The Six Chakra and Opening The Third Eye* by Suzanne Lie, Ph.D. http://www.multidimensions.com/the-conscious/thoughts-door/the-sixth-chakra-and-opening-the-third-eye/
[218] Pineal Gland - The Transcendental Gateway http://humanityhealing.net/wp-content/uploads/2010/08/Pineal-Gland-The-Transcendental-Gateway.pdf page 6
[219] https://en.wikipedia.org/wiki/Eye_of_Horus
[220] Pineal Gland: The Transcendental Gateway http://humanityhealing.net/wp-content/uploads/2010/08/Pineal-Gland-The-Transcendental-Gateway.pdf page 1
[221] Pineal Gland: The Transcendental Gateway http://humanityhealing.net/wp-content/uploads/2010/08/Pineal-Gland-The-Transcendental-Gateway.pdf page 1
[222] https://en.wikipedia.org/wiki/Third_eye
[223] Pineal Gland - The Transcendental Gateway http://humanityhealing.net/wp-content/uploads/2010/08/Pineal-Gland-The-Transcendental-Gateway.pdf page 6
[224] Pineal Gland - The Transcendental Gateway http://humanityhealing.net/wp-content/uploads/2010/08/Pineal-Gland-The-Transcendental-Gateway.pdf page 6
[225] Pineal Gland - The Transcendental Gateway http://humanityhealing.net/wp-content/uploads/2010/08/Pineal-Gland-The-Transcendental-Gateway.pdf page 5
[226] Pineal Gland - The Transcendental Gateway http://humanityhealing.net/wp-content/uploads/2010/08/Pineal-Gland-The-Transcendental-Gateway.pdf page 6
[227] *The Pineal Gland: Is It the Seat of the Soul?* by Gary Vey http://www.viewzone.com/pineal.html
[228] Pineal Gland: The Transcendental Gateway http://humanityhealing.net/wp-content/uploads/2010/08/Pineal-Gland-The-Transcendental-Gateway.pdf page 8
[229] *The Pineal Gland - The Bridge to Divine Consciousness* by Scott Mowry http://www.miraclesandinspiration.com/pinealgland.html part 2
[230] Pineal Gland: The Transcendental Gateway http://humanityhealing.net/wp-content/uploads/2010/08/Pineal-Gland-The-Transcendental-Gateway.pdf page 7
[231] Pineal Gland: The Transcendental Gateway http://humanityhealing.net/wp-content/uploads/2010/08/Pineal-Gland-The-Transcendental-Gateway.pdf pages 2-3
[232] *The Pineal Gland – Biology and Consciousness* By Saskia Bosman, Ph.D. https://inspiradiance.nl/wp-content/uploads/2017/04/PinealTIGpaperupdated.pdf
[233] *The Piezoelectric Effect and the Pineal Gland in the Human Brain* by Debbie Edwards https://physics.knoji.com/the-piezoelectric-effect-and-the-pineal-gland-in-the-human-brain/
[234] *The Piezoelectric Effect and the Pineal Gland in the Human Brain* by Debbie Edwards https://physics.knoji.com/the-piezoelectric-effect-and-the-pineal-gland-in-the-human-brain/
[236] *528Hz and Zero Point Energy* by Leonard G. Horowitz, DMD, MA, MPH, DNM, DMM http://www.528revolution.com/528-hz-and-zero-point-energy/
[236] EEG During Absent Healing by Norman Shealy, MD http://journals.sfu.ca/seemj/index.php/seemj/article/viewFile/310/273
[237] Sisterhood of the Emerald Fire Handbook by Mary Hardy https://templeofsakkara.com
[238] https://en.wikipedia.org/wiki/Piezoelectricity
[239] Alternating Current (AC) http://whatis.techtarget.com/definition/alternating-current-AC
[240] https://en.wikipedia.org/wiki/Piezoelectricity
[241] https://en.wikipedia.org/wiki/Transformer
[242] https://en.wikipedia.org/wiki/Piezoelectricity
[243] https://en.wikipedia.org/wiki/Piezoelectricity
[244] https://en.wikipedia.org/wiki/Piezoelectricity
[245] https://en.wikipedia.org/wiki/Piezoelectricity
[246] *The Piezoelectric Effect and the Pineal Gland in the Human Brain* by Debbie Edwards

247. https://physics.knoji.com/the-piezoelectric-effect-and-the-pineal-gland-in-the-human-brain/
248. *The Body Electric: Electromagnetism and the Foundation of Life* by Robert O. Becker, MD and Gary Seldon page 126
249. *The Piezoelectric Effect and the Pineal Gland in the Human Brain* by Debbie Edwards
https://physics.knoji.com/the-piezoelectric-effect-and-the-pineal-gland-in-the-human-brain/
249. *The Piezoelectric Effect and the Pineal Gland in the Human Brain* by Debbie Edwards
https://physics.knoji.com/the-piezoelectric-effect-and-the-pineal-gland-in-the-human-brain/
250. http://www.ancient-code.com/ancient-power-sources-of-the-gods-advanced-technology-and-our-ancestors/
251. Pineal Gland: The Transcendental Gateway http://humanityhealing.net/wp-content/uploads/2010/08/Pineal-Gland-The-Transcendental-Gateway.pdf page 8
252. *Piezoelectric Basins for Acoustic Levitation Identified at Megalithic Sites: Focusing the Heartbeat of the Sun* by Alex Putney for http://www.human-resonance.org/levitation_basins.html
253. http://www.ancient-code.com/ancient-power-sources-of-the-gods-advanced-technology-and-our-ancestors/
254. *Orion Infrasound Pyramid at Resonance* by Alexander Putney Collec-tion https://archive.org/stream/AlexanderPutneyLightwater/Alexander%20Putney/Alexander%20Putney%20-%20Phi_djvu.txt
255. *Piezoelectric Basins for Acoustic Levitation Identified at Megalithic Sites* by Alex Putney for http://www.human-resonance.org/levitation_basins.html
256. David Wilcock on Pineal Consciousness https://www.youtube.com/watch?v=rYn9_8IekC4https://www.youtube.com/user/davidwilcock333/videos
257. *Orion Infrasound Pyramid at Resonance* by Alexander Putney Collec-tion https://archive.org/stream/AlexanderPutneyLightwater/Alexander%20Putney/Alexander%20Putney%20-%20Phi_djvu.txt
258. *Cross Currents: the Perils of Electropollution, the Promise of Electro-medicine* by Dr. Robert O. Becker page 99
259. *The Piezoelectric Effect and the Pineal Gland in the Human Brain* by Debbie Edwards
https://physics.knoji.com/the-piezoelectric-effect-and-the-pineal-gland-in-the-human-brain/
260. *Rays of Truth - Crystals of Light: Information and Guidance for the Golden Age* by Dr. Fred Bell page 120
261. *Rays of Truth - Crystals of Light: Information and Guidance for the Golden Age* by Dr. Fred Bell pages 117-129
262. *Cross Currents: the Perils of Electropollution, the Promise of Elec-tromedicine* by Dr. Robert O. Becker page 187
263. *Cross Currents: the Perils of Electropollution, the Promise of Elec-tromedicine* by by Dr. Robert O. Becker page 188
264. *Cross Currents: the Perils of Electropollution, the Promise of Elec-tromedicine* by by Dr. Robert O. Becker page 188
265. *Cross Currents: the Perils of Electropollution, the Promise of Elec-tromedicine* by by Dr. Robert O. Becker page 195
266. *Cross Currents: the Perils of Electropollution, the Promise of Elec-tromedicine* by by Dr. Robert O. Becker page 249
267. *Rays of Truth - Crystals of Light: Information and Guidance for the Golden Age* by Dr. Fred Bell pages 117-119
268. EEG During Absent Healing by Norman Shealy, MD
http://journals.sfu.ca/seemj/index.php/seemj/article/viewFile/310/273
269. https://inspectapedia.com/emf/Electromagnetic_Frequency_Hertz_Definitions.php
270. https://inspectapedia.com/emf/Electromagnetic_Frequency_Hertz_Definitions.php
271. *The Electromagnetic Response of Human Skin in the Millimetre and Submillimetre Wave Range* by Yuri Feldman, Alexander Puzenko, Paul Ben Ishai, Andreas Caduff, Issak Davidovich, Fadi Sakron and Aharon J. Agranat http://iopscience.iop.org/article/10.1088/0031-9155/54/11/005/meta
272. *The Human Skin as a Sub-THz Receiver - Does 5G Pose a Danger to it or not?* by N. Betzaiel, Paul Ben Ishai and Yuri Feldman https://www.ncbi.nlm.nih.gov/pubmed/29459303
273. https://www.globalresearch.ca/the-same-frequencies-used-for-pain-inflicting-crowd-control-weapons-form-the-foundation-of-the-network-that-will-tie-together-more-than-50-billion-devices-as-part-of-the-internet-of-things/5580280
274. https://ehtrust.org/wp-content/uploads/Scientist-5G-appeal-2017.pdf
275. https://en.wikipedia.org/wiki/Large_Hadron_Collider
276. *Abaddon Ascending: The Ancient Conspiracy at the Center of CERN'S Most Secretive Mission* by Thomas Horn & Josh Peck
277. https://en.wikipedia.org/wiki/Safety_of_high-energy_particle_collision_experiments
278. *HAARP: Secret Weapon Used For Weather Modification, Electromag-netic Warfare* by Fred Burks
http://www.globalresearch.ca/haarp-secret-weapon-used-for-weather-modification-electromagnetic-warfare/20407
279. *Angels Don't Play This HAARP: Advances in Tesla Technology* written by Jeane Manning and Dr. Nick Begich
280. *The Piezoelectric Effect and the Pineal Gland in the Human Brain* by Debbie Edwards
https://physics.knoji.com/the-piezoelectric-effect-and-the-pineal-gland-in-the-human-brain/
281. *The Piezoelectric Effect and the Pineal Gland in the Human Brain* by Debbie Edwards
https://physics.knoji.com/the-piezoelectric-effect-and-the-pineal-gland-in-the-human-brain/
282. *The Piezoelectric Effect and the Pineal Gland in the Human Brain* by Debbie Edwards

https://physics.knoji.com/the-piezoelectric-effect-and-the-pineal-gland-in-the-human-brain/
[283] *Electronic Mind Control* by Rixon Stewart http://www.tearingdownstrongholds.com
[284] https://en.wikipedia.org/wiki/Ultra_high_frequency
[285] *Electronic Mind Control* by Rixon Stewart http://www.tearingdownstrongholds.com
[286] *The Use of Fluoridation For Mass Mind Control: The Truth About Water Fluoridation* by Charles Perkins http://rense.com/general79/hd3.htm
[287] *The Effects of Fluoride on the Physiology of the Pineal Gland* by Jennifer Anne Luke http://www.fluoridealert.org/wp-content/uploads/luke-1997.pdf page 168
[288] *Immunoexcitotoxicity as the Central Mechanism of Etiopathology and Treatment of Autism Spectrum Disorders: A Possible
Role of Fluoride and Aluminum* by Anna Strunecka, Russell L. Blaylock, Jiri Patocka an Otakar Strunecky https://www.ncbi.nlm.nih.gov/pmc/articles/PMC5909100/?report=printable
[289] *The Flouride Deception* by Christopher Bryson http://www.infowars.com/poison-tap-water/
[290] *Fluoride concentrations in the pineal gland, brain and bone of goos-ander (Mergus merganser) and its prey in Odra River estuary in Poland* by Elzbieta Kalisinska, Irena Bosiacka-Baranowska, Natalia Lanocha, Danuta Kosik-Bogacka, Katarzyna Krolaczyk, Aleksandra Wilk, Katarzyna Kavetska, Halina Budis, Izabela Gutowska, and Dariusz Chlubek https://www.ncbi.nlm.nih.gov/pmc/articles/PMC4213386/
[291] *Immunoexcitotoxicity as the Central Mechanism of Etiopathology and Treatment of Autism Spectrum Disorders: A Possible Role of Fluoride and Aluminum* by Anna Strunecka, Russell L. Blaylock, Jiri Patocka an Otakar Strunecky https://www.ncbi.nlm.nih.gov/pmc/articles/PMC5909100/?report=printable
[292] https://www.ewg.org/enviroblog/2011/09/your-best-air-freshener-isnt-air-freshener#.W4Oe_lMvyu4
[293] *Pineal Gland: The Transcendental Gateway* http://humanityhealing.net/wp-content/uploads/2010/08/Pineal-Gland-The-Transcendental-Gateway.pdf page 9
[294] *Alkaline Foods to Help Detoxify the Pineal* by S. Ali Meyers https://www.wakingtimes.com/2013/02/14/alkaline-foods-to-help-decalcify-the-pineal-gland/
[295] *The Environmental Assault on the Pineal* by Gary Vey http://www.viewzone.com/pineal.html
[296] *Pineal Gland: The Transcendental Gateway* http://humanityhealing.net/wp-content/uploads/2010/08/Pineal-Gland-The-Transcendental-Gateway.pdf page 9
[297] *Pineal Gland: The Transcendental Gateway* http://humanityhealing.net/wp-content/uploads/2010/08/Pineal-Gland-The-Transcendental-Gateway.pdf page 9
[298] *8 Supplements to Boost Your Pineal Gland Function* By Anna Hunt, Waking Times http://www.wakingtimes.com/2014/11/16/top-8-supplements-boost-pineal-gland-function/
[299] *Fluoride Special Report - Toxic Waters: The Truth about Water Fluoridation* by Dr. Mercola https://mercola.fileburst.com/PDF/FluorideSpecialReport_ToxicWaters.pdf
[300] *How To Detox Fluorides From Your Body* by Paul Fassa https://www.wakingtimes.com/2012/07/02/how-detox-fluorides-your-body/
[301] *The Secret of Rejuvenation or Professor Brown Sequard's Great Discovery of the Fountain of Youth* by Dr. Raymond W. Bernard page 27
[302] *How To Detox Fluorides From Your Body* by Paul Fassa https://www.wakingtimes.com/2012/07/02/how-detox-fluorides-your-body/
[303] *Pineal Gland: The Transcendental Gateway* http://humanityhealing.net/wp-content/uploads/2010/08/Pineal-Gland-The-Transcendental-Gateway.pdf page 9
[304] *The Complete Master Cleanse: A Step-by-Step Guide to Maximizing the Benefits of the Lemonade Diet* by Tom Woloshyn http://vitagem.com/products/the-master-cleanse/
[305] *Pineal Gland: The Transcendental Gateway* http://humanityhealing.net/wp-content/uploads/2010/08/Pineal-Gland-The-Transcendental-Gateway.pdf page 9
[306] *Endocrine Disruptors* https://www.niehs.nih.gov/health/topics/agents/endocrine/index.cfm
[307] *Solfeggio Scale Effect on the Mind and Body* https://static.secure.website/wscfus/9158863/uploads/Solfeggio_for_Ponder_Final.pdf
[308] *Solfeggio Scale Effect on the Mind and Body* https://static.secure.website/wscfus/9158863/uploads/Solfeggio_for_Ponder_Final.pdf
[309] *Solfeggio Scale Effect on the Mind and Body* https://static.secure.website/wscfus/9158863/uploads/Solfeggio_for_Ponder_Final.pdf
[310] *Piezoelectric Effect and Metaphysical Properties* by Debbie Edwards https://physics.knoji.com/clear-quartz-crystal-crystal-physics-the-piezoelectric-effect-and-metaphysical-properties/
[311] https://www.crystalsgems.com/crystals-that-are-good-for-the-pineal-gland/
[312] *Love Is In The Earth: A Kaleidoscope of Crystals* by Melody page 722
[313] *Pineal Gland: The Transcendental Gateway* http://humanityhealing.net/wp-content/uploads/2010/08/Pineal-Gland-The-Transcendental-Gateway.pdf

314. *The Sixth Chakra and Opening the Third Eye* by Suzanne Lie, Ph. D. http://www.multidimensions.com/the-conscious/thoughts-door/the-sixth-chakra-and-opening-the-third-eye/
315. *The Sixth Chakra and Opening the Third Eye* by Suzanne Lie, Ph. D. http://www.multidimensions.com/the-conscious/thoughts-door/the-sixth-chakra-and-opening-the-third-eye/
316. *The Sixth Chakra and Opening the Third Eye* by Suzanne Lie, Ph. D. http://www.multidimensions.com/the-conscious/thoughts-door/the-sixth-chakra-and-opening-the-third-eye/
317. *Sexology: The Basis of Endocrine and Criminology* by Samuel Aunt We-or https://gnosticteachings.org/books-by-samael-aun-weor/sexology-the-basis-of-endocrinology-and-criminology/1438-the-pituitary-gland.html
318. *The Human Chakra System page 2 Sushumna* by Rick Richards http://www.rickrichards.com/Chakras.htm
319. *The Hidden Powers in Humans - Chakras and Kundalini* by Param-hans Swami Maheshwarananda https://www.yogaindailylife.org/system/en/chakras
320. *Modern Esoteric: Beyond Our Senses (Second Edition)* by Brad Olsen page 289
321. *Self Transcendence Workbook* by T.D.A. Ling http://www.co-bw.com/SelfTranscendenceWorkbook.pdf pages 34-35
322. *How Wrestling God Awakened Jacob's Pineal Gland* by Joshua Tilghman on March 15, 2012 http://www.spiritofthescripture.com/id262-how-wrestling-god-awakened-jacobs-pineal-gland.html
323. *The Celsus Library: 20,000 Scrolls Lost to History but Its Striking Architecture Remains* https://www.ancient-origins.net/ancient-places-europe/celsus-library-20000-scrolls-lost-history-its-striking-architecture-remains-021095
324. *How Wrestling God Awakened Jacob's Pineal Gland* by Joshua Tilghman on March 15, 2012 http://www.spiritofthescripture.com/id262-how-wrestling-god-awakened-jacobs-pineal-gland.html
325. *Music, Stonehenge and the Great Pyramid* by James Furia http://www.greatdreams.com/gem1.htm#References%20For%20Part%20One
326. *Music, Stonehenge and the Great Pyramid* by James Furia http://www.greatdreams.com/gem1.htm#References%20For%20Part%20One
327. *HU The Most Beautiful Prayer* by Harold Klemp
328. https://thirdeyepinecones.com/history-symbolism
329. https://thirdeyepinecones.com/history-symbolism
330. https://en.wikipedia.org/wiki/Kizhi_Pogost
331. *There's an Organ in Your Brain Which Seats Your Soul: Meet Your Pineal Gland* by Jeffrey Roberts https://www.collective-evolution.com/2013/12/15/theres-an-organ-in-your-brain-which-seats-your-soul-meet-your-pineal-gland/
332. https://thirdeyepinecones.com/history-symbolism
333. http://cropcircleconnector.com/interface2005.htm
334. *Brain Structures and their Functions* by Patricia Anne Kinser, Haverford College, under the direction of Paul Grobstein, Bryn Mawr College http://serendip.brynmawr.edu/bb/kinser/Structure1.html#cerebrum
335. https://en.wikipedia.org/wiki/Brainstem
336. https://en.wikipedia.org/wiki/Vagus_nerve
337. https://en.wikipedia.org/wiki/Vagus_nerve
338. Lindley, William. *VAGUS NERVE: Learn How to Activate, Stimulate and Treat the Most Important Nerve in Your Body*. Kindle Edition Location 178-336 of 1393
339. Lindley, William. *VAGUS NERVE: Learn How to Activate, Stimulate and Treat the Most Important Nerve in Your Body*. Kindle Edition Location 106, 162, 211-312 and 1009 0f 1393
340. Lindley, William. *VAGUS NERVE: Learn How to Activate, Stimulate and Treat the Most Important Nerve in Your Body*. Kindle Edition Location 336-346 and 862 -913-943 of 1393
341. Lindley, William. *VAGUS NERVE: Learn How to Activate, Stimulate and Treat the Most Important Nerve in Your Body*. Kindle Edition Location 435-576 of 1393
342. Lindley, William. *VAGUS NERVE: Learn How to Activate, Stimulate and Treat the Most Important Nerve in Your Body*. Kindle Edition Location 862-984 of 1393
343. *Evolve your Brain: The Science of Changing Your Mind* written by Dr. Joe Dispenza page 112
344. https://en.wikipedia.org/wiki/Brainstem
345. *Brain Structures and their Functions* by Patricia Anne Kinser, Haverford College, under the direction of Paul Grobstein, Bryn Mawr College http://serendip.brynmawr.edu/bb/kinser/Structure1.html#cerebrum
346. https://en.wikipedia.org/wiki/Brainstem
347. *Brain Structures and their Functions* by Patricia Anne Kinser, Haverford College, under the direction of Paul Grobstein, Bryn Mawr College http://serendip.brynmawr.edu/bb/kinser/Structure1.html#cerebrum
348. Brain Injury https://www.braininjury-explanation.com/consequences/impact-by-brain-area/brainstem
349. https://en.wikipedia.org/wiki/Brainstem
350. *Evolve your Brain: The Science of Changing Your Mind* written by Dr. Joe Dispenza pages 110 - 111

[351] *Evolve your Brain: The Science of Changing Your Mind* written by Dr. Joe Dispenza page 111
[352] *Brain Structures and their Functions* by Patricia Anne Kinser, Haverford College, under the direction of Paul Grobstein, Bryn Mawr College http://serendip.brynmawr.edu/bb/kinser/Structure1.html#cerebrum
[353] Reticular Formation https://en.wikipedia.org/wiki/Reticular_formation
[354] *Brain Structures and their Functions* by Patricia Anne Kinser, Haverford College, under the direction of Paul Grobstein, Bryn Mawr College http://serendip.brynmawr.edu/bb/kinser/Structure1.html#cerebrum
[355] https://en.wikipedia.org/wiki/Brainstem
[356] *The Pineal Gland – Biology and Consciousness* by Saskia Bosman, Ph.D. page 1
[357] *Self Transcendence Workbook* by T.D.A. Ling http://www.co-bw.com/SelfTranscendenceWorkbook.pdf pages 34-35
[358] *The Gospel of Mary Magdalene* translation and commentary by Jean-Yves Leloup page 14
[359] *Separation of Light and Darkness: Another Esoteric Message from Michelangelo* written by Joshua Tilghman
[360] https://en.wikipedia.org/wiki/Eye_of_Horus
[361] Ancient Egypt Online: The Eye http://www.ancientegyptonline.co.uk/eye.html
[362] https://en.wikipedia.org/wiki/Eye_of_Horus
[363] *Raise Your Vibration* by Sabrina Reber http://howtoraiseyourvibration.blogspot.com/2012/01/eye-of-horusra.html
[364] https://en.wikipedia.org/wiki/Eye_of_Horus
[365] *The Gospel of Mary Magdalene translated* by Jean-Yves Leloup
[366] https://en.wikipedia.org/wiki/Vesica_piscis
[367] *Musings of the Vesica Piscis* by Rachel Fletcher Nexus Network Journal Vol. 6, No. 2, 2004 Page 96
[368] *Musings of the Vesica Piscis* by Rachel Fletcher Nexus Network Journal Vol. 6, No. 2, 2004 Page 97
[369] http://en.wikipedia.org/wiki/Flower_of_Life
[370] http://en.wikipedia.org/wiki/Flower_of_Life
[371] http://en.wikipedia.org/wiki/Flower_of_Life
[372] http://en.wikipedia.org/wiki/Flower_of_Life
[373] http://en.wikipedia.org/wiki/Flower_of_Life
[374] *The Ancient Secret of the Flower of Life* by Drunvelo Melchizedek page 14
[375] *The Ancient Secret of the Flower of Life* by Drunvelo Melchizedek page 14
[376] *Vesica Piscis is the Solution* by Roscoe http://grahamhancock.com/phorum/read.php?1,215934,215934
[377] Why 153 Fish is in John 21:11 https://www.defendingthebride.com/ss/fish/153.html#print
[378] The Works of Archimedes https://ia801408.us.archive.org/5/items/worksofarchimede029517mbp/worksofarchimede029517mbp.pdf
[379] https://en.wikipedia.org/wiki/Vesica_piscis
[380] *Vesica Piscis is the Solution* by Roscoe http://grahamhancock.com/phorum/read.php?1,215934,215934
[381] *Magdalene's Lost Legacy: Symbolic Numbers and the Sacred Union in Christianity*, Margret Starbird pages 134 - 141
[382] *The Great Pyramid and a 153 Fishes in the Net* by Joseph E. Mason http://www.greatdreams.com/numbers/jerry/153.htm
[383] *The Ancient Secret of the Flower of Life* by Drunvelo Melchizedek page 3
[384] *Flower Of Life: Ancient Sacred Geometry Symbol And Blueprint Of The Universe* by Ellen Lloyd, AncientPages.com October 8, 2017http://www.ancientpages.com/2017/10/08/flower-of-life-ancient-sacred-geometry-symbol-and-blueprint-of-the-universe/
[385] *The Ancient Secret of the Flower of Life* by Drunvelo Melchizedek page 43
[386] *Flower of Life* by Andrew Monkman https://web.archive.org/web/20120326100526/http://www.world-mysteries.com/sar_sage1.htm
[387] *Flower of Life* by Andrew Monkman https://web.archive.org/web/20120326100526/http://www.world-mysteries.com/sar_sage1.htm
[388] *Flower of Life* by Andrew Monkman https://web.archive.org/web/20120326100526/http://www.world-mysteries.com/sar_sage1.htm
[389] *The Ancient Secret of the Flower of Life* by Drunvelo Melchizedek page 31
[390] *The Ancient Secret of the Flower of Life* by Drunvelo Melchizedek page 43
[391] http://en.wikipedia.org/wiki/Flower_of_Life
[392] *Flower Of Life: Ancient Sacred Geometry Symbol And Blueprint Of The Universe* by Ellen Lloyd, AncientPages.com October 8, 2017http://www.ancientpages.com/2017/10/08/flower-of-life-ancient-sacred-geometry-symbol-and-blueprint-of-the-universe/
[393] *Flower of Life* by Andrew Monkman https://web.archive.org/web/20120326100526/http://www.world-mysteries.com/sar_sage1.htm
[394] http://en.wikipedia.org/wiki/Flower_of_Life

[395] *Flower of Life* by Andrew Monkman https://web.archive.org/web/20120326100526/http:/www.world-mysteries.com/sar_sage1.htm
[396] *Flower of Life* by Token Rock https://www.tokenrock.com/explain-flower-of-life-46.html
[397] *Sacred Geometry Introductory Tutorial* by Bruce Rawls https://www.geometrycode.com/sacred-geometry/
[398] The Torus - Dynamic Flow Process http://cosmometry.net/the-torus---dynamic-flow-process
[399] Toroidal Space: Dynamic Expressive Surface Topolgy - A Real World Practical Use of Toroidal Space http://www.theportacle.com/the-science/
[400] The Torus - Dynamic Flow Process http://cosmometry.net/the-torus---dynamic-flow-process
[401] Toroidal Space: Dynamic Expressive Surface Topolgy - A Real World Practical Use of Toroidal Space http://www.theportacle.com/the-science/
[402] The Torus - Dynamic Flow Process http://cosmometry.net/the-torus---dynamic-flow-process
[403] The Torus - Dynamic Flow Process http://cosmometry.net/the-torus---dynamic-flow-process
[404] Fractals in Nature https://cosmosmagazine.com/mathematics/fractals-in-nature
[405] Toroidal Space: Dynamic Expressive Surface Topolgy - A Real World Practical Use of Toroidal Space http://www.theportacle.com/the-science/
[406] *The Field of Form* by Lawrence Edwards pages 127-153
[407] Shadows of the Messiah - Where God's Name is Written https://promisedlandministries.wordpress.com/2010/03/14/shadows-of-the-messiah-where-gods-name-is-written/

Chapter 6:
The Glia Brain

> *"Our entire biological system, the brain and the Earth itself, work on the same frequencies."*
> — NIKOLA TESLA

I am going to get a bit more technical with anatomy, the brain and biology before I move back to the Spiral Breath. As you can see from the previous chapter, the connection between biology, science, spirituality, along with healing the emotional, mental and physical body are all interconnected. The glia brain information goes hand in hand with the limbic system. It can increase your well being and access to your Higher Consciousness. Woven among the technical information are extraordinary precious nuggets of wisdom and enlightenment.

For me, the knowledge of the limbic system and the glia brain gave me the understanding of how the working parts of the mind, body and spirit interact with each other. This knowledge allowed me to see how my Spiral Breath was being effective. The blending of biology, science, quantum physics and spirituality streamlined my healing process and also, gave me the 'why and how' I access Higher Knowledge and achieved my Light Body. Knowing how things worked and what I could do to enhance the process, gave me a path that I could use to achieve 'better than I was' before my head injury. It also allows me the ability to share this technique and the wisdom that I have acquired through my life experiences.

The Spiral Breath, accompanied by the limbic system and glia brain knowledge; marinated with my spiritual experiences and understanding brought me back into Harmony with greater Grace and Ease. Let's continue…

THE GLIA BRAIN

Within our body, we have two brains that interact with each other as one unit: the neural brain and the glia brain.

The neural brain consists of 'grey matter' also known as the neocortex or the cerebral cortex. Only 3 to 5 millimeters deep, this thin outer layer of the brain is densely populated with neurons and synapses.[409] Next to the cerebellum, the cerebral cortex contains the most neurons (nerve cells) than any other region of the brain.[410]

Neurons transmit both electrical impulses and neurotransmitter molecules between other neurons through synapses. Neurotransmitters are bio-chemical communicators. A synapse is a tiny structure that transmits and receives an electrical impulse or a chemical signal neurotransmitter between one neuron to another or to a secretory cell or to a specific region of a muscle.[411] This transmitter or receiver synapse connects neurons into neural circuits that allows us to think, feel, remember and hope.[412]

Grey matter is found at the inner core of the spinal cord and forms the outer surface layers of the brain's cortex.[413] The grey matter addresses awareness, language, motor function, reasoning, consciousness in the physical world and free will.[414]

The glia brain is the 'white matter'. The white matter consists of millions of tightly packed nerve axon fibers that are insulated with myelin sheath and glial cells.[415]

These nerve axon fibers are long, slender wire-like projections of a nerve cell (neuron) and lay just below the grey matter. They send electrical impulses back and forth between neurons in a relay circuit, connecting the neurons to the various parts of the brain.[416]

Glia cells, also called glial cells or neuroglia, are nervous system cells that are not neurons and are not part of any other tissue present in the brain.[417] Glia cells are found in the central nervous system (CNS), brain, spinal column and peripheral nervous system. There are several types of glial cells, all with unique and specialized functions. They maintain homeostasis, provide support, nutrients, oxygen and protection for neurons, form insulating myelin and destroy harmful pathogens.[418]

One of the key functions of glia cells, is that they help facilitate the forming of synaptic connections within the brain. Every time you learn or experience something, you form a synaptic connection.[419] Every time you revisit the memory of an experience or repeat the learned practice in thought or action, you strengthen that synaptic connection. Eventually, the frequently visited memory behavior becomes a conditioned and reflex response.[420]

The corpus callosum is the largest white matter structure in the brain, containing the largest number of nerve bundles within the body and the brain. It consists of 200 to 250 million contralateral axonal projections.[421] It is the bridge of communication that joins the two hemispheres of the brain together.[422]

It was discovered through MRI's that children who suffered childhood neglect had approximately 17% decrease of glia cells in their corpus callosum area.[423] Fortunately, glia cells and white matter can be increase dramatically with daily practice of creativity, meditation, breath work, holding the frequency of unconditional love within your heart, incorporating the use of pure essential oils and nutritional support with quality essential fatty acids.[424]

The white matter gets its color from the electrical insulation made up of luminescent glial cells that wrap the nerve axons called myelin. Using a focused light microscope, the reflected light of the myelin resembles a branch of a tree encased in ice crystals.[425] Myelinating glia cells extend from the toes up into and around the brain wrapping the nerves, organs and spinal cord with a coating of myelin protection.

Glia cells do not communicate through the rapid firing of electrical impulses as seen in neurons. Glia cells communicate through the spread of chemicals, such as glutamate and calcium waves.[426] This glutamate and calcium wave communication allows glial cells (astrocytes) to broadcast like a wireless cell phone, verses a neural synaptic connection similar to that of a land line telephone.[427]

Dr. Theodore Schwann discovered and documented glia cells in the nerves known as Schwann cells. Although his contributions and achievements were great, his career only lasted from 1834 – 1839.[428]

In 1856, pathologist Rudolf Virchow documented more non-neuronal cells which he naively termed neuroglia (glia for short).[429] Glia is Greek and Latin for glue.[430]

In 1886, Fridtjof Nansen suggested that glia might be "the seat of intelligence, as their number increased in size from the lower to the higher forms of animals." R. Douglas Fields, Ph.D. states that the law of increasing ratio of glia to neurons ascending the ladder from lower to higher vertebrates holds true today.[431]

In 1906 Santiago Ramon y Cajal won a Nobel Prize for his research and drawings of the Glia cells. Cajal shared the Prize with his rival Camillo Golgi, who developed the staining process in which Cajal based his work.[432]

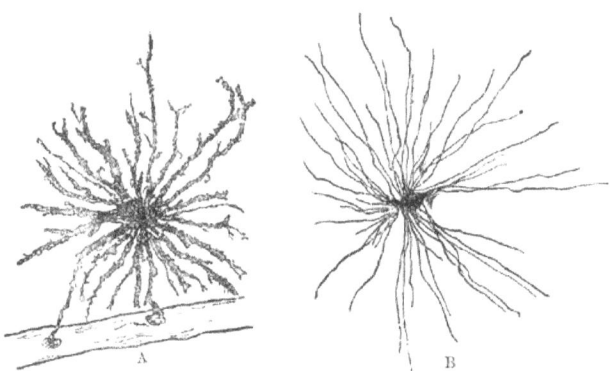

6.1 Glia Cells drawing by Santiago Ramón y Cajal using the Golgi stain

Until recently, most people, including many doctors, have never heard of glia cells. One reason for this is that from 1924 - 1949, Morris Fishbein became the president of the American Medical Association (AMA) and the Journal of the American Medical Association. During this time, he edited the glia brain out of the medical books, along with medical cures, therapies and technology.[433] Motivated solely by money and power, this professional clown-turned-doctor prevented the population from knowing the amazing benefits of the glia and inexpensive, alternative medical advances.[434]

Glia cells are so much more than neural glue. Dr. R. Douglas Fields writes in his book *The Other Brain: The Scientific Breakthroughs That Will Heal Our Brains and Revolutionize Our Health*, that "they [glia] can build the brain of a fetus, direct the connection of its growing axons to wire up the nervous system, repair it after it is injured, sense impulses crackling through axons and hear synapses speaking, control the signals the neurons use to communicate with one another at synapses, provide the energy source and substrates for neurotransmitters to neurons, couple large areas of synapses and neurons into functional groups, integrate and propagate the information they receive from neurons through their own private network, release neuro-toxic or neuroprotective factors, plug and unplug synapses, move themselves in and out of the synaptic cleft, give birth to new neurons, communicate with vascular and immune systems, insulate the neuronal lines of communication and control the speed of impulse traffic through them."[435] Whew! That's a lot of technical words and functions with still more to reveal.

Glia cells cover the blood vessels and capillaries in the central nervous system leading to the brain to create a seal known as the blood brain barrier. The glial cells are so tightly packed that they prevent cells, molecules, debris and circulating pathogens from penetrating the brain.[436] When healthy, the blood brain barrier separates the blood that circulates in the body from entering the brain and the extracellular fluid in the central nervous system. The blood brain barrier allows water, some gases and lipid-soluble molecules to pass, as well as, glucose and amino acids that are crucial for neural function. The blood brain barrier can become leaky and permeable with inflammation, and select neurological disorders.[437]

Glia cells produce more glia cells within the brain and protect neurons by removing toxic and deteriorated cellular debris. As you can see, glia cells organize, synchronize, manage and direct all forms of information within the brain, which include, glial, hormonal, immunological, neuronal, vascular, hardwires and rewires the brain and repairs the brain after injury or infection. The glia brain and glia cells orchestrate all the cellular components of the nervous system through a massive communication network.[438]

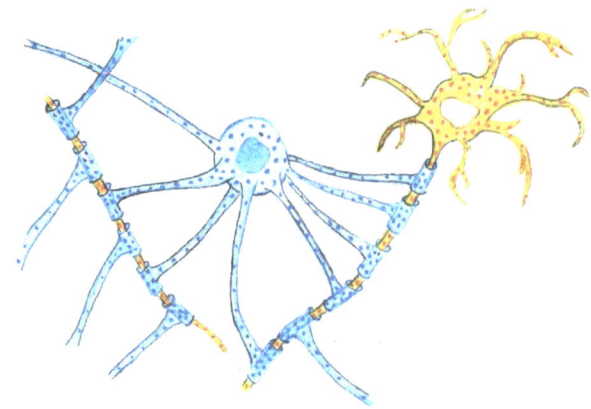

6.2 Glial Cells Creating Connections and Protection illustration by Gayle Mack

In addition to the above functions, glia cells wrap the nerves and peripheral nerves with a protective electrical insulation called the myelin sheath. In the central nervous system, the myelin sheath is formed from oligodendrocytes. In the peripheral nervous system, myelin is formed from the Schwann cells.[439]

There are four major groups of glial cells: Schwann, Microglia, Oligodendrocytes and Astrocytes.[440]

✡ ✡ ✡

SCHWANN CELLS

Schwann cells are a type of nerve cell and are only found in the central nervous system and peripheral nervous system of the body, but not found in the brain. They are classified as myelinating, nonmyelinating and terminal Schwann cells.[441] Each classification has specific tasks that they perform. Besides executing some of the same functions as the other glia cells in the central nervous system, they also create the myelin insulation, with the exception of the nonmyelinating cells. If any one of these Schwann cells were flawed or malfunctioning, it would hinder our nerves from working properly.[442]

Myelinating cells look like 'pearls' on a string. Nonmyelinating cells look like "a fistful of spaghetti."[443] Terminal Schwann cells (also called "perisynaptic" cells) surround the synapse and seal off the nerve junction and nerve endings like shrink-wrap.[444]

✡ ✡ ✡

MICROGLIA CELLS

Microglia cells (micro-glue) are considered the 'special forces' for the brain. They are always on duty. When microglia cells sense a threat of infection or in the case of injury, they shift from docile, stationary cells into warrior cells that seek, find and destroy bacterium, viruses and cellular debris.[445]

Microglia cells defend the healthy environment of our brain by releasing cytokines, like the excitatory neurotransmitter glutamate; reactive oxygen and nitrogen, which forms a 'chemical warfare' that neutralizes potentially harmful cells.[446]

In the grey matter of the brain, Microglia cells are bushy in appearance and extend their branches out in every direction symmetrically. In the white matter, their cellular branches create a protection grid that runs parallel and perpendicular to the axons.[447]

Microglia cells are formed within the embryo that becomes the brain during the gestation period of a fetus. Shortly after birth they colonize in specific areas of the brain and begin a rapid division of their cells.[448] Microglia make up 5 to 20 percent of the glia cells that are found in the brain and continue to replenish themselves through cell division as they are needed.[449]

✡ ✡ ✡

OLIGODENDROCYTES

Oligodendrocytes and Astrocytes are found inside the brain and spinal cord. They have not been found in the nerves of our body like the Schwann cells. Oligodendrocytes are extremely numerous in the white matter and are known for their exceptional high-speed impulse conduction of the myelin. Under a microscope, oligodendrocytes look like flat pearls on a string. They were given this name for they appeared to be short stubby dendrites.[450]

Ironically, when P. del Rio-Hortega altered the Golgi stain with different metallic salts, the oligodendrocytes lit up to reveal long, slender tentacles that stretched exceptionally long in distances. Oligodendrocytes resemble an octopus and their long tentacles wrap the axons to form and repair the myelin sheath (see image 6.2).[451]

Nerve and brain axons within the brain are covered by a multitude of oligodendrocyte tentacles that grip the axons. Dr. R. Douglas Fields describes them like stacked hands on the length of a baseball bat. This myelin coverage allows nerve impulses, as well as, neuron to glial communication to take place between nerves, axons and glial cells. Oligodendrocytes are always listening to the 'firing' of the axons.[452]

✡ ✡ ✡

ASTROCYTES

Astrocytes were the first major glia cell to be discovered.[453] Some scientists thought they resembled stars, thus they were named 'astrocytes.' Ramon y Cajal called them "spider cells."[454] Astrocytes, like oligodendrocytes, are only found in the brain and spinal cord; never in the nerves of our body.[455] Depending on the area, they are two to ten times more abundant than neurons.[456] In the human frontal cortex, the ratio of astrocytes to neurons is four to one.[457] Astrocytes make up more than half the brain cells.[458]

Astrocytes are found in the optic nerve. The eye is actually part of the brain and develops from the brain during embryonic development.[459] Astrocytes also control the blood flow to the various regions of brain activity.[460]

Although astrocytes are void of axons and dendrites, they support neurons by removing their waste products and delivering energy. Neurons create potassium ions when they fire their synapses. Astrocytes maintain a balance of ions by removing excess potassium in the space between cells in the brain. Controlling the charged ions that are around the neurons allows the glia to recharge the cells' battery and maintain a proper power supply for the neurons.[461] Without astrocytes absorbing the potassium ions, the brain would not be able to maintain power or recharge its energy and would quickly run out of electrical power.[462]

Astrocytes have an electrical voltage but they do not fire an electrical nerve impulse like neurons. Astrocytes communicate between themselves in the cortex through the release of calcium waves instead of electrical ions. They chemically send information to neurons, which cause neurons to 'fire' and modulate neuronal behavior.[463]

The signal frequencies of each chemical message are sent along the overlapping glia cells that form the myelin at speeds up to 200 miles per hour.[464] The myelin insulation acts as an antenna, which allows frequencies to be sent throughout our entire body instantaneously.

I would like to point out that with most things in life, there are multiple aspects of every situation. With glia and health, there is harmony, disharmony and the journey back to harmony. It too is a trinity. Glia can be at the center of both an out-of-balanced immune or nervous system, as well as, the center of maintaining wellness.[465] In certain instances, loss of the precious, protective myelin can cause dysfunction within the body. When glia cells become infected, they can become rogue cells and cause destruction.[466] For me and within this book, I am addressing the glia when in a harmonious state and the journey back to harmony.

Back to creating harmony and activating higher consciousness...

Recent research has discovered that immature glial cells can act like stem cells and mature astrocytes can activate dormant stem cells to form replacement neurons and glia cells. This is good news for anti-aging and the healing process.[467]

Glia cells are beneficial in brain injuries, such as mine. Astrocytes support the brain after injuries by forming scar tissue.[468] They move to the area of injury and begin multiplying through a division of cells. As was stated above, glia cells can defend against infectious organisms, they can stimulate the repair of damaged nerve fibers and myelin, improve communication between neurons and muscle, in addition to, increase higher intelligence, creativity and extrasensory perceptions.[469]

The Glia brain addresses the autonomic, unconscious and 'super-unconscious' functions of our body, along with motor control and muscle memory. It works outside our conscious mind and shapes the circuitry of the neural brain, the subconscious, the energetic, spiritual and emotional realms.[470]

The white matter covers the outer layer of the spinal cord and makes up the inner core of the brain directly under the cerebral cortex or grey matter.[471]

It is interesting that the grey matter runs from the center of the spinal cord to the outer layer of the brain, while the white matter forms the outer layer of the spinal cord and progresses to the center of the brain.[472] It appears to me that the two 'matters' cross at the brain stem like a macrocosm of the standing columnar waves of our DNA and the tacking motion of tachyon particles.

My friend Gandalf, who introduced me to the glia brain, taught me that the core of the glia brain operates from the heart and accesses the mind *through* the heart, while the neural brain operates from the mind within the brain itself. HeartMath Institute Research Center studies the physiological mechanisms of how the heart and brain communicate. They explore how the heart processes information and how it influences emotions, perception and health.

HeartMath found during their research that the heart does in fact, have a 'little brain' within it called the heart-brain or intrinsic cardiac nervous system. This heart-brain is made up of an elaborate system of complex ganglia, neurotransmitters, proteins and support cells, exactly like those found in our head brain. The heart-brain is capable of acting on its own to learn, to remember both short-term and long-term memory, make decisions, to feel and to sense. The little heart-brain can influence the frontal cortical areas that address attention levels, motivation, perceptual sensitivity, emotions, resilience, values, behaviors, attitudes and intuition.[473]

There are four major ways that the heart communicates with the brain and the body: 1) neurologically through the nervous system and nerve impulses, 2) biochemically through hormones and neurotransmitters, 3) biophysically through pulse waves and 4) energetically through electromagnetic fields.[474] The communication directives are sent from the heart-brain to the brain through spinal column and vagus nerves, where they engage the medulla, hypothalamus, thalamus, amygdala and cerebral cortex.[475]

The frequencies of the heart measure approximately 60 times higher in electrical amplitude than the brain and 5,000 times higher magnetically. The electromagnetic fields that are produced from our heart and brain can be measured using electrocardiograms (ECG) and electroencephalograms (EEG). When the heart is in a harmonic "coherence," it is exponentially more powerful than the neural brain.[476]

Using the technology above, science can measure the electromagnetic response that is generated from the brain and also the electromagnetic response that is generated between one person to another. When therapeutic touch modalities are performed with a sincere caring attitude, the coherence is measurably increased in the cardiac field.[477]

I recently saw a video of a Chinese baby, whose mother had passed during childbirth. The baby was very fussy and cried a lot. The family of the baby put the child into the hands of the man who had received its mother's heart. Within a few moments, the baby stops crying, as it recognizes the frequency of his mother's heart.[478]

Transplanted organs carry the original identity receptors of the donor on the cell membrane's outer surface. These identity receptors are called human leukocytic antigens (HLA) and maintain psychological and behavioral memory, as well as the personal frequency identity of the donor. The original frequency and cellular memory downloads into the transplant recipient and acts like a broadcasting antenna. Personality traits, memory and yes, even the loving frequency of a mother still resonates within the body of another.[479] The baby recognized the frequency that it was surrounded by in the womb and that courses through its veins.

The heart is a powerful thing and the energy that it generates (whether joyful or of suffering) can effect lives, emotions and wellbeing within seconds.

Remember, the heart generates the strongest electromagnetic field produced by the body. The measurement of electrical activity or signal of one person's heart using an electrocardiogram (ECG) can be registered in another person's brain using an electroencephalogram (EEG). This transfer of energy between the heart and the brain can be registered within other places of their body, whether they are touching, in the same room or at a distance.[480]

Our glia brain can be immediately stimulated with the frequency of sound, smell, pure essential oils, touch, thought, breath work and visualization.

Just one synapse is all it takes to deliver a 'lightening-speed' response at 200 plus miles per hour from an axon to nerve endings within the spine. In our spinal cord, one single synapse can determine whether the response within our body becomes a sensory neuron or a motor neuron.[481] Take the sense of smell, for instance. It requires just one synapse to send the message or frequency through the body to create a change. Frequency is immediately transported from the scent of a substance through the olfactory bulbs in the nasal passages to a synapse. It is then sent along the glia cells and myelin to the amygdala, which relays the sensory information to the highest centers of our brain, which is the limbic system.

A synapse transmits signals and receives signals; acting like switches and volume controls.[482] One tiny synapse vessel can hold thousands of neurotransmitters.[483] One astrocyte glia cell can wrap one hundred thousand synapses.[484]

This is why the use of pure essential oils and aromatics are so effective for an immediate shift in frequency, mood and clarity.

If you place a spilt clove of garlic on the bottom of your bare feet, you will taste the garlic in your mouth within minutes. My grandmother used to rub our feet with garlic and put the slices of garlic in our socks during the winter months to support our wellness. Placing pure essential oils on the feet or body can have the same response on the body and the brain. This is due to the transdermal absorption[485] and the glia's myelinating sheath.

The glia brain allows the frequency of the cells in the body to make an energetic shift within seconds of inhalation or application of a pure essential oil. Electrical impulses are sent from our sense organs to our brain along the myelinated nerve fibers of our nervous system, thus effecting a quick bodily response. These electrical impulses have been measured at speeds of 200 miles per hour.[486] Myelinating glia cells are responsible for the increased speed of neurological communications and the rapid frequency response that is transmitted between the glia cells and the glia brain.[487]

In the 1930's, Ichiji Tasaki found that myelin changed the way that electricity is transmitted along an axon. Instead of the electrical wave shooting down the fiber, as previously believed, Tasaki discovered that myelin forced the electrical impulses to jump from one node of Ranvier to the next with rapid speed. He found that myelinated axons transmit information one hundred times faster than unmyelinated axons.[488]

✡ ✡ ✡

FRACTALS, DNA AND GLIAL CONNECTION TO BODY, MIND AND SPIRIT

Glia cells also play a major role in creating synaptic circuits that are necessary for learning, changing our behaviors, our thought processes, as well as, storing our long term memory. This is known as neuroplasticity.[489]

Glial cells measure 85% of our total brain cells, while the neurons are only 15%.[490] In the nervous system, glia cells outnumber neurons six to one. In the white matter of the brain, glia cells can be 100 to one! In the frontal cortex of our brain, the ratio of glial cells (astrocytes) to neurons are four to one.[491]

Researchers examined Einstein's brain years after he had passed. They wanted to know what made him so brilliant. Upon thorough investigation, they found only one difference between his brain and the average brain. Einstein had an exceptional amount of glia cells in his frontal lobes.[492]

When you stimulate your amygdalae and pineal gland, you stimulate the growth of glia cells that can remodel tissue, repair the brain, increase learning and elevate consciousness.[493] Glia cells are a gateway to higher consciousness and the possibility of becoming a *Fully Realized Human Being!*

Einstein knew that the we are 'One' with Universal Energy. His $E=MC^2$ equation reveals that energy (E) equals matter/mass (M) multiplied by the speed of Light squared (C^2). Matter and energy are equal. They are different forms of the same thing.[494] Atoms are made of invisible energy that are not tangible matter, yet they make up tangible matter.[495] Also, matter can be transmuted and turned into energy and visa versa. Matter and energy are equal and interchangeable.[496]

Each cell of our body and brain is a macrocosm fractal of a microcosm fractal of Universal energy. The mathematics of fractal geometry is the creation of never ending, "self-similar" patterns that recur in progressively smaller or larger scales. These patterns repeat in physical matter, as well as, in energy through infinity. With fractals, the whole looks like a part. Our circulatory, respiratory, renal and neural systems are all based on fractals and are reflected throughout nature.[497]

Our DNA is a double helix fractal of chromosomes and cell division. Taken further, within the genetic material of our DNA are fractals of a toroidal energy field that nests within another toroidal electromagnetic energy field. When the toroidal energy field effects are properly lined up in harmony, they form the 'X'. Harmonic energy is funneled out through the top and bottom of this 'X', creating a wave that moves faster than the speed of Light.[498]

Fractals demonstrate through quantum physics that we are more than three dimensional beings.[499] Quantum physics encompasses Energy, Matter, Spirit and 'Superconsciousness,' all which mirror the make up of our human body, nature and the Universe. Quantum physics and fractal energy reflects our ability to achieve higher consciousness and our energetic Light Bodies.[500]

Imagine what we could accomplish if we would allow ourselves to generate the amount of glia cells that Albert Einstein had. How much more joy and meaning could we bring into our lives if we would allow ourselves to became 'fully accessed' – FULLY REALIZED like Jesus and Mary Magdalene?[501]

The information that is being shared in this chapter, show us that glia cells, DNA and energy can help us activate our TRUE Consciousness within our frontal lobes. It also demonstrates our ability to access our spiritual freedom through our glia brain and limbic system. Glia cells and DNA appear to be the interconnection between our physical body, quantum energy and our Divine 'I AM' Selves.

You can easily increase the concentration of glia cells in your frontal lobe and activate your glia brain with daily stimulation of breath work like the Spiral Breath, meditation and getting good, restful sleep. During REM (rapid eye movement) sleep, hundreds of genes are regulated and synthesized in our brain.[502] We can also nourish our glia cells and brain by taking quality essential fatty acids.[503]

As you strengthen your glial cell and glia brain activity, you can activate and stimulate your DNA. Quite possibly, our glia brain can activate the higher frequency strands of DNA that have been unseen in the physical third dimensional realm.

Research has proven that our DNA can be an antenna, a transmitter, a transducer and can store information, all at the same time. DNA emits an ultra-low electromagnetic radiation (EMR). The electromagnetic energy emitted from our DNA can actually create a hologram and a complete energetic projection of itself.[504]

In 1962, John A. Wheeler published a treatise on relativity entitled Geometrodynamics, (Academic Press, NY), where he used quantum physics to support his theory on the energy within the hole of a spherical toroid. I addressed the Torus and Toroidal Fields in Chapter 5 and toroidal energy will continue throughout the rest of the book. Wheeler explained how "wormholes act as transducers for higher dimensional energy to influx into our fourth dimensional space/time reality and he suggested that DNA had the same energy pattern and topology."[505]

Continuing on with Wheeler's research, Dr. Glenn Rein put forward the Toroid Antennae Model of DNA function. Rein submitted that the toroidal shape of DNA allows it to act as an antenna to sense the subtle energies within our environment; acts as a transducer by converting the subtle energy into electromagnetic energy and then behaves as a transmitter by radiating the converted electromagnetic energy from the DNA, to create a biochemical change on intracellular processes.[506]

Dr. Rein also found that the DNA he was viewing under a Laser Correlation Spectroscopy machine had left its energy template behind after he had physically removed the DNA from the machine. The image and energy were still present and viewable. This discovery became known as the DNA Phantom Effect.[507]

In 2010, a group of researchers (which included Nobel Laureate Dr. Luc Montagnier) published a paper entitled DNA Waves and Water. They discovered that human DNA, when placed in pure water and then removed, had left its energetic hologram in the water. *When this water was placed in a tube that contained the components that make up DNA, the original DNA sequence was recreated. The pure water retained the integrity of the DNA's original electromagnetic signal in the form of memory. The pure water not only stored the DNA's information, it transmitted it from the hologram into being.*[508]

This is an interesting tidbit of information, considering that our brain and heart are composed of 73% water, our lungs are approximately 83% water, muscles and kidneys are 79%, our skin is 64% water and our bones are 31% water. The average overall composition of water in the human body is approximately 60%.[509] So, if the original DNA sequence can recreate itself from a hologram in a test tube, why can't we recreate healthy DNA within our own bodies?

The above research group found that DNA signaling is stimulated by the Schumann wave resonance of 7 Hz, which is the natural occurring frequency of the Earth and the same wave frequency that is produced in our brain when we are in an Alpha brain wave state.

In 1996, Dr. Glenn Rein working with HeartMath Institute (HMI) in Boulder Creek, CA published a paper, "Effect of Conscious Intention on DNA." His research revealed that only the people (healers) who generated a genuine state of unconditional love could resonate with and alter DNA with focused intention.[510]

Recently, using a new imaging technology, lead researcher Christof Koch and his scientific team, discovered three neurons (grey matter) that overlaid both hemispheres of a brain. The largest neuron was wrapped around the entire brain's circumference like a "crown of thorns." The three giant neurons were attached to the claustrum, which has been shown to be a direct connection to human consciousness.[511]

When I read this article, I saw in my mind's eye, the 'Trinity.' I interpreted that the neurons which wrapped the left and right hemispheres of the brain to be the Divine Feminine and the Divine Masculine. The 'crown' that wrapped the entire brain was the Divine Oneness - I AM.

The claustrum is like a neural 'Grand Central Station'. Christof Koch wrote in a 2014 article for Scientific American, that "Almost every region of the cortex sends fibers to the claustrum."[512]

Christof Koch, along with Francis Crick (known for his research of DNA double helix) refer to the claustrum as a "conductor of consciousness." They believe that it connects all of our external (visual, sound, hearing, touch) and internal perceptions together into a single unified experience, like a conductor would synchronize an orchestra.[513]

With discipline and regular practice of the Spiral Breath, as well as, incorporating some of the various modalities mentioned within this book, you have the ability to activate the multidimensional aspects of your DNA strands, activate your glia brain, increase the amount of glia cells in your frontal lobes and activate your limbic system. Activating your limbic system and frontal lobes can open the doorway to the transformational realms of the 'knowing' - Gnosis and the 'realm of imperishable stars.'

I know this to be true, as this is the realm that I achieved when I was lying in the sarcophagus in the Kings Chamber of the Great Pyramid in 1991.

For several years prior to that trip, I had been working on healing my emotional wounds and being the best person that I could be. Something sparked within me when I heard about this spiritual tour to Egypt and its temples. I knew with every fiber of my being that I had to be there and that it was going to change my life.

We spent several days of ceremony at different temple sites along the Nile River, preparing us for the final initiation at the Great Pyramid. At each temple site, we focused on transforming the mental, emotional and spiritual wounds that we, each individually, carried within the corresponding chakra and our personal energy. During this trip, I was able to sincerely shift my emotional, mental and physical wounds through Forgiveness, Compassion, Faith and Divine Unconditional Love.

At the Temple of Isis on the Island of Philae, I became my Light Body during our ceremony. Later on that week, in our final ceremony, I laid in the sarcophagus in the Kings Chamber of the Great Pyramid. I felt that I had been there before and that I was merely awakening my memory of my past achievements. I opened my heart and mind to the possibility of reactivating that higher resonance within me, both from the experience at the Temple of Isis and from my past life remembrance. I took a deep breath. As I exhaled, I saw my "Light" travel down from my head along my body. When the Light reached my toes, I moved into a higher vibrational realm that was equally as dark as it was light.

I was free of physical form, yet I was quite conscious and acutely aware of my surroundings. Although I had no form, I could sense where my energetic body was. I was connected to the physical realm by a silver cord where my navel would be.

There was a blend of formless souls and bright star souls that encompassed me. Besides their formless 'Essence' or Light, the Souls were living consciousness. They were individuals yet, they were the 'Oneness' - a part and the whole at the same time. I was in a realm of Communion - Gnosis.

I was being rejoiced for achieving or rather returning to this 'state of being.' I was schooled with wisdom; infused with Light and a pure Love that I had not experienced in the physical realm. This was the realm where the Subtle Organizing Energy Field existed just before becoming form. This was the 'Imperishable Realm' - the 'Realm of Imperishable Stars.' It was an amazing experience! I wish that everyone would be able to experience the depth of Peace, Joy and Love that I had. This experience set the course of my life. I made it my mission to help others achieve this degree of Divine Love.

When I received the Spiral Breath and then experienced the Bliss that came with it, I knew that I had something I could share that would help others achieve a higher consciousness and Bliss.

Activating our glia brain, limbic system and DNA through our senses, the Spiral Breath technique and by holding the frequency of Unconditional Love is a key and a way to do so.

[407] Shadows of the Messiah - Where God's Name is Written   https://promisedlandministries.wordpress.com/2010/03/14/shadows-of-the-messiah-where-gods-name-is-written/
[409] *Evolve Your Brain: The Science of Changing Your Mind* written by Joe Dispenza, DC page 127
[410] *The Other Brain: The Scientific Breakthroughs That Will Heal Our Brains and Revolutionize Our Health* by R. Douglas Fields, Ph. D. page 19
[411] https://www.medicinenet.com/script/main/art.asp?articlekey=9246
[412] *The Other Brain: The Scientific Breakthroughs That Will Heal Our Brains and Revolutionize Our Health* by R. Douglas Fields, Ph. D. page 52
[413] *Evolve Your Brain: The Science of Changing Your Mind* written by Joe Dispenza, DC page 127
[414] *Evolve Your Brain: The Science of Changing Your Mind* written by Joe Dispenza, DC page 69, 99, 259
[415] *The Other Brain: The Scientific Breakthroughs That Will Heal Our Brains and Revolutionize Our Health* by R. Douglas Fields, Ph. D. page 18, 321
[416] *The Other Brain: The Scientific Breakthroughs That Will Heal Our Brains and Revolutionize Our Health* by R. Douglas Fields, Ph. D. page 18, 19, 312
[417] *The Other Brain: The Scientific Breakthroughs That Will Heal Our Brains and Revolutionize Our Health* by R. Douglas Fields, Ph. D. page 315
[418] https://en.wikipedia.org/wiki/Glia
[419] *Evolve Your Brain: The Science of Changing Your Mind* written by Joe Dispenza, DC page 127
[420] *The Biology of Belief:Unleashing the Power of Consciousness, Matter & Miracles* by Bruce H. Lipton Ph.D. page 103 - 105
[421] https://en.wikipedia.org/wiki/Corpus_callosum
[422] *Evolve Your Brain: The Science of Changing Your Mind* written by Joe Dispenza, DC page 128
[423] *The Other Brain: The Scientific Breakthroughs That Will Heal Our Brains and Revolutionize Our Health* by R. Douglas Fields, Ph. D. page 285
[424] *The Other Brain: The Scientific Breakthroughs That Will Heal Our Brains and Revolutionize Our Health* by R. Douglas Fields, Ph. D page 293
[425] *The Other Brain: The Scientific Breakthroughs That Will Heal Our Brains and Revolutionize Our Health* by R. Douglas Fields, Ph. D. page 33
[426] *The Other Brain: The Scientific Breakthroughs That Will Heal Our Brains and Revolutionize Our Health* by R. Douglas Fields, Ph. D. page 52 - 61, 267
[427] *The Other Brain: The Scientific Breakthroughs That Will Heal Our Brains and Revolutionize Our Health* by R. Douglas Fields, Ph. D. page 57
[428] *The Other Brain: The Scientific Breakthroughs That Will Heal Our Brains and Revolutionize Our Health* by R. Douglas Fields, Ph. D. page 26
[429] *The Other Brain: The Scientific Breakthroughs That Will Heal Our Brains and Revolutionize Our Health* by R. Douglas Fields, Ph. D. page 306
[430] *The Other Brain: The Scientific Breakthroughs That Will Heal Our Brains and Revolutionize Our Health* by R. Douglas Fields, Ph. D. page 7
[431] *The Other Brain: The Scientific Breakthroughs That Will Heal Our Brains and Revolutionize Our Health* by R. Douglas Fields, Ph. D. page 30 - 31
[432] *The Other Brain: The Scientific Breakthroughs That Will Heal Our Brains and Revolutionize Our Health* by R. Douglas Fields, Ph. D. page 10
[433] Morris Fishbein - AMA Enemy of American Health by Bob Wallace   https://rense.com/general19/enemy.htm
[434] The Cancer Diaries Part Five: Morris Fishbein by Rick Archer September 2013 http://www.ssqq.com/stories/cancerfight05.htm
[435] *The Other Brain: The Scientific Breakthroughs That Will Heal Our Brains and Revolutionize Our Health* by R. Douglas Fields, Ph. D. page 306
[436] *The Other Brain: The Scientific Breakthroughs That Will Heal Our Brains and Revolutionize Our Health* by R. Douglas Fields, Ph. D. pages 172 - 173
[437] Wikipedia
[438] *The Other Brain: The Scientific Breakthroughs That Will Heal Our Brains and Revolutionize Our Health* by R. Douglas Fields, Ph. D. page 24, 309
[439] *The Other Brain: The Scientific Breakthroughs That Will Heal Our Brains and Revolutionize Our Health* by R. Douglas Fields, Ph. D. page 15, 19, 35
[440] *The Other Brain: The Scientific Breakthroughs That Will Heal Our Brains and Revolutionize Our Health* by R. Douglas Fields, Ph. D. page 23
[441] *The Other Brain: The Scientific Breakthroughs That Will Heal Our Brains and Revolutionize Our Health* by R. Douglas Fields, Ph. D. page 32

[442] *The Other Brain: The Scientific Breakthroughs That Will Heal Our Brains and Revolutionize Our Health* by R. Douglas Fields, Ph. D. page 32
[443] *The Other Brain: The Scientific Breakthroughs That Will Heal Our Brains and Revolutionize Our Health* by R. Douglas Fields, Ph. D. page 31
[444] *The Other Brain: The Scientific Breakthroughs That Will Heal Our Brains and Revolutionize Our Health* by R. Douglas Fields, Ph. D. page 31-32
[445] *The Other Brain: The Scientific Breakthroughs That Will Heal Our Brains and Revolutionize Our Health* by R. Douglas Fields, Ph. D. page 42 - 44
[446] *The Other Brain: The Scientific Breakthroughs That Will Heal Our Brains and Revolutionize Our Health* by R. Douglas Fields, Ph. D. page 44
[447] *The Other Brain: The Scientific Breakthroughs That Will Heal Our Brains and Revolutionize Our Health* by R. Douglas Fields, Ph. D. page 43 - 44
[448] *The Other Brain: The Scientific Breakthroughs That Will Heal Our Brains and Revolutionize Our Health* by R. Douglas Fields, Ph. D. page 43
[449] *The Other Brain: The Scientific Breakthroughs That Will Heal Our Brains and Revolutionize Our Health* by R. Douglas Fields, Ph. D. page 42
[450] *The Other Brain: The Scientific Breakthroughs That Will Heal Our Brains and Revolutionize Our Health* by R. Douglas Fields, Ph. D. pages 32 - 35
[451] *The Other Brain: The Scientific Breakthroughs That Will Heal Our Brains and Revolutionize Our Health* by R. Douglas Fields, Ph. D. pages 34
[452] *The Other Brain: The Scientific Breakthroughs That Will Heal Our Brains and Revolutionize Our Health* by R. Douglas Fields, Ph. D. page 34 - 35
[453] *The Other Brain: The Scientific Breakthroughs That Will Heal Our Brains and Revolutionize Our Health* by R. Douglas Fields, Ph. D. page 45
[454] *The Other Brain: The Scientific Breakthroughs That Will Heal Our Brains and Revolutionize Our Health* by R. Douglas Fields, Ph. D. page 11
[455] *The Other Brain: The Scientific Breakthroughs That Will Heal Our Brains and Revolutionize Our Health* by R. Douglas Fields, Ph. D. page 33
[456] *The Other Brain: The Scientific Breakthroughs That Will Heal Our Brains and Revolutionize Our Health* by R. Douglas Fields, Ph. D. page 45
[457] *The Other Brain: The Scientific Breakthroughs That Will Heal Our Brains and Revolutionize Our Health* by R. Douglas Fields, Ph. D. page 24
[458] *Evolve your Brain: The Science of Changing Your Mind* written by Dr. Joe Dispenza page 181
[459] *The Other Brain* written by Douglas Fields, Ph. D. *The Other Brain: The Scientific Breakthroughs That Will Heal Our Brains and Revolutionize Our Health* by R. Douglas Fields, Ph. D. page 45
[460] The Root of Thought: What Do Glial Cells Do? https://www.scientificamerican.com/article/the-root-of-thought-what/
[461] *The Other Brain: The Scientific Breakthroughs That Will Heal Our Brains and Revolutionize Our Health* by R. Douglas Fields, Ph. D. page 45-46
[462] *The Other Brain: The Scientific Breakthroughs That Will Heal Our Brains and Revolutionize Our Health* by R. Douglas Fields, Ph. D. page 47
[463] The Root of Thought: What Do Glial Cells Do? https://www.scientificamerican.com/article/the-root-of-thought-what/
[464] *The Other Brain: The Scientific Breakthroughs That Will Heal Our Brains and Revolutionize Our Health* by R. Douglas Fields, Ph. D. page 19
[465] *The Other Brain: The Scientific Breakthroughs That Will Heal Our Brains and Revolutionize Our Health* by R. Douglas Fields, Ph. D. page 132
[466] *The Other Brain: The Scientific Breakthroughs That Will Heal Our Brains and Revolutionize Our Health* by R. Douglas Fields, Ph. D. page 66-77
[467] *The Other Brain: The Scientific Breakthroughs That Will Heal Our Brains and Revolutionize Our Health* by R. Douglas Fields, Ph. D. page 65
[468] *The Other Brain: The Scientific Breakthroughs That Will Heal Our Brains and Revolutionize Our Health* by R. Douglas Fields, Ph. D. page 45
[469] *The Other Brain: The Scientific Breakthroughs That Will Heal Our Brains and Revolutionize Our Health* by R. Douglas Fields, Ph. D. page 65
[470] *The Other Brain: The Scientific Breakthroughs That Will Heal Our Brains and Revolutionize Our Health* by R. Douglas Fields, Ph. D. pages 253 - 258
[471] *The Other Brain: The Scientific Breakthroughs That Will Heal Our Brains and Revolutionize Our Health*

by R. Douglas Fields, Ph. D. page 321
[472] *The Other Brain: The Scientific Breakthroughs That Will Heal Our Brains and Revolutionize Our Health* by R. Douglas Fields, Ph. D. page 321
[473] *Science of the Heart: Vol 2* (1993-2001) Exploring the Role of the Heart in Human Performance page 5, 9 https://www.heartmath.org/resources/downloads/science-of-the-heart/
[474] *Science of the Heart: Vol 2* (1993-2001) Exploring the Role of the Heart in Human Performance page 3 https://www.heartmath.org/resources/downloads/science-of-the-heart/
[475] *Science of the Heart: Vol 2* (1993-2001) Exploring the Role of the Heart in Human Performance page 5 https://www.heartmath.org/resources/downloads/science-of-the-heart/
[476] *The Energetic Heart: Bioelectromagnetic Interactions Within and Between People* written by Rollin McCraty, Ph.D. HeartMath Research Center
[477] *The Energetic Heart: Bioelectromagnetic Interactions Within and Between People* written by Rollin McCraty, Ph.D. HeartMath Research Center
[478] https://www.youtube.com/watch?v=Fa_B2nJoBZE
[479] *The Biology of Belief:Unleashing the Power of Consciousness, Matter & Miracles* by Bruce H. Lipton Ph.D. pages 160 - 163
[480] *The Energetic Heart: Bioelectromagnetic Interactions Within and Between People written* by Rollin McCraty, Ph.D. HeartMath Research Center
[481] *The Other Brain: The Scientific Breakthroughs That Will Heal Our Brains and Revolutionize Our Health* by R. Douglas Fields, Ph. D. page 22
[482] *The Other Brain: The Scientific Breakthroughs That Will Heal Our Brains and Revolutionize Our Health* by R. Douglas Fields, Ph. D. pages 19 - 23
[483] Cell Biology By the Numbers http://book.bionumbers.org/how-big-is-a-synapse/
[484] *The Other Brain: The Scientific Breakthroughs That Will Heal Our Brains and Revolutionize Our Health* by R. Douglas Fields, Ph. D. page 308
[485] *The Chemistry of Essential Oils Made Simple* by David Stewart Ph.D, D.N.M. page 26 - 27
[486] *The Other Brain: The Scientific Breakthroughs That Will Heal Our Brains and Revolutionize Our Health* by R. Douglas Fields, Ph. D. page 19
[487] *The Other Brain: The Scientific Breakthroughs That Will Heal Our Brains and Revolutionize Our Health* by R. Douglas Fields, Ph. D. page 299 - 300
[488] *The Other Brain: The Scientific Breakthroughs That Will Heal Our Brains and Revolutionize Our Health* by R. Douglas Fields, Ph. D. page 299 - 300
[489] *Evolve your Brain: The Science of Changing Your Mind* written by Dr. Joe Dispenza page 181 - 182
[490] *The Other Brain: The Scientific Breakthroughs That Will Heal Our Brains and Revolutionize Our Health* by R. Douglas Fields, Ph. D. page VII Preface
[491] *The Other Brain: The Scientific Breakthroughs That Will Heal Our Brains and Revolutionize Our Health* by R. Douglas Fields, Ph. D. page 24
[492] *The Other Brain: The Scientific Breakthroughs That Will Heal Our Brains and Revolutionize Our Health* by R. Douglas Fields, Ph. D. page 7
[493] *The Other Brain: The Scientific Breakthroughs That Will Heal Our Brains and Revolutionize Our Health* by R. Douglas Fields, Ph. D. page 24
[494] *The Chemistry of Essential Oils Made Simple* by David Stewart Ph.D, D.N.M. page 87
[495] *The Biology of Belief:Unleashing the Power of Consciousness, Matter & Miracles* by Bruce H. Lipton Ph.D. page 71
[496] *The Chemistry of Essential Oils Made Simple* by David Stewart Ph.D, D.N.M. page 86
[497] Fractal the Hidden Dimension https://www.youtube.com/watch?v=xL.gaoorsi9U
[498] Fractals, DNA, Golden Ratio with Dan Winters https://www.youtube.com/watch?v=4Rx35q-zJRk
[499] *The Biology of Belief:Unleashing the Power of Consciousness, Matter & Miracles* by Bruce H. Lipton Ph.D. page 166
[500] *The Biology of Belief:Unleashing the Power of Consciousness, Matter & Miracles* by Bruce H. Lipton Ph.D. pages 131, 159 - 165
[501] *The Gospel of Mary Magdalene* translated by Jean-Yves Leloup page 29
[502] *The Other Brain: The Scientific Breakthroughs That Will Heal Our Brains and Revolutionize Our Health* by R. Douglas Fields, Ph. D. page 260
[503] *Building Lipids for Myelin* by Laura Montani and Ueli Suter https://www.ncbi.nlm.nih.gov/pmc/articles/PMC5990396/
[504] *A Review of Psi Activity in the DNA* by Bradley Y. Bartholomew Universal Journal of Psychology 5(1): 22-29, 2017 http://www.hrpub.org/download/20170228/UJP4-19408753.pdf
[505] *A Review of Psi Activity in the DNA* by Bradley Y. Bartholomew Universal Journal of Psychology 5(1): 22-29,

[505] 2017 http://www.hrpub.org/download/20170228/UJP4-19408753.pdf
[506] *A Review of Psi Activity in the DNA* by Bradley Y. Bartholomew Universal Journal of Psychology 5(1): 22-29, 2017 http://www.hrpub.org/download/20170228/UJP4-19408753.pdf
[507] *A Review of Psi Activity in the DNA* by Bradley Y. Bartholomew Universal Journal of Psychology 5(1): 22-29, 2017 http://www.hrpub.org/download/20170228/UJP4-19408753.pdf
[508] *A Review of Psi Activity in the DNA* by Bradley Y. Bartholomew Universal Journal of Psychology 5(1): 22-29, 2017 http://www.hrpub.org/download/20170228/UJP4-19408753.pdf
[509] The Water in You: Water and the Human Body https://www.usgs.gov/special-topic/water-science-school/science/water-you-water-and-human-body?qt-science_center_objects=0#qt-science_center_objects
[510] A Review of Psi Activity in the DNA by Bradley Y. Bartholomew Universal Journal of Psychology 5(1): 22-29, 2017 http://www.hrpub.org/download/20170228/UJP4-19408753.pdf
[511] *A Giant Neuron Has Been Found Wrapped Around the Entire Circumference of the Brain* http://www.sciencealert.com/a-giant-neuron-has-been-found-wrapped-around-the-entire-circumference-of-the-brain
[512] *Neuronal "Superhub" Might Generate Consciousness* written by Christof Koch https://www.scientificamerican.com/article/neuronal-superhub-might-generate-consciousness/
[513] *What is the function of the claustrum?* written by Christof Koch and Francis Crick article: https://www.ncbi.nlm.nih.gov/pmc/articles/PMC1569501/

Chapter 7:
Emotions

Along with the physical healing that I experienced, the Spiral Breath also became a wonderful tool to balance my emotional discomforts. The Spiral Breath enables me to quickly move through the issues that bind me to discord and conflict. Shifting my emotional discomforts to a more forgiving and loving state of being brings more Light, Compassion and Wisdom into my spiritual realm and my daily life. The Spiral Breath is a windfall of Grace for body, mind, emotions and spirit.

When you move into a higher vibrational frequency, the unaddressed emotional, mental and spiritual blocks that are locked within your chakras and cellular memory will begin to surface. The lower frequency emotions cannot exist in the same space as the higher frequencies of Divine Unconditional Love. Can you recall a time when your frustration or anger quickly dissipated when you experienced something joyful and kind?

Having the knowledge of the glia brain and the limbic system allowed me to fully understand the true process that we undergo when healing our emotions. This knowledge justifies how quickly we can shift, change and heal the emotional wounds that have been obstacles in our lives for decades. Having the ability to blend our physical, mental and emotional bodies with science, biology, physiology, physics, quantum physics, chemistry and spirituality all at the same time to support our healing is profoundly amazing! It demonstrates the brilliance of God's 'Given Gifts.'

Remember that you may experience a bit of momentary uncomfortability as your old or chronic emotional issues come forth. You will find within the forthcoming pages, several ways to enhance the Spiral Breath when addressing these issues to promote healthy, graceful healing. From experience, I know the joy and relief that you will experience when you do address your emotional issues is well worth the time, energy and any discomfort it takes to clear them!

When you realize that we create and co-create our circumstances with our thoughts, wether conscious or unconscious, we can begin to heal, shift and reprogram our desired circumstance and outcomes. At times, when our emotional issues begin to surface, out of habit we ask God, "Why are you doing this to me?"

A better question to ask might be, "Why am I creating this again?" or become your personal detective and ask, "What is the core emotional issue that needs to be addressed?" "When was the first time I felt this?" "What am I getting out of this circumstance?" "How has this served me in the past?" "How am I getting in the way of my healing?"

Truly, there is no better time to look at the chaos in your life than right now. Are you ready to make a shift into a more harmonious state of being?

If you are, take a moment to look at what actions, behaviors, thoughts or habits no longer serve you in achieving your greatest good. What is getting in your way of you being truly happy? Are you too judgmental of yourself and others? Are you angry? Do you have trouble finishing a task? Do you sabotage yourself and your happiness? Take note of anything that you would change in your personality or your 'way of being.'

Write them down. It really does help with the healing process to put issues and aspects of behavior on paper. It takes it out of the mind and makes it physical and tangible. Sometimes, you just need to acknowledge that you have an aspect of behavior that could use shifting or that an event from the past has happened to you in order to start the healing process. Writing it down can be the first huge step you need to begin shifting the energy of the issue. It also gives you an opportunity to be honest with yourself. Eventually, you may feel comfortable with speaking it out loud and sharing it with someone your trust.

Number the items on your list in the order of their intensity. You can choose to address the most intense issues first and in doing so, you may find that the lesser ones dissolve on their own. If the most intense issues are a bit overwhelming, start with the lesser ones and work through the list. You could dowse or muscle test which one to begin with or you could simply do an "eenie, meenie, minie, mo." It's your choice. You always have a choice.

You can choose to Love yourself enough to make a change with those difficult emotions and thought patterns that rise up in your life or you can hang on to them. If you choose the later, they become weights that drag you down and anchor you to the third dimension and habits of survival. These difficult emotional anchors will continue to create chaos and discomfort in your life until you address them.

One time, I found an old list of aspects that I wanted to change within myself and a few desires that I wished to bring into my life. The list was about three years old. I had to laugh at myself, because what I thought was so important at the time, was not even on my new list. Some of the desires had already been achieved and with others, I had achieved even greater than I had asked for. The aspects that I wanted to change had shifted themselves out of my daily lifestyle and the items that I wanted to bring into my way of being had manifested. I had achieved my goals. Even though I had not consciously noticed the change, I was able to see my 'betterment' on paper in my own hand writing.

There is a wonderful book called *Do One Thing Different: Ten Simple Ways to Change Your Life* by Bill O'Hanlon. We have the divine power of choice. We can choose to make the same choices and keep complaining or we can choose to change our circumstances by making different choices. Doing one thing different is a simple way to break a pattern and make a change.

In his book, Bill O'Hanlon references a woman who had not left her home in a couple of years. He had her walk to the front door and back to where she had been sitting. After doing this for a couple of days, he asked her to open the door and stand in the doorway. A couple of days later, he asked her to walk to the front porch; then eventually, to the bottom of the steps and then to the mailbox. Each day she went a little bit farther than she had the day before and if she didn't, there was no judgement. Soon, she was walking the neighborhood and enjoying the sunlight and being social. It started by doing one thing different.

Sometimes, little or seemingly insignificant things can contribute to our personal sabotage of happiness. Do you find that you stretch the truth to make the conversation more exciting? Do you have a tendency to gossip or make someone look bad in order to make yourself feel more important? Do you put yourself down or sabotage your progress to reinforce that you are unworthy of success or happiness? Even though you may hesitate and your own little voice is saying "don't do that…," you do it anyway?

Make a choice to change, even a small change is a beginning. Choose to stop the unfavorable words from passing across your lips. Do it once and the second time is easier. If you revert back to old habits, then recommit to yourself and begin again. There is great personal power that arises within you when you speak words that praise and uplift people. It can be very transformational for you and for those who hear your words and experience your actions.

On the flip side, do you find yourself not speaking up and then being upset with yourself for not? Again, the first time might be a little scary, but the second time is easier. Eventually, people will know you for giving your opinion and speaking your truth. I know this from personal experience also.

Each time you make a choice, you open yourself up to allow more opportunities to come in. If your choice only works for a short while; then make another choice. Making a choice is taking an action. Action is movement and movement is change.

The Spiral Breath technique is my favorite way to clear stressful emotional and mental energy, especially when accompanied with a pure essential oil or sound (i.e. Solfeggio tones, binaural beats, etc). I'll show you how to utilize the Spiral Breath technique with other modalities shortly.

While you are healing your issues, do not become disillusioned if a situation that you are working on or one that you thought you cleared comes back around. I call this *'same scene, different play.'* It is where the same scenario repeatedly takes place; with the same or different people playing the roles. Repeated situations will afford you an opportunity to show you where you stand with an issue and how you have grown.

Take note on how you handled the situation this time it came around, as compared to how you handled it before in the past. How will you know that you have healed or made a shift if you do not have an opportunity to check your reactions?

Some people say it is difficult or too hard to face their fears or issues. At times, the conscious mind is simply not ready or able to be pushed to address an emo-tional issue. This is where the Spiral Breath in conjunction with a pure essential oil is beneficial. Just breathe and let the Grace assist you to achieve peace of mind and heart.

Sometimes, people don't have the necessary tools or know how to address an emotional, spiritual or mental wound. That is where this book and the Spiral Breath come into play.

Making the choice to do nothing only keeps one from moving forward into a more loving way of being. Speaking from experience, sometimes we grow accus-tom to our circumstances and even though we are uncomfortable or unhappy with them, we take no action to change our circumstances. It is what we have come to know. At times, what we are familiar with will override the unknown and keep us complacent in an unpleasant life.

> *This is why you become sick and why you die:*
> *It is the result of your actions.*
> *What you do takes you further away.*
> *Those who have ears let them hear.*
> THE GOSPEL OF MARY[514]

It has been scientifically proven that 90 – 95% of our behavior and uncon-scious beliefs are subconscious programs that we acquired before the age of seven. Science has also shown that 95% of the time we are living or reacting to life from those unconscious beliefs.[515, 516]

The quality of the experiences that we encounter between 0 and 7 years of age can predetermine our choices, behaviors, beliefs and destiny. Experiences that enforce heavy emotions and feelings of fear, anxiety or a lack of self worth, etc., can drive the direction of our choices, behavior and beliefs, BUT ONLY until we learn that we have a way to shift that direction.

We have the extraordinary ability to change the 'less than harmonious' subconscious programming that we acquired during our childhood and life expe-riences. When we choose to make a change in our behavior and beliefs, we are making a change in our destiny and taking our personal power back. When we ask for a way to move us through a situation, Divine always shows us a 'way.'

'Life stuff' happens to all of us in one way or another. My grandmother would say that these were the threads that made the fabric of our life stronger. She would recite the old adage, "God never gives us more than we can handle." At times, she would also say that she sometimes wished that God didn't think so highly of her. Then she would chuckle, take a deep breath and get on with her day.

When we choose to take responsibility for the outcome of our own lives, we can stop blaming our childhood, our parents, another person or circumstance, luck or lack of it, society, the "times," the church or the devil and most importantly – 'ourselves.' 'Life stuff' happens. If we want a change in the way our life is unfold-ing, we must take responsibility for the direction and the outcome.

Fortunately for us, there is a lot of good direction being offered up these days. There are many roads to the mansion of 'Happiness' to choose from. I am offering up, through the Spiral Breath, what helped liberate me from my physical, emotional and mental burdens.

I have found that we often define ourselves by our past experiences. We can get stuck in the woundedness, sorrow or anger of an experience and let the energy of that experience become our focus.

We also have a tendency to define ourselves by someone else's negative opinion or spoken words upon us, such as "being worthless." Those negative words and opinions can become our "self-imposed truth" or mis-truths. If we hear them enough, we start to believe them and every time we think those negative words about ourselves, we strengthen our belief in them.

As an example, my step-father heard me say that I wanted to be a doctor. "Oh lord, you're not smart enough to be a doctor. You'll probably kill someone. No way would I let you be my doctor." This became a familiar taunt and often used phrase from him. Eventually, I believed him and did not even try. I became a hair designer instead. And I was very good at it! I became an educator for a world known product and was on their design team. I opened my own salon and did well, but my yearning was in wellness.

I took classes and certifications, read books and studied herbs and nutrition. One day, a hair client (who was also a medical doctor in family practice) commented that she was getting a procedure done and asked me to take her hair a little bit shorter than normal. Having my iridology certification and her permission, I took a look into her eyes. "It appears that your colon is prolapsed. Are you constipated?" She replies, "Terribly and all my life." I asked if she had considered doing a colon cleanse? Two weeks later, she walks into my salon and gives me a very large hug. She no longer required the procedure and felt great. She hands me a piece of paper and says, "You're in the wrong business. Give this school a call. I've already contacted them and they are expecting you."

Her words ignited the fire within me. She spoke confidence and faith over me. She believed in me. Her words and actions replaced those of my stepfather's. Soon, I was fulfilling my dream. As I turned the key in the front door of my salon for the last time, it began to snow. It was the end of one chapter and the beginning of a new one.

The blessings that I have experienced with this new chapter of my life have deeply touched my heart. The rewards have been many and priceless!

✡ ✡ ✡

THOUGHTS ARE ENERGY

Thoughts hold a frequency that vibrates within our cells.[517] Chemicals are formed within our brain, whenever we have a thought or an experience with any of our senses (sight, hearing, touch/feeling, taste or scent). Every thought holds a chemical energy that generates an emotion. Earlier I mentioned, that the Hypothalamus actually produces a chemical to match every emotion that we experience.[518]

When we continue to repeat the energetic thoughts and the *'same scene - different play'*, neurons generate synapses and axons that create a web-like energetic pattern that can overlay onto our original vibrational pattern of balance. The imposed trauma can create an energy pattern that can disrupt our own personal signature vibration. This energetic pattern can unconsciously direct our thoughts, actions and our lives.[519]

If the repetitive patterns are destructive, such as anger, abandonment, distrust, lack of self worth, etc., they can unconsciously interfere with our ability to live our lives the way we *would like* to live them.

If the repetitive patterns are constructive and positive; they will generate happiness and inner peace.

The subconscious mind is a million times more powerful
than the conscious mind.[520]

Repressed traumas, overwhelming emotions, unhealthy thought processes and behaviors become chemically programmed and can be stored in our subconscious mind and body.[521] They can undermine our efforts to change our life experiences and habits.

The conscious mind is in charge maybe 5% of the time.
The subconscious mind is in charge the other 95%.[522]

The limbic system converts biochemical communication signals into encoded memory.[523]

This biochemical memory can be stored in our brain, as well as, in our body in a psychosomatic network within the receptors between nerves and bundles of cell bodies called ganglia. The biochemical memory can be distributed in and around the spinal cord and along pathways to our internal organs and the surface of our skin.

Through emotion-driven unconscious or conscious reactions, neuropeptides trigger our mind and body to retrieve or suppress the encoded emotions and behaviors.[524]

Remember, a present experience can be influenced by a past or inherited emotional response. We sometimes use those negatively charged past experiences or beliefs to justify our current bad behavior or circumstances.

Fortunately for us, disempowering negatively charged thought and emotional programs can be easily and quickly rewritten.[525] With the grace of our body-mind connection, there is always a biochemical potential to support change and emotional growth.[526]

In absolute truth, if we can self-impose an energy or thought process that is out of harmony and negatively affects us; we can just as easily self-impose a thought process and energy that brings us *into* harmony with a positive effect. It simply has to do with our perception.

✡ ✡ ✡

CHANGING OUR PERCEPTION

I learned during a seminar with Dr. Joe Dispenza, that it takes 72 hours for a positive thought to generate a new synapse in our brain that energetically and chemically supports that positive thought. It is how we change our perception from being a victim to being victorious!

This piece of information from Dr. Dispenza gave me the why and how the process of 'change' works both scientifically and biochemically. In his seminars and book *Breaking the Habit of Being Yourself: How to Lose Your Mind and Create a New One*, Dr. Joe Dispenza explains in great detail how our emotions become chemically locked or "hardwired" into our body and how we can break the habit of automatic response.

In short, a biochemical reaction takes place every time we have a thought. Our brain produces chemical messengers (mostly from the hypothalamus) to fortify the thought and then releases the generated biochemicals into the body. In turn, our body immediately creates reactions to match the thought and we find ourselves feeling the way we are thinking.[527]

When we enforce our thoughts with repetitive thinking, we strengthen the neural pathways to how we are feeling. When what we are feeling becomes synchronized with what we are thinking, the body-mind connection creates a *state of being*. Over time, we memorize these states of being. We become conditioned to respond a certain way when we experience a similar thought or feeling.[528]

Our memorized feelings keep us anchored in the past. As long as we are driven by our memorized feelings and reactions, we will continue to create *same scene, different play.*[529]

If we find ourselves in a state of being that we do not enjoy, we can change our perception and our way of reacting by changing our inner dialogue. Create a clear, precise new thought to replace the old one. When we consciously commit to make a change, the process begins.

As we give our focus to the new thought, we begin to create new chemical memory and new neural pathways. Repeatedly enforcing the new thought, along with an enhanced positive feeling, the new thought begins to take root *within 72 hours!* The more we reinforce the new thought, the stronger the connection becomes.[530]

The old automatic patterning begins to loose its strength, because our mind and body are no longer producing the biochemical messengers required to keep the old patterning active. Eventually, we retrain our thoughts, feelings and reactions with the new biochemical memory and strengthen the neural pathways that enforce new habits and a new joyful state of being.[531]

If we can condition ourselves to be unhappy, we can certainly condition ourselves to be joyful.

I know from my own past experiences, that when I sincerely chose to make a change in my behavior and thoughts, I also had to back it up with action. When I held myself accountable for my thoughts and actions, making the change came more easily. It is not a one time action. I have to remind myself to keep focused on the end result.

I get a little help from my subconscious mind, which likes to be in control. I give it a task. I sincerely ask my subconscious mind to quickly and easily alert my conscious mind every time I go into autopilot mode. I notice that I will begin to catch myself as I slide into autopilot emotions or reactions. Then I restate my chosen new thought and reinforce it with a heightened state of joy.

If I mis-step; then I re-step. I re-center myself and re-affirm my intended thought, behavior or response. I do this as long as it takes to ensure that my desire becomes my automatic thought process and behavioral pattern. The first 72 hours are crucial. Remember, it takes 72 hours of repeated reinforcement of the new thought to create a new neural pathway. It takes a minimum of 21 days of continued reinforcement for the old thought process to dissolve and up to 66 days for a new behavior or thought to become an automatic, unconscious habit.[532]

It is not always easy to persevere. Your memorized habits will try to sabotage your efforts to change. When this happens, just re-center. Take a breath (a slow Spiral Breath is very beneficial); re-affirm your intention and re-step, moving forward towards your goal. I can attest, that the effort you put into making a change is *definitely worth it!* Walk Forth!

Another thing that helped me shift my behaviors and emotions more easily was learning to lighten up with myself. This was a huge accomplishment for me! I have learned to laugh with myself. I laugh at how quickly I can sometimes be moved off my center of harmony. I will dialogue with myself, "Wow, that didn't take long to get triggered." "Wrrrrrerwrr! Down girl!" "Seriously! You let that trip you up?" or "What do you need to look at?"

When you ask your self or rather, ask your brain a question, like a computer, it searches for an answer. Your answer could be as simple as being hungry or having a lack of sleep. It could be more complex, like having been emotionally triggered from earlier in the day or week.

Sometimes, when I ask myself what triggered my reaction, I get a quick glimpse of a past experience. Then, I ask myself to show me the first time that I felt 'that' emotion (whatever it is) so I can shift it with Compassion, Forgiveness or Grace. I breathe the Spiral Breath until I feel centered or have made a shift.

I have trained myself to make light of my reaction, because it is showing me what I have yet to work on. That is, I do my best not to get angry at myself for reacting or place guilt or shame for my reaction. I simply acknowledge that I have something that requires some attention. I re-center myself, give apologizes when necessary and re-step.

I have a better chance of achieving an emotional healing, when my heart and my mind work together in unison and I am focused on my goal. I found that doing the Spiral Breath, while holding a positive desire or outcome, helped my intentions manifest more quickly. I hold that desire with all my senses engaged. I visualize my desired outcome and I see myself rejoicing for having achieved it. I take note of how it emotionally feels; I notice how things feel to the touch, I smell the environment around me and I hear the sounds around me.

With myself and those whom I have shared my Spiral Breath technique, we have found that when we change our perception, we can step out of autopilot mode and stop being a victim of circumstance.

Here is another aspect of changing your perception that I find equally as important. Instead of focusing on your weakness, shift your focus to your strength, courage and fortitude.

True, our experiences are what we create through our repetitive thinking and our memorized state of emotional being. We do tend to manifest what we are focused on. So why not let the positive energy that is generated when we focus on our strength, courage and fortitude move us forward into peace and harmony?

Bad things can happen to good people. It's part of "Life." These experiences give us an opportunity for personal growth; to learn, to push our boundaries and show us our strength. How will we know our level of strength, courage or compassion if we are not given an opportunity to push our limits?

In 1986, I was in a bad car accident. While stopped at a traffic light, I was hit from behind by a drunk driver. Nearly every bone in my body was shifted out of place, although none were broken. As I lay in the emergency room, the doctor leaned in; patted me on the shoulder and said, "Well… You will just have to come to terms with your disfigurement. In time, you'll get used to it. You're a pretty girl. Someone will take pity on you and marry you anyway."

A fire rose within me, as his words echoed in my head, "Take pity on me…" "get use to it…." If I could have moved my arm, I would have made him sing out like a soprano. Seeing where my focus was, he quickly backed up.

I could have given up, felt sorry for myself and stayed disfigured, but his comments burned at my soul. It made me want to prove him wrong. I chose to change my focus from being a victim of circumstance to being victorious over those circumstances.

I recalled the movie 'Resurrection' with Ellen Burstyn, where she healed herself and went from wheelchair to walking. That movie was based on a true story. I chose to believe that if she could do it, then I could do it! I did everything I could to restore my previous wellbeing.

It took several years, but I did it. I have one rib that sticks out a little in the front of my chest above my heart. It reminds me of what I overcame. I used my emotions to fuel a positive outcome. The doctors disdaining remarks became my motivation and ultimately, I came to see it as a blessing.

Often, we forget to acknowledge the fact that we *came through* a tough experience. The experience may have been traumatic, but we moved through it with the tools and the knowledge that we had at the time. We do not always give ourselves credit for getting *through* an incident or experience. We tend to focus on the trauma instead of the triumph.

I also have noticed, that we tend to look back on a past childhood experience with our adult mind and our current life knowledge. We judge what we did or did not do as a child or in a past traumatic moment with the life experience that we did not have at the time.

I believe in Divine Accordance – everything in life happens the way it does for the purpose of growing and learning. If it wasn't supposed to happen – it wouldn't have or to put it another way, if it was supposed to happen; then it would have.

Everyone experiences differently and will heal differently. I have found that, even if two people have the same or similar experiences, they will move through the healing process based on their own individual emotional foundation and their accumulated life wisdom.

When we sincerely ask for a change to take place, and expect an answer, a 'way' will come through a book, a technique, a person, etc. When we can stop feeling sorry for ourselves, we are able to take action. One action, even a small action gives way to another. Step by step, thought after thought and action by action creates movement towards healing. Soon, you realize that an issue has become yesterday's news and the energetics of that event no longer holds you as an emotional hostage.

Taking responsibility for our actions (and in some cases, for the lack of action) will determine how quickly we move into balance. This includes being responsible and accountable for what we have created and co-created through our thoughts, as well as our actions. Whatever we place our focus on, whether in our thoughts, words or actions is what we create more of in our lives.

I share this wisdom because I know it to be true. Earlier, I shared about my healing process from a car accident, where I could have felt sorry for myself and stayed disfigured. I chose to do what it took to return as close as I could to the way I was before the accident. This I accomplished.

From another experience more of an emotional nature, when I was six, my mother remarried. My stepfather turned out to be 'not-so-nice.' I endured physical, mental and sexual abuse from him.

I had many conversations with God, Jesus and the Mary's during this time for guidance and strength. One day, at age thirteen, I had enough and I stood up for myself. It almost ended my life, but God's hands intervened. Like two sides of a coin, my weakest point was also the point I stepped into my courage. That moment changed my life. In that moment, I took back my personal power.

While sharing this with a friend, I discovered that she too was dealing with abuse. My courage sparked her courage. Each day we strengthened each other and took another step towards healing. Each day my faith grew stronger. Little by little I made change, which made a huge difference in my life and for those around me.

✡ ✡ ✡

COURAGE

The disciples were in sorrow. Shedding many tears and saying:
"How are we to go among the unbelievers and
announce the Kingdom of the Son of Man?
They did not spare his life, so why should they spare ours?"
Then Mary arose, Embraced them all
and began to speak to her brothers,
"Do not remain in sorrow and doubt,
for his Grace will guide and comfort you.
Instead, let us praise his greatness, for he has prepared us for this.
He is calling upon us to become fully human – Anthropos."
　　The Gospel of Mary Magdalene [533]
"This is why you become sick and why you die,
it is the results of your actions;
what you do takes you further away.
Those who have ears, let them hear."
　　The Gospel of Mary Magdalen [534]

Our unhappiness is the consequence of our thoughts and our actions. Our actions are the consequence of our choices! Do your thoughts, actions and reactions take you further away from Divine and your Divine I AM?

We can either focus on our Joy that will bring us closer to the Light or we can focus on the chaos that moves us farther away. When you choose to address your emotional issues, you are focusing on your joy, even though you might go through a bit of uncomfortability to get there. It comes down to our choice and having tools that can help facilitate a graceful change.

When I channel Divine Mother and the Mary's, they have shared repetitively, "Once you make a decision to change, whatever it is you wish to change, *in that moment*, you set forth the energy that begins to make change. You birth into creation a course of action that will bring change. Change can be as difficult or as easy as you choose. We ask that you choose ease. Grace and Ease."

It does take courage to address your own emotional issues, though I have found that the actual amount of courage required is far less than what I had imagined it would take. Once I make a firm decision to shift my circumstances, the way and the courage always come.

Your heart and mind have to be in synch with your decision. If you think you should shift an issue, but really don't want to, then you won't. If you feel that you should shift an issue, but don't think you can, then you won't. The power to make a change comes when both the heart and the mind are in harmony with your decision.

When you become single focused within the heart and the mind, stepping across the threshold of change becomes easier and moves you from fear or habit into Faith and Joy. Making a consistent change in your thoughts and actions stimulates the process of resetting your previous patterns with new harmonious ones.

Action begins the process of unfolding Freedom! Make a choice and take an action. Within that action you will find your Courage!

Here are a couple experiences where I took action in Faith and let it unfold into Freedom:

The day that I decided to step out of the abusive environment from my step-father, that decision - that action set forth the energy of 'change.' That night, the abuse had escalated to a very dangerous level. The following morning, my mother and I went to find an apartment.

We drove past several places that just didn't seem 'right.' Then one small complex stood out as if it were lit up with flood lights. It glowed. "That one!" I said, pointing to it. At the apartment office, a sweet older woman came to the door and ushered us in.

As she touched my back, I winced. She raised my shirt and saw the open strap marks and bruises. She called her husband into the room and said, "This mother needs a safe place for her and her children. We are giving her the upstairs apartment at no cost until she can afford to pay." Without hesitation, he agreed. They unfolded their compassion and grace, as well as their protection.

On the first Sunday that we were in our new safe apartment, there was a knock on the door. Cautiously, we opened the door to find one of our neighbors with a chair in her hands. She said, "We heard that you could use a few things..." We looked out behind her to find a line of people (that we did not know) extending out into the parking lot. Each had something in hand – a bed, a table, blankets, food, etc.

By the time the last one emptied their hands, our empty apartment was completely furnished. A basket of money donations sat on the counter and the kitchen was FULL of food! So much so, that the entire apartment complex had full freezers, as well.

Our lives started new and safe, with God's unfolding Grace. Friendships were made that are as deep and strong today, as they were in that time.

A choice to change was made and that action transformed fear into Faith. *Action brought us into Freedom and there we found when we looked back on our Action that we had exercised our Courage!*

On a lighter note of action, freedom and courage, I participated in my first fire walk several years ago and walked across burning coals.

I knew to my core that I could do it, but I was also in fear of being burned.

During the instructional class, I was having this back and forth conversation in my head. It was like having the devil on one shoulder and an angel on the other. I would think, "What if I get burned?" Then I heard, "Stay in Faith! You KNOW you can do it!" Then my ego kicked in, "I'm a facilitator here. What will people think if I get burned?" "You KNOW you can walk the fire! Look what you have overcome in your life! Trust!"

During this mental volley of 'what if,' someone asked me to be their focus person. This is the person who stands on the other side of the fire and holds the fire walkers' gaze as they cross the coals. This person was looking for me to give them their added courage. The (self imposed) pressure was on!

As the fire burned down to coals, we walked around it chanting, "I am one, I am one; I am one with the fire." How appropriate! We were speaking the words that Divine Source has given us from the beginning of time, "I AM ONE ! I AM ONE with Nature and the Elements. I AM ONE with ALL THAT IS!"

When the coals were ready, I walked around the fire several times before I decided that it was my time. I approached the fire path and hesitated. I heard, "Trust! Go! Walk!" I recognized that I was not fully trusting in Divine or myself. I took a deep breath and stated out loud, "Cool spiritual fire. I AM ONE with the fire!" With that, I stepped into my Faith and onto the coals; reaching the other side with Grace and Ease.

A feeling of elation swept over me. There I was, jumping for joy and laughing! I was grinning like a child who just received everything they wanted for Christmas. I quickly got in line to walk again. Each time I crossed the coals, I gave the fire an emotional issue that I wanted to heal or I gave a blessing for someone I loved.

Symbolically, I was burning up or rather, transmuting that which no longer served me. We walked those coals until they were tamped out completely. The only thing that surpassed my own elation was seeing that look of elation on the faces of the others who also chose to take a leap into their Faith.

I (we) had mastered mind over matter and were unscathed. I looked back over the fire path and realized that, as with life, the hardest step was the first one. And what an amazing step that was!

I became aware that I had spent SO much energy on the "what if?" and the "what if" did not happened! I once was told by a lovely elderly minister that 90% of "what if's" never happen. A better way to spend my time would be to think about a positive outcome.

Standing on the threshold of a decision or making a change in your life can be scary. Again, most of the time, I have found that the thought of making a decision or taking an action was more frightening and took much more energy to think about it, than to *actually do it!*

In the moment that I stepped onto the burning coals, I re-confirmed that I can do anything that I set my heart and my mind to.

You don't have to walk a fire to heal your emotions. Healing does, however, require the implementation of an action to set forth the energy that brings about change. The Spiral Breath and the other modalities presented in this book will give you some options to choose from. It is up to you to do one thing different; to make the choice and take the first step.

FORGIVENESS

Forgiveness is also a very powerful tool! It is a key component to our healing process. This was a big one for me! In my struggle to truly be able to give forgiveness and mean it, I was graced with this teaching. I shared it in an article on my website www.keystoascension.com. It deserves being reprinted in this section. Forgiveness has become one of my greatest tools for personal healing.

Forgive as IF You Have Forgotten

I am often asked about forgiveness, especially after my newsletter entitled "Emotional Threads."[535] As we are being infused with Divine Feminine

Consciousness, our old emotional issues are coming up to be healed – through forgiveness.

One of the main keys to enlightenment and ascension is healing your childhood and emotional wounds. These unaddressed wounds keep us in turmoil. They are the anchors that weigh us down and lock us in the third dimensional survival issues and in a lack of joy.

No matter what your circumstances are, the more you address your childhood and emotional wounds, the easier your journey through life will be. Sometimes, the wounds are deep and simply saying "I forgive you" just doesn't seem to be enough.

I do understand this one well! I struggled with forgiveness towards my stepfather; the people who knew about the abuse and did nothing and the people who knew and took advantage of the situation.

Forgiveness was difficult, at the time, because the abuse encompassed so many emotions. The anger, fear, guilt and shame that I felt was creating a serious lack in my self-worth. My faith and protecting other family members and friends was what enabled me to cope with the abuse.

My inner voice strongly urged me to forgive, so that I could become truly happy and at peace. Taking measures to heal my woundedness, I prayed, read the Bible, had a priest pray over me and talked with counselors. I tried everything that I knew to do, but I just couldn't get these emotions to shift into forgiveness. I even got scrappy and mouthy for a while, but that only made things worse. At one point, I ran away from home, though I didn't get far.

One day, I had a serious 'heart to heart' with God. "It says in the Bible to forgive and forget. I can say I forgive, but I can't forget! I have not been able to do that. What am I doing wrong? Please, show me how to forgive completely, so that I can heal my body, my mind and my heart!"

Then I got still and listened. In the silence, I heard, "My dear daughter, this particular phrase has been mis-quoted. I said, Forgive as IF you have forgotten. Forgetting can keep you naive. Find compassion and you will find the Blessing of

Forgiveness. Forgive him because he is a child of God and he is wounded. Forgive as IF you have forgotten and I will show you even greater Love."

This I could do and it made a big impact on my healing process! I had to find compassion first. To find compassion, I had to find some understanding. I asked myself, "What would make a person be so mean and hurtful?" Then I answered myself, "Someone who was hurt and angry."

I asked God if I could "see" what happened, so I could have more understanding; if it was for the greatest good. Being a psychic child, I saw in my mind's eye that my stepfather was indeed a wounded boy. I saw the scenario that caused his anger. This was later confirmed by his mother when she came, out of the blue, to ask my forgiveness. She said she knew the abuse was going on, but did nothing. Her husband didn't want to 'sully' the family name, so she had kept silent until he passed.

When he was a young teenager, my stepfather was angry at his mother for something she had done. He played out his anger and his woundedness, by hurting little girls and later on, women. This made him feel strong and gave him a false sense of being in control. Doesn't make it right – it just was.

Having an understanding of "why", I could now move into compassion. Whether you are graced with the reason or not, by simply asking what would cause someone to act in unfavorable ways, allows some kind of understanding to come forth.

By forgiving him as IF I had forgotten, I was sincerely able to forgive his trespasses. Forgiving him did not excuse him from being responsible for his actions. Forgiving him freed me from *my* anger, my embarrassment and my shame. I found my voice, my self-worth and my self-love. And yes, as God had promised, a greater Love than I had known.

I learned, early on, that all situations are a co-creation. For every experience, the people involved have a lesson to learn or an opportunity to heal and grow. For some reason along our life's journey, we have to experience what we do. Some call it karma.

In Divine Accordance, we are setting up the foundation of who we will become. Maybe the experience was setting up our career choice in order to benefit many. It could be that the sharing of our personal pain would be the blessing that kept another from harming themselves or others, and knowing that they are not alone. It could be that, on some level, we were simply a catalyst to create a healing on a grander scale.

Once I have an understanding of why someone would act in an inappropriate way, I am able to move into compassion. With compassion, I find it easier to forgive. The more I practiced the process of understanding, compassion and forgiveness, the easier it became to forgive myself and others.

The more I can forgive; the more compassion fills my heart. The more compassion that fills my heart; the greater the understanding I gain of my own actions and the actions of others.

I found immense personal freedom, when I could truly forgive myself and others in our co-created experience. And I certainly am most grateful when someone can forgive me when it is I who has misstepped.

As far as forgetting, I have not forgotten. These experiences happened. They encompass much of my childhood and early teens. They were part of the foundation that made me who I am today.

My experiences, traumatic as they were at times, became amazing blessings for me, which I now 'pay forward' as tools to assist myself and others in healing. Through forgiveness, those harmful experiences stopped ruling my reactions and my life.

The faster that you can forgive yourself for what you said or did not say and for what you did or did not do; the faster that you can forgive others for what they said or did not say and what they did or did not do.

Remember, that it is our choice for how long we choose to hang on to our issues and emotional wounds and how quickly or gently we choose to heal. It is also our choice on how much integrity we apply during the process.

Live your life by focusing on the blessings and the joy that have graced your journey thus far. Emotional issues may still pop up. When they do, choose to move through them quickly and with ease. Apply the process of asking for understanding, moving into compassion and forgiving as IF you have forgotten.

✡ ✡ ✡

GRATITUDE

"Gratitude opens the door to the power, the wisdom; the creativity of the Universe. You open the door through Gratitude."
Deepak Chopra

"If you want to find happiness, find Gratitude."
Steve Maraboli

One message of guidance that comes up often is Gratitude. Gratitude is the key to manifesting! Gratitude is the quality of being thankful; the readiness to show appreciation for and to return the kindness received.

It has been proven that gratitude is strongly connected to a healthy mental and emotional well being. Grateful people have a tendency to experience more joy, be more enthusiastic, motivated, more gracious, cope better with stress, have lower blood pressure and are generally more successful than those who do not live in gratitude.[536]

Gratitude has been known to turn depression and anxiety around with remarkable speed. Gratitude can even lift the feelings of unworthiness, greed, envy and bitterness.[537]

Through channelled messages, Divine Mother and the Mary's ask that we give thanks for that which we desire and require, as *IF* we have already received it. This is the 'art' of Gratitude.

My favorite minister, Joel Osteen, shares in his services, when we ask God for something we *want*, we are affirming that we are without it. Energetically, we are affirming our state of lack.

When we give thanks for what we wish, as if we have already received it, our affirmation is confirming our blessing! Energetically, confirming our blessing means that it has *already* been birthed into creation. A prayer of 'wanting' becomes a 'prayer of giving thanks' – a prayer of Gratitude.

The art of Gratitude is multifold. When we use all of our senses (taste, scent, touch, hearing, sight and knowing) as we express our prayer or desire, it can manifest with greater ease and speed.

First, the thought of what we desire is birthed. In Chapter Ten: Tachyon and Energy, I will share the science of how 'thought' is birthed into creation.

Secondly, hold the *feeling* of gratitude within your heart, as if you have already received what you desire. Feel the gratitude intensify within your heart and then expand it out to permeate all the cells of your being – physically, mentally, emotionally and energetically.

Hold the *vision* of receiving your intention. When we hold the vision of what we desire or require, with the addition of incorporating our sense of touch, taste, smell, sight and hearing, our prayer of gratitude becomes more real. When we can see it, touch it, hear it and smell it, even if it is in our mind, it becomes more physical. When we add the joy of receiving it, we allow our prayer or intention to manifest more quickly.

I also include in my prayer of gratitude 'For My Greatest Good.' When I allow God to deliver 'my greatest good,' I often will receive greater than what I originally desired. Why not let *Divine All That Is* deliver our blessings to our fullest favor?

The final part of praying with gratitude is Trust. Trust can be a big 'hot' button when you have little trust to give. Do your best to muster up some trust anyway. Let trust multiply by putting it into practice.

Once you have given thanks for having already received your desires; shift your Hope that it will come to pass into *Belief* that it will come to pass and *'Expecting'* it to. Let your intention manifest as you wait with expectancy. Expectancy can easily shift into Trust and Faith.

One Sunday with friends, I was asked if I had a busy week ahead of me. I answered, "Not at the moment, but I trust God will fill my schedule for my greatest and highest good." One of my friends commented, "You really believe that's going to happen?" "Absolutely!" I continued, "I proclaimed my prayer of gratitude for already having done so and I expect God to deliver my favor." My friend replied, "Aren't you being a bit arrogant?" I countered with a smile, "Not at all! It is called *Faith!*"

Within an hour of being in my office on Monday morning, I was not only booked for the week, I was booked for 2 ½ weeks out. And I gave Thanks!

Joel Osteen, reminds us to put action behind our beliefs. He says, *"When you have nothing to stand on in the natural and you start acting as though God's Word is true; being positive and hopeful – you are putting action behind your Faith. That gets God's attention. That's what causes Him to work supernaturally in your life. You go from Believing to Expecting."*[538]

A few years back, I was a bit worn out from the multitude of "things on my plate." I commented to a friend, "When this event is finished I am taking a vacation!" My friend inquired, "Where are you going?" "I don't know." I replied, "I trust that God will drop something into my lap." Then I laughed and went about my day. Two days later, another friend called to see if I would be her traveling companion on a trip. She needed assistance with luggage and driving, etc. Of course I said 'yes,' then quickly gave thanks to God for 'dropping' my vacation into my lap.

Gratitude is a virtue that requires cultivating and action. When you begin to 'practice' gratitude, you begin to receive more things to be grateful for. A grateful heart is like a magnet.

> *"Gratitude is not only the greatest of the virtues,*
> *but the parent of all others."*
> MARCUS TULLIUS CICERO

Counting your blessings helps you focus on the goodness in your life and not on the lack. When life becomes chaotic; I refocus on my 'gratitudes' and life quickly begins to smooth out. I get an "Attitude of Gratitude!"

Gratitude empowers us to be more motivated, inspired and happy. When you begin your day with gratitude and carry it through the day, life becomes very pleasant.

I like to start the day by giving thanks that God gave me another day to share and receive the bountiful blessings that will unfold as I go throughout my day. I then set my intention for the day and visualize it unfolding in my mind. I allow myself to imagine my intention with all my senses. I take note how it feels and how it looks. In the surroundings of my vision, I imagine the sounds, the colors and the excitement of having received my intention. I hold the feeling of gratitude in my heart as I do my Spiral Breath technique. When I am filled with Grace, Love and Gratitude, I step out of bed and step into my blessed day.

When I walk in the mornings, I give thanks for everything that greets me: the sun that warms me, the birds that sing for me, the flowers that have bloomed for my eyes to behold and the wind that whispers in my ears. I am grateful that my legs allow me to power up the hills and for the cheerful waves from neighbors. My walks are a continual prayer of gratitude in motion. When you consciously focus and put forth the action of gratitude, it begins to multiply.

Throughout the day, as I express my gratitude, it becomes a wave of goodness that unfolds as I go along. The beauty of expressing gratitude is that it is contagious!

> *"Feeling gratitude and not expressing it*
> *is like wrapping a present and not giving it."*
> William Arthur Ward

One day I stopped at my local grocery store. As I passed by the courtesy desk and the very long line of disgruntled people, I noticed that my friend, who was working the desk, was a bit frazzled. I got in line and sincerely complimented the woman in front of me and smiled. She looked at me for a moment before replying a thank you and smiled back. Her agitation of waiting started to ease.

She asked me what I was returning. I replied, "A hug." She smiled and said that she could use one, so I gave her one. As she thanked me, the person in front of her said that he could use one. So she gave the young man a hug. It started a chain reaction. Soon, people were coming down the aisles to participate in giving and receiving hugs, sharing smiles and giving thanks.

When I got up to the counter, my friend (who was so busy that she had not noticed me or the unfolding gratitude wave) asked how she could help me. I said, "I would like to return a hug." It took her a few moments to process the request. Then her eyes lit up as she realized it was me. A smile broadened her face and she ran around the counter to receive her hug.

Everyone who had been in that line was now sharing grace, consideration and gratitude throughout the store. The energy within the store quickly became electrified with joy and laughter in a matter of minutes.

> "As we express our gratitude, we must never forget that the highest appreciation is not to utter words but to live by them."
> JOHN F. KENNEDY

Sometimes, life gets hectic and it is easy to forget our gratitudes. It definitely is true, that what we place our focus on is what we will manifest more of! When you are feeling heavy hearted and nothing seems to be going your way; this is the most perfect time to start counting your blessings and change the direction of your day and life. Do whatever you can to change your situation and then, let God do what you can't.

Remember the beautiful and powerful verse of John 16:23-24 in the Aramaic translation from the *Prayers of the Cosmos: Meditations on the Aramaic Words of Jesus* by Neil Douglas-Klotz:

> "All things that you ask straightly, directly, that you desire –
> like an arrow to its mark, from the Breathing Life of All,
> Father-Mother of the Cosmos, with my Shem – my experience,
> my Light and Sound, my Atmosphere,
> my Word from inside my Name – you will be given.
> So far you have not done this.
> So ask without hidden motive and be surrounded by your answer –
> Be enveloped by what you desire that your gladness be full –
> That the joy of goals met here may continue its story to
> perfection in Unity." [539]

It is really one of my favorite sayings as it truly encompasses Gratitude, Compassion, Trust, Faith and Action.

I like the phrase, *"Be surrounded by your answer – Be enveloped by what you desire that your gladness be full."* It is saying to 'Be' your answer! Feel what you desire with all your senses.

The last line states, *"Be full – that the joy of goals MET here may continue its story to perfection in Unity."* Once again, be full of joy that your goals - your requests - your desires have 'already' been MET, as if you have already received them!

Every experience that you create and co-create will eventually unfold into a blessing. You may not see it right away. Know that there is always a 'Divine Plan.' I found my courage and my strength through my tough experiences. Through them, I also cultivated compassion, forgiveness and a true appreciation for Life, Love, Happiness and Gratitude! As I am full of *"Joy for goals MET,"* God continues to unfold His perfection in Unity through my story.

Had I not experienced trauma to my brainstem and cerebellum, I might not have been given the Spiral Breath technique that facilitated my healing. Sure, I would have preferred not to be hit in the head and sustain the injuries that I had, but the experience unfolded a blessing that I can share to benefit others, as well as myself and for that blessing – I am grateful.

> *"Thankfulness is the beginning of gratitude.*
> *Gratitude is the completion of thankfulness.*
> *Thankfulness may consist merely of words.*
> *Gratitude is shown in acts."*
> HENRI FREDERIC AMIEL

✡ ✡ ✡

INNER PEACE

Inner Peace refers to a conscious and intentional state of being that reflects both mental and spiritual peace despite the potential presence of stress.[540] Inner Peace is a learned practice that is achieved by mindfully focusing on remaining calm through a present chaos. Inner Peace is a practice of being *'at Peace,'* having 'Peace of Mind' and 'Peace of Heart.'

Ancient cultures and religious traditions including Hinduism, Buddhism, Taoism, the Egyptians and Native Americans, as well as, texts from the Bible to the teachings of Hermes, have been guiding humanity to find their unshakable 'peace within.'

> *And the Peace of God, which transcends all understanding*
> *will guard your hearts and your minds in Christ Jesus.*
> PHILIPPIANS 4:7

The Spiral Breath, along with a focused intent, can help you achieve Inner Peace. The Spiral Breath helps to activate your anterior amygdala, as does meditation, toning, and the use of pure essential oils. In the previous chapters, we talked about how to switch on your amygdala and frontal lobes. Activating the anterior amygdala can move you into a state of calm, which then stimulates your frontal lobe, as well as positive emotions, improved decision making and greater intelligence. With consistent practice, you can retrain your reactions and build strong, unshakable Inner Peace.[541]

Studies have shown that people who meditate on a regular basis, not only increase their own physical and psychological wellbeing, by achieving Inner Peace, they can also increase their compassion, as much as 50 percent within an eight week period of time.[542]

When you seek Peace, you will find it.[543]

"Peace is giving up the love of power for the power of Love.
With peacefulness, everyone wins." [544]

When we utilize Virtues, such as, Compassion, Forgiveness, Gratitude, Courage and Discernment, we can more easily find Inner Peace. This reminds me of the Teachings of Hermes from The *Corpus Hermeticum*. Hermes taught 'Be still and in solemn silence keep! Thus shall the mercy that flows on us from God not cease." [545] He is saying that when we go within and still our mind and actions, we open ourselves to receive God's continual Grace.

"... After saying all this, the Blessed One greeted them all saying,
"Peace be with you – may my peace arise and be fulfilled within you!
Be vigilant and allow no one to mislead you by saying
'Here it is' or there it is!' For it is within you the Son of Man dwells.
Go to Him, for those who seek him, find him.
Walk forth and announce the gospel of the Kingdom."
THE GOSPEL OF MARY MAGDALENE [546]

Here we are being asked to get still and breathe, when we are experiencing chaos, feeling rushed or feeling discomfort in our life. In the stillness, we can become aware of what is pulling us out of harmony. In the stillness, we can make a more appropriate decision on our response or action, rather than one from habit, fear or anger. It is in finding our Inner Peace that we can be fulfilled.

> *"I go now into Silence.*
> *Having said all this, Mary became silent,*
> *for it was in the silence that the Teacher spoke to her."* [547]

Sometimes, inner peace can come simply by stopping to take a slow, deep, spiraled breath the moment we recognize that chaos is happening. Taking a slow, deep breath allows us to step back and create a separation of the energies, therefore, giving us a moment to regroup. Stepping back gives an opportunity to evaluate a situation before taking action or reacting.

Finding peace within can come by forgiving ourselves or others. Inner Peace may be as simple as surrendering control of how something should look or how something should happen and we just let the circumstance unfold in Divine Accordance.

When you stop resisting change and stop getting in your own way, you can let go and let God unfold your blessings.

I am reminded of the Serenity Prayer:

God grant me the serenity to accept the things I cannot change,
courage to change the things I can and the wisdom to know the difference. [548]

When Inner Peace becomes our primary objective and we give time to the daily practice of it, the enormous 'heaviness' of the heart and soul can quickly shift into Virtues of Harmony, such as: Compassion, Discipline, Generosity, Gratitude, Honesty, Humbleness, Joy, Justice, the Love of Knowledge, Respect for Life, Self-Control, Truth, and Unconditional Love.

And yes, my favorite essential oil company, Young Living Essential Oils has a pure essential oil blend for each of the above aspects to help you add another energetic layer to your Inner Peace and Harmony.

These are the Virtues of Inner Peace and Harmony and the corresponding Pure Essential Oil blends that I utilize to enhance the Spiral Breath:

Virtue	Essential Oil Blends
Compassion	*Forgiveness™, Hope™*
Discipline	*Magnify Your Purpose™, Motivation™, Believe™*
Generosity	*Abundance™, The Gift™*
Gratitude	*Gratitude™*
Honesty	*Acceptance™, White Angelica™*
Humbleness	*Humility™, Grounding™, Egyptian Gold™*
Joy	*Joy™, Live With Passion™, Live Your Passion™*
Justice	*3 Wise Men™, Common Sense™, Valor™*
Love of Knowledge	*Brain Power™, Dream Catcher™, Awaken™*
Peace	*Peace & Calming™, Hope™, Inspiration™*
Respect for Life	*3 Wise Men™, Sacred Mountain™*
Self-Control	*Gathering™, Surrender™, Transformation™*
Truth	*Clarity™, Acceptance™, Awaken™, Envision™*
Unconditional Love	*Joy™, Harmony™, Fulfill Your Destiny™, Highest Potential™*

✡ ✡ ✡

BE VIGILANT

"No one can make you feel inferior without your consent."
ELEANOR ROOSEVELT

"Be vigilant and allow no one to mislead you."
GOSPEL OF MARY MAGDALENE

Walk forth in your Peace; allow no one or 'no' thing to shake you from your Inner Peace and your Truth.

There are times when someone's attitude, comments or actions can spin you out, especially, when you are caught 'off guard.' I have often found that the person's unpleasant actions rarely have anything to do with me. The individual may have circumstances going on in their lives that are affecting the way that they react. Sometimes you can diffuse a situation by recognizing that the person is having a bad day and simply grace them with kindness. At times, the situation does require you to make a decision or take an action.

This is where Discernment comes into play. Discernment is the ability to judge well; to contemplate when it is appropriate to simply know what you know and when to share what you know. It is also knowing when to act verses when to observe.

Using discernment, I ask myself, "Is it my place to engage or observe?" Is it best to stand my ground or step back knowing it's not my battle? Is it best to speak my truth or just let it roll off? I use Discernment to assist me in making a choice. Wisdom is used to know the difference.

Years ago, I worked at a restaurant, where a manager had a mission to make the female employees cry. Sadly, it empowered him. I recognized this quickly and committed to hold my inner peace, which empowered me. The lengths that he would go to in his efforts to make me cry became comical. The more unaffected I was, the more agitated he became with his lack of success and the more determined he became in his actions.

One day, he yelled, "What will it take to make you break?" I simply responded that he hadn't a clue what I've been through in my life. And that his antics were not worth the energy it would take to react. He stomped off in a rant, but he also set down his mission.

A couple of weeks later, I gave my two week notice, as I had graduated from Naturopathic school and was able to purchase the equipment that I required to start my practice. The manager said that he had never met anyone he could not break. I spoke sincerely and said that he had a beautiful opportunity to make a difference in people's lives by raising them up. How sad that he chose to use that opportunity to tear them down.

Keeping his eye contact, I added compassionately, "You must have had a terrible childhood. I hope, one day, you find the courage to heal." With that, I slid my last paycheck from his hand and walked out the door.

How did I keep my inner peace? I did not take his actions personally. It was not easy at first, but the more I refocused my inner peace, the easier it became. I knew that his actions and anger were not about me. I recognized that he was a wounded boy in an adult body trying to feel important and powerful.

I don't know what he went through in his life, but it was obvious that he either did not have the tools to heal his emotional wounds or he chose not to.

Did my words make a difference for him? Maybe – maybe not. The important lesson here is that I was vigilant with my own inner peace and was in the end, not shaken from it.

In the Gospel of Mary Magdalene (page 8), Mary Magdalene is not only asking us to seek Inner Peace, she is also asking us to be Vigilant. When we make a commitment to ourselves – *we must keep it!* When we step onto the path of Enlightenment – we must be vigilant about it! Not just vigilant on Sunday's, at church functions, spiritual gatherings, conferences or when we are with a certain friend or group. Be steadfast with your commitment to yourself in every moment.

When I channel Divine Mother and the Mary's, She (respectively) always asks that we "go with Love – Divine Unconditional Love and choose Grace and Ease in every moment, with every thought, every action, every step and with every breath."

Living in Unconditional Love with every moment does not mean that you become passive or a doormat. It is exercising Self-Love, Self-Worth and Self-Respect, as well as, love and respect for All that God has created.

You can have exponential growth within an instant on your path to enlightenment, when you choose to live every moment in Unconditional Love. When you mis-step, then re-step without judgment or guilt. Take note of your actions, make adjustments and re-step onto your path. Keep reinforcing your desired actions and outcome until it is second nature. Be Vigilant with your actions, thoughts and goals.

Utilizing the Spiral Breath, along with pure essential oils and re-enforcing the Virtues into your daily Inner Peace, will help you achieve your desires. It will be as difficult or as easy as you choose. So why not choose Grace and Ease.

The difference between I AM and 'I am not' is our own perception of ourselves and our own choice of action![549]

514 *The Gospel of Mary Magdalene* translated by Jean-Yves Leloup page 7
515 *Bruce Lipton: Biology of Belief Interview* by Evelyn Einhaeuser, Synergies In Healing Journal
http://www.synergies-journal.com/synergies/2015/3/30/bruce-lipton-the-biology-of-belief
516 *The Biology of Belief: Unleashing the Power of Consciousness, Matter & Miracles* by Bruce H. Lipton, Ph. D. pages 125-151
517 *The Biology of Belief: Unleashing the Power of Consciousness, Matter & Miracles* by Bruce H. Lipton, Ph. D. page 95
518 *Evolve your Brain: The Science of Changing Your Mind* written by Dr. Joe Dispenza pages 114-115, 329-330
519 *Evolve your Brain: The Science of Changing Your Mind* written by Dr. Joe Dispenza pages 114-115, 329-330
520 *The Biology of Belief: Unleashing the Power of Consciousness, Matter & Miracles* by Bruce H. Lipton, Ph. D. page 98
521 *Molecules of Emotion: The Science Behind Mind-Body Medicine* by Candace B. Pert, Ph. D. page 141
522 *The Biology of Belief: Unleashing the Power of Consciousness, Matter & Miracles* by Bruce H. Lipton, Ph. D. page 98
523 *The Biology of Belief: Unleashing the Power of Consciousness, Matter & Miracles* by Bruce H. Lipton, Ph. D. pages 98, 102
524 Pert, Candace B.. *Molecules of Emotion: The Science Behind Mind-Body Medicine* (pp. 143-144). Scribner. Kindle Edition.
525 *The Biology of Belief: Unleashing the Power of Consciousness, Matter & Miracles* by Bruce H. Lipton, Ph. D. page 98
526 Pert, Candace B.. *Molecules of Emotion: The Science Behind Mind-Body Medicine* (p. 146). Scribner. Kindle Edition.
527 *Breaking the Habit of Being Yourself: How to Lose Your Mind and Create a New One* by Dr. Joe Dispenza page 53
528 *Breaking the Habit of Being Yourself: How to Lose Your Mind and Create a New One* by Dr. Joe Dispenza pages 58-61
529 *Breaking the Habit of Being Yourself: How to Lose Your Mind and Create a New One* by Dr. Joe Dispenza pages 71-74
530 *Breaking the Habit of Being Yourself: How to Lose Your Mind and Create a New One* by Dr. Joe Dispenza page 70
531 *Breaking the Habit of Being Yourself: How to Lose Your Mind and Create a New One* by Dr. Joe Dispenza pages 70-75
532 *How Long Does It Actually Take To Form a New Habit? (Backed by Science)* by James Clear Behavioral Psychology, Habits https://jamesclear.com/new-habit
533 *The Gospel of Mary Magdalene* translated by Jean-Yves Leloup page 9
534 *The Gospel of Mary Magdalene* translated by Jean-Yves Leloup page 7
535 *Forgive As If You Have Forgotten* written by Gayle Mack www.keystoascension.com
536 Sansone, Randy A and Lori A Sansone. "*Gratitude and well being: the benefits of appreciation*" Psychiatry (Edgmont (Pa. : Township)) vol. 7,11 (2010): 18-22.
537 Wood, A. M., et al., *Gratitude and wellbeing: A review and theoretical integration*, Clinical Psychology Review (2010), doi:10.1016/j.cpr.2010.03.005 https://greatergood.berkeley.edu/pdfs/GratitudePDFs/2Wood-GratitudeWellbeingReview.pdf
538 *Become a Better You: 7 Keys to Improving Your Life Every Day* by Joel Osteen page 353
539 *Prayers Of The Cosmos: Meditations on the Aramaic Words of Jesus Translated and Commentary* by Neil Douglas-Klotz pages 86-87
540 https://en.wikipedia.org/wiki/Inner_peace
541 *10 Science-Backed Reasons To Make Inner Peace a Priority* by Gaia Staff - October 12, 2016 https://www.gaia.com/article/10-reasons-make-inner-peace-priority
542 *Can Meditation Make You a More Compassionate Person?* By COS Admin | April 1, 2013 https://cos.northeastern.edu/news/release-can-meditation-make-you-a-more-compassionate-person/
543 *The NAG HAMMADI Scriptures: The Revised and Updated Translation of Sacred Gnostic Texts* edited by Marvin Meyer page 742
544 *The Virtue of Peacefulness* https://www.ppseawa.org/peace-initiatives/virtue-peacefulness
545 Hermes. Corpus Hermeticum (Kindle Location 831). iap. Kindle Edition.
546 *The Gospel of Mary Magdalene* translated by Jean-Yves Leloup page 8
547 *The Gospel of Mary Magdalene* translated by Jean-Yves Leloup page 37
548 *The Serenity Prayer* by American Theologian Reinhold Niebuhr https://en.wikipedia.org/wiki/Serenity_Prayer

Chapter 8:
Chakras and Associated Energies

I have mentioned chakras several times in the chapters preceding this one. For those who are not familiar with chakras, I have designated this chapter for you.

Chakras tie into the body's energy, our emotional well being and personal enlightenment. Our chakras reflect the levels and clarity of our ever expanding consciousness.[550]

Chakra is a Sanskrit word which means "spinning wheel of energy." Each chakra is its own spinning toroidal vortex made of subtle electromagnetic energy.[551] Everything that is manifested and all that is unmanifested is energy. Energy is interconnected on one level or another and woven into the matrix and fabric of life.

The first chakra is the foundation for the other six main chakras. It reflects the foundation of our material world and relates to the solid matter of our bodies like our bones, flesh, large intestines (solid waste), etc. It represents the four elements of which we are made from (carbon, hydrogen, oxygen and nitrogen) and the four directions (north, east, south and west). Kundalini energy resides and rests here in the first chakra.[552]

As we increase the energy within our chakras and raise our consciousness, the vibration of our mass/matter begins to shift into Light.

In the research that I have gathered over the years, I have come to work with this combined knowledge on Chakras. There are seven major chakras on our body that run along the spine from the tailbone to the brain.

These spinning wheels of energy are subtly connected to our central nervous system (CNS), parasympathetic nervous system (PSN) and our sympathetic nervous system (SNS). When you include the two chakras below the base chakra called the Earth Gateway and the Earth Star and the four chakras above the seventh chakra or crown chakra, which are the Soul Star, the Stellar Gateway, the Universal Gateway and the Cosmic Gateway, there would be thirteen main chakras.[553]

Barbara Ann Brennan and Dr. David Tansley, (who wrote *Radionics and the Subtle Bodies of Man*), teach that there are 21 minor chakras on the body that interact with the seven major chakras. They are located at the following places: one just behind each eye, one in front of each ear, one where the clavicles meet, one near the thymus gland, one above each breast, one near the liver, one connected with the stomach, two are connected with the spleen, one near the solar plexus, one related to each gonad, one behind each knee, one in the palm of each hand and one on the sole of each foot.[554, 555] I access these points when I am balancing energy for myself and others.

Chakras are multidimensional toroidal fields of living energy. They are both antennas, which gather energy and transmitters, which disperse the energy outward throughout our body and energy field.[556]

Our chakras take in energy from the Universal Energy Field (UEF), from the collective consciousness and the environment around us. The energy is dispersed between the chakras and our personal energy field (aura).[557] Chakras receive and assimilate millions of bits of information from our surroundings and convert it into knowledge and experience.[558] In turn, this Universal Energy enhances our mental, physical, emotional and spiritual wellbeing.[559]

Each chakra has a certain pattern and a specific frequency at which it vibrates. Each chakra will allow only the frequencies that match its vibration to enter its field. The energy held within our chakras consist mostly of the energetic resonance of the repeated patterns of action and reaction, as well as, our habitual thoughts and the feelings that we accumulate throughout our daily life. The repeated patterns of energy and frequency create an energy field that can either enhance our chakras and wellbeing or impede them.[560]

If our patterns of action create disharmony, the flow of energy within our chakras can become weak. If the chakras are overwhelmed or over stimulated with external or internal stimulus, they will eventually shutdown and close altogether to protect the subtle body. This can result in a feeling of being "stuck."[561]

Chakras can be stuck open or closed. The flow of energy can indicate the degree of openness within an individual chakra. When a chakra is blocked, the energy intake and output is low. When a chakra is blown, the intake and output of energy is excessive.[562]

If there is a blockage of energy or an excess of energy within a chakra, the natural flow of electromagnetic energy is disrupted. This can affect us on a physical, mental, emotional and even a spiritual basis.[563]

If a chakra is stagnant, with a low energy flow, slow in its spin, or if it is overactive and excessive in spin, one might be experiencing physical disturbances in that area of the body or be stuck in unproductive emotional patterns associated with that particular chakra.

Overloaded chakras can be difficult to open. Grounding helps, as does addressing the issues that are associated with that specific chakra. Grounding is a way of defusing energy through breathing exercises like the Spiral Breath. The application of a pure essential oil, putting your bare feet on the Earth, walking, exercising, hugging a tree, a person or a pet and joyful laughter can also be beneficial.

Holding a harmonizing balance within each chakra is one of the keys to enlightenment on many levels. The more you can open your chakra and the more energy that can flow through it, the greater your peace, energy and wellbeing will be.[564]

We have been conditioned through our experiences to react from our emotional wounds, either without thinking or strategically without caring. For many, our self love, love for others and Divine Love have become 'out of balance' due to life experiences. Shifting stagnant energy within our chakras and addressing our emotional issues are essential keys for our transformation.

Each chakra differs in the size and rate of spin. The electromagnetic energy field that makes up a chakra vortex will vary in its rate of vibrational spin depending on its location on the body. This energy field is in essence - frequency and

Light. The colors that we see associated with the chakras and organs are actually frequencies of light that our eyes pick up as color.[565] The varying vibration of light cause the chakra to emanate a particular color according to the rate of its spin. This gives the chakras their associated color.[566]

The lower chakras tend to have a slower spin and are more dense in their color. The vibrational color begins with red at the base or root chakra, then moves to orange at the second chakra. These lower chakras relate to the fundamental survival and emotional issues on the physical realm.[567]

The middle chakras correlate with the emotional and mental realms and emanate yellow at the Solar Plexus (third chakra), green at the heart (fourth chakra) and blue at the throat (fifth chakra).[568]

The higher chakras address the spiritual realm. The sixth chakra (third eye) is indigo/violet, while the seventh crown chakra radiates violet to white when the pineal and Thousand Petal Lotus are activated.[569] The higher the chakras, the higher the increase of their vibrational rate. As you can see in the chart below, the chakra colors also follow the refraction of light through a prism and the colors of the rainbow.[570]

8.1 Chakras CGI by Pan Czakry.png

Chakras are circular in shape and create a sacred geometry 'Seed of Life' pattern called a tube torus, which is a toroidal field (see image below). This toroidal field is a vortex of moving energy that moves both clockwise and counterclockwise at the same time, while folding in upon itself around a central axis - top down to center and bottom up to center. This multidirectional, continuous moving pattern forms a shape like a two-ended trumpet.[571]

Each toroidal chakra structure creates a "white hole" that sends energy out the front of body, and at the same time, creates a "black hole" on the opposite side that brings energy into the back of the body. In her book, *Hands of Light A Guide to Healing Through the Human Energy Field*, Barbara Ann Brennan shares that the front of the chakras relate to one's feelings and the back of the chakras relate to their will.[572]

This sacred geometry formation creates its own individual electromagnetic field of energy. It is a microcosm within the macrocosm. The energy field of a chakra tube torus is a mirror of the energy fields found throughout the universe.

8.2 Tube Torus - Seed of Life By Daniel M. Short (Own work (Original text: Self-made))
[CC BY-SA 3.0 (http://creativecommons.org/licenses/by-sa/3.0)], via Wikimedia Commons

IDA, PINGALA, SUSHUMNA, PRANA TUBE AND KUNDALINI

There are four primary aspects or channels of highly charged Vital Life Force energy that are associated with fully engaged and harmonious chakras. In Swara Yoga, these are Ida nadi (the negative aspect) and Pingala nadi (positive aspect), Sushumna (neutral or androgynous aspect) and Kundalini Shakti (spiritual force).[573]

With any electrical circuit (which the human body is one), three specific wires or channels are required for conduction of energy. They are one negative, one positive and one neutral channel. Our human body does not have physical wires, but it does have an elaborate system of energy channels that brings the Vital Life Force into the body and transports the breath of Life throughout.[574]

Vital Life is called Prana in Sanskrit. The word Prana is derived from two roots: *Pra* is a prefix that indicates 'constance' and *na* which means movement or flow. Prana is a force in constant movement. In Swara Yoga, it is believed that the body is a storehouse of Vital Life Force energy and this energy is the link between the physical and psychic bodies. The ancient Vedas, as well as Albert Einstein, knew that pranic Life Force energy can be converted into matter and matter can be converted into Vital Life Force.[575] Once again, we find that Einstein's equation of $E=MC^2$, where E (energy) equals M (mass) times the speed of light squared (C^2) reflects this belief.[576]

Prana emanates from the original source that has always been. Breathing is the most significant way that we absorb the precious life sustaining prana that circulates through our body. Vital Life Force energy also comes up from the Earth into the soles of our feet and travels up our legs towards our root or first chakra. One aspect is the feminine/magnetic/negative current known as Ida nadi and the other is masculine/electric/positive current known as Pingala nadi.[577]

The negative current (Ida) brings consciousness into every part of the body and activates the *Parasympathetic Nervous System* (PNS). The parasympathetic nervous system's negative current stimulates the internal organs, such as, the heart, lungs, liver, kidneys, pancreas, intestines, etc. The negative energy current governs the left side of the spinal column, the entire left half of the body and the right hemisphere of the brain. The feminine/yin negative current is associated with the moon and has a cooling, relaxing, passive effect on the body.[578, 579]

The positive current (Pingala) is energizing and stimulates the physical body and external awareness. The positive current activates the *Sympathetic Nervous System* (SNS), which is responsible for preparing the body for external activities, releasing adrenaline to stimulate the superficial muscles and cope with stress. The positive energy current governs the right side of the spinal column, the entire right half of the body and the left hemisphere of the brain. The masculine/yang positive current is associated with the sun and is energizing, heating and has an aggressive effect on the body.[580, 581]

The negative energy current (Ida) flows into the left side of the first chakra, just below the base of the spine. Moving up the chakras and spine, it comes to rest at the root of the left nostril, where it merges with the sixth energy center/chakra. The positive current (Pingala) flows into the right side of the first chakra, just below the base of the spine. Moving upward, it comes to rest at the root of the right nostril. Here, the positive energy current merges with the negative current and the sixth energy center/chakra.[582]

At the base of the spine, these two energy channels come together, then separately continue moving up and around the chakra on opposite sides of the seemingly invisible vibrational field. The two energies cross each other at the top of the vibrational field, forming a vortex of energy called the first or root chakra.

The individual electric and magnetic energies continue to move up and around the opposite sides of each chakra and cross each other at the top of the chakra. Then they both change directions and move up the opposite side of the next chakra. The male and female energies are two facets of 'One' chakra. It's like a 9 volt battery. Each rectangular battery contains two currents (+ and -) that run up opposite sides and then meet at the top. One battery containing two synergistic energies. Within the chakra system, the male and female energies create a dance as they snake and spiral their way to the top of our bodies through the brain.[583]

The spiraling energies of the positive and negative currents switch back and forth and cross over the neutral Sushumna and Prana tube. Their energetic pattern replicates the double snake caduceus.[584] In observation, the spiraling energies create a Standing Columnar Wave, as do each individual chakra, the movement of tachyon particles and the refocus of light that emanates from pyramid energy.[585]

We have talked about the opposing energies of the feminine/magnetic/negative current verses the masculine/electric/positive current. What is not often talked about is the neutral or androgynous Sushumna energy. It is the third aspect of energy associated with the chakras and spinal column. Sushumna corresponds with the *Central or Cerebrospinal Nervous System* (CNS), which is one of the primary systems for our body.

The CNS and Sushumna run energy and signals from the base of the spine all the way up to the brain.[586] Sushumna's main purpose is to provide a channel or passage-way for the spiritual energy to freely move.[587] This channel is also known as the Prana Tube or Pranic Passage. It is not a physical part of our body, it is energetic. The Yogi's and ancient master healers have worked with this energetic channel for thousands of years.[588]

With a clear, activated Sushumna and Prana tube, one has the ability to transcend body, mind and the Space-Time continuum.[589]

Like the feminine/magnetic/negative current (Ida) and the masculine/electric/positive current (Pingala), Sushumna also emerges from the base of the spine. Instead of spiraling left or right, Sushumna moves straight through the center of the chakras and is the staff or sword that the negative and positive energies spiral around. As the Sushumna energy moves up the spinal column, it charges the nerve endings along the way, which ultimately affect the organs and body systems, as well as, our mental, emotional and spiritual bodies.[590]

When Sushumna is dormant, only one hemisphere of the brain is functioning at a time, either the right hemisphere governed by the negative (Ida) channel or the left hemisphere governed by the positive (Pingala) channel. When Sushumna flows freely, the brain, as a whole, is activated. Both hemispheres are active simultaneously for a 'full brain' experience and our spiritual power is greatly enhanced.

With the activated full brain Sushumna, the breath flows through both nostrils at the same time.[591]

To influence the *Parasympathetic Nervous System*, focus your breath in the left nostril to activate Ida. To influence the *Sympathetic Nervous System*, focus your breath in the right nostril to activate Pingala. To influence the Central or *Cerebrospinal Nervous System*, focus your breath through both nostrils at the same time.

Having a focused concentration on activating and strengthening Sushumna, while performing the Spiral Breath technique and specific yogic practices, can help you build up an energetic charge that will usher in a Kundalini awakening.

All three energies (Ida, Pingala and Sushumna) rise up from the base of the spine and then merge at the sixth chakra in the area of the medulla oblongata. When the feminine/magnetic/negative current (Ida) and the masculine/electric/positive current (Pingala) come together in harmony, they create the powerful spiritual energy known as Kundalini. Kundalini can rise freely only when the Sushumna passage is open and clear from mental, emotional and spiritual blocks. The Sushumna passage then becomes charged with Kundalini energy. When Kundalini energy rises, you can increase your Vital Life Force, as well as, bring extraordinary heightened states of awareness and a sense of mental, physical and emotional well being.[592]

Kundalini energy is described as a luminous light that lies dormant at the base of the spine until it is activated. The sleeping kundalini lies coiled up three and a half times in the root chakra like a serpent. Upon its awakening, the kundalini energy will uncoil and rise up along the spinal column, through the chakras and the Sushumna channel. When the kundalini lightning reaches the pineal gland within the limbic system, it triggers the release of the spiritual DMT elixir that unfolds the Thousand Petal Lotus and a glorious state of bliss and elevated consciousness.

Sometimes, kundalini energy can be activated spontaneously, when one has a high vibrational or spiritual experience. Most of the time, the awakening of your Kundalini energy must be cultivated through focused breath, intention and practice.[593]

When the Sushumna energy flows within the prana tube for a long period of time, the physical body can transfigure the body, mind and matter. Samadhi can also be accessed when Sushumna is flowing unencumbered.[594] Samadhi is the perfect union of one's individualized soul with Infinite Spirit. It is a concentrated state of awareness where you "hold inner vision." It is an experience of Divine Ecstasy with Superconscious Perception, where the Soul perceives the entire Universe. Samadhi is the state where human consciousness becomes One with Cosmic Consciousness. It has been referred to as the "Mystical Marriage" where the Soul merges into God's presence and becomes One with Him/Her.[595]

Samadhi is the state that I accessed at the Temple of Isis on Philae and while lying in the sarcophagus in the King's chamber of the Great Pyramid.

✡ ✡ ✡

THOUSAND PETAL LOTUS

The Thousand Petal Lotus can be found at the top of the head at the Crown chakra. It gets its name from the thousand nerve endings found within the folds of this extraordinary part of the brain that gently wraps the limbic system. The Thousand Petal Lotus lies dormant; waiting to be nourished with Vital Life Force energy and bloom. The Thousand Petal Lotus is the 'Seat of Consciousness.' It is Pure Consciousness that leads us into the infinite Gnosis of Divine Enlightenment.[596] Opening our Thousand Petal Lotus is our ULTIMATE goal for enlightenment!

I like the phrase that Anodea Judith said in her book Wheels of Life, that *"Our brains, as instruments of awareness, are virtually limitless."*[597] With proper focus and breath, like the Spiral Breath, we can access the Thousand Petal Lotus and turn our brain into an instrument that can enhance our wellbeing and awaken the latent powers of our transcendental and extra-sensory perception.

The lotus petal count for each chakra is related to specific groupings of vertebrae nerve pairs in the peripheral nervous system.[598, 599] The total number of chakra petals are related to the main nerve pairs, including the coccygeal nerve pair, add up to 50. There are 20 layers of 50 petals in the Thousand Petal Lotus. When the nerve pairs and the vertebrae groupings are placed as such, it works:

Throat chakra - 16 petals - 8 pairs - C1, C2, C3, C4, C5, C6, C7, T1

Heart chakra - 12 petals - 6 pairs - T2, T3, T4, T5, T6, T7

Solar Plexus - 10 petals - 5 pairs - T8, T9, T10, T11, T12

Sacral chakra- 6 petals - 3 pairs - L1, L2, L3

Root chakra - 4 petals - 2 pair - L4, L5

Coccyx Chakra - 2 petals - 1 pair - S5

When the twelve cranial nerve pairs are added in, the total count goes to one thousand twenty four (1024). It is interesting, that this number 1024, also shows up in the number sequence of cell division just after fertilization of the female ovum. The embryonic cells multiply in the sequence of 1, 2, 4, 8, 32, 64, 128, 256, 512, 1024, etc.[600]

As Vital Life Force energy is released and travels along the spinal column and prana tube to the brain, the energy activates the spinal nerves that exit between each vertebra. The stimulation of the spinal nerves activates the peripheral nerves, which sends energy to corresponding tissue and organs in the body.[601]

It is suggested that the cells of these main nerve endings contain the frequency and resonance of their original form and that they reset the nervous system when the Thousand Petal Lotus is activated. Thereupon resides the 'Glory' of the crown chakra.[602]

In a radio interview presented October 1, 1983 in Santa Cruz, CA, Shri Mataji Nirmala Devi discussed the significant importance of awakening the seventh chakra and the meaning of the Thousand Petal Lotus. As you recall, the areas of the sixth and seventh chakra contain the Limbic System. This is the place where you find true Freedom and can move beyond the third dimensional Absolute into the Absolute Realization of Heaven on Earth. This is also known as your Self-Realization.

Absolute Realization happens when you awaken your Limbic System and your frontal lobes. Shri Mataji states that *"There are a thousand nerves at the crown chakra and if you were to cut the transverse section of the brain, you can see that all these petal-like structures of the brain are forming a lotus of a thousand petals. The center of the thousand petals cover the limbic area of the brain before Realization, like the closed bud of a lotus."*

Shri Mataji goes on to say that, *"When the Kundalini reaches the Sahasrara (seventh chakra), the lotus petals open and enlightenment takes place. You may feel a pulsation in the crown of the head, followed by a melting sensation and a flow of cool vibrations from the fontanel areas. This is the baptism by which you know that you are truly born again.*

Vibratory awareness begins at this point. As the Kundalini unites our individual consciousness with the Universal Consciousness, we are suddenly tuned in to the Universal Wavelength of Vibrations."[603]

Awakening the Thousand Petal Lotus is our access to multidimensionality, our God-given gifts and cellular rejuvenation.[604]

When your Thousand Petal Lotus opens, it is an *extraordinary* feeling! I access this realm when I channel. In this space, you reach a level of being that makes anything less than this bliss just existing in life. You will definitely want to achieve this feeling on a regular basis!

THE TAILBONE, SACRUM AND CEREBROSPINAL FLUID

I can hear you saying, "What does the tailbone, sacrum and cerebrospinal fluid have to do with the brain and the Thousand Petal Lotus? Actually, a lot!

The coccyx (tailbone) is at the very end of the spine and is attached to the bottom of the sacrum. It is also the anchor for many of the muscles in the pelvic floor and the attachment for the muscles that connect the pubic rami to the sacrum. When the tailbone is injured and displaced, the angle of attachment shifts and can cause tightness, spasms, weakness and discomfort with sitting, lifting, bending or squatting. Displacement or injury can also decrease the tailbones mobility.[605]

The lack of mobility is important because the coccyx/tailbone is an energy pump that helps direct the flow of energy up the spinal column and Sushumna channel. If the spinal/Sushumna channel is blocked, vitality is blocked. The tailbone and sacrum are also pumps for the cerebrospinal fluid (CSF), which flows up to the brain. Cerebrospinal fluid acts as a cushion to protect the brain from bumps and injury. CSF also delivers protein and healthy salts to nourish the brain.

As we breathe, the tailbone and sacrum gently flex back and forth. On our inhalations, the tailbone will flex backwards and as we exhale, it moves forward. Simultaneously, as we inhale, the joints between the plates of our skull called sutures, open slightly. When we exhale, the sutures close.[606]

As you breathe, this coordinated movement between the sacrum and the sutures of the skull create a wave of energy that gently moves the cerebrospinal fluid up and down the spinal column and Sushumna channel to bathe the brain. Cerebrospinal fluid is also a conduit that amplifies the electrical charges in the nervous system. The amplified electrical charge can trigger a full brain experience, which activates the Thousand Petal Lotus. The charged spinal channel plays an important role in homeostasis of the central nervous system.[607]

The tailbone also stimulates your immune system by assisting the lymphatic system in the removal of the waste products from our nervous system and pumps blood flow to the trunk of your body.[608] Lymphatic fluid is pumped to the spleen in order to create lymphocytes and white blood cells that produce antibodies to combat infection. Dr. Andrew Taylor Still wrote, *"The lymphatics are closely and universally connected with the spinal cord and all other nerves, long or short, universal or separate and all drink from the waters of the brain (cerebral spinal fluid)."*[609]

Hanna Kroeger, Ms.D. was a huge advocate for setting the tailbone for optimal health. If the tailbone is displaced and the movement is decreased or blocked, then the pump for our immune system is blocked. Hanna Kroeger believed that everyone should have their tailbone checked and dedicated her life to share her technique.[610] Hanna's tailbone setting technique is simple and very effective.[611] Your chiropractor or a health practitioner schooled in Hanna's technique can help in setting your tailbone, if you feel like yours is off.

✡ ✡ ✡

ROOT LOCK AND THE THOUSAND PETAL LOTUS

There is an exercise in the yoga practice that helps one to increase the flow of cerebrospinal fluid and Vital Life Force energy along the spinal column to the brain, while strengthening your pelvic floor. It is called the 'root lock' or Moola (mula) Bandha. It involves contracting the muscles of your perineum and pelvic floor, including the urinary and anal sphincters, like you are stopping the flow of elimination.[612]

This technique gets its name from locking down on the root chakra (first chakra) at the base of the spinal column. Tighten the muscles at the root chakra as strong and as long as possible or tighten rhythmically with the inhalations and relax with the exhalations.

The root lock contractions in the perineal (pelvic) region, stimulate the parasympathetic nerve fibers that emerge from the spinal cord in the cervical (neck) and the sacral (pelvic) areas of the spinal cord. Contracting the abdomen at the second and third chakras stimulate the sympathetic nervous system and the nerve endings of the lumbar (lower back) and the thoracic (mid back) regions.[613] Contracting and locking down on these three chakras, redirects the Vital Life Force energy, lymphatic fluid and cerebrospinal fluid up the spinal canal; bathing the central nervous system, the brain and the limbic system.[614]

I was taught to contract the root chakra/anal sphincter, second chakra/lower abdomen and then the third chakra/upper abdomen in a squeeze, two, three movement in quick succession. We would squeeze, two, three at the beginning of our inhalations and visualize our breathe, cerebrospinal fluid and Divine Light moving up through our chakras to our Thousand Petal Lotus.

Dr. Joe Dispenza explains that as the protein and salts dissolve into our cerebrospinal fluid, it creates charged molecules, which when accelerated with the assistance of the root lock movement, generates an induction field of electromagnetic energy. The longer you continue the root lock process along with your breath, the greater the charge you create within the induction field. Eventually, the upward moving induction field will reverse its current and flow down the spinal canal simultaneously. This action generates an electromagnetic toroidal field of energy that is reflected throughout the universe and nature.[615]

The charged cerebrospinal fluid and the heightened energy field can trigger your pineal gland to release its sacred nectar. The pineal elixir is the essence that opens the Thousand Petal Lotus. When the Thousand Petal Lotus unfurls, it generates a rapid, full brain wave of energy known as the gamma brain wave.[616] This full brain wave experience is an initiation into the mystical realm of superconsciousness.[617]

The exalted effects of utilizing the root lock, in conjunction with the Spiral Breath, can bring our physical, mental, emotional and spiritual wellbeing into life-sustaining harmony. Mastery of this technique can result in a kundalini awakening and the fullest realization of our highest divine potential.[618] This is our ultimate goal on the quest for enlightenment and harmony.

From experience, I will share this tidbit of wisdom. Before attempting to raise your Kundalini energy, take the time to clear and tune the chakras to allow the powerful Kundalini to rise without causing discomfort.[619] When you concentrate on a chakra and add 'Breath', you stimulate it and increase it's Vital Life Force.

Of course… my favorite way to clear and balance a chakra is to do the Spiral Breath as you place your focus and energy on them. The Spiral Breath unites the heart and the mind as you breathe, which enables you to clear with greater ease.

The step by step Spiral Breath technique has its own chapter. I will address a couple of modalities that compliment the Spiral Breath technique in the upcoming chapters, including incorporating the use of pure essential oils. Each subject and modality presented works in concert with each other to bring about a state of Grace and Inner Peace. You can use them individually or layer them together to meet your individual requirements.

Acquainting yourself with the particular aspects and attributes of each chakra will assist you to achieve greater accuracy and expedite the healing process. Incorporating pure essential oils creates more Grace and Ease when moving emotional, mental and spiritual blocks from your chakras.

I have created a list of aspects and attributes in the section below for your convenience.

✡ ✡ ✡

THE CHAKRAS - ATTRIBUTES AND HARMONIZERS

I have put together a basic compilation of properties associated with the seven major chakras on the body. You can build on this list to make it more comprehensive. The basics will help you to see where you may require some attention on your journey to finding harmony within. I also included the chakra names from Swara Yoga, as the translation gives great insight.

Root Chakra *(also called First Chakra, Kundalini or Base Chakra)* [620]

- *Swara Yoga: Mooladhara: Mool* means Root, *adhara* means Place
- *Four Petalled Red Lotus:* where human evolution begins, foundation
- *Color:* red, brown and black
- *Location:* base of the spine, in the coccygeal region
- *Corresponding Gland:* adrenal
- *Sense:* smell
- *Connected to:* nasal cavity, sense of smell, can be stimulated from tip of nose
  Associated Emotions: survival issues, being a victim, financial issues, greed, selfishness, dependence, primal force, fear
- *Positive Attributes:* security, abundance, good physical health, grounded
- *Corresponding Verbiage:* I have
- *Musical Note:* C
- *Sound:* Lam
- *Element:* Earth
- *Operating Force:* Gravity
- *Gemstones:* Agate, bloodstone, garnet, ruby, red jasper, obsidian, smoky quartz or any red stone that you resonate with
- *Harmonizing Essential Oils:* Abundance™, Acceptance™, Aroma Life™, Northern Lights Black Spruce™, Common Sense™, Gathering™, Grounding™, Light the Fire™, Live with Passion™, Motivation™, Release™, Sacred Mountain™, SARA™, Surrender™, Ylang Ylang, Valor™, Valor II™, White Angelica™

NOTE: The essential oil blends are Young Living Essential Oils (YLO). I have found these to be the purest oils and of the highest quality and integrity.

Sacral Chakra *(also called Second Chakra)* [621]

- *Swara Yoga:* Swadhisthana: Swa means Self, sthana means Place
- *Six Petalled Vermillion Lotus:* represents the Subconscious Mind
- *Color:* orange
- *Location:* lower abdomen approximately 2 inches below the navel
- *Corresponding Gland:* reproductive
- *Sense:* taste, which is dependent on smell
- *Associated Emotions:* abandonment, mother/father issues, sexual, jealousy, blame, guilt
- *Positive Attributes:* creativity, healthy relationships, prosperity
- *Corresponding Verbiage:* I feel
- *Musical Note:* D
- *Sound:* Vam
- *Element:* Water
- *Operating Force:* attraction to opposites
- *Gemstones:* amber, gold topaz, tiger eye, any orange stone
- *Harmonizing Essential Oils:* Abundance™, Northern Lights Black Spruce™, Christmas Spirit™, Dream Catcher™, Forgiveness™, Gentle Baby™, Harmony™, Inner Child™, Light the Fire™, Motivation™, Peace & Calming™, Release™, SARA™, Sensation™, The Gift™, Trauma Life™, White Angelica™

Solar Plexus *(also called Third Chakra)* [622]

- *Swara Yoga:* Manipura: Mani means Jewel, Puri means City - City of Jewels
- *Ten Petalled Yellow Lotus:* concentrate on Inner Fire
- Center where Prana (Vital Life Force) is stored
- *Color:* yellow
- *Location:* upper abdomen, stomach area, under diaphragm
- *Corresponding Gland:* pancreas
- *Associated Emotions:* personal power, self-confidence, self-worth, self-esteem, self-control, anger, ego, shame
- *Positive Attributes:* personal power, worthiness, stability, effectiveness
- *Corresponding Verbiage:* I can, I do
- *Sense:* Sight
- *Musical Note:* E
- *Sound:* Ram
- *Element:* Fire
- *Operating Force:* combustion
- *Gemstones:* citrine, yellow jasper, yellow apatite, amblygonite, Libyan gold tektite
- *Harmonizing Essential Oils:* Awaken™, Northern Lights Black Spruce™, Lemon, Believe™, Highest Potential™, Hope™, Humility™, Inner Child™, Live with Passion™, Motivation™, Present Time™, Release™, Sacred Mountain™, SARA™, Surrender™, Transformation™

Heart Chakra *(also called Fourth Chakra, Heart Center)* [623]

- *Swara Yoga:* Anahata: Ana means No, ahata means Stuck - Unstuck vibration
- *Twelve Petalled Pale Blue Lotus:* realize Pranic potential and activate it
- *Color:* green
- *Location:* chest, heart
- *Corresponding Gland:* thymus, lungs
- *Associated Emotions:* unworthy, sorrow, forgiveness, inability to express emotion
- *Positive Attributes:* compassion, gratitude, love, joy, inner peace, hope, faith, Unconditional Love
- *Corresponding Verbiage:* I love
- *Musical Note:* F
- *Sound:* Yam
- *Element:* Air
- *Sense:* Touch
- *Operating Force:* equilibrium
- *Gemstones:* emerald, jade, malachite, aventurine, rose quartz, peridot, tourmaline
- *Harmonizing Essential Oils:* Abundance™, Acceptance™, Aroma Life™, Australian Blue™, Awaken™, Believe™, Northern Lights Black Spruce™, Build Your Dream™, Christmas Spirit™, Frankincense, Rose, Geranium, Forgiveness™, Gratitude™, Harmony™, Highest Potential™, Hope™, Humility™, Inner Child™, Joy™, Magnify Your Purpose™, Sandalwood, SARA™, Sensation™, Surrender™, Transformation™, Trauma Life™

Throat Chakra *(also called Fifth Chakra)* [624]

- *Swara Yoga: Vishuddhi:* Vi signifies something Great and Beyond Comparison, shuddhi means Purifier
- *Sixteen Petalled Smoky Violet Lotus:* the 'Great Gate of Liberation'
- *Color:* blue
- *Location:* throat
- *Corresponding Gland:* thyroid, parathyroid
- *Associated Emotions:* communication, lies, judgmental, voice-singing, speaking
- *Positive Attributes:* truth, self-expressive
- *Corresponding Verbiage:* I speak
- *Musical Note:* G
- *Sound:* Ham
- *Element:* Ether
- *Sense:* hearing
- *Operating Force:* resonance
- *Gemstones:* sapphire, turquoise, lapis lazuli, aquamarine
- *Harmonizing Essential Oils:* Angelica, Northern Lights Black Spruce™, Clarity™, Gathering™, Gratitude™, Humility™, Inspiration™, Release™, Rosewood, Thyme, Transformation™, SARA™, White Angelica™, 3 Wise Men™

Third Eye Chakra *(also called Sixth Chakra, Brow Chakra)* [625, 626]

- *Swara Yoga:* Ajna: Ajna means Third Eye, Guru
- *Transparent Lotus with Two White Petals or Ninety-six:* where the three rivers meet - Ida, Pingala and Sushamna
- *Color:* indigo
- *Location:* center of forehead in line with the nose
- *Corresponding Gland:* pituitary, hypothalamus
- *Associated Emotions:* intuition, psychic ability, imagination, decision making
- *Positive Attributes:* clarity, spiritual awakening, self-mastery, perception
- *Musical Note:* A
- *Sound:* OM
- *Element:* Time
- *Corresponding Verbiage:* I see
- *Operating Force:* Light
- *Gemstones:* sugalite, purple fluorite, lapis lazuli
- *Harmonizing Essential Oils:* Abundance™, Acceptance™, Awaken™, Basil, Northern Lights Black Spruce™, Brain Power™, Build Your Dream™, Clarity™, Clary Sage, Dream Catcher™, Egyptian Gold™, Envision™, Exodus™, Frankincense, Gathering™, Helichrysum, Highest Potential™, Holy Basil, Humility™, Inspiration™, Into the Future™, Joy™, Live With Passion™, Magnify Your Purpose™, Myrrh, Patchouli, Present Time™, Sacred Mountain™, Sandalwood, The Gift™, Transformation™, White Angelica™

Crown Chakra *(also called Seventh Chakra and Thousand Petal Lotus)* [627, 628]

- *Swara Yoga:* Sahasrara: means Thousand Petal Lotus
- *Thousand Petalled Lotus* or One Thousand Twenty Four
- *Color:* violet
- *Location:* top of the head
- *Corresponding Gland:* pineal
- *Associated Emotions:* peace, faith, inspiration, devotion
- *Positive Attributes:* bliss, enlightenment, spiritual awareness, divine wisdom
- *Corresponding Verbiage:* I Know, Gnosis
- *Musical Note:* B
- *Sound:* Breath
- *Element:* Space
- *Operating Force:* Silence
- *Gemstones:* amethyst, alexandrite, diamond, quartz
- *Harmonizing Essential Oils:* Acceptance™, Australian Blue™, Awaken™, Believe™, Northern Lights Black Spruce™, Cypress, Dream Catcher™, Egyptian Gold™, Envision™, Frankincense, Gratitude™, Harmony™, Highest Potential™, Lavender, Joy™, Neroli, Magnify Your Purpose™, Myrrh, Present Time™, Sacred Frankincense, Spikenard, The Gift™, White Angelica™, 3 Wise Men™

I was asked to include a section on dowsing and the chakras. I often incorporate the use of a pendulum or muscle test to quickly assess the status of a chakra. Muscle testing is a form of dowsing. I then use the Spiral Breath and an appropriate pure essential oil blend to bring about balance.

DOWSING AND CHAKRAS

Dowsing with a pendulum is an easy and beneficial way to determine if a chakra is out of balance.

Knowing which way to spin the directional energy can help facilitate the healing process and encourage harmony. Directional spin can be determined by the sensitivity in your hands (palm chakras), dowsing with a pendulum, muscle testing or sensing. Dowsing with a pendulum will allow you to see the direction of spin, as well as, the intensity of the spin.

I was taught that a clockwise spin reflects an open chakra. A counterclockwise spin suggests the chakra is blocked with energetic emotional debris or it is spinning backwards. The rate of the spin reflects the degree of openness or closure.[629]

To Start, I will cover some basic Dowsing practices:

Hold your pendulum between your palms in order to warm it up and tune it to your personal vibration.

Hold the chain or string of your pendulum approximately 2 to 3 inches above the stone or dangling object that you are using as your pendulum. A hanging pendulum can be an object made of wood, metal, stone, a crystal or any object that is suspended from a string or chain.

Hold the chain or string in your right hand between your thumb, forefinger and middle finger. This forms a Trinity. The middle finger has a positive charge, the forefinger has a negative charge and the thumb is neutral.[630]

There are many different ways to dowse. It depends on your dowsing tool and who taught you. I share how I was taught and what works for me. Hold your pendulum over a neutral area (to the side of the body) and ask for a 'yes' answer to get started. You can have an up and down movement for your 'yes' or it could rotate in a circular clockwise motion. This is why you ask for a 'yes' response, so your pendulum shows you how it is answering. A 'no' answer could be a left to right swing, a counterclock-wise spin or it may just be still.

If you are having trouble with getting movement, try Hanna Kroeger's technique. While holding the pendulum in your right hand, bring the pendulum over the middle finger of your left hand and ask the pendulum to show you a positive 'yes' answer. Be patient and wait for your answer. Then move the pendulum over the forefinger of your left hand and ask the pendulum to show you a negative 'no' response. Now, bring the pendulum over the thumb of your left hand and ask the pendulum to show you a neutral response.

If your pendulum remains still, set your pendulum to the side and stand with your feet shoulder width apart. Raise your left arm straight up pointing to the north and stretch your right arm down pointing to the south. Stand in this position for a couple of minutes to increase the magnetic forces flowing through you from the earth's poles and the ionosphere.[631]

Blocked or suppressed emotions can interfere with the natural energy flow of your chakras. If left unaddressed, the imbalance of energy can create a disturbance and manifest in a physical, emotional, mental or spiritual way.[632]

If the chakra is weak, the pendulum will spin in small, slow circles. A fully closed chakra will have a counterclockwise spin about 6 inches in diameter. A fully open chakra will have a clockwise spin diameter of 6 inches. A clockwise spin draws the Universal Energy Field into the chakra. As the chakra begins to open, the pendulum will swing strong, with even rotations.[633]

A still pendulum with no movement could mean that the chakra is so overused or blocked that it is no longer able to metabolize any energy from the Universal Energy Field.[634]

In her book, *Hands of Light: A Guide to Healing Through the Human Energy Field*, Barbara Ann Brennan shows you what to do and what it means if your pendulum reflects a 'caddywhompus' or elliptical spin.[635]

To assess a chakra, hold a pendulum as previously stated, just above the body without touching it. This allows the pendulum to interact with the persons aura and energy field. Hold the pendulum as still as you can above the chosen chakra. Hold your thoughts as clear and unbiased as possible and let the pendulum move on its own. Do not help it along.[636]

If you are checking the chakras on the front of the body, have your client lie on their back - face up. If you are checking the chakras in the back, have your client lie face down on their stomach.[637] If they are standing, you can also point to the particular chakra, front and back, that is being assessed and watch your pendulum.

When working on yourself, place the hand that is not holding the pendulum over the chakra about an inch above the body or point to the chakra. It is not necessary to touch the body to get an answer.

Within the chakra system, energy flows between the chakras vertically and horizontally. Vertically allows you to check if the flow of energy is open between the connecting chakras that are above and below it. Horizontal flow allows you to see if the energy is flowing into the front chakra from the surrounding environment and out of the back chakras. The flow or lack of it, can help you determine if there are any impediments.[638]

Once you determine the status of the chakra, use the pendulum to dowse for the cause. When dowsing, you would want to ask questions and make statements that require a yes or no answer. Such as, "The imbalance is physical," then pause for an answer. If no movement state, "The imbalance or core issue is emotional," "The imbalance is mental," "The imbalance is spiritual."

The answer would prompt more statements. The answers that you receive become a 'directional map' giving you insight to the possible root of the imbalance of energy.

Allow time after your statement for the pendulum to move in a response. If the imbalance shows to be emotional, then run through a list of emotions related to that chakra to find the one with greatest swing. To make it more efficient, you can use the list that accompanies the individual chakras in the above section.

If you have a list of emotions on a page, group them into columns. Then you can ask, "The emotion is on this page." If yes, pinpoint it. "The emotion is in this column. Point to the designated column. Move to each column until you receive your answer. Once you find the column, split the column in half, "The emotion is in the top half (or bottom half)." Whichever half shows positive, then read the individual emotions until you find your answer.

You might take it farther and ask individually, "The imbalance is inherited; acquired in this lifetime or from a past life." If yes to inherited, dowse which side of the family, as in Mother, Father, Maternal Grandmother/father or Paternal Grandmother/father. Once you find the imbalance and the familial thread, use the Spiral Breath with a complimentary pure essential oil blend to clear the issue forward to the present time and beyond.

Clearing issues through the generations can have a profound effect on all family members. When I have a major emotional or mental clearing, my mother has an epiphany, either in her dreams, a 'drop in' thought or a realization. When my mother has a major clearing, my sister, brother and I have epiphanies.

If an issue is acquired during this lifetime and you (or your client) are not sure where that particular emotion came from, you can go deeper and pinpoint a time frame. State: This emotion/experience/event took place between birth to age five, age five to ten, etc. Say for example, 'age 5 to 10' made the pendulum respond. Go deeper by asking, "age 5" "age 6" "age 7," etc. What ever age is revealed, ask your client (or yourself if working on yourself), "Did anything significant happen to you at age ___?" Usually something pops into their/your mind. If not, ask to clear the block (whatever it is) with Grace and Ease from the moment of experience, on up into the present and into the future. This way, they/you won't walk into it later on.

Spin your pendulum clockwise to bring in the Universal Energy Field/Divine Love to assist you. As you spin the pendulum to generate increased energy, have your client use the Spiral Breath. Hold a positive intention as you/they breathe to clear the energetic threads from the past, specifically from the very first time you/they experienced that thought, feeling or emotion. Once you get a strong clear spin, bring that balanced energy forward into the present time and into the future.

Remember, each chakra is connected to specific attributes, emotions, parts of the body, sound, color, elements, gemstone and essential oils. Keeping it simple, you can choose an appropriate pure essential oil (single oil or blend), crystal or positive affirmation that brings the chakra into balance as you breathe.

If using a pure essential oil, place the essential oil bottle in the person's left hand. Ask if this oil is beneficial. Let your pendulum give you an answer. If Yes, apply a couple drops in the palm of their left hand. Have them swirl the oil in three clockwise rotations with two fingers of the right hand to tune the oil to their DNA and personal frequency. Have them rub their palms together, inhale the scent; then apply the essential oil to the chakra area, wrists or heart.

If working with crystals to help move energy, place the crystal(s) on the body in the area of the chakra being measured to incorporate the frequency of the chosen crystal(s) into their aura field and direct energy from one chakra to another. Get creative by using crystal layout patterns around you and your client. You can find more suggestions for layouts in most books and videos on crystals, chakras and energy healing.

If you are working with an affirmation, have the person repeat the affirmation out load, then silently repeat the affirmation while doing the Spiral Breath to help shift the energy. I have found that speaking out loud addresses the conscious mind and speaking inwardly to yourself addresses your subconscious mind. Speaking both out loud and inwardly addresses both your subconscious and conscious minds and can be more beneficial. Holding the pendulum over the chakra, you can watch the spin increase, which reflects an increase of the energy within the chakra.

Working with chakras and dowsing can be a simple process or extremely intricate. It depends on your preference, as to how intricate you wish to work. Fortunately, there are a multitude of books, classes and techniques available, should you decide to expand your knowledge and energy healing skills in this discipline.

✡ ✡ ✡

CREATING SACRED SPACE

There is one other suggestion that I would like to share before we move out of this chapter on Chakras. I always create Sacred Space in the area around myself and the person(s) or place(s) that I am working on before I start. It is as simple as saying, "I create Sacred Space at this time." Visualize a circle of Divine Light encompassing the area, including you and the person that you are working with.

If you choose, you can also use 'Smudge.' It is used by the Native American and Indigenous cultures. Smudging is a purification technique that has been used since ancient times to cleanse and protect a space, your body, mind and spirit of negativity. It is like washing the negativity out of the air and blesses the space.

A dry Smudge would be placing dried herbs in an Abalone shell or a heat resistant bowl. Cedar, Sage and Lavender or Cedar, Sage, Tobacco and Sweetgrass are what the Elders taught me to use, though the organic herbs will vary upon the culture, intention of ceremony and the herbs available in your region. Pre-made smudge sticks are also available for convenience.

Light the mixture of your chosen herbs on fire, then blow out the flames to create a smoldering smoke. Wave the smoke over you front to back and head to toe. Walk the perimeter of the room in a clockwise direction, while fanning the smoke with your hand or feather. Stop to acknowledge the four main directions, as in, North, East, South and West. Once the perimeter is smudged, wave the smoke over your work area, your tools, crystals, etc., and anyone participating in the Sacred Space.

When you Smudge, you are acknowledging the four elements. The herbs represent the Earth, the Abalone shell represents Water, the flame and smoke represent Fire, the feather represents Air.[639]

Each herb has a special meaning, such as: [640, 641, 642]

Sage: clears negative energy

Cedar: takes your prayers to heaven

Lavender/Sweetgrass/Tobacco: is the sweet gift of Gratitude to Great Spirit

Palo Santo: Inspires creativity, deeper connections to Divine Source

*Copal/Frankincense/Myrrh resin: used to purify and sanctify, pleasing to Spirit

Copal, Frankincense and Myrrh are resins and would be placed in a resin burner or on a charcoal briquette specifically designed for burning incense. Take care to use heat resistant bowls, silicone pads or stones when using charcoal briquettes and smudge.

I use **Smokeless Smudge** in my office. I use a couple of blends and have them made up in spray bottles. In an empty spray bottle add one part vodka and 2 parts water. The vodka helps to evaporate the water. Leave room in the bottle to add your chosen pure essential oils. Place the spray top on the bottle and gently roll the bottle between your palms to blend. This also tunes the liquid smudge to your energy.

Mist yourself, the perimeter of your room and your work area before starting your day. I also refresh the area between clients, as an added layer of purification. This way, all my clients walk into Sacred Space.

Here are some of my favorite combinations. Use as many drops of each as you prefer. You can also use your intuition and preference to make your own custom liquid smudge.

Cedarwood™, Sage and *Lavender*

Frankincense, Cobaiba (Copal) and *Myrrh*

Palo Santo and *Transformation™*

Abundance™, Joy™ and *Gratitude™*

Highest Potential™, Believe and *Present Time™*

I like to fill myself up with the Universal Divine Light before I begin. Energetic currents flow from the highest one to the lowest. If you are in a lower vibrational frequency than your client, you may take on some of their 'stuff'. When you fill yourself up and raise your frequency with Light and Love before you begin, you will deflect the unwanted 'stuff' from sticking to you. You may even receive a healing at the same time as your client, if you have the same energetic threads within your energy field and cells. Raising your own energy first is also being responsible for your own energy and being respectful.

When necessary, I create a specific, designated vortex of energy to the side of me that will quickly and Gracefully transmute any funk that I may pull off of the clients' energy field and place in it. It is a responsible technique that I use to ensure that my client, myself or anyone else does not walk through the 'funk' and pick it up in their energy field.

I simply draw a circle with my hand and visualize it spinning in a toroidal vortex; pulsing with Divine Light to quickly transmute whatever is placed there. Remember, thoughts and words are energy and energy is matter. When I am finished with the vortex, I send it up to the Higher Realms and ask God to take care of it for the Greatest and Highest Good.

When you are finished with your session give Thanks for the healing, the Wisdom, and the energy, etc. Release the Sacred Space that you had created by simply stating it is released.

There is a nice smudging blessing and a formal process that is used when smudging a person before entering Sacred Space. This process would be used after a space has been consecrated and purified with smudge. Each person entering the Sacred Space would be cleansed before entering. Some speak the blessing, others just smudge. It is your choice how you wish to proceed. When appropriate, you can use a drum to represent the heartbeat of Divine Spirit (optional).

The blessing and process is as follows:

First, greet the person being smudged by looking sincerely and reverently into their eyes. Fan the smudge smoke at the heart and tap the heart lightly with the feather:

May your heart be cleansed, that you might hear its messages clearly.

Then fan the smoke upward to the Right side of the person's head, moving clockwise (sun-wise) over to the Left side of their head:

May your thoughts be cleansed, that they manifest beautiful things.

May your you eyes be cleansed, that you might see the signs and wonders of the world clearly.

May your throat be cleansed, that you might speak rightly when words are needed.

Fan the smoke across their Left shoulder; continuing to wash the smoke across the top of their outstretched arm to the fingertips then along the underside of the arm to the armpit:

May your hands be cleansed, that they create beautiful things.

Fan the smoke down the Left side of their torso; down their Left leg and foot. Some like to raise their foot to purify their soles. Say:

May your feet be cleansed, that they might take you where you most need to be.

Fan the smoke to the Right foot and sole; move up the Right leg; brushing the smoke up the Right side of the torso; along the underside of the Right arm to the fingertips, continue fanning the smoke across the top of the arm to their Right shoulder.

I was taught to drift the feather from the top of the head gently down the front center line of the person's body down to their feet. If the feather faltered, then extra clearing was given in that area before smudging the back of their body.

Turn the person to THEIR Right and repeat the process along the back of the body from head to feet and back up to their head. Always moving clockwise with the direction of the sun. Drift the feather to check for residue. Then tap the person on the back with the feather at their heart area.

May this sacred smoke carry your prayers to Heaven.[643, 644]

You can adapt the above blessing when clearing your office before the start of your day.

549 *The Gospel of Mary Magdalene* translated by Jean-Yves Leloup page 75
550 *Swara Yoga: The Tantric Science of Brain Breathing* by Swami Muktibodhananda Saraswati page 83
551 *Swara Yoga: The Tantric Science of Brain Breathing* by Swami Muktibodhananda Saraswati page 60
552 *Wheels of Life* by Anodea Judith page 110
553 *Article 3: Metatrons Cube & the Number 13* by Simone Matthews
   http://www.universallifetools.com/2013/05/metatrons-cube-number-13/
554 *Hands of Light: A Guide to Healing Through the Human Energy Field* by Barbara Ann Brennan page 44
555 *Radionics and the Subtle Bodies of Man* by Dr. David Tansley, D.C. page 31
556 *Swara Yoga: The Tantric Science of Brain Breathing* by Swami Muktibodhananda Saraswati page 60
557 *Radionics and the Subtle Bodies of Man* by Dr. David Tansley, D.C. page 23
558 *Wheels of Life: The Classic Guide to the Chakra System* by Anodea Judith, Ph. D. page 321
559 *Hands of Light: A Guide to Healing Through the Human Energy Field* by Barbara Ann Brennan page 45
560 *Wheels of Life: The Classic Guide to the Chakra System* by Anodea Judith, Ph. D. page 70-71
561 *Wheels of Life: The Classic Guide to the Chakra System* by Anodea Judith, Ph. D. page 24, 70-71
562 *Wheels of Life: The Classic Guide to the Chakra System* by Anodea Judith, Ph. D. page 25-26
563 *Hands of Light: A Guide to Healing Through the Human Energy Field* by Barbara Ann Brennan page 45, 133-145
564 *Wheels of Life: The Classic Guide to the Chakra System* by Anodea Judith, Ph. D. page 66-73, 94-98, 182
565 *Hands of Light: A Guide to Healing Through the Human Energy Field* by Barbara Ann Brennan page 34
566 *Swara Yoga: The Tantric Science of Brain Breathing* by Swami Muktibodhananda Saraswati page 60-63
567 *Swara Yoga: The Tantric Science of Brain Breathing* by Swami Muktibodhananda Saraswati page 60-64
568 *Swara Yoga: The Tantric Science of Brain Breathing* by Swami Muktibodhananda Saraswati page 64-65
569 *Hands of Light: A Guide to Healing Through the Human Energy Field* by Barbara Ann Brennan page 34
570 *Swara Yoga: The Tantric Science of Brain Breathing* by Swami Muktibodhananda Saraswati page 65-67
571 *Hands of Light: A Guide to Healing Through the Human Energy Field* by Barbara Ann Brennan page 46-49
572 *Hands of Light: A Guide to Healing Through the Human Energy Field* by Barbara Ann Brennan page 45
573 *Swara Yoga: The Tantric Science of Brain Breathing* by Swami Muktibodhananda Saraswati page 48-59
574 *Swara Yoga: The Tantric Science of Brain Breathing* by Swami Muktibodhananda Saraswati page 49
575 *Swara Yoga: The Tantric Science of Brain Breathing* by Swami Muktibodhananda Saraswati pages 12-14
576 https://www.britannica.com/science/E-mc2-equation
577 *Swara Yoga: The Tantric Science of Brain Breathing* by Swami Muktibodhananda Saraswati pages 12-15, 49-52
578 *Swara Yoga: The Tantric Science of Brain Breathing* by Swami Muktibodhananda Saraswati page 51-54
579 *Hands of Light: A Guide to Healing Through the Human Energy Field* by Barbara Ann Brennan page 31
580 *Swara Yoga: The Tantric Science of Brain Breathing* by Swami Muktibodhananda Saraswati page 51-54
581 *Hands of Light: A Guide to Healing Through the Human Energy Field* by Barbara Ann Brennan page 31
549 *The Gospel of Mary Magdalene* translated by Jean-Yves Leloup page 75
550 *Swara Yoga: The Tantric Science of Brain Breathing* by Swami Muktibodhananda Saraswati page 83
551 *Swara Yoga: The Tantric Science of Brain Breathing* by Swami Muktibodhananda Saraswati page 60
552 *Wheels of Life* by Anodea Judith page 110
553 *Article 3: Metatrons Cube & the Number 13* by Simone Matthews
   http://www.universallifetools.com/2013/05/metatrons-cube-number-13/
554 *Hands of Light: A Guide to Healing Through the Human Energy Field* by Barbara Ann Brennan page 44
555 *Radionics and the Subtle Bodies of Man* by Dr. David Tansley, D.C. page 31
556 *Swara Yoga: The Tantric Science of Brain Breathing* by Swami Muktibodhananda Saraswati page 60
557 *Radionics and the Subtle Bodies of Man* by Dr. David Tansley, D.C. page 23
558 *Wheels of Life: The Classic Guide to the Chakra System* by Anodea Judith, Ph. D. page 321
559 *Hands of Light: A Guide to Healing Through the Human Energy Field* by Barbara Ann Brennan page 45
560 *Wheels of Life: The Classic Guide to the Chakra System* by Anodea Judith, Ph. D. page 70-71
561 *Wheels of Life: The Classic Guide to the Chakra System* by Anodea Judith, Ph. D. page 24, 70-71
562 *Wheels of Life: The Classic Guide to the Chakra System* by Anodea Judith, Ph. D. page 25-26
563 *Hands of Light: A Guide to Healing Through the Human Energy Field* by Barbara Ann Brennan page 45, 133-145
564 *Wheels of Life: The Classic Guide to the Chakra System* by Anodea Judith, Ph. D. page 66-73, 94-98, 182
565 *Hands of Light: A Guide to Healing Through the Human Energy Field* by Barbara Ann Brennan page 34
566 *Swara Yoga: The Tantric Science of Brain Breathing* by Swami Muktibodhananda Saraswati page 60-63
567 *Swara Yoga: The Tantric Science of Brain Breathing* by Swami Muktibodhananda Saraswati page 60-64
568 *Swara Yoga: The Tantric Science of Brain Breathing* by Swami Muktibodhananda Saraswati page 64-65
569 *Hands of Light: A Guide to Healing Through the Human Energy Field* by Barbara Ann Brennan page 34
570 *Swara Yoga: The Tantric Science of Brain Breathing* by Swami Muktibodhananda Saraswati page 65-67

571 *Hands of Light: A Guide to Healing Through the Human Energy Field* by Barbara Ann Brennan page 46-49
572 *Hands of Light: A Guide to Healing Through the Human Energy Field* by Barbara Ann Brennan page 45
573 *Swara Yoga: The Tantric Science of Brain Breathing* by Swami Muktibodhananda Saraswati page 48-59
574 *Swara Yoga: The Tantric Science of Brain Breathing* by Swami Muktibodhananda Saraswati page 49
575 *Swara Yoga: The Tantric Science of Brain Breathing* by Swami Muktibodhananda Saraswati pages 12-14
576 https://www.britannica.com/science/E-mc2-equation
577 *Swara Yoga: The Tantric Science of Brain Breathing* by Swami Muktibodhananda Saraswati pages 12-15, 49-52
578 *Swara Yoga: The Tantric Science of Brain Breathing* by Swami Muktibodhananda Saraswati page 51-54
579 *Hands of Light: A Guide to Healing Through the Human Energy Field* by Barbara Ann Brennan page 31
580 *Swara Yoga: The Tantric Science of Brain Breathing* by Swami Muktibodhananda Saraswati page 51-54
581 *Hands of Light: A Guide to Healing Through the Human Energy Field* by Barbara Ann Brennan page 31
582 *Swara Yoga: The Tantric Science of Brain Breathing* by Swami Muktibodhananda Saraswati page 51-52
583 Personal observation
584 *The Chakras* by C.W. Leadbeater page 27
585 *Pyramid Energy: The Philosophy of God, The Science of Man* written by Mary and Dean Hardy with Kenneth and Marjorie Killick pages 238-247
586 *Swara Yoga: The Tantric Science of Brain Breathing* by Swami Muktibodhananda Saraswati page 55-59
587 *Swara Yoga: The Tantric Science of Brain Breathing* by Swami Muktibodhananda Saraswati page 50
588 *Becoming Supernatural: How Common People Are Doing The Uncommon* by Dr. Joe Dispenza page 134
589 *Swara Yoga: The Tantric Science of Brain Breathing* by Swami Muktibodhananda Saraswati page 55-59
590 *Swara Yoga: The Tantric Science of Brain Breathing* by Swami Muktibodhananda Saraswati pages 55-59
591 *Swara Yoga: The Tantric Science of Brain Breathing* by Swami Muktibodhananda Saraswati page 51-59
592 *Swara Yoga: The Tantric Science of Brain Breathing* by Swami Muktibodhananda Saraswati page 56-59
593 *The Chakras* by C.W. Leadbeater pages 73-75, 100-106
594 *Swara Yoga: The Tantric Science of Brain Breathing* by Swami Muktibodhananda Saraswati page 59
595 https://www.ananda.org/yogapedia/samadhi/
596 *Swara Yoga: The Tantric Science of Brain Breathing* by Swami Muktibodhananda Saraswati page 67
597 *Wheels of Life: The Classic Guide to the Chakra System* by Anodea Judith, Ph. D. page 321
598 *Wheels of Life: The Classic Guide to the Chakra System* by Anodea Judith, Ph. D. page 318
599 The Kundalini Process: Chakras and Their Petals   http://thekundaliniprocess.blogspot.com/view/sidebar
600 The Kundalini Process: Chakras and Their Petals   http://thekundaliniprocess.blogspot.com/view/sidebar
601 Becoming Supernatural: How common People Are Doing the Uncommon by Dr. Joe Dispenza page 267
602 The Kundalini Process: Chakras and Their Petals   http://thekundaliniprocess.blogspot.com/view/sidebar
603 Shri Mataji 1983 TV Interview (Houston, Tx USA) https://www.youtube.com/watch?v=RCOSmcBlh24
604 Personal experience
605 https://www.foundationalconcepts.com/the-pelvic-chronicles-blog/why-is-the-tailbone-coccyx-so-important/
606 *Becoming Supernatural: How common People Are Doing the Uncommon* by Dr. Joe Dispenza page 125
607 http://neuropathology-web.org/chapter14/chapter14CSF.html
608 https://www.foundationalconcepts.com/the-pelvic-chronicles-blog/why-is-the-tailbone-coccyx-so-important/
609 *Manual Techniques Addressing the Lymphatic System: Origins and Development* by Bruno J. Chikly, MD. DO. *The Journal of the American Osteopathic Association*, October 2005, Vol. 105, 457-464. https://jaoa.org/article.aspx?articleid=2093148
610 *Free Your Body of Tumors and Cysts* by Rev. Hanna Kroeger, Ms. D. page 70-73
611 Hanna Kroeger's YouTube video How to Set the Tailbone https://www.youtube.com/watch?v=MRYX5D6ZlcA
612 https://yogainternational.com/article/view/tone-your-pelvic-floor-in-2-minutes by Sandra Anderson, Himalayan Institute
613 *Moola Bandha: The Master Key* by Swami Buddhananda page 3
614 *Becoming Supernatural: How common People Are Doing the Uncommon* by Dr. Joe Dispenza page 135
615 *Becoming Supernatural: How common People Are Doing the Uncommon* by Dr. Joe Dispenza page 128-130
616 *Becoming Supernatural: How common People Are Doing the Uncommon* by Dr. Joe Dispenza page 131-135
617 Shri Mataji 1983 TV Interview (Houston, Tx USA) https://www.youtube.com/watch?v=RCOSmcBlh24
618 Moola Bandha: The Master Key by Swami Buddhananda pages 3-6
619 *Swara Yoga: The Tantric Science of Brain Breathing* by Swami Muktibodhananda Saraswati page 62
620 *Swara Yoga: The Tantric Science of Brain Breathing* by Swami Muktibodhananda Saraswati page 63
621 *Swara Yoga: The Tantric Science of Brain Breathing* by Swami Muktibodhananda Saraswati page 63-64
622 *Swara Yoga: The Tantric Science of Brain Breathing* by Swami Muktibodhananda Saraswati page 64-65
623 *Swara Yoga: The Tantric Science of Brain Breathing* by Swami Muktibodhananda Saraswati page 65
624 *Swara Yoga: The Tantric Science of Brain Breathing* by Swami Muktibodhananda Saraswati page 65-66

[625] *Swara Yoga: The Tantric Science of Brain Breathing* by Swami Muktibodhananda Saraswati page 66-67
[626] The Kundalini Process: Chakras and Their Petals
http://thekundaliniprocess.blogspot.com/2009/11/updated-view-of-chakras.html
[627] *Swara Yoga: The Tantric Science of Brain Breathing* by Swami Muktibodhananda Saraswati page 67
[628] The Kundalini Process: Chakras and Their Petals
http://thekundaliniprocess.blogspot.com/2009/11/updated-view-of-chakras.html
[629] *Hands of Light: A Guide to Healing Through the Human Energy Field* by Barbara Ann Brennan page 71-72
[630] *The Pendulum Book* by Hanna Kroeger page 4
[631] *The Pendulum Book* by Hanna Kroeger page 5
[632] *Hands of Light: A Guide to Healing Through the Human Energy Field* by Barbara Ann Brennan page 71-72
[633] *Hands of Light: A Guide to Healing Through the Human Energy Field* by Barbara Ann Brennan page 71, 82
[634] *Hands of Light: A Guide to Healing Through the Human Energy Field* by Barbara Ann Brennan page 82
[635] *Hands of Light: A Guide to Healing Through the Human Energy Field* by Barbara Ann Brennan page 81-88
[636] *Hands of Light: A Guide to Healing Through the Human Energy Field* by Barbara Ann Brennan page 81
[637] *Hands of Light: A Guide to Healing Through the Human Energy Field* by Barbara Ann Brennan page 81
[638] *Hands of Light: A Guide to Healing Through the Human Energy Field* by Barbara Ann Brennan page 365
[639] *Clear Your Energy and Lift Your Spirits With the Sacred Art of Smudging* by Bess O'Connor
https://chopra.com/articles/clear-your-energy-and-lift-your-spirits-with-the-sacred-art-of-smudging
[640] Smudging http://www.crystalinks.com/smudging.html
[641] *The Science Behind Smudging* by Tanja Taljaard on Wednesday August 9th, 2017
https://upliftconnect.com/science-behind-smudging/
[642] Sacred & Blessing Herbs & Smudging https://www.taosherb.com/store/sacred-herbs.html
[643] Sacred & Blessing Herbs & Smudging https://www.taosherb.com/store/sacred-herbs.html
[644] similar to *Clear Your Energy and Lift Your Spirits With the Sacred Art of Smudging* by Bess O'Connor
https://chopra.com/articles/clear-your-energy-and-lift-your-spirits-with-the-sacred-art-of-smudging

Chapter 9:
Color / Sound / Frequency / Sacred Geometry

I put Color, Sound, Frequency and Sacred Geometry together as they are each a part of the other. I constantly marvel at God's brilliance in the simplistic-complexity of life. I will address each topic on it's own and you will find at the end of this section how they too are individual, yet part of a greater whole.

COLOR

Sunlight is full spectrum color. Colors within the full spectrum range from infrared to ultraviolet. Color is electromagnetic energy and it exists throughout our universe. Whether human, plant or animal, light and sunlight are vital to sustain life.[645]

The various wavelengths and speed of the energies' particle rotation determines its color and whether it is visible or invisible to the naked eye. As we raise our frequency, we will open ourselves up to experience colors that are not visible in the third dimensional realm. Whether the wavelengths of color are visible or not, the frequency of each color of light penetrates our body down to our individual cells.

When sunlight is absorbed into our body, it separates into the prismatic colors just like light does when it passes through a prism. Each individual cell is its own living organism that produces and emits energy, as well as, light. This is known as its "aura." [646]

Each organ in our body generates a specific light frequency. For example, the liver vibrates the color red, the pituitary vibrates green, the spleen vibrates violet, the circulation system vibrates magenta and the lymphatic system vibrates yellow.
[647]

Color therapy introduces a certain color to a specific part of the body or the body as a whole. It is done by placing colored films, glass or crystals in front of a light and directed onto the body. Color has been known to either stimulate an organ or body system if it is underactive, calm one that is overactive and/or bring about an overall sense of balance.[648]

Color and light are key components for life. Each color has qualities that are beneficial to our well being. The color frequency and the intensity of the light has been found to have an immediate response within the brain. Color even correlates to the planets in our solar system, metals, minerals and essential elements.[649]

Each of our chakras corresponds to a specific color. I listed several of the colors in the section regarding chakras.

The importance of color has been documented and studied for centuries. In the 13th century, Roger Bacon theorized that rainbows were created by light waves passing through glass, crystals or water particles.

In the 17th century, Sir Isaac Newton observed that prisms could disassemble and reassemble white light and wrote about his findings with color in his book, Opticks in 1704.[650] It contains his experiments and findings related to the order of color reflected by a prism, as well as his circle color chart that reflects the colors and their corresponding vibrational tones.[651] Here are his color and sound findings.

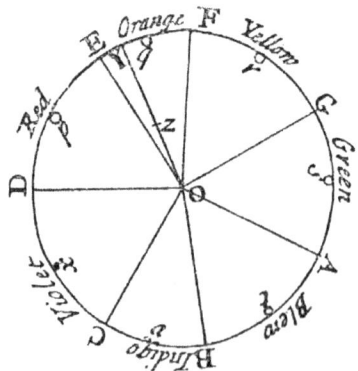

9.1 Sir Isaac Newton's Circle Color Chart from Opticks[652]

Sir Isaac Newton also recognized that the different colors of light move at different speeds, with red moving more quickly than violet. Even though red has a longer wave pattern than violet, which has a very short wave, when passing through a prism, water droplet or medium, red travels faster (more bent) than violet. This opened up research that gave us infrared and ultraviolet light technology.

In 1802, Thomas Young proposed that the human eye contained three types of photoreceptor cells (now known as cone cells) that were each receptive to a particular range of visible Light.

Hermann von Helmholtz continued Thomas Young's theory and in 1850, classified the photoreceptor cells according to the cells response to the wavelength of light as it penetrated the retina. They are referred to as short-preferring (which responds to blue), middle-preferring (responds to green) and long-preferring (responds to red).

In 1878, Dr. Edwin D. Babbitt published a treatise entitled, *Principals of Light and Color*. It was this information upon which Dinshah based his research.

In 1920, Dinshah P. Ghadiali (preferring to be called 'Dinshah') evolved the research of Dr. Babbitt and developed the *Spectro-Chrome System* that provided a safe, natural and effective color therapy to support wellness. Dinshah created a light box lamp with changeable colored slides to bath his clients with various colored light.

When color is beamed into the aura of a living cell, it initiates an electrical reaction that brings about a change. Color Therapy can energize the inherent ability to initiate repair and a normalcy in our physiological bodies.[653] Dinshah correlated the four main elements of living tissue with their resonating color. They are Oxygen – blue, Carbon – yellow, Hydrogen – red and Nitrogen – green. These four elements make up 97% of our physical body.[654]

Color goes along with sound, as it is also frequency and has a measurable speed. Sir Isaac Newton had discovered that each color frequency resonates to a specific tone. Each note of the harmonic scale resonates to a specific color frequency.[655]

The first list is based on the Pythagorean musical scale, where originally the musical note A was equal to the resonance of 432 Hertz.

Pythagorean scale:

Note	Frequency	Color	Measurement of Light (wavelength measurement of light)
G	384Hz	Red	7099 Angstroms
A	432Hz	Orange	6310 A
B	486Hz	Lemon	5609 A
C	512Hz	Green	5324 A
D	576Hz	Blue	4733 A
E	648Hz	Indigo	4207 A
F	683Hz	Violet	3993 A

Using the Standard scale (which is commonly used today) the musical note A equals 440 Hertz. The color and note frequencies are skewed and fractured.

G	391.996 Hz	Red	6954.1727 A
A	440 Hz	Orange	6195.4725 A
B	493.883 Hz	Lemon	5519.5419 A
C	523.251 Hz	Green	5212.2522 A
D	587.330 Hz	Blue	4641.3565 A
E	659.255 Hz	Violet	4134.9825 A
F	698.457 Hz	deep Violet	3902.9001 A

Dinshah accomplished amazing things with his *Spectro-Chrome System* light box. He based his work on the Standard Scale with the musical note A being 440 Hertz. He used more tones and rounded the frequency of the tones up or down to generate Spectro-Chrome Color and Sound equivalents.

G	392 Hz	Red
A	440 Hz	Orange
A#	466 Hz	Yellow
B	494 Hz	Lemon
C	523 Hz	Green
C#	554 Hz	Turquoise
D	687 Hz	Blue
D#	622 Hz	Indigo
E	659 Hz	Violet
A# & E	562*	Purple
G & E	525*	Magenta
G# & D	501*	Scarlet

Dinshah taught that Red, Orange, Yellow and Lemon were INFRA-GREEN colors because they come before Green on the color spectrum. These colors are also considered to be stimulating to the physiology of the body. Green is the median or center color of the spectrum and considered to be the physical equalizer. Turquoise, Blue, Indigo and Violet come after Green on the color spectrum and are defined as being ULTRA-GREEN colors. These colors have a tendency to calm and decrease stimulation with the physiology of the body.[656] Purple, Magenta and Scarlet are a blend of tones and carry both sides of the color spectrum. They possess unique qualities and properties. Purple decreases, Scarlet stimulates and Magenta is an equalizer.[657]

Dinshah believed that Light energy contains a considerably higher potential to increase wellness than sound. However, he did incorporate sound in conjunction with his Spectro-Chrome Color therapies.[658]

SOUND

Sound is primordial. It has been around since God spoke matter into being. Quite possibly, even before.

Sound is an intricate and important part of our harmonious wellbeing. The multi-aspects and benefits of sound are so plentiful and encompassing on so many levels that it is worth exploring in detail.

Sound is electromagnetic frequency transmissions that contain both positive and negative charges within quantum space and subspace. The positive and negative aspects of electromagnetic sound energy set up a toroidal spin that draws matter into it and manifests form. Sound also possesses the properties of both mathematics and physics.[659, 660]

The most elemental state of vibration is sound. Ancient mystics, spiritual teachers, alchemists and philosophers have taught us that *everything* is in a constant state of vibration. Utilizing sound, vibration and frequency, we can open up the 'secrets' of the universe and return to a state of harmony and balance.[661]

Humans can perceive sound when the frequencies range from approximately 20 Hz to 20,000 Hz (also written 20 kiloHerrtz - kHz).[662] Sound is a vibration that generates an audible wave of pressure when it passes through a transmission medium, such as air, water, liquid, gas or solid matter.[663]

The wave length and the speed of the wave determines the pitch or frequency of the sound. The longer the wavelength, the lower the pitch. The 'height' of the wave is called the amplitude. The amplitude determines how loud the sound will be. Thus, the greater the amplitude, the louder the sound.[664]

The Great Hermes understood the need to use sound to 'retune' our bodies to the natural harmonics of the earth. He brought stringed instruments into existence when he created a four stringed lyre and dedicated it to the sun god Apollo.

His lyre produced the natural tones of the four basic elements on this planet. The base string was tuned to the frequency note of E, which reflected the resonant tone of the Earth. The second string was tuned to G, the tone of Fire. The third string was tuned to A, the tone of Air and fourth string was tuned to D, the tone of Water.

Hermes gave the lyre to his disciple Orpheus. The lyre was passed around between colleagues and eventually came to Pythagoras with the addition of two extra strings. Pythagoras experimented with the updated lyre adding a 7th and 8th string creating the Apollonian heptachord (hepta = 8). He believed that this completed the octaves and created, what was termed, the "perfect of all intervals." [665]

Pythagoras created the Pythagorean Kanon, a stringed instrument that amplified the overtones. These overtones generated a precise wheel of intervals with exact 3/2 proportions (Perfect Fifth) that generated a sonic resonance. These sonic resonant overtones mathematically mirrored the sacred geometry Flower of Life pattern, which also mirrors the laws of Universal Creation at its Source.

Pythagoras believed that these sacred resonate tones could shift matter and anti-matter allowing us to move through time and space.[666] He believed that music was the purification for the soul, just as medicine was the purification of the body.

Pythagoras of Samos (c.570 - c.496 BC) went on to bridge mathematics and music.[667] He was an ancient Ionian Greek philosopher, lover of wisdom and founder of Pythagoreanism. Pythagoras was influenced by Orpheus, the Hermetic teachings of ancient Egypt, the Eleusinian Mysteries and the Vedic Scriptures of India. His teachings spanned many topics from politics and religion; to mysticism, numerology, music and vegetarianism.

Pythagoras was credited with numerous mathematical and scientific discoveries, which included the Pythagorean Theorem, Pythagorean Tuning, Pythagorean Musical Scale and the doctrine of Musica Universalis (which is the belief that the planets move according to mathematical equations and produce an inaudible symphony of music). He identified the five platonic solids, which are the tetrahedron with 4 triangular sides, the cube with 6 square faces, the octahedron with 8 triangular sides, the dodecahedron with 12 triangular sides and the icosahedron with 20 triangular sides. He gave us the mathematical Tetractys triangle that reflects the dimensions of the great pyramid, the Theory of Proportions, the sphericity of the Earth and identified the morning and evening stars as the planet Venus.

Pythagoras also taught metempsychosis (the 'transmigration of souls'), where souls are immortal and return upon death into another body, which we know as reincarnation. The teachings of Pythagoras went on to influence the philosophies of Plato, Aristotle and Western Philosophy.[668, 669]

The Pythagorean musical scale is the original musical scale, where the note A has a resonance of 432 Hertz. The Pythagorean musical scale is based on a whole number progression of 8 Hertz. 8 Hz is the frequency of the musical foundation note "C". When the note C at 8 Hz is raised 6 octaves, it has a frequency of 512 Hz. This drops the pitch of middle C from the Standard Scale at 523 Hz to 512 Hz, which in turn, returns the frequency of the note A to 432 Hz. The note A at 432 Hz tunes the pineal gland and the highest areas within the head chakra.[670]

It is interesting that our planet Earth pulses at 7.82 to 8 cycles per second like a heart beat, which is measured as 8 Hz.[671] The Pythagorean musical scale reflects the harmonic signature frequencies of the Earth, which science came to reference as the Schumann Resonance.[672]

Cathedrals, churches, temples and strongholds of historic past, as well as, sacred sites like the Great pyramids of Egypt and Stonehenge were tuned to the Pythagorean scale of 432 Hz. This was achieved by using sacred geometry measurements, angles and shapes that set up a specific resonant frequency within the individual rooms and with the buildings in their totality. They were also built on a natural energy vortex in order to amplify the resonance that was created. These structures became antennas that received and transmitted energy.[673, 674, 675]

It is worth noting, that the distance from the center of the earth to the average height of the atmosphere has a value of 4320 arcminutes. This value can be harmonically reduced down to 432.[676]

432 is also, the square root of the classical speed of Light (186624 miles per second). Our original music scale was based on the frequency of the speed of Light. Once again, I marvel at God's brilliance in the simplicity of complexity.[677]

Continuing with the Pythagorean tuning frequencies, we find that the other notes have significant mathematical relationships. Such as:

- A# = 57.29578 = Radian (180/π) measure for angles defined by an arc of a circle

- B = 240.17358 = One half the height of the Great Pyramid

- D = 288 = Diameter of the outer circle of Stonehenge

- D# = 152.89924 = Multiplied by Pi = Height of the Great Pyramid

- G# = 101.93282 = Difference in height of Chephren and the Great Pyramid[678]

These pitch frequencies are important for retuning the energetic frequencies of our bodies back into a harmonic resonance.

We receive and transmit frequencies in several ways. One way is through the cochlea, which is part of our inner ear. It is a tightly wound, natural Phi spiral that is mathematically shaped in a Fibonacci and Golden Ratio spiral. Chas Stoddard explains in *A Short History of Tuning and Temperament* that the fractal recursiveness of the cochlea allows octaves to be decoded at the same point in each layer of the spiral. This lets us detect and identify the different tones and levels of octaves. It works off the 432 Hz. frequencies.[679]

Another way we receive and transmit frequency is through our DNA. Our DNA receives frequencies in the form of sound and transforms the tones into light energy signals, such as phonons and protons. Our DNA then transmits these wave-particles of sound and light frequencies throughout our cellular structure and energetic being.[680]

The spiral structure of our DNA is similar to a Tesla coil. It also reflects the Golden Means and Fibonacci Spiral with its angstrom measurements. These contributing factors enhance the capability of our oscillating DNA to be powerful transmitters and receivers.

While being light and sound sensitive, our DNA and body are also bio-acoustic. Bio-acoustic involves the detection and production of biological, neurophysiological and anatomical sounds within our body, such as our heart beat, the whooshing sound as blood flows through the arteries, the sound of the breath as it passes through our nostril into our lungs; the sound of joints creaking, the growling of our stomach when we are hungry and the sounds of our digestive track after we have eaten, to name a few.[681]

Our RNA and DNA are bio-acoustic. They are covered with protein that hold the same properties of quartz crystal. The piezoelectric effect of this crystalline substance compels the DNA to emit high frequency sound and to be sensitive to high frequency sounds.[682]

Each body has a primary frequency that is determined by the length of the DNA. Every part of the body, from cells to organs, has their own unique individual vibrational tone when it is in optimal condition. These individual frequency tones create a symphony of sound within and around the body. Solfeggio Frequencies tuned to the Pythagorean scale generate sound frequencies that can return our 'out of balance', skewed frequencies into our original and more harmonious state.[683]

Being light and sound sensitive allows our body to come into balance with the appropriate harmonic sound, light, frequency and resonance. Genetic biochemists are studying the tones in the Pythagorean Scale and Solfeggio Frequencies as they appear to repair broken DNA.

Every organ and cell absorbs and emits sound. The original harmonic tones of the Earth, the universe and nature can assist us with a return to optimal wellness.[684]

On the flip side, our DNA and overall wellbeing can also be pulled out of balance with disharmonic sound, light and frequency. The use of the Standard Scale with the note of A resonating at 440 Hz; the overload of Wi-Fi and electromagnetic fields and our exposure to 5G are just a few of the known disharmonic frequencies that negatively affect our wellbeing.

In 1939, the British Standards Institute (BSI) implemented the shift of the musical scale from the note A above middle C resonating at 432 Hz to an increased resonance of 440 Hz. This small increase negated the sacred harmonics and overtones that facilitate healing and spiritual awakening. Music tuned to the Standard Scale with A tuned to 440 Hz is based on skewed frequencies that create disharmony within our cells and energy field. The adopted Standard scale at 440

Hz has been known to negatively affect our brain chemistry, create a disconnect between the mind and heart, as well as, suppress creativity and intuition.[685]

The Rockefeller Foundation and the Nazi Third Reich instigated the 'push' to alter the original sacred harmonic scale. Britain adopted and enforced the change just weeks prior to the start of World War II. The Rockefeller Foundation had been conducting extensive research into the psychological impact of certain sound frequencies that would shift emotions into fear, uneasiness, agitation and hysteria in order to manipulate the masses during wartime. As Germany bombed cathedrals, the Rockefeller Foundation rebuilt and retuned them.[686, 687]

In his book *The Book of 528: Prosperity Key of Love*, Dr. Leonard Horowitz discusses in great detail how music can bio-energetically affect our body chemistry, psychoneuro immunology and our wellbeing. He shares how the 440 Hz standard scale musically, audibly and subliminally imposes a frequency that instills aggression and dissonance rather than vibrating in harmony with Love.

Fortunately for us, the 432 Hz scale is making a comeback.

✡ ✡ ✡

432 AND GEMATRIA

The number 432 is equivalent to the word 'Consecration' using Gematria. Gematria is a unique system, originally created by the AssyroBabylonian, that assigns a numerical value to the 22 letters of the Hebrew and Greek alphabets. Individual words, sentences, phrases, Bible verses, essential information, personal references and names, as well as, angelic and holy names were deliberately worded or spelled to add up to a precise number that represented a specific energy.

Certain numbers are symbolic and have extended hidden meaning. It is believed that words and phrases, which have the same numerical value, possess the same resonance, frequency and stature as sound.[688]

There are two main forms of gematria. That of the "revealed" form, common with the hermetic writings associated with the Rabbinic literature and the "mystical" form that is mainly associated with the Kabalistic writings.[689]

When the Bible and sacred texts were translated into Latin, the gematria and numerical values were lost. However, the Hebrew and Greek translations stayed intact.

Hidden number symbology is closely related to sacred geometry (which means "sacred measurements of the earth") and includes correlations with our galaxy and cosmos. It is amazing how complex and precise the ancient bearers of wisdom were in these areas. I will share a few references based on the number 153, which is a sacred number and ties into music, sound and frequency.

✧ ✧ ✧

THE NUMBER 153

Mary Magdalene's epithet "η Μαγδαληνή" is written in Greek. The corresponding numbers are 8+40+1+3+4+1+30+8+50+8, which add up to 153. This number reflects that she is of elevated importance.[690]

153 is also the symbolic number for the "Sacred Feminine" and you recite 153 Hail Mary's (3 + 15 sets of 10) when saying the Rosary.

The number 153 is found in conjunction with the numbers 3 and 17. Remember that the ratio of the width of the Vesica Piscis to its length is 153:265 and is the nearest whole number to the square root of 3 or 1.7320508. If you draw a straight line connecting the center of each circle that make up the Vesica Piscis to the point where they meet or intersect, they form two equilateral triangles. The ratios are 265:153 = 1.732061 and 1351:780 =1.7320513.

If you added the numbers between 1 and 17, they will equal 153.

1+2+3+4+5+6+7+8+9+10+11+12+13+14+15+16+17 = 153

The Great Pyramid is based on 153 (152.89924). If you arrange the numbers 1 through 153 in a triangle like this:

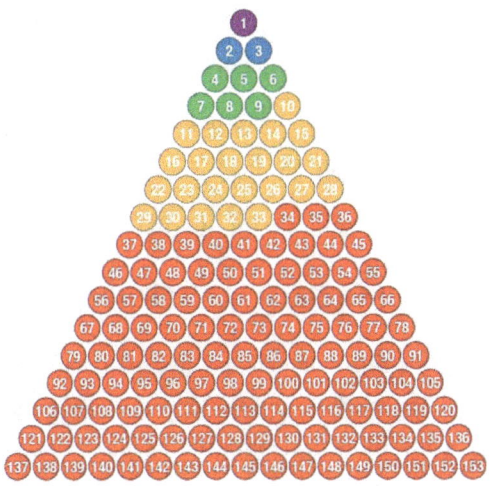

9.2 Triangle of Numbers graphic by Steve Valdeck

You have 17 rows. If you multiply 17 by 9 (the total number of pyramids at the Giza complex) you get 153. Three hundred sixty (360) feet up the side of the Great Pyramid is the 153rd course or level. The length of the grand gallery inside the Great Pyramid is 153 feet.

In gematria the words 'three sixty' equal 153. Michael the Archangel equals 153, as does Quetzalcoatl.

There are 153 Tetragrammaton found in the Book of Genesis. In the original Hebrew, the proper or sacred name of God was transliterated in four letters to YHWH (sometimes written in the older style as YHVH) as Yahweh or JHVH as Jehovah. The ancients believed that God's name was too sacred to speak aloud. The four letters of the Tetragrammaton form the root meaning "to be" and some have understood the original meaning as "He-Who-IS" or "He-Who-Brings."

The square root of 153 is the number of full moons in one year - 12.369316876853.

Here are a couple more important 153 numbers that relate to the Limbic system and the Glia brain:

The musical note D# resonates at 152.89924 cycles per second. Divide this number by pi and you have the radius of the inner circle of Stonehenge. Multiply 152.89924 by pi and you have the height of the Great pyramid.

These formulations only work when D# is based on the Pythagorean scale verses the modern Standard scale.[691, 692]

✧ ✧ ✧

SOLFEGGIO TONES

The Solfeggio Tones fit nicely here, as they go along with the Pythagorean Scale. I mentioned them briefly in the sections addressing the pineal gland and sound. Here, I'll go a little more in-depth with the information.

The Solfeggio Scale tones were Divinely given to a Benedictine Monk, Guido D'Arezzo. He found that the Solfeggio Tones impart a feeling of joy, opens your connection with Divine Source, increases the natural Life Force energy, repairs DNA, as well as, harmonizes the soul, awakens intuition and increases the ability to manifest.[693]

The Solfeggio Scale tones were used in the Ancient Gregorian Chanting. Just listening to Gregorian Chants enable people to heal emotional, mental, physical and spiritual wounds. The tones facilitate healing on a grand level and raise the resonance within ones personal energy and facilitates the 'way through' limiting thought, as it elevates higher consciousness.

The original Solfeggio tones were protected by ancient pre-Egyptian mystics and the Levitical priesthood. Eventually, the Church suppressed the use of Solfeggio Tones around 1050AD and adopted the Twelve-Tone Equal Temperament. Using the adopted Standard Scale, the octave is divided into 12 equal mathematical parts on a logarithmic scale, which results in an equal pitch distance between two tones.

As was mentioned above, the slight difference in pitch between the original Pythagorean and the adopted Standard Scale made an enormous difference in stifling our process towards enlightenment.

The Solfeggio Tones were preserved in the ancient megalithic Temple of Mnajdra, on the island of Malta. Mnajdra (pronounced Nahdra) was constructed in the fourth millennium BC and is considered to be the oldest spiritual site on Earth. The Solfeggio Tones were rediscovered by Dr. Joseph Puleo in the 1970's.

Using the Pythagorean method of numeral reduction, which turns large numbers into single digits, Dr. Puleo was able to unlock the six mathematically encoded patterns found in the Book of Numbers, Chapter 7, verses 12 through 83 of the Bible. The numbers were: 396, 417, 528, 639, 741 and 852.

The values of the digits in each number were added together until a single digit remained. Take the tone 'LA' at 852 Hz = 8 + 5 + 2 = 15, then add 1 + 5 = 6. All the frequency numbers add up to 3, 6 or 9 and are the fundamental root vibration of all the Solfeggio frequencies. Pythagorus called these numbers sacred.

> *"If you only knew the magnificence of the 3, 6, and 9, then you would hold a key to the universe."*
>
> NIKOLA TESLA[694]

The individual Solfeggio tones correspond to specific Hertz frequencies, as well as, to the frequency of our organs, emotions, attributes, syllables and the chakras. They are as such:

63 Hz

174 Hz - appears to be a natural anesthetic, removing energetic and physical discomfort, promoting a sense of safety and security within the body.

285 Hz - helps repair damaged tissue (cuts, wounds, burns, etc.)

UT *396 Hz* - Liberation from Fear - Liberates guilt, fear, insecurity and survival issues - linked to the 1st Chakra (Root) and the vibration of the color Red.

RE *417 Hz* - Transmutation - Undo situations & facilitates change, overcoming limiting beliefs - linked to the 2nd Chakra (Sacral) and the vibration of the color Orange.

MI *528 Hz* - Miracles - Transformation & Miracles, DNA repair, increases energy, creativity, clearer thinking and brain function, confidence and wellbeing - linked to the 3rd Chakra (Solar Plexus) and vibration of the color Yellow.

FA *639 Hz* - Relationship and Harmonization - Connecting relationships, self love and emotional stability - linked to the 4th Chakra (Heart) and the vibration of the color Green.

SOL *741 Hz* - Consciousness Expansion - Awakening Intuition, enhances communication - linked to the 5th Chakra (Throat) and the vibration of the color Blue.

LA *852 Hz* - Awakening Intuition and Returning to Spiritual Order - activates pituitary, increases concentration and intuition - linked to the 6th Chakra (Third Eye) and the vibration of the color Indigo.

SI *963 Hz* - Oneness - Activates the pineal and is a direct source to Divine - it is linked to the 7th Chakra (Crown Chakra) and the vibration of the color Violet

1074 Hz

1185 Hz

1296 Hz

1317 Hz and so on…

Each of the intervals between the previous frequency is equal to a 111Hz change. Each of the individual stone rooms in the Temple of Mnajdra resonate between 110 Hz and 111 Hz frequencies.

The syllables that reference each Solfeggio Tone, as in UT, RE, MI, FA SOL, LA, SI come from the first stanza of the Hymn to St. John the Baptist. In Latin it is as such:

Ut queant laxis **Re**sonare fibris

Mira gestorum **Fa**muli tuorum

Solve polluti **La**bii reatum

Sancte **I**ohannes

The translation is: "In order that the people might resonate (resound) the miracles (wonders) of Your creations with loosened (expanded) vocal chords, Wash the guilt from (our) polluted lip, Saint John." [695, 696]

Dr. Puleo knew that there were six verses to St. John's sacred hymn and that each verse was sung in its corresponding Solfeggio tone. He also believed that these sacred tones could shift the frequency of water. Our physical body, being mostly water, could raise its resonance simply by resounding these sacred tones.[697]

Singing Ut, Re, Mi Fa, So, La, SI with its appropriate tone was a way of voicing the frequency of the full prayer.

Dr. Puleo recognized that the creative/etherical/spiritual music of the original six Solfeggio Tones reflects a 639 primordial mathematical matrix that generates a standing wave. Russia's leading space/time physicist, Dr. Hartmut Müller confirmed that the six sacred Solfeggio tones, or "energy nodes," are sub-waves within the Standing Gravitational Wave (SGW) that produce sustaining energy and holographic reality.[698]

✡ ✡ ✡

I believe the Solfeggio Tones were the tones used to heal at the pyramid of Sakkara in Egypt. There are stepped platforms behind the pyramid that I believe were used for healing, as were the individual chambers. When I was there in 1993, I intuitively saw Priests and Priestesses standing on the various steps. Left, right and center of each step was a different tone. The center of the step was the whole or pure tone. Standing to the left of the center, the tones became the half tone down the scale or flats - as in Eb. Standing to the right of the center generated the half tone up or sharps - as in D#.

People stood on the top of the platform and I moved other participants around on the steps and had them tone what I heard. The sound was for the most part harmonious. The multiple tones being 'sounded' created various chords that fluctuated between Major, Minor, Augmented and Diminished chords.

Occasionally, a tone was resounded that created a strong vibrating wave as a note clashed with another. This intense pulsing actually helped break up crystalized emotion that was locked solid in someones energy or cells. When the blockage was clear, the tones returned to being harmonic. Everyone who was present received a healing in some degree.

9.3 Temple of Sakkara Egypt [699]

ISO-PRINCIPLE

We can use sound, key, tempo, beats per minute (bpm), resonance and frequencies to balance our chakra system, to shift emotions, change our physiology and activate the glia brain, limbic system and frontal lobe.

Musical Entrainment has the capability to resonate with a listener's feelings. The tones, harmonics, rhythm and melody can move a person into an emotional response. This is done by moving the musical notes and chord between major, minor, diminished and augmented chords. Musical entrainment can shift a person from negative feelings into positive emotions, can invoke a sense of fear or promote an uplifting emotional state or one of serenity and calm. This technique is known as 'iso principle.'

As a therapeutic practice, "iso-principle is a technique by which music is matched with the mood of a client, then gradually altered to affect the desired mood state. This technique can also be used to affect physiological responses such as heart rate and blood pressure." (Davis, Gfeller & Thaut, 2008)

Iso-principle is also used in movies to emotionally enhance and support the scene.[700]

✡ ✡ ✡

ENTRAINMENT

Entrainment is when two or more interacting oscillating vibrations lock into phase and assume the same rate and vibrate in harmony. It is a natural compromise, as the two or more vibrational or rhythmic cycles become synchronized. Entrainment is also known as the Universal Law of Harmony or the Transformation Principle.

Basically, any two or more vibrating bodies will eventually entrain or synchronize themselves if opposed to each other long enough. The principle of entrainment is a universal phenomenon. It not only occurs in nature, but also, in physics, chemistry, biology, pharmacology, medicine, psychology, sociology, and astronomy.[701]

Here are a few examples of entrainment:[702, 703]

1. In 1665, Dutch scientist, Christian Huygens, filled a room with pendulum clocks and started them one at a time. Each pendulum swung at a different pace. When he returned to the room a day later, all the pendulums had synchronized. Every pendulum was swinging at the same time for the same duration.

2. Research suggests that our circadian rhythm (biological clock) is entrained and synchronized to the rhythms of the earth relative to the sun giving us our wake sleep cycle.

3. Brainwave entrainment is called Frequency Following Response (FFR). This is when an external sound frequency (audio stimuli) is repeatedly played using headphones. The brainwaves eventually assume that particular sound frequency, such as with binaural beats of gamma, beta, alpha, theta and delta frequencies. I will go into more detail with brainwave patterns in the next section. Brainwave entrainment can be extremely useful and beneficial. However, as was discussed in the section *Harmful EMF Fields and our Pineal,* entrainment to extremely high or extremely low radio and electromagnetic frequencies can produce negative effects on our brain. It is healthful to know the difference.[704]

4. Women who live in the same home have a tendency to cycle their menses at the same time.

5. When two people come together in intimacy, their individual heart beats tend to move into the same pulse, beat or rhythm.

6. Pure, natural therapeutic grade essential oils can also be entrained. In perfect accordance of God's design, natural therapeutic grade essential oils are mathematically 'tuned' in frequencies that are similar to a musical scale. When blended together, they naturally adjust their frequencies to form a molecular coherence that bings harmony to our body, mind and spirit.[705] Take for example, the essential oil blend of Abundance™. The entrained frequency is 78 MHz. Even though the frequency of just two of the oils, Frankincense (147 MHz) and Myrrh (108MHz) are higher as

individual oils. When blended together the oils will find or entrain to a vibrational range that is unique and may not be the sum of the combined frequencies or even the ratio of the combined frequencies divided by the number of oils used in the blend.

7. During my previously mentioned 8:8 spiritual event in Egypt in August of 1993, I experienced an entrainment with my heart rhythm at the Sakkara Pyramid. I went into one of the chamber rooms by the stepped platforms. Tuning dimensions were carved on the center front wall of each chamber as you entered. The wall to the left had a cut out shelf that measured to my shoulder level height. I was guided to lean against the wall with my face in the open shelf space. I could feel a pulse like a heart beat in the wall. I sensed that it was the heart beat of Mother Earth. It was off beat or out of synch with my own heartbeat.

I began taking slow deep breaths and was intuitively guided to tone 'Om' several times. My tone echoed and amplified in this small space, as if it was moving down a hollow tunnel to the core of the earth. I could feel the reverberation of sound in the stone wall as it resonated within my chest as I toned. On the fourth 'Om,' my heartbeat jumped into the rhythm of Mother Earth and a gentle bliss filled my body. Many in our tour group were able to experience this, including the temple guard.

9.4 Tuning dimensions in Sakkara Pyramid chamber courtesy of Mary Hardy

8. Here is another example of entraining the heart beat to the earth. On one of my Mary Magdalene/Black Madonna tours, we went to the beautiful city of Collier, France. They have a magnificent Cathedral and Black Madonna there. After our visit to the Cathedral, we spent some time on their picturesque beach. As I lay on the blanket I could feel a pulse like a heart beat underneath me. I dug out a space in the sand where I could lay comfortably and had my friends cover me with sand from my shoulders down. I could feel the earth's heart beat and then mine. Like in Egypt, my heartbeat was out of synch with the earth.

I began taking slow meditative breaths. In the packed sand that covered my body, we could see the synchronization process taking place. The sand at my heart area began to pulse with my heartbeat ever so slightly. The sand around the bottom edge of my body pulsed with the earth. As soon as my heartbeat synchronized with the earth, the sand that covered me jumped from head to toe as the electromagnetic frequency aligned me on an energetic and cellular level. We literally could see the pulse of my unified heartbeat in the sand along the entire length of my body.

Once again, a feeling of gentle bliss encompassed me and all my friends wanted to experience it. Within a few minutes we had several holes dug out and everyone on the beach was 'synching up.'

✡ ✡ ✡

BRAIN WAVES AND BINAURAL BEATS

There are five main brain wave patterns. From the highest Hertz frequencies to the lowest, they are: Gamma, Beta, Alpha, Theta and Delta. All five patterns are active within the brain at all times. However, one wave pattern will be dominant over the others. Throughout the day, the dominating wave will move between each of the five brain waves. The dominating brain wave pattern determines your state of consciousness, your mood and activity level.[706]

Brain activity is electrochemical. Do you remember the thalamus from the limbic system and the astrocytes? When the astrocytes inside the thalamus are triggered by glutamate, they release a wave of calcium that propels the voltage in the neurons to generate activity, which influence the cycles of brain waves. The electrochemical activity produces electromagnetic wave patterns. These brain wave patterns are so strong that they can be measured by an electroencephalogram (EEG) with electrodes that are attached to your scalp.[707]

The electrical voltage of one thalamic neuron instantaneously triggers other neurons that are in tandem with it. This generates a relay of electrical energy that continues to trigger other neurons that are connected to the large network of neurons within our brain. This electrochemical wave can fire the neurons in unison and in cycles, to propel the activity of brain waves in our cerebral cortex.[708]

When we speak of brainwave patterns, cycles and Hertz, we are referencing the number of times an electromagnetic wave peaks in amplitude and frequency per second. Amplitude is the measured distance from peak to peak on a wave of sound or electricity at the strongest repeating part of the wave.[709] Amplitude is the "push" or power of the electrical impulse and is measured in microvoltage.[710]

Frequency refers to the speed of the oscillations and how many times the wave peaks per second. It is the frequency the designates one brainwave from the other, such as Beta, Alpha, Theta, Delta and Gamma. The brainwave frequency determines your state of consciousness.[711]

In the diagram below, you will notice with the 'In Phase' wave that the sinusoidal wave peaks above the midline and below it. The peaks are equal distance from each other. In image 9.5, if the measurement of time was one (1) second, then the wave would have a measurement of 4 Hertz (Hz), meaning that it peaks 4 times per second.[712]

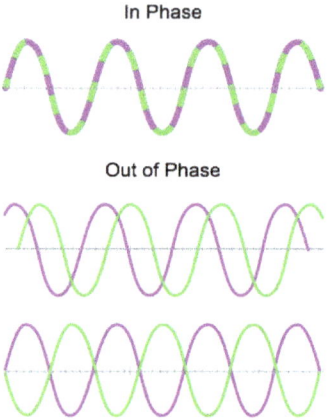

9:5 In Phase - Out of Phase wave forms graphic by Steve Valdeck

Brain wave activity can be recorded once the glia cells have coated the nerve fibers with their insulating layers of myelin sheathing.[713] Brain wave activity within the human brain follows a progression through the developmental stages. They are:

Delta, which is mostly at an EEG frequency between 0.5 to 4 cycles per second (0.5-4 Hertz), is the predominate brain wave pattern from birth to two years of age, with periodic bursts of higher brainwave activity.

Theta (4-8 Hz) is the main operating brain wave between the ages of two and six. Theta is the most suggestible and programmable state of mind. Children can download incredible amounts of information from their environment and their parents at this stage. This is a crucial time in the programming of our basic fundamental beliefs, behaviors and skill sets. These observations are directly downloaded in the child's subconscious memory and can unconsciously influence the behavior, potential and direction of their life. Theta is also the state that hypnotists use with their clients.

Alpha waves (8-12 Hz) begin to operate between the ages of six and twelve.

Beta brain waves (12-35 Hz) become predominate around the age of twelve. By adolescence, children have become automatically programmed from their environment and learned behaviors.

Gamma waves (35 Hz and higher) are the 'peak performance' states. Gamma brain waves engage the entire brain for a synchronized, high functioning state of awareness.[714]

Every state of consciousness contains four of the major brainwaves - Beta, Alpha, Theta and Delta. They work in combination with each other like an orchestra with the dominant brainwave pattern acting like the conductor. The combination of brainwaves can create a harmonious state of being or disharmony in a state of varied chaos.[715] Ultimately, our goal is to strategically use them all in order to live, manifest and express ourselves in a state of harmony.

What I find intriguing, is that each of us have our own unique 'signature pattern' that is a constant, even when we are moving through one state of consciousness to another.[716]

Each individual brain wave state has its advantages and disadvantages depending on your current circumstances. Fortunately, we can enhance a brainwave pattern in order to achieve a specific outcome. If you are studying for an exam, Alpha and low Beta are good for focus. If you wish to be calm and relaxed, increase your Alpha or Theta brain waves. Theta and Delta brainwave patterns can influence better sleep and rejuvenation. If you are too relaxed and unmotivated, then increase your low Beta or Gamma brain waves.[717]

Here are descriptions of the brain wave patterns and some of their associated characteristics. Having a basic understanding of each brain wave pattern can assist you in your journey to a more harmonious life.

Beta Brain Waves

Beta Brain Waves involve the thinking process that is focused on the external environment and are influenced by the ego.[718] Beta brain waves can take you from logical thought and problem solving to panic.[719] Beta brain waves run in the range of 12 Hz to 40 Hz.

There are three classifications of Beta Brain Waves. High Beta waves vibrate from 18 Hz to 40 Hz, Mid-Range Beta Waves vibrate from 15 Hz to 20 Hz and Low Beta Waves, vibrate from 12 Hz to 15 Hz.[720]

High Beta waves are sometimes referred to as "Beta 3" waves. High Beta brain waves have been associated with muscle tension, negative thinking, fear, intense or chronic anxiety, excessive stress, sleep issues, paranoia, sadness, nervous energy, fatigue, aggression, short fused, excessive thinking or worrying, insecurity, competition and addictions. When someone becomes angry, they move into High Beta brain waves. It is the spike of High Beta activity that prevents them from reasoning and calming down.[721, 722]

Your body and brain produce survival bio-chemicals in the High Beta mode that are intended for short term emergency situations. Sometimes, the brain can become stuck in a dominant High Beta brain wave. Being locked in a continual mode of High Beta takes a tremendous amount of energy and can keep you in a fight-or-flight mode or in a continuous state of hyper-drive. Those locked in High Beta can feel that they are powerless and a victim of circumstance or be obsessive, pushy or compulsive.[723]

"Alpha blocking" is a brain wave process where the excessive High Beta waves block the production of Alpha waves and inhibit a shift into the more calming Alpha wave activity.[724]

If you are experiencing any of the above issues, try listening to Alpha or Theta brain waves, while doing the Spiral Breath technique to achieve a more calming presence.

The *Mid-Range Beta* waves are sometimes referred to as "Beta 2" waves.

Mid-Range Beta waves are associated with increased energy, slight anxiety, higher performance and may increase your IQ by enhancing concentration, as well as, how your brain receives and processes information.[725]

The *Low Beta* brain waves are sometimes referred to as "Beta 1" and are the slower of the Beta wave cycles. Low Beta brain waves promote focused learning, calculating, problem solving, language learning and creativity.[726] Children begin to move into a natural Beta state around the age of twelve.

When Beta brain waves are functioning at their best, they enhance our active attention on the environment around us; logical, focused and complex thinking and decision making. Learning how to utilize Beta waves to benefit our circumstances will bring about a more harmonious and productive life.[727, 728]

If you are experiencing a lack of mental energy, problem solving, concentration or focus, an increase of Low Beta or Gamma brain waves could be beneficial. If you are too wired, increase your Alpha brain waves.

✡ ✡ ✡

Alpha Brain Waves

Alpha Brain Waves vibrate between 7 Hz and 12 Hz and are associated with meditative states, relaxation, visualization, daydreaming, creativity, self-awareness, stronger intuition and "super learning."

Alpha brain waves are considered to be a bridge between the conscious and the subconscious, our external world and our internal world, as well as our waking state and our sleeping state.[729, 730, 731]

Increased Alpha brain wave activity can boost your mood and initiate calmness, which can reduce your stress and anxiety levels. When we are in a relaxed state, we tend to naturally increase our production of Serotonin. Increased Alpha brain waves can also improve your study skills, as both mind and body are relaxed, yet the mind retains focus.[732] Alpha waves can enhance positive thinking, which can improve your optimism and your outlook on life.[733] Consciously practicing 'mindfulness' can also increase our Alpha brain waves.[734]

Images that are generated by Alpha brain waves during visualization and meditation are clearer, sharper, stronger and are more vivid in their colors.[735]

When you utilize slow, deep breathing, as with the Spiral Breath, you activate your Alpha brain waves.[736]

Your body and your brain require that you drop into an Alpha brain wave state in order to download, compartmentalize and store the information that you acquired throughout your day. Without Alpha brainwaves, you would not remember or recall information, dreams or insights. When you take time to rest and reflect throughout the day or experience an idle mind your Alpha brain waves commit information and your experiences into memory. Same as when you sleep. Whether you take a power nap or sleep during the night, obtaining good restful sleep and moving through all five brain wave patterns are important for memory and retention.[737, 738]

When you close your eyes, you reduce the sensory, external input up to 80 percent. Reducing the external input enables you to activate your Alpha brain waves. Meditating, visualizing, daydreaming or deep focused breathing with your eyes closed, increase the natural production of your Alpha wave activity. The moment that you open your eyes you shift into a low Beta state.

It has been found that those who endure prolonged stress, such as, anxiety, nervousness, rapid repetitive thinking, long work hours and over stimulation of electro-magnetic fields have a tendency to become introverts and/or experience sleep issues and often have low Alpha wave activity. Sometimes, people under stress do not cycle through all the wave patterns and get stuck in High Beta. Instead of moving into a relaxing Alpha state, they stay over stimulated in High Beta, which depletes their Alpha waves and makes it difficult to relax, fall asleep or stay asleep.[740]

Those who are more logical and have difficulty visualizing tend to have lower levels of Alpha brain waves.

If someone who is experiencing lethargy, moodiness, is unmotivated, unable to focus or spends to much time daydreaming becomes more so with the introduction of Alpha waves, they are over stimulated in Alpha waves and would do better listening to low Beta or Gamma brain waves.[741]

I have found that people who can easily move in and out of Beta and Alpha are generally less stressed, have better coping skills; have greater memory recall and are more social and outgoing.

Alpha brain waves are most often produced by the right hemisphere, though they can also be found synchronized and evenly generated in both hemispheres of the brain. When both hemispheres of the brain are in synch, they communicate with each other more efficiently. When we are relaxing, during closed eye rest or when drowsy or sleeping, Alpha waves are generated mostly from our occipital lobe. During REM sleep (Rapid Eye Movement), the Alpha brain wave activity is mostly generated in the frontal-central region of the brain.[742]

If you want to increase your energy, improve your learning, memory, recall and brain function; become more productive and positive in your thinking, heighten your creativity and intuition, activate your glia brain, increase your quality of life and simply be in the "flow;" then increase your Alpha brain waves.

✡ ✡ ✡

Theta Brain Waves

Theta Brain Waves oscillate from 4 Hz to 7 Hz. Theta brain waves are slower wave frequencies, oscillating 4 to 7 times per second. They are high in amplitude and can be rhythmic or arrhythmic, while engaging the entire brain. They are associated with the early stages of sleep and the dreaming process.

Like Alpha waves, Theta waves are also considered to be a "super learning" wave. If you want to learn a new language, listen to Theta waves during your lesson. Young children between the ages of 2 to 6 years of age can easily learn an additional language, as they generally have higher Theta brain wave activity than adults. Children can absorb and download vast amounts of information from their environment and their parents.[743]

In Theta dominance, children observe and absorb directly into their subconscious. Complex skills can be observed and quickly put into action. Parental behaviors, beliefs, attitudes and words are programmed into a child's subconscious and become "hard-wired" into their foundation just through observation. These subconscious programs become our "truths" (beneficial or harmful) that influence and control us throughout our lives until we make a conscious effort to make a change (if necessary) and reprogram our thoughts, behaviors and beliefs. Theta is a very powerful brain wave state. It can be both a hindrance and a benefit.[744]

Hypnotherapists drop their patients into a Theta brain wave state, which puts them into a more suggestive and re-programmable state. In a Theta state, there is no veil between the conscious and subconscious minds.[745] When you move from a conscious mind into your subconscious, you have shifted from Beta to Theta. You also move from a fight-or-flight mode and a dominant sympathetic nervous system into your parasympathetic nervous system and a restful state.[746]

Adults have a tendency to lose their Theta wave activity as they become submerged in the mental Beta frequencies that are required for most of the work day. Add in a stressful lifestyle with family, finances and a lack of joy and you will probably find diminished Theta brain wave activity.

Most people can easily transition from Beta to Alpha to Theta then back to Alpha and Beta as needed. On occasion, people get over stimulated with Theta waves and this can cause a lack of concentration and focus. Those with attention issues may find that they do better if they enhance their Alpha or low Beta brain waves.[747]

Theta brain waves are also known to stimulate creativity, can enhance the processing of vast amounts of information and are present with brainstorming. People with higher levels of Theta waves are able to become 'hyper-focused' on a specific task and are excellent problem solvers. Exceptional musicians, designers, artists, inventors and quick learners have higher levels of Theta brain wave activity. In a Theta state, **Theta brain waves connect the conscious mind to the subconscious mind and help you access your inner self.**[748]

When you are choosing to reprogram your thought process, automatic emotional responses or tap into suppressed emotions, it is extremely beneficial to be in a Theta brain wave pattern.

Sometimes, positive affirmations are just not enough. You have to get to the root cause and core emotional issue. Often times, that root cause anchored itself into your subconscious during your very impressionable Theta based years. Those years between the ages of 2 and 6.

To make a lasting change to an unhealthy thought process, pattern or learned behavior, it is necessary to go deep into the subconscious Theta realm to where the emotion, thought or behavior was first created and anchored itself as a foundational truth. It is here, in the subconscious, that we can truly make a change.[749, 750]

95 percent of what makes up who we are lies in our subconscious mind. The subconscious is made up of our programs and habits.[751] Using meditation and breath work like the Spiral Breath technique, we can access the Theta brain wave realm and make significant change.

As we move from our thinking, conscious Beta state into a meditative Alpha state, we start to slow our thinking process. Remember, when we close our eyes, we shut out up to 80 percent of the environmental input around us. Restful attention, slow deep breaths and mindful intent allows us to move into a peaceful state where we are still conscious, yet very relaxed. In the Alpha brain wave state, our frontal lobe quiets the brain activity and we move into a peaceful, creative state of being.[752]

Continued breathing with the Spiral Breath, along with the assistance of listening to Theta wave entrainment can help you attain your results with greater ease.

Once you have reached the Theta brain wave level, you can change the preprogrammed subconscious thoughts, emotions or behavior patterns that have kept you from harmony. In the Theta brain wave mode, you are free to manifest your desires without interference from your 'busy' mind and old programming.[753]

Guided meditation with imagery is another way to achieve access to the Theta realm. Visual images that use directional movement are extremely beneficial. Visual images that guide you to walk through nature and outdoor environments tend to access your Alpha brain waves. It is easier to enhance Theta waves once you have reached the Alpha state. Visual images that guide you to walk into a house or structure access your Theta brain waves.

The images that work best for Theta access are those that take you on a long journey. Key words that will take you deeper are those with directional movement, such as, walk *through* a doorway, *down* the hall, *into* a room, temple or sacred place, *up* or *down* and *around* the spiral staircase, *under* an archway, look *inside* the box or step *inside* the secret room hidden behind the vine encrusted wall, step *over* the wooden box, lean *up* and *over* the window sill, walk *along* the narrow tunnel, etc.

The long journey helps generate and increase the Theta brain waves. Allow enough time with each suggestion to visually complete the task.[754]

At the end of the guided journey, I sometimes visualize myself arriving to stand before a Master Teacher or a Spiritual/Religious figure of my choosing. You can stand before yourself as a child, teenager, yourself before or after an event, your present self, your future self or someone whom you have unresolved issues with. Ask your chosen figure if they have a message for you or take time to rewrite an event or conversation to one that is supportive and positive. Forgive what requires forgiving, heal what requires healing and then rewrite your programming.

Before I begin my meditations, I like to set an intention. If I am rewriting an automatic response or emotion, I will bring that issue forward into my conscious attention. Say for example, being defensive. I connect to a recent experience where I felt defensive. Then I ask to heal the very first time I felt that way and then bring the healing of that feeling up through my life into the present and on into the future.

With my intentions stated, I set it aside and begin my meditation and breath work. I will often incorporate a pure essential oil blend that supports my intention.

If I have a question that requires and answer, I state my question as my intention. I begin my meditation and wait for the answer to be manifested as I breathe the Spiral Breath. Get creative and be precise in your wording. Your possibilities are vast!

Theta waves also promote deeper relaxation, restorative sleep, dream activity, lucid dreams and are associated with REM (Rapid Eye Movement) sleep. Increased Theta activity improves long-term memory, improves your immune system and can accelerate the healing of our brain and our body.[755]

On the bio-chemical side, our brain cells reset their sodium and potassium ratios when the brain is in a Theta state. The sodium and potassium levels are required for the process of transporting chemicals into and out of our brain cells. Being active or locked into a Beta/High Beta brainwave state for an excessive period of time can cause a depletion and an imbalance in the ratio of potassium and sodium. This can cause mental fatigue, brain fog and/or excessive thinking. Listening to a Theta brain wave for five to fifteen minutes can restore balance, mental clarity and acts like a power nap without the sleep.[756]

I have found that Theta waves are excellent to listen to as you are doing the Spiral Breath technique. as they can stimulate the glia brain, activate the pineal gland, awaken your third eye and increase your extra-sensory skills.

Theta brain waves are high when you experience powerful surges of emotion and are known to increase intuition. Theta waves are heightened when you get that "gut feeling." When a mother senses that something is wrong with her child; when a friend or spouse stops what they are doing to check on their loved one, they are 'tuning in' using Theta waves.[757]

Theta waves are the mental/emotional telepathy connection that is present between loved ones. It is common for me to sense that a friend is in need of one and I will call asking, "How are you? What is going on?" I also see events in my minds' eye before they happen. Sometimes, I am able to give warning; other times my call is the first response.

One afternoon, I saw in my minds' eye that a friend was a passenger in a car and was involved in a terrible accident. As soon as the scene flashed through my thoughts, I immediately surrounded them with 'White Light' and asked God to keep them safe from harm. Then I called him. He did not answer so I left a message about what I saw and asked him to let me know that he was alright.

A couple minutes later, my friend reported that my call came through just before the impact. With the ring, everything went into slow motion and a sense of peace enveloped them. They were pulled from the totaled car miraculously unscathed.

The brain and the power of love are mighty!

✡ ✡ ✡

Delta Brain Waves

Delta Brain Waves are the slowest brain frequency oscillating at .5 Hz to 4 Hz per second. Delta brain waves have the greatest amplitude (longest wave length) of all the brain wave patterns and can be rhythmic or arrhythmic.

Delta is your deep sleep, deep healing and rejuvenation stage. Increased Delta wave activity stimulates the natural release of our anti-aging hormones, DHEA, human growth hormones, serotonin, melatonin and DMT.[758]

Elevated Delta brain waves have been reported to reduce Cortisol and adrenalin levels in your body. High levels of stress produce excess adrenaline, which require cortisol to diminish its production. This leaves an excess of cortisol in the body, which can increase inflammation, harm the body and diminish brain cells. Excessive cortisol has also been found to accelerate aging.

Delta waves help with the repair of muscle and brain cells. People who have encountered brain damage have higher Delta brain wave activity, as well as, those who have had Near-Death-Experiences (NDE).[759]

Delta brain waves are dominant with babies during the final stages of pregnancy while still in the womb and continue up to 2 years of age. Delta waves are the final brain waves that we produce just before we die, which would explain the final surge of DMT that generates the 'rally' and helps with the transition.

Increased Delta brain waves enable the deepest state of relaxation to be obtained and is said to provide access to God, as well as, 'Infinite Intelligence.' This is the state that Monks reach with their advanced states of meditation.

With practice, you can achieve an Alpha-Delta State. During which, you can tap into Delta brain waves while in an Alpha meditative state and be slightly wakeful during deep sleep. Alpha-Delta State brain waves are observed across the anterior-posterior region of the brain.[760]

Delta brain waves are both a radio transmitter and a receiver. With higher levels of Delta wave activity, you have your own personal radar system. Delta waves can send and receive information and messages on an unconscious level. In a Delta wave dominance, you can know when the phone is about to ring and who is calling even before you answer. You answer someones question before it is asked. Complete conversations can be had without speaking a single word. Medical intuitive's access higher than normal Delta brain waves.[761]

People with an excess of Delta waves can sometimes have heightened receptivity and empathy. They can feel overly sensitive and bombarded with the thoughts and feelings of others. At times, they hear what everyone is thinking.[762]

Accessing Delta brain waves during meditation allow you to stimulate the glia brain, access higher states of spiritual consciousness and paranormal experiences, such as, increased intuition, out of body experiences (O.O.B.E), bilocating, astral projection, teleportation and quantum jumping.

It takes practice, but it can be done.

✧ ✧ ✧

Gamma Brain Waves

Gamma Brain Waves have the fastest oscillating frequency with the smallest amplitude (shortest wave height) of the five patterns. Gamma Brain Waves (not to be confused with Gamma rays) range from 40 Hz – 100 Hz plus in humans. They are present in both waking consciousness and during your deep REM sleep.

Higher levels of Gamma brain waves are equated to those with higher intelligence; who are hyper focused, faster processors of information, phenomenal memory and recall, have greater amounts of self-control, are more compassionate and have a tendency to be happy people.[763]

Gamma brain waves heighten the acuity of your six senses of taste, touch, hearing, sight, smell and thought. Increased sense of thought elevates extra sensory perception, telekinesis and states of paranormal and higher consciousness. Gamma waves are our 'superconsciousness.'[764]

Gamma brain waves originate in the thalamus and move from the back of the brain to the frontal lobe and back again 40 plus times per second. This full sweeping, rapid pulsing motion engages the entire brain at the same time, instead of one specific section. Gamma brain waves activate the glia brain and the limbic system.

I often slide into 'full-brain' Gamma waves when I am doing the Spiral Breath technique. For me, I internally hear a 'wooshing' sound, as the brain waves travel at a rapid speed back and forth from my brainstem to my frontal lobes. Then I move into a heightened state of awareness. I am peaceful and energized at the same time. It is a joyful experience when I achieve it. I have to say, it startled me the first time I experienced this. I recall saying out loud, "What just happened?" Fortunately, I was able to return to the 'full-brain' state when I resumed the Spiral Breath.

When musicians and athletes are in the "zone," they have initiated their Gamma brain waves. It has been found that visually practicing the music or routine in their mind (seeing themselves in action) improves their performances, locks in their memory response and entrains their reflexes.[765]

Gamma brain waves are responsible for acutely remembering every detail of a memorable event. They bind all the senses together, such as sight, smells and sounds, for vivid recall of an event or experience.[766] For example, the night that your 'special someone' told you that they loved you. You can remember what you were wearing, what song was playing and every detail of the surrounding environment. You recall the feel of their breath on your ear as those special words were spoken and the static in the space between your lips just before you kissed. Your heart begins to race in this moment, recalling the memory like it happened yesterday, instead of thirty years ago.[767]

Those with lower amounts of Gamma brain wave activity might be experiencing learning disabilities, memory issues, depression or a lack of focus.

If you are lacking in a particular brain wave pattern, there are several ways to increase them. I have found that focused breathing, like the Spiral Breath technique stimulates brain wave activity, especially when you enhance the breath while listening to Alpha, Theta, Delta or Gamma brain wave patterns. Meditation, listening to Solfeggio tones and being at high vibrational sacred places are also effective. Using brain wave entrainment with binaural beats can be beneficial when you wish to increase, decrease or balance brain wave activity.

✡ ✡ ✡

Binaural Beats

Brain wave entrainment allows one to enhance a desired state of being, tap into inner wisdom and access altered states of consciousness by influencing a specific brainwave response.[768]

Binaural beats (also called beat frequencies) are considered to be an 'audio hallucination.'[769] The word binaural means 'having or relating to two ears.' Binaural beats are auditory brainstem responses that initiate when two different pure-tone sine waves are introduced one in each ear. Both frequencies must be lower than 1000 Hz and have less than a 30 Hz difference between them. For example, a 200 Hz pure tone is presented to a person's right ear, while a 205 Hz pure tone is simultaneously presented to the left ear. The listener would perceive a third tone in addition to the other two tones. The third tone is called the beat frequency or binaural beat and correlates to a frequency of 5 Hz, which is the difference between the two original pure tones and in the Theta zone.[770, 771]

Below 1000 Hz, the wave length of the frequency is longer than the diameter of the human skull. Lower frequencies produce longer wave lengths. Therefore, incoming frequencies that are below 1000 Hz will curve around the skull and are heard by both ears. Due to the distance between the ears, the brain "hears" the input from the ears as being 'out of phase' with each other (see image 9.5). As the sound wave moves around the skull, each ear receives a different portion of the wave. The brain has the ability to detect a difference in a waveform phase, which allows it to perceive binaural beats.[772]

The beat frequencies/binaural beats are the result of the two different pure tone frequencies that are not even multiples or harmonics of one another. The tones alternately reinforce and cancel each other out to produce a new different frequency or tone that is much lower. These interacting tones create an amplitude modulated standing wave, that moves back and forth between an 'in phase' and 'out of phase' vibrational pattern. They come together and oppose each other.

The binaural beat is not heard in the normal human range of hearing, which is 20 Hz to 20,000 HZ. It is 'perceived' as an audible beat within the superior olivary nuclei of the brainstem. The brain follows along with the new 'perceived' frequency, producing brainwaves at the same rate or oscillation as the perceived Hertzian frequency. This neural brain rhythm entrainment is known as the 'frequency following response' (FFR). Meaning that, we could use a specific binaural beat frequency to achieve a particular dominate brainwave pattern as a conscious management technique.[773, 774]

Frequency Follow Response (FFR) has been used for centuries. Ancient cultures knew that rhythmic sound repetition could induce a trance-like state that would enhance a powerful healing or spiritual experience. Using repetitive drumming and chanting at 4.5 beats per second, Tibetan monks, Native American Indians, master healers and Yogis could generate a Theta brainwave state that would transcend consciousness and facilitate healing, concentration and spiritual growth.[775] Music in 4/4 time tends to make us feel good because the musical rhythm beat creates a Theta Wave pattern that can entrain our brain waves.[776]

Listening to binaural beats is best experienced with head phones or ear buds, although it can also be achieved with dual speakers. Listening to binaural beats is a fast and easy way to shift your brain waves. Incorporating brain entrainment with binaural beats and other modalities, like the Spiral Breath, can greatly increase your desired results of relaxation, easier emotional balancing, heightened study abilities and higher levels of consciousness.

As you can see, color, sound, sacred geometry, frequency and brain wave patterns are extremely important to our health and higher consciousness. Daily practice of the Spiral Breath technique and incorporating any of the above modalities with it, can assist your progress to strengthen your glia activity, improve mental clarity, increase joy, extra sensory perceptions, higher consciousness and simply enhance your life.

645 *Let There be Light* written by Darius Dinshah page 7-8
646 *Let There be Light* written by Darius Dinshah page 8
647 *Let There be Light* written by Darius Dinshah pages 37-40
648 *Let There be Light* written by Darius Dinshah page 40
649 *Let There be Light* written by Darius Dinshah pages 96-97
650 *Opticks - A Treatise of the Reflections, Refractions, Inflections and Colours of Light* written by Sir Isaac Newton http://www.gutenberg.org/files/33504/33504-h/33504-h.htm[7/9/12 9:44:47 AM]
The Project Gutenberg eBook of Op-ticks:, by Sir Isaac Newton, Knt.
651 http://www.gutenberg.org/files/33504/33504-h/33504-h.htm[7/9/12 9:44:47 AM]
The Project Gutenberg eBook of Opticks:, by Sir Isaac Newton, Knt. page 223
652 *Opticks - A Treatise of the Reflections, Refractions, Inflections and Colours of Light* written by Sir Isaac Newton http://www.gutenberg.org/files/33504/33504-h/33504-h.htm[7/9/12 9:44:47 AM]
The Project Gutenberg eBook of Opticks:, by Sir Isaac Newton, Knt.
653 *Let There be Light* written by Darius Dinshah page 118
654 *Pyramid Energy: The Philosophy of God, The Science of Man* by Mary and Dean Hardy, Kenneth and Marjorie Kil-lick page 205
655 *Let There be Light* written by Darius Dinshah pages 94-95
656 *Let There be Light* written by Darius Dinshah page 16
657 *Let There be Light* written by Darius Dinshah pages 39-40
658 *Let There be Light* written by Darius Dinshah page 95
659 Bell, Dr Fred. *Rays of Truth – Crystals of Light: Information & Guidance for The Golden Age* . Kindle Edition loca-tion 3651
660 Horowitz, Leonard G.. *DNA: PIRATES OF THE SACRED SPIRAL* . UNKNOWN. Kindle Edition.
661 Sacred Frequencies: The Cycle of Time Number 432 https://altered-states.net/barry/update205/
662 https://en.wikipedia.org/wiki/Sound
663 https://en.wikipedia.org/wiki/Sound
664 *The Physics of Sound* by Benjamin Hollis https://method-behind-the-music.com/mechanics/physics/
665 *Intervals, Scales, Tones and the Concert Pitch C* by Maria Renold page 20
666 *Tha Pythagorean Harp (Kanon) Renaissance of Resonance* by Jim Doney Mandalatrece http://www.thakanon.org/pythagorean-harp-kanon.html
667 Pythagoras https://en.wikipedia.org/wiki/Pythagoras
668 Pythagoras https://en.wikipedia.org/wiki/Pythagoras
669 *Pyramid Energy: The Philosophy of God, The Science of Man* by Mary and Dean Hardy, Kenneth and Marjorie Killick page 269
670 Bell, Dr Fred. *Rays of Truth – Crystals of Light: Information & Guidance for The Golden Age* . Kindle Edition. Location 4173
671 Sacred Frequencies: The Cycle of Time Number 432 https://altered-states.net/barry/update205/
672 *Planetary Harmonics &Neurobiological Resonances in Light, Sound & Brain Wav Frequencies, Including the Influence of Color* by Nick Anthony Fiorenza http://www.lunarplanner.com/Harmonics/planetary-harmonics.html#
673 *The Venus Blueprint: Uncovering the Ancient Science of Sacred Spaces* by Richard Merrick page 20-43
674 *Magdalene's Lost Legacy: Symbolic Numbers and the Sacred Union in Christianity*, Margret Starbird pages 29-32
675 Music of the Pyramids https://altered-states.net/barry/update205/
676 Sacred Frequencies: The Cycle of Time Number 432 https://altered-states.net/barry/update205/
677 Arithmetic Relating to the Number 432 http://web.archive.org/web/20030623014504/ http://wordmax.com/gallery432/432meas.htm
678 *James Furia's Music Scale Symmetry* http://web.archive.org/web/20030623014635/ http://wordmax.com/gallery432/432musi.htm
679 440 Hz Music - Conspiracy To Detune Us From Natural 432 Hz Harmonics? https://www.shiftfrequency.com/george-orwells-ghost-440hz-music-conspiracy-to-detune-us-from-natural-432hz-harmonics/
680 Horowitz, Leonard G. *DNA: PIRATES OF THE SACRED SPIRAL*. UNKNOWN. Kindle Edition.
681 Sacred Frequencies: The Cycle of Time Number 432 https://altered-states.net/barry/update205/
682 Bell, Dr Fred. *Rays of Truth – Crystals of Light: Information & Guidance for The Golden Age* . Kindle Edition. Location 2528 - 2534
683 Bell, Dr Fred. Rays of Truth – Crystals of Light: Information & Guidance for The Golden Age . Kindle Edition. Loca-tion 3651
684 Music of the Pyramids https://altered-states.net/barry/update205/
685 440 Hz Music - Conspiracy To Detune Us From Natural 432 Hz Harmonics? https://www.shiftfrequency.com/george-orwells-ghost-440hz-music-conspiracy-to-detune-us-from-natural-432hz-harmonics/

[686] 440 Hz Music - Conspiracy To Detune Us From Natural 432 Hz Harmonics? https://www.shiftfrequency.com/george-orwells-ghost-440hz-music-conspiracy-to-detune-us-from-natural-432hz-harmonics/
[687] Horowitz, Leonard G. *The Book of 528: Prosperity Key of Love* (p. 136-141). Tetrahedron Media. Kindle Edition.
[688] *The Code of the Ancients: Introduction to Gematria and Code-Related Numbers* by Joseph E. Mason
[689] https://en.wikipedia.org/wiki/Gematria
[690] *Magdalene's Lost Legacy: Symbolic Numbers and the Sacred Union in Christianity*, Margret Starbird page 139-141
[691] The Number 153 - The Symbolism and Spiritual Significance http://www.greatdreams.com/153.htm
[692] *The Great Pyramid and a 153 Fishes in the Net* by Joseph E. Mason http://www.greatdreams.com/numbers/jerry/153.htm
[693] Solfeggio Scale Effect On The Mind and Body http://www.kryschendo.com/uploads/Solfeggio_for_Ponder_Final.pdf
[694] Horowitz, Leonard G. *The Book of 528: Prosperity Key of Love* (p. 44). Tetrahedron Media. Kindle Edition.
[695] Solfeggio Scale Effect On The Mind and Body http://www.kryschendo.com/uploads/Solfeggio_for_Ponder_Final.pdf
[696] What are Solfeggio Frequencies? https://attunedvibrations.com/solfeggio/
[697] Horowitz, Leonard G. *The Book of 528: Prosperity Key of Love* (p. 37). Tetrahedron Media. Kindle Edition.
[698] Horowitz, Leonard G. *The Book of 528: Prosperity Key of Love* (p. 43-44). Tetrahedron Media. Kindle Edition.
[699] http://www.francescoraffaele.com/egypt/hesyra/new/ntrykht1.jpg
[700] *Let's Talk About ISO-Principle: The Introduction* by Erin Seibert, MA, MT-BCMusic Therapy https://musictherapytime.com/2015/05/19/lets-talk-about-iso-principle-the-introduction/
[701] Entrainment: The universal law of harmony http://meditationiseasy.com/meditation-techniques/entrainment-the-universal-law-of-harmony/
[702] https://en.wikipedia.org/wiki/Entrainment_(chronobiology)
[703] Entrainment: The universal law of harmony http://meditationiseasy.com/meditation-techniques/entrainment-the-universal-law-of-harmony/
[704] Entrainment: The Universal Law of Harmony   http://www.meditationiseasy.com/binaural-beats/entrainment-the-universal-law-of-harmony/
[705] *The Chemistry of Essential Oils Made Simple* by David Stewart Ph.D, D.N.M. page 180-181
[706] 5 Types Of Brain Waves Frequencies: Gamma, Beta, Alpha, Theta, Delta https://mentalhealthdaily.com/2014/04/15/5-types-of-brain-waves-frequencies-gamma-beta-alpha-theta-delta/
[707] *Evolve your Brain: The Science of Changing Your Mind* by Dr. Joe Dispenza page 462
[708] *The Other Brain* by Douglas Fields, Ph. D. page 260-261
[709] https://dictionary.cambridge.org/us/dictionary/english/amplitude
[710] *The High Performance Mind: Mastering Brainwaves For Insight, Healing and Creativity* by Anna Wise page 3
[711] *The High Performance Mind: Mastering Brainwaves For Insight, Healing and Creativity* by Anna Wise page 3
[712] In Phase/Out of Phase: http://mcat-review.org/waves-periodic-motion.php
[713] *The Other Brain* by Douglas Fields, Ph. D. page 152
[714] *The Biology of Belief:Unleashing the Power of Consciousness, Matter & Miracles* by Bruce H. Lipton Ph.D. page 134
[715] *The High Performance Mind: Mastering Brainwaves For Insight, Healing and Creativity* by Anna Wise page 9, 235
[716] *The High Performance Mind: Mastering Brainwaves For Insight, Healing and Creativity* by Anna Wise page 9
[717] 5 Types Of Brain Waves Frequencies: Gamma, Beta, Alpha, Theta, Delta https://mentalhealthdaily.com/2014/04/15/5-types-of-brain-waves-frequencies-gamma-beta-alpha-theta-delta/
[718] *Alpha-Theta Therapy and the Neurobehavioral Treatment of Addictions, Disorders and Trauma* by Nancy P. White, Ph.D., Leonard M. Richards, Th.D., in Introduction to Quantitative EEG and Neurofeedback (Second Edition), 2009 pages 143-166 https://www.sciencedirect.com/topics/agricultural-and-biological-sciences/brain-waves
[719] *The High Performance Mind: Mastering Brainwaves For Insight, Healing and Creativity* by Anna Wise pages 3-4
[720] 5 Types Of Brain Waves Frequencies: Gamma, Beta, Alpha, Theta, Delta https://mentalhealthdaily.com/2014/04/15/5-types-of-brain-waves-frequencies-gamma-beta-alpha-theta-delta/
[721] 5 Types Of Brain Waves Frequencies: Gamma, Beta, Alpha, Theta, Delta https://mentalhealthdaily.com/2014/04/15/5-types-of-brain-waves-frequencies-gamma-beta-alpha-theta-delta/
[722] *Breaking The Habit of Being Yourself: How to Lose Your Mind and Create a New One* by Dr. Joe Dispenza page 192-200
[723] *Breaking The Habit of Being Yourself: How to Lose Your Mind and Create a New One* by Dr. Joe Dispenza page 192-193
[724] 5 Types Of Brain Waves Frequencies: Gamma, Beta, Alpha, Theta, Delta   https://mentalhealthdaily.com/2014/04/15/5-types-of-brain-waves-frequencies-gamma-beta-alpha-theta-delta/
[725] 5 Types Of Brain Waves Frequencies: Gamma, Beta, Alpha, Theta, Delta   https://mentalhealthdaily.com/

726 2014/04/15/5-types-of-brain-waves-frequencies-gamma-beta-alpha-theta-delta/
726 5 Types Of Brain Waves Frequencies: Gamma, Beta, Alpha, Theta, Delta https://mentalhealthdaily.com/2014/04/15/5-types-of-brain-waves-frequencies-gamma-beta-alpha-theta-delta/
727 *Your Subconscious Brain Can Change Your Life* by Dr. Mike Dow page 77
728 *The High Performance Mind: Mastering Brainwaves For Insight, Healing and Creativity* by Anna Wise pages 3-4
729 *The High Performance Mind: Mastering Brainwaves For Insight, Healing and Creativity* by Anna Wise page 4
730 *Alpha-Theta Therapy and the Neurobehavioral Treatment of Addictions, Disorders and Trauma* by Nancy P. White, Ph.D., Leonard M. Richards, Th.D., in Introduction to Quantitative EEG and Neurofeedback (Second Edition), 2009 pages 143-166 https://www.sciencedirect.com/topics/agricultural-and-biological-sciences/brain-waves
731 5 Types Of Brain Waves Frequencies: Gamma, Beta, Alpha, Theta, Delta https://mentalhealthdaily.com/2014/04/15/5-types-of-brain-waves-frequencies-gamma-beta-alpha-theta-delta/
732 This Is How Brain Waves Contribute To The State of Mind https://blog.mindvalley.com/brain-waves/
733 5 Types Of Brain Waves Frequencies: Gamma, Beta, Alpha, Theta, Delta https://mentalhealthdaily.com/2014/04/15/5-types-of-brain-waves-frequencies-gamma-beta-alpha-theta-delta/
734 https://www.psychologytoday.com/us/blog/the-athletes-way/201504/alpha-brain-waves-boost-creativity-and-reduce-depression
735 *The High Performance Mind: Mastering Brainwaves For Insight, Healing and Creativity* by Anna Wise page 94, 103
736 *The High Performance Mind: Mastering Brainwaves For Insight, Healing and Creativity* by Anna Wise page 87
737 *The High Performance Mind: Mastering Brainwaves For Insight, Healing and Creativity* by Anna Wise page 4
738 5 Types Of Brain Waves Frequencies: Gamma, Beta, Alpha, Theta, Delta https://mentalhealthdaily.com/2014/04/15/5-types-of-brain-waves-frequencies-gamma-beta-alpha-theta-delta/
739 *Breaking The Habit of Being Yourself: How to Lose Your Mind and Create a New One* by Dr. Joe Dispenza page 188
740 5 Types Of Brain Waves Frequencies: Gamma, Beta, Alpha, Theta, Delta https://mentalhealthdaily.com/2014/04/15/5-types-of-brain-waves-frequencies-gamma-beta-alpha-theta-delta/
741 5 Types Of Brain Waves Frequencies: Gamma, Beta, Alpha, Theta, Delta https://mentalhealthdaily.com/2014/04/15/5-types-of-brain-waves-frequencies-gamma-beta-alpha-theta-delta/
742 5 Types Of Brain Waves Frequencies: Gamma, Beta, Alpha, Theta, Delta https://mentalhealthdaily.com/2014/04/15/5-types-of-brain-waves-frequencies-gamma-beta-alpha-theta-delta/
743 *The Biology of Belief:Unleashing the Power of Consciousness, Matter & Miracles* by Bruce H. Lipton Ph.D. page 132-133
744 *The Biology of Belief:Unleashing the Power of Consciousness, Matter & Miracles* by Bruce H. Lipton Ph.D. page 132-133
745 *Breaking The Habit of Being Yourself: How to Lose Your Mind and Create a New One* by Dr. Joe Dispenza page 189
746 *Your Subconscious Brain Can Change Your Life* by Dr. Mike Dow page 76
747 5 Types Of Brain Waves Frequencies: Gamma, Beta, Alpha, Theta, Delta https://mentalhealthdaily.com/2014/04/15/5-types-of-brain-waves-frequencies-gamma-beta-alpha-theta-delta/
748 *Breaking The Habit of Being Yourself: How to Lose Your Mind and Create a New One* by Dr. Joe Dispenza page 189
749 *Breaking The Habit of Being Yourself: How to Lose Your Mind and Create a New One* by Dr. Joe Dispenza page 203-205
750 Evolve your Brain: The Science of Changing Your Mind by Dr. Joe Dispenza pages 463-465
751 *Breaking The Habit of Being Yourself: How to Lose Your Mind and Create a New One* by Dr. Joe Dispenza page 203
752 *Breaking The Habit of Being Yourself: How to Lose Your Mind and Create a New One* by Dr. Joe Dispenza pages 203-210
753 *Breaking The Habit of Being Yourself: How to Lose Your Mind and Create a New One* by Dr. Joe Dispenza pages 203-210
754 *The High Performance Mind: Mastering Brainwaves For Insight, Healing and Creativity* by Anna Wise pages 71-76
755 5 Types Of Brain Waves Frequencies: Gamma, Beta, Alpha, Theta, Delta https://mentalhealthdaily.com/2014/04/15/5-types-of-brain-waves-frequencies-gamma-beta-alpha-theta-delta/
756 5 Types Of Brain Waves Frequencies: Gamma, Beta, Alpha, Theta, Delta https://mentalhealthdaily.com/2014/04/15/5-types-of-brain-waves-frequencies-gamma-beta-alpha-theta-delta/
757 5 Types Of Brain Waves Frequencies: Gamma, Beta, Alpha, Theta, Delta https://mentalhealthdaily.com/2014/04/15/5-types-of-brain-waves-frequencies-gamma-beta-alpha-theta-delta/
758 5 Types Of Brain Waves Frequencies: Gamma, Beta, Alpha, Theta, Delta https://mentalhealthdaily.com/2014/04/15/5-types-of-brain-waves-frequencies-gamma-beta-alpha-theta-delta/
759 5 Types Of Brain Waves Frequencies: Gamma, Beta, Alpha, Theta, Delta https://mentalhealthdaily.com/2014/04/15/5-types-of-brain-waves-frequencies-gamma-beta-alpha-theta-delta/
760 5 Types Of Brain Waves Frequencies: Gamma, Beta, Alpha, Theta, Delta https://mentalhealthdaily.com/2014/04/15/5-types-of-brain-waves-frequencies-gamma-beta-alpha-theta-delta/
761 *The High Performance Mind: Mastering Brainwaves For Insight, Healing and Creativity* by Anna Wise pages 198-200

[762] *The High Performance Mind: Mastering Brainwaves For Insight, Healing and Creativity* by Anna Wise pages 7-8, 204-207
[763] *Breaking The Habit of Being Yourself: How to Lose Your Mind and Create a New One* by Dr. Joe Dispenza pages 190-191
[764] What are Gamma Waves https://blog.mindvalley.com/gamma-brain-waves/
[765] What are Gamma Waves https://blog.mindvalley.com/gamma-brain-waves/
[766] 5 Types Of Brain Waves Frequencies: Gamma, Beta, Alpha, Theta, Delta https://mentalhealthdaily.com/2014/04/15/5-types-of-brain-waves-frequencies-gamma-beta-alpha-theta-delta/
[767] What are Gamma Waves https://blog.mindvalley.com/gamma-brain-waves/
[768] *Awakening the Mind: A Guide to Mastering the Power of Your Brain Waves* by Anna Wise page 122-123
[769] https://www.healthyhearing.com/report/51394-How-the-brain-processes-binaural-beats
[770] https://blog.mindvalley.com/what-are-binaural-beats/
[771] https://www.binauralbeatsmeditation.com/the-science/
[772] What are Binaural Beats http://web-us.com/thescience.htm
[773] What are Binaural Beats http://web-us.com/thescience.htm
[774] https://www.binauralbeatsmeditation.com/the-science/
[775] https://www.binauralbeatsmeditation.com/the-science/
[776] *Your Subconscious Brain Can Change Your Life* by Dr. Mike Dow page 75

Chapter 10:

Tachyon and Energy

Tachyon energy is the "origins of matter."

✡ ✡ ✡

SUBTLE ORGANIZING ENERGY FIELD

Every atom, molecule and cell has a Subtle Organizing Energy Field (SOEF), which exists just below the speed of light. The Subtle Organizing Energy Field is the perfectly organized, non-manifested state of subtle vibrational energy that exists before it is manifested or condensed into matter or mass.

"The scientific community has shown that matter is nothing more than the condensation of a vibrating, universal substrate of subtle energy. This is the virtual condition that is known as zero-point-energy. Matter is created when zero-point-energy is transformed into tachyon energy. The tachyon energy is then transformed by the Subtle Organized Energy Fields (SOEF)."[777]

The material universe is merely the highest, refined subtle energy that has been condensed into a multitude of dense forms of matter.

✡ ✡ ✡

ZERO-POINT-ENERGY

Zero-Point-Energy, also known as Free Energy or Quantum Vacuum Energy is formless, unmanifested and infinite. It is the energy that remains after all other energy, such as particles, molecules and light are removed within the thermodynamic temperature of Absolute Zero.[778] Zero Point Energy (ZPE) is what the Bible refers to as the *firmament*. This physical vacuum is densely saturated with "virtual particles" that vibrate, fluctuate and permeate all of space/time.[779]

✡ ✡ ✡

ABSOLUTE ZERO

When matter is cooled to the temperature of Absolute Zero, motion is undetected. Absolute Zero is measured at minus 273 degrees Celsius (on a Kelvin scale this temperature is set at zero) or minus 459.67 degrees Fahrenheit (on the Rankine scale this temperature is set at zero). Absolute Zero is the point at which all fundamental particles of nature appear to have no movement or oscillation. However, even though no movement is detected from these particles, there still exists an omnipresent energy field. The kinetic energy (vibration) cannot be removed.[780]

Zero-Point-Energy is formless and Tachyon is Form.

✡ ✡ ✡

TACHYON ENERGY

Pythagoras called this energy *pneuma*. Baron Dr. Carl Von Reichenbach called it *od*. Dr. Franz Mesmer called it *animal magnetism*. The founder of homeopathy, Dr. Samuel Hahnemann called this energy *vital force*. The movie Star Wars called it *The Force*. The Russians call it *bioplasma*. Pre-Relativity physicists called it *ether* and post-Relativity physicists call it the *superquatum field*.[781]

So what is it? Tachyon Energy is the very first energetic structure that emerges out of the non-structured, formless and unlimited Zero-Point-Energy. Dr. Hans Nieper says that, *"The Tachyon field exists on the boundary between energy and matter."*

Matter begins when Zero-Point-Energy starts to slow down and condense into faster-than-the-speed-of-light Tachyon Energy. Once the Tachyon Field is energized, the Subtle Organizing Energy Field converts Tachyon Energy into frequencies that generate physical form.[782]

Tachyon comes from the Greek word *takhys*, which means "swift, rapid, hasty." It is related to *takhos* meaning "speed swiftness." In sailing terms, *tacking* is a maneuver by which a sailing vessel, whose desired course is into the wind, turns its bow (front of the boat) towards the wind so that the direction that the wind blows alternates from one side of the boat to the other. This zigzag action allows progress in the desired direction.

Even though Tachyon and Zero-Point-Energy are relatively new to the scientific world, the knowledge of this energy and matter goes back to ancient cultures around the world. The following is an excerpt from the ancient text *'The Gospel of Mary.'* Jesus is teaching the Disciples about the origins of matter.

Peter asks Jesus,

"What is matter? Will it last forever?"
The Teacher answered, "All that is born, all that is created;
All the elements of nature are interwoven and united with each other.
All that is composed shall be decomposed.
Everything returns to its roots;
matter returns to the origins of matter.
Those that have ears let them hear."
THE GOSPEL OF MARY [783]

Ancient texts from the 2nd century AD by Hermes Trismegistus presented dialogues discussing the mastering of energy. These compilations were translated and became the Corpus Hermeticum. The Emerald Tablet written by Hermes appeared in the 4th century with the Gnostic Library that was found in Nag Hammadi. The Kybalion simplified The Seven Great Hermetic Principles to Self-Mastery, which talk about matter, light and energy in the same or similar wording to that of Tachyon Energy.

This is the field of Light that Jesus refers to as the spiritual "White Light."

The qualities of Tachyon's are much like Zero-Point Energy, varying only in that Tachyon is a structured energy field.

Faster-than-the-speed-of-light Tachyon energy continues to condense with the help of the Subtle Organizing Energy Field until it transforms itself into matter and form.[784]

This is also how a thought manifests itself into reality. Being electromagnetic in our physical makeup, when a thought or prayer is birthed into the Realm of All That Is, it creates an electrical charge. This charge triggers an energetic response that begins the condensing of Zero-Point-Energy into Tachyon Energy. The Subtle Organizing Energy Field joins in to convert the structured energy of the Tachyons into a vibrational energy that manifests itself into being. It is art of manifestation.

Nikola Tesla had also reduced the auric field down to the same faster-than-the-speed-of-light Tachyon energy. The auric field is the electromagnetic energy field that surrounds a 'living' thing, be it human, plant, animal, etc.

Tesla believed that the Tachyon particle pairs are the absolute building blocks and foundation of all creation. Tachyon energy is ever present and ever changing.

Kenneth Killick, scientist, author, teacher and designer of pyramids spelled Tachyon with an "i" instead of a "y." He described Tachion/Tachyon Energy as "a charged electromagnetic field that is the glue of the universe" and that "Tachion Energy is the bond between the spiritual and the physical realms."

"Tachion particles are not physical. They are charged, structured energy fields that form the sub-atomic particles of the atom. Tachion particles always operate simultaneously in pairs, such as, + +, - -, + - or - + pairs." Kenneth believed that the electromagnetic charges of the pairs make up the three great planes of consciousness. The (- -) pairs form the physical world, the (- +) or (+ -) pairs form the mental world and the (+ +) pairs form the spiritual world.[785]

Between the physical consciousness of the negative/negative particles and the spiritual consciousness of the positive/positive particles, you will find the mental consciousness of the negative/positive and the positive/negative pairs.

Tachyon particles oscillate in their pure energy fields. When Tachyons are refocused into light, the movement of opposite energy creates a spiraling effect as they rotate and refocus their direction. At each point of crossover, the field of rotation changes direction and the polarity charge changes, creating the three pairs or combinations.

This action of movement creates the pattern of an infinity sign. One half of the spiral has a positive frequency and the other half has a negative frequency. The two opposite frequencies come together to create one blended frequency before refocusing to their original and opposing frequencies. Here, the continual physical consciousness and the continual spiritual consciousness constantly empower the mental consciousness. The more you focus on spiraling your energy and increasing your Tachyon Field, the faster you will be able to achieve mind over matter and ultimately to overcome matter into light.

The clocking action of the positive/positive pair is clockwise (CW). The clocking action of the negative/negative pair is counter-clockwise (CCW). The positive/negative or negative/positive pairs rotate either CW or CCW, but always at 90 degrees to the plane of the positive/positive or negative/negative pairs.[786]

Kenneth Killick taught us that within the course of the *"Tachion (Tachyon) motion, all motions have a path of 240 degrees. Unlike electron spin, there is no centrifugal force, thus no gravity. Tachions are of the nature whereby they can pass through matter and/or other fields of energy without being effected or affecting such fields or matter."*[787]

Kenneth also shared that this clocking action pattern of the Tachyon motion is the same pattern that the Hopi Indian's use in their rain dance. It is also believed to be the pattern used by the Israelites to take down the walls of Jericho. The motion path of the Tachyon, as well as the pattern movement of the dance, create a Standing Columnar Wave. When the trumpet sounded at Jericho, the sound frequency fractured the standing wave, which crumbled the walls. On a side note, it is believed that the Hopi Indians are the lost tribe of Israel.[788]

Kenneth Killick taught us that *"when you change the energy, you change the manifestation of mass."* Once we understand the principles of Hermetic Law, we can learn to master 'mind over matter,' which is mastering Tachyon Energy.[789]

It is amazing that the principles which Hermes developed so many thousands of years ago are as true today as when they were written. Hermes Trismegistus was regarded by the Ancient Egyptians as the 'scribe of the gods,' the 'master of the masters' and thrice great for knowing three parts of the wisdom of the universe. Only fragments of his teachings have been discovered and are considered to be the earliest of all alchemical works to have survived. They are estimated to have been written as early as c.650. Translations have been used by Plato, secret societies, to advise kings and as the foundation of many esoteric cultures.

Hermes was known as the father of Wisdom, the founder of Astrology and discoverer of Alchemy. He shared the teachings that he evolved, so humanity would know and practice the 'Principles of Truth." Temple trained Hierophants and Masters traveled the earth freely sharing the wisdom to those who were willing to learn and understand. [790]

> *"Oh let not the flame die out! Cherished age after age in its dark cavern - in its holy temples cherished. Fed by pure ministers of love - let not the flame die out."*
>
> HERMES TRISTMEGISTUS [791]

Science is proving what Hermes knew and taught. The best part of this Wisdom is that we can achieve a higher state of being with the knowledge; the practice of raising our energy and holding a Higher Resonance and level of Consciousness.

> *"The Principles of Truth are Seven.*
> *He who knows these, understandingly, possesses the Magic Key before whose touch all the Doors of the Temple fly open."*
>
> THE KYBALION

The 7 Principles of Hermetic Law are:

1. The Principle of Mentalism
2. The Principle of Correspondence
3. The Principle of Vibration
4. The Principle of Polarity
5. The Principle of Rhythm
6. The Principle of Cause and Effect
7. The Principle of Gender

Because the 7 Principles of Hermetic Law express the action and properties of Tachyon Energy, I decided to include them in this chapter. I will use the Principles from *The Kybalion* written by the Three Initiates, as they are written in wordage that is easy to understand. Here they are:

7 PRINCIPLES OF HERMETIC LAW

The First Principle of Hermetic Law is Mentalism:

"The Mind is All; The Universe is Mental."

For anything to exist, a thought had to form first, which sparks an electrical charge that triggers the Tachyons to begin the formation of physical reality or manifestation.[792] "Your thoughts are seeds, plant positive seeds in your mind garden."[793]

This Principle addresses the outward manifestations that we know as 'matter.' It encompasses Matter, Energy, that which we experience with our Senses, Thought and anything pertaining to the Material Realm of the Universe. That which is Seen and Unseen - Form and Formless - Manifest and Un-Manifest - Known and UnKnown.

With the knowledge of the Tachyon Field, we can influence the subatomic particles of Tachyon Energy to manifest our desires; to do what we think we can do, to be who we think we can be; to access Higher Consciousness and increase our personal energy, so as to transform ourselves back into Light and travel the Universe.[794, 795]

Having personally raised my energy to become a column of Light and my Light Body on several occasions is what put me on my path to discover and teach Enlightenment. My search to explain how I became Light and how I could share the 'how to' with others led me to teachings in many forms and to these Principles of Truths from Hermes.

The Second Principle of Hermetic Law is Correspondence:

"As Above, So Below; So Below. As Above."
Simply put, 'Everything is Connected.'

From The Emerald Tablet of Hermes Trismegistus, he writes, *"That which is Below corresponds to that which is Above and that which is Above corresponds to that which is Below, to accomplish the miracle of the One Thing."*

It means that there is always a correspondence between the laws of phenomena of the various 'planes' of being and life. Whatever happens on any level of reality, whether it is physical, mental or spiritual planes, it also happens on every other level.

This concept is founded upon the mirror image of all things, such as, the stars and planets reflect their properties and aspects on earth, God created man in his own image; the microcosm is as the macrocosm and visa versa, what we create in the spiritual realm, will manifest in the physical realm and visa versa.

In context to the above, the scientific world was surprised to discover that an atom proved strikingly similar to a solar system. Both are comprised of particles kept in orbit by the gravity of an energetic core. Modern technology had mirrored the wisdom of the Hermes *As Above, So Below*.[769, 797, 798]

The Third Principle of Hermetic Law is Vibration:

"Nothing rests, everything moves; everything vibrates."

Whether in a light beam or a rock, all molecules of matter move. Rotations can be so slow that the matter appears to have no movement. On the opposite side, objects can spin so fast, as to actually appear to be still, like the Earth. Yet, light beams and rainbows are visible, but their molecules are not touchable.[799, 800]

Tachyon Energy never rests, every particle of Light and every molecule of matter oscillates, vibrates or resonates. The only difference between The Infinite ALL of Pure Source before form (Energy), be it Zero-Point-Energy, Tachyon Energy, Subtle Organizing Energy Field, Matter, Thought/Mind, Light or Spirit is vibration and the rate of its speed, intensity or rapidity.

The higher you can attune your frequency and resonance, the more Light you can bring into your energy and the greater access of Higher Consciousness you will achieve.

The Fourth Principle of Hermetic Law is Polarity:

"Everything is Dual, everything has poles, everything has its pair of opposites, like and unlike are the same; opposites are identical in nature, but different in degree; extremes meet; all truths are but half truths; all paradoxes may be reconciled."

Throughout the universe there are degrees of polarity. This comes back to Tachyon Energy. Remember that Tachyon pairs have a polarity of energy that move opposite from each other but in unison. The negative/negative Tachyon particle relates to the physical frequencies and the positive/positive particle relates to the spiritual. These particles can also be viewed as matter and anti-matter.

This positive or negative charge makes up the many frequencies of electrical energy. Polarity can be viewed in magnetic energy. When placing two magnets together, 'like' poles will repel each other, while the opposite poles will attract each other.

Polarities are also present in everything from life to emotions, such as hot/cold, wet/dry, night/day, failure/success, love/hate, self-worth/worthless, fear/anger or agree/disagree.

The difference of opposites consists merely of the difference of degrees of the same thing. Like night and day for instance, where darkness leaves off, light begins. They are varying degrees between the opposite poles of that phenomenon.[801, 802]

The Fifth Principle of Hermetic Law is Rhythm:

"Everything flows, out and in; everything has its tides, all things rise and fall; the pendulum swing manifests in everything; the measure of swing to the right is the measure of swing to the left; rhythm compensates."

Rhythm is any measured flow or movement; a strong, repeating pattern of movement or sound; an ordered recurrent alternation of strong and weak elements in a flow of sound and silence.

Everything in life has a flow and a natural, measured rhythm or pace, whether it is of the Universe, solar systems, humans, animals, plants, molecules, energy, matter or anti-matter.

We inhale and exhale. We have our circadian rhythm; the rise and fall of the tide, as well as, the moon cycles, which are in an ordered recurrent measurement, as is our seasons and the orbital movement of the planets and stars. All have a flow, a measure and a rhythm.

We have 12 paired meridians and they have an innate daily cycle that they follow. Every two hours, one of the meridians comes into its highest action at a specific time of the day, while its paired meridian is at its lowest action.

Atoms, molecules and sound oscillate, resonate and vibrate in measured waves or rotations, which create a rhythm.

The wave phase of the Tachyon pairs rotate in unison and create a rhythm that is ever present and infinite flowing. It is when we learn how to USE Rhythm and Energy to benefit, instead of being Used by it, that we find Mastery through Alchemy. "Change the energy, you change the manifestation of mass (matter)." [803, 804]

The Sixth Principle of Hermetic Law is Cause and Effect:

"Every Cause has its Effect; every Effect has its Cause; everything happens according to Law; Chance is but a name for Law not recognized; there are many planes of causation but nothing escapes the Law."

This is also called the Law of Karma. For every action, there is a reaction. Whatever you focus on, you manifest more of it. Show kindness, kindness is shown to you. Show Gratitude, Gratitude multiplies. Ask and you shall receive. Practice improves your skills.

With Tachyon Energy, an energetic spark, whether thought or action, triggers Tachyon Energy to be birthed from the All or Zero-Point-Energy. The Cause has an Effect and that Effect has an Affect on something else, that Causes that Affect to have an Effect on another something else and so on.

Your actions, your thoughts and your words have an Effect on you and those around you. Take care that your actions are a benefit, your thoughts are positive and your words are uplifting. It is then that you will find Harmony and Freedom.[805, 806]

The Seventh Principle of Hermetic Law is Gender:

"Gender is in everything; everything has its Masculine and Feminine Principles; Gender manifests on all planes."

Everything and everyone contains these two elements, principles or energies. Gender is reflected through the Yin/Yang concept and in the polarity poles of a magnet. Gender is also expressed in energy as electric (+) is Masculine and magnetic energy (-) is Feminine. Together in unison, they create electromagnetic energy.

With Tachion Energy, the Feminine negative/negative (- -) field of the physical plane is returning to the spiritual plane to be regenerated. The Masculine positive/positive (+ +) field of the spiritual plane returns to the physical plane to raise its resonance in order to return to the spiritual plane.[807]

The Feminine principle expresses the aspects of responder and receiving energy, while the Masculine expresses the aspects of the initiator and dispenses energy. Masculine energy is active, Feminine is passive; Masculine is analytical, Feminine is intuitive; Masculine is left-brain, Feminine is right-brain. The Masculine initiates creation and the Feminine brings it into fruition.[808]

In the *Book of Revelations* (1:8), God says, "I AM the Alpha and the Omega," "the first and the last;" "the beginning and the end."

The Alpha or "Great A" is the archetypal symbol of the Sacred Masculine and the Omega "Ω" or the "Great Om" is the archetypal symbol for the Sacred Feminine. The "Great A," is also represented by the triangle △ with the point up.

The "Great OM" is the counterpart and is represented by the triangle ▽ with the point facing down.

Together the △ (masculine) and ▽ (feminine) create the Star of David ✡. The two intertwining equilateral triangles symbolically represent the cosmic dance of opposite energies, union in harmony and sacred marriage.[809]

Learning how and when to utilize both masculine and feminine energies to achieve maximum balance is an art. Mastering the art of influencing Tachyon Energy will help you achieve Higher Consciousness and a true sense of Peace and Harmony. The Spiral Breath technique and the modalities mentioned in this book, whether separate or in tandem, will assist you in raising your Tachyon Energy to FULLY participate in the Tachyon Field of Higher Consciousness.

---

[777] *Tachyon Energy: A New Paradigm in Holistic Healing* written by David Wagner and Dr. Gabriel Cousens
[778] Zero Point Energy www.calphysics.org/zpe.html
[779] *Zero Point Energy: The Fuel of the Future* by Thomas F. Valne, PhD, PE page 13-14
[780] https://en.wikipedia.org/wiki/Absolute_zero
[781] *Tachyon Healing and the Physics of Love* copyright 1995 by Gerry Wolke
[782] *Tachyon Energy: A New Paradigm in Holistic Healing* with David Wagner and Dr. Gabriel Cousens
[783] *The Gospel of Mary Magdalene* translated by Jean-Yves Leloup page 7
[784] *Paramagnetism: Rediscovering Nature's Secret Force of Growth* by Philip S. Callahan Ph.D.
[785] *Pyramid Energy: The Philosophy of God, The Science of Man* by Mary & Dean Hardy and Kenneth Killick page 41
[786] *Pyramid Energy: The Philosophy of God, The Science of Man* by Mary & Dean Hardy and Kenneth Killick page 51
[787] *Pyramid Energy: The Philosophy of God, The Science of Man* by Mary & Dean Hardy and Kenneth Killick page 42
[788] *Pyramid Energy: The Philosophy of God, The Science of Man* by Mary & Dean Hardy and Kenneth Killick page 42
[789] *Pyramid Energy: The Philosophy of God, The Science of Man* by Mary & Dean Hardy and Kenneth Killick page 27
[790] *The Kybalion: A Study of The Hermetic Philosophy of Ancient Egypt and Greece* by Three Initiates pages 11-14
[791] *The Kybalion: A Study of The Hermetic Philosophy of Ancient Egypt and Greece* by Three Initiates page 8
[792] *The Kybalion: A Study of The Hermetic Philosophy of Ancient Egypt and Greece* by Three Initiates pages 15-16
[793] https://en.wikipedia.org/wiki/The_Kybalion
[794] *Pyramid Energy: The Philosophy of God, The Science of Man* by Mary & Dean Hardy and Kenneth Killick pages 27-28, 43
[795] *The Kybalion: A Study of The Hermetic Philosophy of Ancient Egypt and Greece* by Three Initiates pages 15-16, 23-26
[796] *The Kybalion: A Study of The Hermetic Philosophy of Ancient Egypt and Greece* by Three Initiates pages 16-17, 55-63
[797] https://arkintime.com/as-above-so-below/hermes-trismegistus/
[798] *Pyramid Energy: The Philosophy of God, The Science of Man* by Mary & Dean Hardy, Kenneth Killick pages 27-28
[799] *The Kybalion: A Study of The Hermetic Philosophy of Ancient Egypt and Greece* by Three Initiates pages 17, 65-69
[800] *Pyramid Energy: The Philosophy of God, The Science of Man* by Mary & Dean Hardy, Kenneth Killick pages 23-29
[801] *The Kybalion: A Study of The Hermetic Philosophy of Ancient Egypt and Greece* by Three Initiates pages 18-19, 71-74
[802] *Pyramid Energy: The Philosophy of God, The Science of Man* by Mary & Dean Hardy and Kenneth Killick page 27-30
[803] *The Kybalion: A Study of The Hermetic Philosophy of Ancient Egypt and Greece* by Three Initiates pages 19-20, 74-79
[804] *Pyramid Energy: The Philosophy of God, The Science of Man* by Mary & Dean Hardy and Kenneth Killick pages 27-30
[805] *The Kybalion: A Study of The Hermetic Philosophy of Ancient Egypt and Greece* by Three Initiates pages 20-21, 81-85
[806] *Pyramid Energy: The Philosophy of God, The Science of Man* by Mary & Dean Hardy and Kenneth Killick pages 27-31
[807] *Pyramid Energy: The Philosophy of God, The Science of Man* by Mary & Dean Hardy and Kenneth Killick pages 27-33, 45, 152-155
[808] *The Kybalion: A Study of The Hermetic Philosophy of Ancient Egypt and Greece* by Three Initiates pages 21-22, 87-100
[809] *Magdalene's Lost Legacy: Symbolic Numbers and the Sacred Union in Christianity*, Margret Starbird pages 12-18

Chapter 11:

Incorporating Pure Essential Oils

Pure Essential Oils are a perfect compliment with the Spiral Breath. I start each day with the application and inhalation of an essential oil on my wrists, heart chakra, third eye and crown chakra before I begin my Spiral Breath and morning prayer of Gratitude. It takes a quick moment to apply.

I put a couple of drops of my chosen essential oil in the palm of my non-dominant hand and spiral it clockwise three times with my index and middle finger of my dominant hand. This activates the oils and tunes it to my DNA. I anoint my crown chakra, third eye and heart chakra with my fingers that I dipped and swirled into the oil. I swipe my palms across my wrists. Then I rub my palms together and take a couple long deep inhalations of the fragrant energy as I state my intention for the day. Something like, "I am open to receive the bountiful Blessings that come my way today. I walk through this day with Grace, Compassion, Gratitude, Discernment, Wisdom and Ease."

I get into a comfortable seated position. I begin spiraling my breath and do so for 20 minutes letting my intentions energetically spread through my body.

I like to use Frankincense, Sandalwood, Highest Potential™, Magnify Your Purpose™, Gratitude™ or Harmony™ depending on which aspect of prayerful intent I wish to excel in that particular day.

Therapeutic grade essential oils are truly gifts from Divine and nature. Every plant, flower, tree or bush has their own unique properties of natural chemical compounds.[810] When properly grown, harvested and distilled, therapeutic grade essential oils retain the pure essence of nature and their phenomenal healing properties.[811]

Pure therapeutic grade essential oils are plant derived and contain messenger molecules that can act as neurotransmitters, hormones, enzymes, vitamins, peptides, steroids and ligands. Pure essential oils can help restore, protect and maintain wellness within our body, emotions, mind and spirit.[812, 813]

What makes pure essential oils so amazing and effective is the fact that they carry the exact six sided aromatic benzene chains and vital life force as our DNA and RNA. Pure essential oils are comprised of the same natural elements and compounds that are found in our human bodies. The five main elements are Carbon (C), Hydrogen (H), Oxygen (O) and Nitrogen (N), which make up 96% of our human body weight and Sulfur (S), which is a minor element. Dr. David Stewart Ph.D, D.N.M. calls these five elements the "CHOSN Ones."[814]

Dr. Stewart is a brilliant, good hearted man with a gentle spirit, who has blessed us with many books to increase our knowledge and understanding of essential oils. In his book, *The Chemistry of Essential Oils Made Simple*, Dr. Stewart points out that God used these five natural elements in countless combinations when He was creating life. Each combination is uniquely different, with no two alike.[815]

Of these 'CHOSN' five elements, carbon is the greatest contributor, as it is essential in creating and maintaining life. Not only does carbon comprise 70-80 percent of the weight in every pure essential oil, carbon and carbon compounds are found in our heart, brain, DNA, enzymes, hormones, lymph, proteins and tissue, including our blood, sweat and tears. Carbon compounds are part of every process that takes place within our physical, mental, emotional and even our spiritual body.[816]

Essential oils are of such significant importance that the Bible makes 1,031 references to them, as well as, at least thirty three aromatic oil producing plants, including the application of some of these healing oils.[817]

Pure essential oils are extremely concentrated and contain over 40 mil-lion-trillion tiny molecules. Written out that is 40,000,000,000,000,000,000. Our human body contains approximately 100 trillion cells. Just one drop of therapeu-tic grade essential oil contains enough molecules to cover every cell in our body 400,000 times. That is impressive!

Every living cell contains thousands of receptor sites, that act as portals or doorways, which allow communication between itself and neighboring cells. Receptor sites are miniature locks. When the proper signal, molecule or 'key' is introduced and accepted, the cell opens a doorway, which allows the signal/message to be delivered into the DNA.[818] Thank goodness, it only takes one molecule in the right receptor site to signal our DNA to make a change on a cellular level.[819]

Most of the chemical compounds found in pure essential oils are made from unique "aromatic" and "benzene rings." These "rings" or "chains" are comprised of hydrocarbon molecules.[820] When carbon forms rings to build molecules, the possibilities of creation soar into the trillions of trillions.[821]

In his book, *Quantum Physics, Essential Oils & the Mind-Body Connection*, Dr. Stewart shares that these chemical compound ring formations are actually energetic waveforms that can manifest as particles of matter (which is chemistry) or as waves of energy (which is physics) or both at the same time.[822] The aromatic benzene rings in pure essential oils reflect Einstein's relativity and quantum physics. The aromatic rings surpass the blend of physics and chemistry, as they display multidimensional properties of consciousness and spiritual laws.[823]

Dr. Stewart defined pure essential oils perfectly when he said they are *"Vehicles of Living Energy."*[824] The molecules with benzene rings have a higher resonance energy and the behavior of these wave forms impart the electromagnetic frequencies to the oils.[825] Pure essential oils are the same subtle bio-energy that flows through all life. They possess the identical original life force energy or chi that connects all living things in our universe.[826]

Being "living energy," pure therapeutic grade essential oils have electrical properties. This is due to their electron activity that generates 'resonance energy.'[827] Every chemical and neural process that takes place within our body involves electron activity. Our thoughts also have electrical properties. Therefore, we can influence pure essential oils with our thoughts and emotions and in turn, we can use their living energy to elevate our wellbeing, increase our intention and assist with our spiritual journey to higher consciousness. This is referred to as the "mind-body connection."[828]

Pure essential oils become both receivers and transmitters of thought. They can receive and respond to our thoughts and prayers, as well as broadcast or transmit our thoughts, intention and prayer to our body, mind and spirit. Whether we are working on ourselves or someone else, our prayer and intention amplifies the gently, yet powerful effect of the essential oils.[829]

We can increase the therapeutic effectiveness of our chosen essential oils by making three clockwise circles in the pure essential oil with our fingers, as we state our intentions and prayers. This action is a form of sign language that communicates, prepares and tunes the essential oil molecules to rotate in the same direction as the protein molecules within our body and our DNA. Pure essential oils have an innate intelligence that understands our intentions and they respond by transmitting or receiving our prayer. As was stated above, with your chosen essential oil in the palm of your non-dominant hand, simply, place one or more fingers from your dominant hand into the essential oil. Make three clockwise circles. Then anoint or apply topically to the area of your choice.[830]

Why clockwise? Because the proteins, DNA and major molecules of all living things on our planet are helical with a clockwise twist. All life forms on Earth and in our universe turn in a clockwise direction that is synchronized with the earth's magnetic field. People with degenerative health issues are found to have reverse twisted proteins in their blood. In certain situations, electromagnetic fields and other forces can actually unwind some of our proteins, including our DNA and make them turn backwards.[831]

Why three times? It could have something to do with Nikola Tesla's quote, *"If you only knew the magnificence of the 3, 6 and 9, then you would have a key to the universe."*[832] The practice of spiraling the essential oils clockwise three times has been observed to energize the oils and increase their effectiveness. Remember, pure essential oils have consciousness and an innate intelligence that can amplify and broadcast our intention.[833]

Like the benzene rings in essential oils, RNA/DNA's double ringed bases are made up of perfect six sided hexagonal rings and are living energy. This means that **our DNA are also energetic waveforms** and they too can be influenced by electromagnetic frequency, in either a beneficial or harmful way.[834]

As was mentioned earlier, essential oils have properties that employ both physics and chemistry. On the physics side, essential oils display the principle laws of both classical physics and quantum physics. Classical physics address the dimensional properties that are the size of an atom or larger and can be measured and experienced with our five senses of taste, touch, hearing, smell and sight.[835]

Quantum physics address the action of that which is dimensionally smaller than an atom, such as electrons, neurons, protons, quarks and subatomic particles, to name a few. These molecular signal frequencies are so small that we cannot see them, yet they are powerful enough to make a cellular and vibrational change within seconds.[837, 838]

Remember the olfactory bulb in the limbic system? When pure essential oils come to room temperature, they vaporize. All the molecules of an essential oil can then enter our body through the nose and the olfactory system with inhalation, whether you can smell them or not. The molecular messengers are immediately transported either directly into our blood stream by way of our lungs or they go directly into the central brain. Any oil that has molecules less than 500 amu (atomic mass unit) in size can penetrate the skin, move through nerve pathways and meridians, pass through the blood-brain barrier and create a harmonizing effect at cellular levels, including our DNA.[839]

Our human body is made up of approximately 100 trillion cells and each cell has an impressive six gigabytes of memory within it. Each individual cell contains a copy of the master DNA blueprint within it, which includes a complete image of our original body within a projection of light like a hologram. In the brilliance of God's creation, each fractal of that image of light is whole and complete within itself![840] This is why prayer, breath, intent, energy, frequency and even pure essential oils can have such a powerful effect on our physical, mental, emotional and spiritual bodies.

Our DNA is the intelligence of our cells and our cellular memory. DNA stores its original design and information within its structure. When our DNA receives the proper molecular messengers, it can reprogram, repair and restore our cells by manufacturing biochemicals, turning on or shutting down certain functions, instructing a response to other parts of our body; it can assimilate nutrients, eliminate wastes, release antibodies and engage in a multitude of additional actions.[841]

On the chemistry side, essential oils contain chemical compounds. These chemical compounds consist of several classes of oxygenating hydrocarbons, such as phenolics, sesquiterpenes and monoterpenes. They also include acids, alcohols, aldehydes, coumarins, esters, ethers, furanoids, ketones, lactones and oxides, which are oxygenated hydrocarbons that provide a gentle balance to the other chemical compounds. In pure essential oils, the most important group of hydrocarbons are the terpenes.[842]

Organic esters are synthesized from acids and alcohols. They are known for their soothing and stress-releasing properties. Natural esters provide many fruity flavorings like banana, cherry, grape and strawberry. Natural esters are among the most pleasant of fragrances and are highly prized by perfumers and aromatherapist for balancing and attraction.[843]

Phenolics can be therapeutic and are among the most important compounds in pure essential oils. Phenolics are powerful antioxidants that protect us from aging and degenerative diseases, as they combat harmful free radicals.[844] Phenolics can protect us from bacteria, heavy metals, microbes, parasites and viruses, while protecting the healthy flora in our bodies. They can also stimulate, tone, anesthetize and cleanse receptor sites.[845] Without clean receptor sites, cell are unable to communicate with each other. Miscommunication can result in sickness.[846] Not only do phenolics protect our immune system, they also have calming properties that can support our nervous system and gently assist in balancing emotional unease.[847]

Sesquiterpenes oxygenate our cells and can flush misinformation that become trapped or locked within our cellular memory. They also increase the 'half-life' of smaller molecules making them linger longer, both aromatically and therapeutically. Thus, sesquiterpenes are also called 'fixing' molecules.[848]

Monoterpenes are found in every essential oil. They are the balancing components of an oil and work on both a sub-cellular and an intracellular level. Monoterpenes awaken and restore the correct original information in our strands of RNA and DNA, which is our cell's memory.[849] They also help with proper cell-to-cell communication.[850]

Phenolics, Monoterpenes and Sesquiterpenes are a powerful trio that cleanse, erase and restore. This trio is called the PMS Paradigm. It is the trio's collective properties that can create the instant harmonious healing when a pure essential oil is applied or inhaled. The Phenolics cleanse, the Sesquiterpenes erase the bad or mis-information from out cellular memory and the Monoterpenes restore the original cellular intelligence within our DNA.[851]

Pure therapeutic essential oils contain the lightest and smallest of plant molecules and by Divine Grace, they are known to pass through our skin, the cellular membrane wall and the blood-brain barrier (providing that they are lipid soluble). Lipid soluble means that the substance will dissolve in oil.[852] When pure therapeutic essential oils are applied topically, inhaled or taken internally (GRAS approved essential oils), the 'frequency' of the active ingredients can travel along the myelinating glia cells, our nerves, into our blood circulation; through the protective barrier for the brain and have a healing effect on a cellular level from head to toe.[853]

When our cellular communication is cleansed and restored, we naturally begin to return to a natural order of health.[854] For this reason, I believe that pure essential oils, along with focused breath and sincere prayerful intentions are very important when activating the limbic system, frontal lobes, glia cells and the white matter of our brain. Restoring cellular communication was exceptionally beneficial for me and my return to a natural order of health after my head injury.

Natural molecular ring formations can be measured in hertz frequencies, amplitudes and phases.[855] As electrons rotate around an aromatic ring, they generate an electromagnetic frequency that can be measured. Each full revolution is a cycle and units of cycles are measured by the number of times a full revolution is made per second. These frequency cycles manifest additional energy and create waveforms that are also measured in oscillating cycles, amplitude and phases. These measured units of cycles-per-second (cps) are called Hertz (Hz) frequencies, named after the German physicist, Heinrich Rudolph Hertz, who discovered them.[856]

1 Hertz (Hz) means that the particular unit or wave being measured rotates or oscillates once during a one second time frame. 1 Megahertz (MHz) is equivalent to 1,000,000 Hertz (one million times per second). 1 Mega-Megahertz measures a million-million times per second.[857]

Therapeutic grade essential oils contain molecules that vibrate with living electromagnetic frequencies and they can be measured.[858] Therapeutic grade essential oil of Rose has a frequency vibration of 320 MHz. It oscillates 320 million (320,000,000) times per second.[859]

Everything in creation responds to or is affected by frequency! The Third principle of Hermetic Law states, "Nothing rests; everything moves; everything vibrates." [860]

Every cell of our physical body and the molecules of pure organic essential oils are bio-electromagnetic in their nature. This is why pure essential oils are so beneficial and effective. When we apply pure essential oils through inhalation, topically or by ingestion our cells, tissue, organs, emotions, thoughts and our body in its totality, all begin to resonate with the healing frequency and living energy of the vibrating oils. The vibration of pure essential oils can increase the electromagnetic fields, bring coherence and restore harmony to our physical, mental, emotional and spiritual well being. This is called 'sympathetic vibration" or "vibrational energy transfer." [861]

A healthy human body (overall) vibrates between 62 MHz–68 MHz. A healthy human brain vibrates between 71-90 MHz. Healthy human cells begin to change when their frequency drops below 62 MHz. When our body frequency drops below 60 MHz, our healthy cells are deprived of oxygen and nutrients; the pH of our blood lowers and becomes more acidic. The imbalance begins to undermine our resistance and make us susceptible to illness.[862]

It is my opinion, that with the overwhelming chemical toxicity in our environment and our food supply; as well as, the excessive electromagnetic bombardment from cell towers, 5G towers, smart meters, electronics, ELF, HAARP and CERN particle generators, our bodies cannot help but drop from our natural and 'Divine' vibrational frequency.

Pure essential oils can increase the electrical frequencies in our blood, which in turn enables the transport of nutrients and oxygen to be delivered to our cells.

The primary ingredient within a pure organic essential oil is revitalizing oxygen. When cell walls become thick, it is difficult for oxygen to penetrate. Oxygen deprived cells begin to fall from optimal performance and duplicate unhealthy cells during cell division. Pure essential oils can penetrate cell walls and deliver the necessary oxygen for vital life. Therapeutic grade essential oils can restore cells to normal in 7 seconds.[863]

It has been found that therapeutic essential oils in the lower Hertz frequencies tend to effect the physical aspects of our body; the middle range Hertz frequencies tend to shift our emotional aspects, while the higher Hertz frequency essential oils are exceptional for spiritual shifts in our being[864] and for ceremonial purposes.

In 1992, Bruce Tainio, head of the Department of Agriculture at Eastern Washington University, in Washington State, developed technology called Calibrated Frequency Monitor (CFM) that could measure the frequency of plants. He discovered that he could also measure food, essential oils and pathogens that cause disease. Mr. Tainio was able to determined the average frequency of the human body and could even measure the frequency of our organs. Here are the frequencies that he recorded during the hours of 6:00 am to 6:00 pm.

The Human Body:

Human Body	62 – 68 MHz
Human Body from Neck up	72 – 78 MHz
Brain Frequency Range	71 – 90 MHz
Genius Brain Frequency	80 – 82 MHz
Human Body from Neck down	60 – 68 MHz
Thyroid and Parathyroid Glands	62 – 68 MHz

Thymus Gland	65 – 68 MHz
Heart	67 – 70 MHz
Lungs	58 – 65 MHz
Liver	55 – 60 MHz
Pancreas	60 – 80 MHz
Stomach	58 – 65 MHz
Descending Colon	58 – 62 MHz
Ascending Colon	50 – 60 MHz

The above table is a compilation from AROMATHERAPY ESSENTIAL OIL FREQUENCY by D. Gary Young https://www.ralfkollinger.de/wp/wp-content/uploads/2013/05/Frequency-Charts-Aromatherapy-essential-oil-frequency.pdf, The Chemistry of Essential Oils Made Simple by David Stewart Ph.D, D.N.M. page 182, The Healing Oils of the Bible Book and DVD by David Stewart Ph.D, D.N.M. page 32

A living, healthy cell oscillates at 27, 000,000,000,000 Hz (twenty seven trillion times per second) and DNA within the cell resonates at 8,540,000,000,000 Hz (eight trillion five hundred forty billion times per second).[865]

According to Dr. Royal Raymond Rife, every cell, tissue and organ has its own signature vibrational resonance. Dr. Rife created his Rife frequency generator in the late 1920's. Through his research, Dr. Rife discovered that specific beneficial frequencies could cancel out harmful cells and support restorative balance to our body.[866]

Nikola Tesla (1856 – 1943) believed that if we eliminate certain outside frequencies that interfere with our bodies wellbeing, we would have a greater resistance towards disease.[867]

Unfortunately, most of Rife and Tesla's work was confiscated and hidden from humanity. In Divine Accordance however, their technology has begun to surface and we are, once again, able to access and utilize it.

Previously I mentioned that the human body vibrates between 62 MHz and 78 MHz. An overhead light resonates at 60 Hertz. Electrical outlets, appliances, television, phones; etc, are AC (Alternating Current) frequencies, which are either incoherent or chaotic, as the electrical charge will periodically change direction.

With Direct Current (DC), the electrical charge only flows in one direction and is more or less an even flow. The cellular functions within our body are controlled by our own DC fields that generate supportive electromagnetic effects.[868] It was found that our personal DC system is directly involved with every phase of mental activity.[869]

Abnormal exposure to electromagnetic fields and frequencies can fracture our energy field and create substantial abnormalities in our physiology and functions; increased stress response, weakened immune system and lower vibratory rates in our body.[870]

Therapeutic grade essential oils have frequencies that are tuned in mathematical precision, which brings calm, coherence, organization and harmony to the electrical fields of our body to promote healing and maintain wellness. Synthetic oils do not. When we introduce a pure essential oil into our energy field with its high frequency rate, our lower physical frequency can't help but increase.[871]

Chemists have attempted to duplicate the aromatic rings in laboratories, but *have not* been able to achieve the harmonious vibrational response that is found in pure organic essential oils and the DNA ringed bases. Even if their synthetic chemical components have the exact measurements and properties as in a natural substance, the 'living energy' is not present in synthetic aromatic rings. Without the 'living energy' synthetic compounds have a tendency to create toxicity within our body's environment and lower our natural vibrational frequencies.[872]

Simple synthetic proteins that have been created in a laboratory spin counter-clockwise and they contain no living energy.[873]

Because of the potential toxicity with adulterated or synthetic oils, it is extremely important to ensure that you are using pure, therapeutic grade essential oils when taking essential oils internally or applying them topically to your skin. The FDA has published a list of essential oils that they deem safe for consumption. It is called the GRAS list (Generally Recognized As Safe).[874] The website link for the list is printed in the back of the book.

Only 2 percent of essential oils are distilled for internal use. The essential oils that are distilled in the ancient ways carry the 'living energy' and can improve the physical frequency of our body. Ninety-eight percent of essential oils are distilled for perfume, food flavorings or commercial grade aromatherapy purposes.[875]

They are often distilled with chemical solvents to maximize the yield. These contaminated oils are not therapeutic grade essential oils and must be added to a carrier oil, such as almond oil, to lessen harmful reactions.[876]

Proper distillation is also important. If the steam is too hot or has too much pressure, it can burn the oil and/or break down the aromatic compounds that carry the beneficial properties. Burnt oil can be harmful to your skin and body. If it is not hot enough, the precious chemical properties may not be released. Some companies do a second and third distillation of the same plant material, often with alcohol and chemicals to produce a yield. This process renders a weakened and contaminated oil.[877]

Unfortunately, many companies dilute a lower grade essential oil with inexpensive petrochemical solvents that are colorless and odorless to increase their yield and profit. The U.S. FDA (Food and Drug Administration) allows these unethical companies to label their products as 'genuine' or even 100% pure.[878]

Then there are the synthetic oils, which are created in a laboratory using chemical substances that smell or taste like a natural, made by God substance. These you will find in your air and fabric fresheners, as well as candles and room deodorizers. Synthetic oils and scents can wreak havoc in a multitude of areas concerning your wellbeing including respiratory, endocrine and brain fog.[879]

You can see why the use of pure, quality essential oils are beneficial and necessary to our well being. *"First do no harm"* (in Latin, *"Primum non nocere"*) is associated with the Greek physician Hippocrates (460 BC - 370 BC) author of The Hippocratic Oath.

✡ ✡ ✡

ESSENTIAL OILS FOR HIGHER CONSCIOUSNESS

Each pure essential oil has its' own signature frequency that vibrates between 52 and 580 MHz plus. Until recently, it had been thought that Rose oil had the highest vibrational frequency at 320 MHz. However, it was discovered that Australian

Blue Cypress™ essential oil measures 522 MHz[880] and Idaho Blue Spruce™ has a vibrational frequency of 580 MHz.[881] To date, Idaho Blue Spruce is the highest vibrational pure essential oil and it is exceptional for raising the frequency of the pineal, pituitary, amygdalae, glia and white matter of the brain.

There are many reported cases where people smell the scent of Roses when they feel the presence of or see apparitions of Angels, Mother Mary (Our Lady of the Roses), Mary Magdalene, Our Lady of Fatima, Our Lady of Guadalupe, Our Lady of Lourdes or Jesus. The Catholic Church refers to this as the 'Odor of Sanctity' and is thought to be a sign that God's presence or His blessing is upon us.[882]

On many occasions when I am doing healing work or I am channeling the Divine Mother or the Mary's, a sweet floral scent will drift through the air. I take this as a sign that I have raised my frequency to a pure state of Unconditional Love, which is what God, Mother Mary, Mary Magdalene, Jesus and master teachers from multiple cultures teach us to achieve. *"But thanks be to God who always leads us in triumph in Christ and manifests through us the odor of the knowledge of Him in every place."* (2 Corinthians 2:14) It comes back to frequency.

I heard D. Gary Young, founder of Young Living Essential Oils, say that, *"Essential oils carry the consciousness of the Creator."*

We are more than just a physical body. We are consciousness, which encompasses feelings, emotions and thoughts. We are human consciousness returning to Christ Consciousness.

Thoughts and emotions are energetic vibrations that can be measured in Hertz frequencies. A negative thought or mental state can lower our total body frequency by 10-12 MHz. A positive thought or attitude, as well as, meditation and prayer can raise our frequency by 10-15 MHz.[883]

We know that the frequencies of pure essential oils can affect us on a cellular level. Because of that, they can help move old trauma that has become locked into our tissue, cells and DNA out of the unconscious into our conscious mind to be addressed, transmuted and healed.

During a personal wellness session, the practitioner placed an essential oil blend on my forehead. As he slowly swiped the essential oil across my forehead from right to left, I started to weep. I asked with a curious chuckle, "What oil did you just place on me?" He gently smiled and said, "Forgiveness™" and then walked out of the room.

The tears kept rolling. I was not sobbing, just softly shedding the tears that I had held back in silence. Starting on the right side of my forehead and moving to the left took me from the present moment through the past of unforgiven, unacknowledged and unaddressed emotions. When the tears finished I got up. I felt unburdened and deeply in gratitude.

One of my friends shared with me a layering technique that he likes to use to balance emotional discomforts. He placed a couple drops of the essential oil blend SARA™ in the palm of my hand. I rubbed my palms together and inhaled the fragrance through cupped hands. He then placed a couple drops of Hong Kuai essential oil in my palm. I repeated the process of rubbing my palms together and inhaling the blended scents. Then he asked how I was feeling. A noticeable, yet subtle wave of peace was sweeping through my body. I finished the process by layering a few drops of Dorado Azul™ essential oil to enhance the energetic crescendo of this process.

The beauty of pure essential oils is their ability to be subtle, yet powerfully effective at the same time. I was reminded that the 'Divinely inspired' essential oil blend SARA™ is an acronym for Sexual Abuse Ritual/Religious Abuse. The energetic resonance of those particular essential oil blends inspired a pleasant sense of peace and spiritual wellbeing within me.

Pure essential oils amplify intent. Both the intent of the the person who is applying the essential oils and the intent of the person who is receiving the essential oils. It is a good practice to pray or project a positive intention into your essential oils before application.[884] Dr. David Stewart calls pure essential oils 'packets of probabilities and possibilities.' The probabilities are determined from the chemical composition of an essential oil. "The Chemistry determines what is possible and quantum physics determines which possibilities actually happen."[885]

The frequency of the pure essential oils can raise our personal frequency, which can shift the energy within our cells, our body, our thoughts, emotions and our spirit. It is the principle of alchemy and the universal law of electrical frequencies: Change the Energy, you change the manifestation of Mass. Mass is Matter. Matter is condensed Energy.[886]

✡ ✡ ✡

ANOINTING

The above essential oil experiences can be viewed as anointments.

One technique found in the Bible instructs the priest to take some oil and anoint the person's right ear, the right thumb and the right big toe. (Leviticus 14:17) This anointing was directed for those with leprosy. How apropos to discover that these are reflexology and emotional release points. Synchronistically, these points all reference and effect the right brain and our emotions and feelings.

Trigger points in the upper portion of the right ear help release emotional issues that address mother and father issues. Emotional release points on the right thumb help release the fear of the unknown and emotional blocks that prevent us from moving forward and making change. Trigger points on the right big toe help support the clearing of addictions, compulsive behavior and/or bad habits, which can include continual replay of excessive thoughts.[887]

I used this anointing process often with my Spiral Breath session to assist in clearing the emotions that I had anchored in my energy field and cellular memory from my head injury. The negative emotions that I acquired from that incident were 'eating me up' inside and effecting my healing process. These emotional release points, also encompassed those emotional frequencies and tendencies that I acquired throughout my life or inherited from my parents and lineage. Stimulating these release points, in combination with pure essential oils and the Spiral Breath, was a blessing for me on many levels.

I also used the suggested oils from the Bible of Hyssop, Cedarwood™ and Cypress. Hyssop is excellent for cleansing the missteps of the past, helps with releasing stuffed emotions and mis-information that is stored in the cells or DNA. Cedarwood™ is a humbling oil. It helps clear out conceit and excessive pride, while improving brain cognizance. Cedarwood™ can deprogram mis-information on a cellular level. Cypress reprograms cellular memory and DNA to their correct and original signature frequency. Cypress can correct scrambled programming due to trauma at the level of cellular intelligence and promote permanent healings on a cellular level.[888, 889, 890]

Another simple application is to apply a drop of pure essential oil to the pad of your right thumb and press the thumb against the roof of your mouth. This opens the cranial sutures and is a powerful way to amplify the benefits and change the feelings.[891]

I have found that the easiest way to clear emotional, mental and spiritual wounds is to activate our amygdalae, limbic system, frontal lobes and glia brain. We can do this with pure essential oils, focused breath work (such as the Spiral Breath), as well as, incorporating meditation, imagery, sound, and resonance. Using and combining any of the given modalities in this book can enhance the process to emotional, mental and spiritual stability.

THERAPEUTAE

Mary Magdalene is one of the most painted women in history. She is always referenced with a jar of essential oils. Jesus, High Priest/Priestesses of the ancient orders and those trained in the Egyptian Therapeutae used pure essential oils in their healing and ceremonial work.

The Essene Healers of Alexandria were a pre-Christian Essene order known for being "the best" of a kind given to "perfect goodness"and "one who is attendant to the gods" [892] Female healers were called Therapeutridae or Therapeutrides in Greek. Jewish philosopher, Philo of Alexandria describes the Therapeutae (plural) as 'physicians of the soul,' who were known for their mystic values, philosophy, meditations, superior healing arts and simplistic monastic life.

The healing temples were known as Asclepeions in association with the followers of Asclepius (Father of Medicine). They used the precious oils and prayer to help move themselves and those they interacted with into the higher realms of consciousness.[893] Many recipes of medicinal oils were inscribed on marble tablets.[894] According to the *De Vita Contemplativa*, the Therapeutae were widely distributed in the Ancient World, among the Greeks and beyond and were known to be traveling spiritual healers.[895] Other known Therapeutae included Hippocrates, Apollonius of Tyana, Aelius Aristides, Plato, Dionysius of Halicarnassus and Galen.[896]

As I connect the information from what I have learned and experienced throughout my life, it is my belief that the Therapeutae taught how to activate the amygdalae, pineal, limbic system, frontal lobes and our glia brain in order to trigger our "Soul memory" and strengthen our "nous" - the connection between our Body, Soul and Spirit.

Our soul, cellular energy and DNA have been encoded with the 'Knowing' of the ancient teachings of *Wisdom* in order to return to our vibrational Light body when we get 'heavy with matter.' Pure essential oils are "Vehicles of Living Energy" that assist us in aligning with the same subtle bio-energy that flows through all life. Therapeutic grade essential oils, along with breath, help unlock and open the gates to higher consciousness and true 'Knowing.' Once the 'gates' are opened, all we have to do is allow ourselves to enter.

Activating our glia brain, frontal lobes, limbic system and pineal will help us consciously remember our soul's ability. Awaken the higher realms of consciousness and your entire perception of life will reflect amazing Goodness!

Adding quality, pure essential oils to your Spiral Breath session and daily life can be extremely beneficial and enlightening. Especially, when you incorporate the pure essential oil blends that support a particular emotion that you wish to shift or excel in. As you can see, I *really* love my pure essential oils!

[810] *The Chemistry of Essential Oils Made Simple* by David Stewart Ph.D, D.N.M. page 51
[811] *The Chemistry of Essential Oils Made Simple* by David Stewart Ph.D, D.N.M. page 52
[812] *The Chemistry of Essential Oils Made Simple* by David Stewart Ph.D, D.N.M. page 59 - 60
[813] *Essential Oils Desk Reference Seventh Edition* by Life Science Publishing pages 309 - 312
[814] *The Chemistry of Essential Oils Made Simple* by David Stewart Ph.D, D.N.M. page 121-141
[815] *The Chemistry of Essential Oils Made Simple* by David Stewart Ph.D, D.N.M. page 166
[816] *The Chemistry of Essential Oils Made Simple* by David Stewart Ph.D, D.N.M. page 166 - 167
[817] *The Healing Oils of the Bible* Book and DVD by David Stewart Ph.D, D.N.M. pages 96 - 113
[818] *The Healing Oils of the Bible* Book and DVD by David Stewart Ph.D, D.N.M. pages 27 - 28
[819] *The Chemistry of Essential Oils Made Simple*e by David Stewart Ph.D, D.N.M. page 482
[820] *Quantum Physics, Essential Oils & the Mind-Body Connection* by David Stewart Ph.D, D.N.M. page 3
[821] *The Chemistry of Essential Oils Made Simple* by David Stewart Ph.D, D.N.M. page 174
[822] *Quantum Physics, Essential Oils & the Mind-Body Connection* by David Stewart Ph.D, D.N.M. page 3
[823] *The Chemistry of Essential Oils Made Simple* by David Stewart Ph.D, D.N.M. pages 132, 177, 419
[824] *Quantum Physics, Essential Oils & the Mind-Body Connection* by David Stewart Ph.D, D.N.M. page 2
[825] *The Chemistry of Essential Oils Made Simple* by David Stewart Ph.D, D.N.M. page 353
[826] *The Chemistry of Essential Oils Made Simple*by David Stewart Ph.D, D.N.M. page 121 - 123,177, 628 - 629
[827] *The Chemistry of Essential Oils Made Simple* by David Stewart Ph.D, D.N.M. page 177
[828] *Quantum Physics, Essential Oils & the Mind-Body Connection* by David Stewart Ph.D, D.N.M. page 9 - 12
[829] *The Chemistry of Essential Oils Made Simple* by David Stewart Ph.D, D.N.M. page 733
[830] *The Chemistry of Essential Oils Made Simple* by David Stewart Ph.D, D.N.M. pages 474 - 479, 491
[831] *The Chemistry of Essential Oils Made Simple* by David Stewart Ph.D, D.N.M. pages 474 - 479
[832] http://blog.world-mysteries.com/science/why-did-tesla-say-that-369-was-the-key-to-the-universe/
[833] *The Chemistry of Essential Oils Made Simple* by David Stewart Ph.D, D.N.M. page 474 - 479
[834] https://en.wikipedia.org/wiki/DNA
[835] *Quantum Physics, Essential Oils & the Mind-Body Connection* by David Stewart Ph.D, D.N.M. page 4
[836] *Quantum Physics, Essential Oils & the Mind-Body Connection* by David Stewart Ph.D, D.N.M. page 4
[837] *The Chemistry of Essential Oils Made Simple* by David Stewart Ph.D, D.N.M. pages 110 - 112
[838] *The Healing Oils of the Bible* Book and DVD by David Stewart Ph.D, D.N.M. pages 15 -16
[839] *The Chemistry of Essential Oils Made Simple* by David Stewart Ph.D, D.N.M. page 111-112
[840] *The Chemistry of Essential Oils Made Simple* by David Stewart Ph.D, D.N.M. page 202
[841] *The Chemistry of Essential Oils Made Simple* by David Stewart Ph.D, D.N.M. page 211
[842] *The Chemistry of Essential Oils Made Simple* by David Stewart Ph.D, D.N.M. page 290
[843] *The Chemistry of Essential Oils Made Simple* by David Stewart Ph.D, D.N.M. pages 356 - 360
[844] *The Chemistry of Essential Oils Made Simple* by David Stewart Ph.D, D.N.M. page 223
[845] *The Chemistry of Essential Oils Made Simple* by David Stewart Ph.D, D.N.M. page 129, 268, 291
[846] *The Healing Oils of the Bible* Book and DVD by David Stewart Ph.D, D.N.M. page 28
[847] *The Chemistry of Essential Oils Made Simple* by David Stewart Ph.D, D.N.M. page 191-193
[848] *The Chemistry of Essential Oils Made Simple*e by David Stewart Ph.D, D.N.M. page 279
[849] *The Chemistry of Essential Oils Made Simple* by David Stewart Ph.D, D.N.M. page 108,272, 291
[850] *The Healing Oils of the Bible* Book and DVD by David Stewart Ph.D, D.N.M. page 30
[851] *The Chemistry of Essential Oils Made Simple* by David Stewart Ph.D, D.N.M. page 291-308
[852] *The Chemistry of Essential Oils Made Simple* by David Stewart Ph.D, D.N.M. page 447
[853] *The Chemistry of Essential Oils Made Simple* by David Stewart Ph.D, D.N.M. page 305
[854] *The Chemistry of Essential Oils Made Simple*e by David Stewart Ph.D, D.N.M. page 292
[855] *Quantum Physics, Essential Oils & the Mind-Body Connection* by David Stewart Ph.D, D.N.M. page 3
[856] *The Chemistry of Essential Oils Made Simple* by David Stewart Ph.D, D.N.M. page 177
[857] *The Chemistry of Essential Oils Made Simple* by David Stewart Ph.D, D.N.M. page 178
[858] *The Chemistry of Essential Oils Made Simple* by David Stewart Ph.D, D.N.M. pages 176 -177
[859] *The Healing Oils of the Bible* Book and DVD by David Stewart Ph.D, D.N.M page 33
[860] *Pyramid Energy: The Philosophy of God, The Science of Man* by Mary and Dean Hardy, Kenneth and Marjorie Kil-lick page 43
[861] *The Chemistry of Essential Oils Made Simple* by David Stewart Ph.D, D.N.M. pages 181, 187 - 189
[862] *The Chemistry of Essential Oils Made Simple* by David Stewart Ph.D, D.N.M. pages 181 - 183
[863] *AROMATHERAPY ESSENTIAL OIL FREQUENCY* by D. Gary Young https://www.ralf-kollinger.de/wp/wp-content/uploads/2013/05/Frequency-Charts-Aromatherapy-essential-oil-frequency.pd
[864] *AROMATHERAPY ESSENTIAL OIL FREQUENCY* by D. Gary Young

https://www.ralf-kollinger.de/wp/wp-content/uploads/2013/05/Frequency-Charts-Aromatherapy-essential-oil-frequency.pdf

[865] *AROMATHERAPY ESSENTIAL OIL FREQUENCY* by D. Gary Young
https://www.ralf-kollinger.de/wp/wp-content/uploads/2013/05/Frequency-Charts-Aromatherapy-essential-oil-frequency.pd

[866] *Pyramid Energy: The Philosophy of God, The Science of Man* by Mary and Dean Hardy, Kenneth and Marjorie Kil-lick page 210-211

[867] *AROMATHERAPY ESSENTIAL OIL FREQUENCY* by D. Gary Young
https://www.ralf-kollinger.de/wp/wp-content/uploads/2013/05/Frequency-Charts-Aromatherapy-essential-oil-frequency.pd

[868] *The Body Electric: Electromagnetism and the Foundation of Life* by Robert. O. Becker, M.D. and Gary Selden pages 80, 269

[869] *The Body Electric: Electromagnetism and the Foundation of Life* by Robert. O. Becker, M.D. and Gary Selden page 241

[870] *Cross Currents: The Perils of Electropollution, The Promise of Electromedicine* by Dr. Robert O. Becker pages 187-217

[871] *The Chemistry of Essential Oils Made Simple* by David Stewart Ph.D, D.N.M. pages 180-181, 189

[872] *The Chemistry of Essential Oils Made Simple* by David Stewart Ph.D, D.N.M. pages 145-146

[873] *The Chemistry of Essential Oils Made Simple* by David Stewart Ph.D, D.N.M. page 475

[874] FDA GRAS List Section 182.20 https://www.accessdata.fda.gov/scripts/cdrh/cfdocs/cfcfr/CFRSearch.cfm?fr=182.20

[875] *Essential Oils Desk Reference Seventh Edition* by Life Science Publishing page 22

[876] *The Chemistry of Essential Oils Made Simple* by David Stewart Ph.D, D.N.M. page 52

[877] *The Chemistry of Essential Oils Made Simple* by David Stewart Ph.D, D.N.M. pages 4-13

[878] *The Chemistry of Essential Oils Made Simple* by David Stewart Ph.D, D.N.M. page 12

[879] *The Chemistry of Essential Oils Made Simple* by David Stewart Ph.D, D.N.M. pages 6-13

[880] *Vibrant Health Now! How to use essential oils, aromatherapy and natural health products to detox your body and reach optimal health* by Casey Conrad and Alan Simpson page 56

[881] http://nebula.wsimg.com/3df693629be325312047828d440f96c1?AccessKeyId=3DA3A5DAEA3BB2E11125&disposition=0&alloworigin=1

[882] *Mother Mary and the Scent of Roses* by Catherine Mendenhall-Baugh https://catholicmom.com/2018/07/11/mother-mary-and-the-scent-of-roses/ and https://www.thoughtco.com/rose-miracles-and-angel-signs-3973503

[883] *The Healing Oils of the Bible* Book and DVD by David Stewart Ph.D, D.N.M. pages 33-34 and *The Chemistry of Essential Oils Made Simple* by David Stewart Ph.D, D.N.M. pages 183-184

[884] *Quantum Physics, Essential Oils & the Mind-Body Connection* by David Stewart Ph.D, D.N.M. pages 10-11

[885] *Quantum Physics, Essential Oils & the Mind-Body Connection* by David Stewart Ph.D, D.N.M. page 13, 14, 18

[886] *Pyramid Energy: The Philosophy of God, The Science of Man* by Mary and Dean Hardy, Kenneth and Marjorie Killick page 27

[887] *The Healing Oils of the Bible* Book and DVD by David Stewart Ph.D, D.N.M. pages 51-52

[888] *The Healing Oils of the Bible* Book and DVD by David Stewart Ph.D, D.N.M. page 52

[889] *Healing Oils of the Bible* by David Stewart Ph.D. page 288-289

[890] *Quantum Physics, Essential Oils & the Mind-Body Connection* by David Stewart Ph.D, D.N.M. page 16

[891] *Essential Oils Desk Reference Seventh Edition* by Life Science Publishing page 332

[892] https://en.wikipedia.org/wiki/Therapeutae and https://en.wikipedia.org/wiki/Therapeutae_of_Asclepius

[893] The Therapeutae and the Miracles of Jesus http://www.thenazareneway.com/therapeutae_jesus.html

[894] *Vibrant Health Now! How to use essential oils, aromatherapy and natural health products to detox your body and reach optimal health* by Casey Conrad and Alan Simpson page 75

[895] The Therapeutae and the Miracles of Jesus http://www.thenazareneway.com/therapeutae_jesus.html

[896] https://en.wikipedia.org/wiki/Therapeutae_of_Asclepius

Chapter 12:

Spiral Breath Technique Instructional

The Spiral Breath is a powerful, effective technique. It is simple and can be done practically anywhere. The benefits can be felt immediately and it can open the doorway to blissful living.

With frequent practice of the Spiral Breath technique, you can quickly defuse negatively charged emotional energy with Grace and Ease. The Spiral Breath activates the glia brain, limbic system and frontal lobes, as well as supports the body, mind, emotions and spirit. It connects the heart and the mind in a 'Mystical Marriage' to function as one divine unit (unite) in Harmony.

With consistent use, the Spiral Breath can increase your esoteric qualities, such as Precognition (foreknowledge of an event), Claircognizance (clear knowing), Clairvoyance (clear seeing), Clairaudience (clear hearing), Clairempathy (clear emotional feeling), Clairsentience (clear physical feeling), Clairtangency (clear touching), Clairgustance (clear tasting), Clairsalience (clear smelling), Telekinesis (ability to move objects at a distance), Telepathy (mind-reading or the ability to transfer thoughts without using the main known senses), and Astral Projection (a willful out-of-body experience), etc. It can also increase your ability to transcend time, space, energy and matter through conscious intent.

Use the picture below for guidance. Go slow with your visualization in the beginning. As you become familiar with the pattern and movement, you can envision your breath and the emerald green Light spiraling with the speed of your own inhalations.

To help with the visualization, I have created an animated Spiral Breath Technique DVD that can be purchased separately or with the soft cover book. The first part is a tutorial with guided directions. The second part is a 20 minute looped video of the animated Spiral Breath in motion accompanied by the sweet transformational music of David Young.

After the basic instructions, I have included a chapter on incorporating other modalities that I have used with the Spiral Breath technique. Enjoy!

Here is the process:

SPIRAL BREATH TECHNIQUE

Visualize your inhalation as an emerald green Light coming into your heart.

See the emerald Light swirl left to right, right to left, up and over; down and around, all at the same time. Allow the Light to swirl around until every space within your heart is saturated.

Then visualize the beautiful emerald green Light moving up from your heart into your brainstem at the base of your skull. In your mind's eye, see this brilliant green Light swirling around from left to right and right to left, up and over; down and around, all at the same time, as it illuminates the entire area of the brainstem.

When the brainstem area is saturated, move the emerald Light up past your occipital ridge (which is the protruding part of the back of your skull). Then continue to move the emerald Light upwards to the top of your head. This is your Crown Chakra. See the Light swirl left to right, right to left, up and over; down and around, all at the same time until the Crown Chakra is saturated with the emerald green Light.

Continue the flow of the emerald green Light around to your forehead and Third Eye. Allow the brilliant emerald Light to swirl around in all directions in the same toroidal motion until this area is saturated with Light.

Continue moving your breath, as you visualize the emerald green Light flowing downwards to enter your nostrils. Curve the emerald green Light up past your teeth and through the roof of your mouth into the center of your brain. This is where your Limbic System resides. This curling movement also creates the Fibonacci Spiral pattern.

Allow the Divine emerald green Light to saturate every aspect of the Limbic System. See the Light swirl left to right, right to left, up and over; down and around, all at the same time. Visualize your emerald green healing breath activating your pituitary and pineal glands.

This completes the inhalation movement of the Spiral Breath.

Hold your breath for two heart beats (2 seconds) before releasing it into your exhalation. This allows the oxygen to permeate your lungs more fully.

As you exhale, visualize the emerald green Light moving out from your Limbic System through your amygdalae that are located on both sides of your Third Eye.

As the emerald green Light passes through your amygdala and out from your forehead, it shifts in color to a glistening golden hue. Here, the glistening, golden Light blends with your personal auric field that shimmers an iridescent Mother of Pearl in color. Your auric field is fed by the All Encompassing Divine Light that surrounds your body and all things in Creation. As the Light re-enters your heart, it returns to it's brilliant emerald green Light.

The entire inhalation spirals up from your heart to your brainstem at the base of your skull, into your occipital lobe, up to the top of your head and Crown Chakra; around to your third eye, continuing down into your nostrils and curving back up through the roof of your mouth into your limbic system (located an inch inwards from your temples) in the center of your brain.

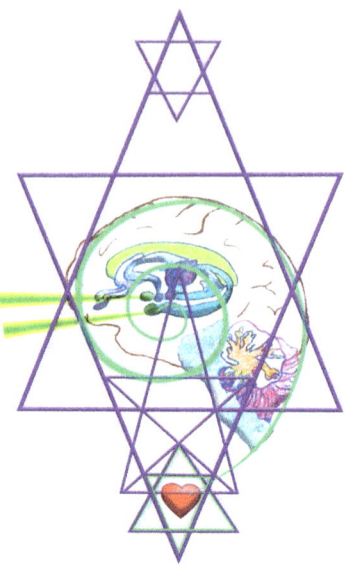

12.1 Spiral Breath Illustration by Gayle Mack

I have found that when I touch my heart as I breathe in, I activate the sense of touch and my breath appears to be coming into my heart instead of my nose. Now that I have been doing the Spiral Breath for a while, when I feel rushed or off center, I can touch my heart and begin a slow inhalation and my energy will begin to shift with the cellular memory of the Spiral Breath. My brain says, "I remember this… We are centering" and I immediately begin to shift into a calm, focused mode. Often, by the time I exhale my first breath, my body and mind are relaxed as if I had been breathing for 20 minutes.

The inhalation should be approximately 5 - 7 seconds or heartbeats long. At the end of your inhalation, hold your breath for 2 seconds or 2 heartbeats and then exhale for 5 - 7 seconds or heartbeats. Stretching your inhalations and exhalations to the count of 7 seconds or heartbeats helps put you into a safe, relaxed state.

If 5 seconds is too long for your inhalation at first, do what is comfortable and gradually work up to 7 seconds.

As you inhale, focus on breathing through both nostrils at the same time. Allow your breath to be audible in the beginning. The sound of your breath as it gently brushes the back of your throat, will help to balance the lobes of your brain and move you into a calm state of being. For those familiar with yoga, it is referred to as the Pranayama breath. For those who are not, make your breath sound like Darth Vader from the movie Star Wars.

Use your diaphragm to assist with the audible exhale. Slowly contract your diaphragm towards your spine on your exhalation. The audible breath will also give the conscious mind something to focus on and helps to calm the mind chatter.

It is important to breathe correctly for this exercise. Incorporate the "Complete Breathing" technique spoken of in Chapter Three. It may take some practice until your body remembers its original, innate breathing pattern. With practice, it will become your normal way of breathing.

Feel your slow, controlled breath moving into your heart in unison with the emerald green Light. Sense your breath and the emerald green Light moving up into your brainstem at the base of your skull.

Visualize your emerald green breath sweeping through your brainstem and collecting any unfavorable emotion or experience that has been trapped in your cells and memory. Give yourself permission to transmute any negatively charged thought, emotion or action that is running like a CD on continuous play. Ask that your subconsciousness bring forward any energetic imprint that you have used in the past or present to protect your woundedness and anything that is keeping you in the perception that you are a victim of its circumstance. Proclaim that you shift and balance any emotions or thoughts that come up for you with Grace and Ease. As you place your intention, the process begins.

As you continue your inhalation, visualize your breath and the healing emerald green Light moving up into your occipital area and up around to your crown chakra at the top of your head. As your emerald green healing breath circulates and permeates your Crown Chakra, be aware without loosing your focus of any sensations you begin to feel. Sometimes, when the Crown Chakra and your Thousand Petal Lotus opens, it feels like a flutter, a cool breeze, a vibration or a melting sensation. If you should experience this, continue to breathe and give yourself permission to experience the bliss of 'Oneness.'

Continue to bring your seamless breath and the illuminating emerald Light from your crown chakra around into your third eye and down into your nostrils and up past the roof of your mouth into the limbic system that rests between the left and right hemispheres of your brain to complete the Fibonacci spiral.

As you hold your breath for two heartbeats or 2 seconds, allow your breath and emerald Light to permeate the entire limbic system. Visualize your emerald green healing breath awakening your pituitary, pineal and your third eye. See them all with your mind's eye vibrating with energy and the brilliant emerald Light.

As you exhale your breath through your amygdalae, that sit on either side of your third eye, see the emerald green Light transform into a golden glistening Light. Remember to use your diaphragm by contracting it towards your spine in order to concentrate the energy as you exhale.

As you breathe, you will begin to feel sensations in the area of your Third Eye, like a vibration, whirling, humming or tickling. Don't be surprised if you hear the popping or muffled clicking sound as you activate your anterior amygdalae, frontal lobe and your Glia Brain.

The more you breathe, the 'heartier' the sensations become in the third eye area. When your heart and pituitary unite with your pineal you will have achieved the 'Mystical Marriage' of the physical heart and the Heavenly Heart. With the activation of the "Mystical Marriage," your Thousand Petal Lotus can unfold. As it does, it will act as an antenna that is receiving higher resonant frequencies and Wisdom. Equally, your Thousand Petal Lotus can broadcast your radiance and intention.

Eventually, you will achieve Hieros Gamos and come into your bliss. In your Divine Bliss, you will become aware that the chakra known as the 'eighth gate' is open. In this state, your opportunities to access your God given gifts are limitless.

**Continue the Spiral Breath for 10 to 20 minutes
each day or longer, if you choose.**

As your Pituitary, Pineal, Amygdalae, Frontal Lobes and Glia activate, you will connect with the 8th Gate. You will find that as you tap into these higher frequencies on a regular basis, your own Divine Light and Higher Consciousness will elevate. Soon, you will notice that when you think about someone, they will call or when you express a desire and it manifests within days or hours; sweet opportunities grace your path daily and your intuition becomes heightened and is spot on. With daily practice, your life opens up to an elevated joy of receiving and sharing.

I like to start my day with the Spiral Breath and end the day with it. If I find myself getting off center throughout the day, I stop for a moment and do the Spiral Breath to recenter. I have noticed that I can come into balance very quickly the moment I shift my focus off the chaos and into my Spiraled Breath. With conscious focus and redirection, my life runs smooth, my experiences are amazing and life is joyful bliss.

Chapter 13:

Spiral Breath
(expanded version suggestions)

The Spiral Breath is a powerful technique on its own. It reconnects the heart and the mind, so that the mind is operating through the heart, instead of void of it. In this section, I have included a couple modalities that I have incorporated with the Spiral Breath to enhance my experience. Try them when you are ready. I believe you will enjoy adding them to your Spiral Breath session.

✧ ✧ ✧

ADDING THE ROOT LOCK

When you feel comfortable with the breath flow of the Spiral Breath and you have synchronized your heart and mind, add the lower chakras to your Spiral Breath.

As you inhale, see your breath and the tail of the emerald green Spiral flow through your heart and down into your Solar Plexus. On your exhale, squeeze your perineum and sphincter muscle, like you are stopping the flow when you urinate and the evacuation of your bowel. This locks the energy flow within the spinal canal, hence the name root lock. Remember to "squeeze, two, three," as you contract the muscles around your first, second and third chakras in a quick succession.

Send the energy quickly up through your spinal canal and prana tube and out through your crown chakra. Take several breaths into your Solar Plexus chakra, repeating the process with each breath.

When you feel open and energized in this chakra, take your breath and the emerald green Light down into your second chakra, which sits approximately two inches below your navel. As you inhale, see your breath and the tail of the emerald green Spiral flow from your heart down into your second chakra.

On your exhale, squeeze your perineum and sphincter muscle and "squeeze, two, three." Send the energy quickly up through your spinal canal and prana tube and out through your crown chakra. Take several breaths into your second chakra, repeating the process until you feel open and energized in this chakra.

After several breaths, continue moving your emerald green breath flow down into your first chakra, which is the area at the end of your tailbone and your sleeping Kundalini. As you inhale, see your breath and the tail of the emerald green Spiral flow from your heart down into your first chakra.

With your exhale, squeeze your perineum and sphincter muscle and "squeeze, two, three" as you send the energy quickly up through your spinal canal and prana tube and out through your crown chakra. Take several breaths into this chakra, repeating the process until you feel open and energized in the first chakra.

Continue breathing and running the emerald green Light and Vital Life Force into your heart and down to your first chakra and squeeze, two, three, as you send your charged Vital Life Force energy up through your heart chakra, throat chakra, third eye/sixth chakra and out through your seventh chakra and top of your head with a fairly quick succession. Take care not to hyperventilate in the process. This breath is a faster paced breath than the original Spiral Breath, but not as fast as a panting dog.

When you are ready and feel like your prana tube and spinal canal are charged with Vital Life Force energy, you can visualize your healing breath and the emerald green Light connecting down to the core of the Earth. Taking the energy into the earth grounds you, yet it allows you to soar into the higher realms at the same time. Bring your charged breath back up through the chakras of your body and your spinal canal. Continue to direct your charged breath out through the top of your head to connect with the eighth gate chakra and beyond. Continue the upward and downward flow of your charged breath.

Enjoy the Bliss!

EMOTIONAL BALANCE AND HARMONY

Here is a wonderful application for bringing Harmony to your emotional body. I have used this for years and it works exceptionally well with the Spiral Breath. These two modalities go hand in hand beautifully.

Create an intention to program your energy. Say it silently to yourself and also out loud. This cues your subconscious mind to work with your conscious mind in order to bring the intention into fruition.

Begin the Spiral Breath technique as you charge the pure essential oils and place them on the designated areas.

Place 4 - 6 drops of Valor™ into your left hand. Dip your fingertips of your right hand into the oil. Gently make three clockwise circles with your fingertips to energize the essential oil and tune it to your intention and personal frequency. Apply Valor to the sole of your left foot. Repeat process using the right hand and apply to the right foot. Place right hand to right foot and left hand to left foot and hold until you feel a strong pulse in the palm of each hand. Cup your hands together and inhale the frequency of the scent.

Remember, if you are working on someone who is face up, cross your arms in front of you to ensure that the right hand is on the right foot and left hand is on the left foot.

Place 4 - 6 drops of Harmony™ into your hand and charge the oil with your fingertips in three clockwise circles. Apply to the area of your belly button and gently massage into your abdomen. Remember that all your nerves, veins and blood vessels begin and end at your naval. Cup your hands together and inhale the frequency of the scent.

Place 4 - 6 drops of Joy™ into your hand and charge the oil with your fingertips in three clockwise circles. Apply to the area of your heart. Cup your hands together and inhale the frequency of the scent.

Place 4 - 6 drops of White Angelica™ into your hand and charge the oil with your fingertips in three clockwise circles. Apply to the area of your throat, back of neck, shoulders and crown chakra. Cup your hands together and inhale the frequency of the scent.

Continue the Spiral Breath for 10 to 20 minutes or as long as you require to energetically shift into a Peaceful and Harmonious state of being.

SPINNING YOUR MERKABA

13.1 Merkaba Body Illustration by Gayle Mack

A Merkaba (also spelled Merkabah, Merkavah and Mer-Ka-Ba) is an aspect of our Spiritual Light Body in a fluid, rotating light. The Ancient Egyptians defined **Mer** as two interconnecting, counter-rotating fields of light spinning within itself, **Ka** as spirit and our individual spirit and **Ba** as body or physical reality.[897]

A Merkaba is our soul-body vehicle of Light that was Divinely designed to give us the ability to travel through the Higher Universal Realms with Perfect Freedom. It allows one level of intelligence to directly connect with a series of other higher resonating intelligences.

A Merkaba is a *self* generated, multidimensional living energy field of Light that transports you through space, time (past, present, future, parallel realities) and dimensions like a vehicle. It is also known as a Vehicle of Ascension and a Chariot of Light.[898, 899]

A Merkaba is a combination of electromagnetic energy, Tachyon Energy and the same higher dimensional Light energy that is found within the stars and the universe. Because our DNA is also made up of these substances, we have the ability to activate and personally generate this Energy Field within and around us. When we are consciously in this multidimensional living field of Light, our radiant Light energy can be measured 20 – 60 feet out from your physical body.[900]

It is suggested that when we became locked into the third dimension, we changed the pattern of how we breathed in Vital Life Force or Universal Prana. Our original breathing pattern reflected the directional patterns of the electromagnetic energy fields that surround our body and forms an interlocking tetrahedron or Merkaba.[901]

The sacred texts describe the Merkaba as having multiple layered heavens. Whereby, there are Seven Heavens protected by angels and encircled by flames and lightning. The Highest Heaven is said to contain seven palaces or temples. Here within the innermost temple dwells a supreme divine image of God's Glory seated on a throne.

The Seven Heavens represent the seven chakras; with the seventh chakra's innermost temple being the pineal, also known as the Seat of the Soul. When you activate your pineal and third eye through your heart chakra, you awaken the 'nous' that connects you to your Divine Image of God's Glory.

Your Merkaba becomes a doorway to greater experiences of higher consciousness. The African Zulu tribes define a Merkaba as a space/time/dimension vehicle. Once you master this divine technique, you can activate your Merkaba at your desire. It is powered through your own Divine Consciousness.

The Bible mentions the Merkaba 44 times in the Old Testament. One of my favorites is Ezekiel 1:19 – 21. *"And when the living beings went, the wheels went by them: and when the living beings were lifted up from the earth, the wheels were lifted up. 1:20 Whithersoever the spirit was to go, they went, thither was their spirit to go; and the wheels were lifted up over against them: for the spirit of the living beings was in the wheels. 1:21 When those went, these went; and when those stood, these stood; and when those were lifted up from the earth, the wheels were lifted up over against them: for the spirit of the living beings was in the wheels."*

Not only is the Merkaba mentioned in the Bible, but also in many esoteric and mystic texts, such as Pistis Sophia, the Dead Sea Scrolls, the Talmud, Torah, Kabala, Books of Enoch and Gnostic texts. It is recognized in many cultures worldwide.

In the Pistis Sophia IV:134, it says this about the Merkaba, *"After visiting Paradise, Enoch had the privilege of returning to earth to bring back these records before being taken up to walk with God. In his privilege of walking with God, Enoch was also shown how his body permanently was able to be transformed cell-by-cell: Through the Merkabah, his body's cellular array could make a complete transformation as he changed his energy frequency from physical to spiritual garments of Glory, showing the power to pass through the zero-point fields. He preserved his image codes to go, literally, into the heavenly worlds."*

The original books of Enoch were of Light encodings that recorded the codes that established this creation; the scientific principles of how the creation operated. *"... for Christ in the narration tells us Enoch wrote the Books of Yeu, while Christ was discoursing with him from the tree of Knowledge (Gnosis) and from the Tree of Life."*[902]

When we clear the negative influences from our lower vibrational emotions, such as survival, fear, anger and hate, we begin to move our cellular structure into the higher vibrational emotions of Joy, Harmony and Unconditional Love. As our cells vibrate with the higher resonance, we find ourselves resonating with the higher dimensional realms, such the fifth, sixth, seventh and eighth dimensions. Within the seventh and eighth dimensions, we begin to experience our Light bodies. Within the ninth dimension, we go beyond the gates of space and time into the more subtle forms of matter and energy.[903]

A Merkaba appears in a multitude of forms.[904] A Merkaba could be an envelope of Light, an Orb, a toroidal vortex energy field that resembles a space craft or a star tetrahedron. The star tetrahedron, which is a sacred geometry shape, is what I saw when the Spiral Breath presented itself to me. It is two tetrahedrons overlapping each other with one pointing up and one pointing down. The beautiful addition to the spinning Merkaba was that several counter-rotating Merkaba's appeared as I cleared and raised my resonance.

The Great Pyramid is a tetrahedron. It is a four sided pyramid or triangle with three sides coming together at an apex and one side as a base. Actually, if you will notice, each side of the Great Pyramid inverts ever so slightly at the exact center point. It is more noticeable from above than standing before it.

Remember the Star of David? It is a Merkaba. The dot in the center signifies that it is three dimensional, but it also represents you in the center of your Merkaba and toroidal field.

Jesus and Mary Magdalene taught the Disciples, Priestess and Priesthood to spin a Merkaba from their heart center. You can manifest your Merkaba when you can hold the resonance of Unconditional Love in your heart and use it to activate your pineal, third eye and glia brain.[905] It is the Divine Unconditional Love that we hold within our hearts that transforms our Merkaba into a living field of Light.[906]

It was with this Merkaba resonance that the Mary's and their families were able to sail their boat (vessel) without oars or paddles. They raised their Merkaba and glided along the natural electromagnetic grids and Ley lines of the Earth.

The Spiral Breath technique is an excellent way to activate your pineal, third eye, frontal lobes and glia brain, while envisioning your personal Merkaba. When the Spiral Breath was presented to me, the emerald green spiral was spiraling within a Merkaba that was spinning in a multi-directional toroidal pattern, with smaller Merkaba's spinning at the points. I drew what I saw through my physical and minds' eye.

EMPOWER YOUR PERSONAL MERKABA

Here are the instructions that I used to empower my personal Merkaba. I received them during a channeled meditation. They will help get you started with the visualizing, creating and charging you own personal Merkaba.

This one takes some focus. Once you are comfortable with the Spiral Breath it is easy to incorporate.

Breathe - Visualize - Manifest and Enjoy!

Get into a comfortable position. As you spiral your breath, set your intention that your breath is continually spiraling from your heart up into your brainstem and crown chakra; around to your third eye, then down in through your nostrils, up through the roof of your mouth, into your limbic system and out through your amygdalae.

After a while, this breathing pattern will become second nature and you will not have to focus on visualizing the spiral. It is just continual and present.

When you are comfortable with your spiral breathing, visualize an emerald green Merkaba over your heart chakra. See your heart in the center of it, radiating your Unconditional Love – Divine Love. Visualize or sense your Merkaba as Light.

Visualize the tetrahedron or pyramid that is pointing upward at your heart center rotating in a counterclockwise direction. This is the masculine electric energy that expands and manifests. This pyramid channels Universal Omnipresence down from the higher realms and concentrates it into our third dimensional realm.

Now visualize the downward pointing tetrahedron or pyramid rotating in a clockwise direction. This is the feminine magnetic energy that receives; contracts and sends us back to Divine Source. This pyramid channels the Universal Omnipresence up from matter into the higher realms.

Together, the two counter-rotating pyramids create electromagnetic energy in a unified field. This is the Tachyon Field. This is creation. This is Life!

The rotating pyramids are equal in size and equal in importance. If you view Earth from a satellite, the space above Earth is equal to that below it. Time/Space is all encompassing.

Continue your Spiral Breath while you are spinning your Merkaba. Increase the Love and Joy within your heart. See your Divine Love becoming stronger and more concentrated. When you are 'full' and feel complete, radiate your Divine Love and Joy out from your heart. See in your minds eye that your Divine Love is permeating your body. Visualize that every little cell is absorbing, awakening and vibrating with Divine Love and Joy.

As you increase your level of Divine Love, you raise your vibration, which in turn increases your Light. Remember, Unconditional Love vibrates the color of emerald green, so don't be surprised if you start to see an emerald green glow about you with your eyes closed or open.

Rub your palms together briskly for a few moments, as if you were warming your hands on a chilly day. Now separate your palms with 2 - 3 inches of space between them. Feel the energy between your hands. This is Vital Life Force or Chi. You should feel a slight sensation of electromagnetic energy vibrating between your palms.

Keeping your hands relaxed as if holding a ball, gently push against the edge of the energy plasma. You are looking to feel a slight energetic resistance or 'push back' as you slowly move your hands closer in small increments. The energy between your palms will begin to increase in its' warmth.

If you do not feel anything at first, keep trying. Take care that you are not over thinking it. Get out of your 'head' and into your heart. Let your energy flow.

Move your palms out to the edge of your counter-rotating Merkaba that is over your heart. Feel the edge or circumference of your Merkaba.

When you are ready, enlarge your energy Merkaba without diminishing the level of concentrated Love emanating from your heart and the center of your Merkaba. Expand your Merkaba out to your shoulders.

Imagine the energy flowing from your heart into your energy Merkaba. You are charging your Merkaba with the Unconditional Love that is radiating out from your heart. If you feel the intensity of the energy lessen as you increase the size of your Merkaba, then hold the dimensions of your Merkaba and build up your concentrated Divine Love.

Continue to expand your Merkaba until you see yourself inside of it. Your head is in the point of the upward facing pyramid and your feet are in the point of the downward facing pyramid. Your arms are now out stretched with palms up. Feel the energy coming into your palms. Allow yourself to feel the shift of energy, as you turn one palm down, while keeping the other palm side up. Then both palms facing down. Return to palms facing up.

Maintain the counter-rotating spin of your pyramid tetrahedrons. You are now within a field of constant motion.

Keeping the rotational spin balanced in both directions, visualize the counter-rotating spin of your Merkaba increasing in it's speed until it is moving faster than you can see. Tachyon particles move faster that the speed of Light. This is where you begin to shift the energy of 'matter.'

Continue to raise your frequency of Love and Light. Your chakras are aligned and are tightly compacted wheels of energy. These chakra wheels generate a Tachyon spiral that runs through the center of your body, along your spine and raise your Kundalini to ignite your pineal and your Thousand Petal Lotus.

Your physical body may begin to vibrate, feel tingly or numb. You may feel heat rising or you might feel light headed. Everyone experiences differently. Notice what you are experiencing, while holding your main focus on your Merkaba. Continue to hold the energetic level or intensity of your Divine Love frequency within your Merkaba.

You may notice that your personal Merkaba might begin to shift from emerald green to pink to blue to violet and back. This is a normal process as your energy activates and raises the frequency of your pink emanating Feminine Flame and your blue emanating Masculine Flame. The rotating colors will transfigure into a vibrant violet color as the Divine Feminine Flame unites with the Divine Masculine Flame and creates the unified flame of Hieros Gamos - the Sacred Union.

When you are fully aligned, a circular disc of energy will radiate out from the base of your spine. This is where the downward masculine electric energy meets the upward feminine magnetic energy creating a disc of unified energy and a toroidal force - As Above, So Below.

This disc of energy can radiate out 20 – 60 feet from the body. The stronger and more concentrated your Divine Love, the greater the radius of your energy disc.

The pattern that is created by this energy disc within your Merkaba is a mirror image and a microcosm of the Milky Way.

When your electromagnetic spin moves into a thermodynamic frequency (Kelvin), you will have the ability to move through space, time and dimensions with the use of your Light Body Merkaba. This is Zero-Point-Energy.[907]

The energetic pattern of the Merkaba is a natural sacred geometric form that encompasses every living being. In humans, it is always present, but lays dormant until it is activated with the frequency of Divine Love. People who emanate Divine Love and tap into their Divine Higher Consciousness can activate their Merkaba field innately. Even though they may not be aware of it, their Merkaba field of energy can be felt by those around them.

The electromagnetic field of Divine Love is something that you can physically feel and measure. Have you ever been in the presence of someone who is radiating a pure level of unconditional love or witnessed an act of compassion that intensely moved you to joyful tears?

Have you ever looked into the face of a child who is in such a state of joy that it touches your heart? Your heart swells and you can feel the joy radiate through you.

As was previously mentioned, emotional qualities such as love, faith and compassion can be measured in wave frequencies. Emotional qualities are living energy that can be cultivated to benefit or harm.

Using a Random Number Generator in a program called Global Consciousness Project; Princeton University researchers proved that human consciousness (collective consciousness) and emotions can be measured. The project began in 1998 and continues today. Global Consciousness Project had placed 37 REG devices (Random Event Generators) called EGG's (ElectroGaiaGram), which is based on the EEG technology. The premise is to capture and measure human consciousness through brain wave activity by the electrode devices (EGG's) placed around the world. The project currently has approximately 70 EGG's worldwide.

While reviewing data, they noticed a significant spike of electromagnetic energy coming from the earth on September 11th, 2001 ten minutes after the first plane hit the towers in New York. They determined that the minds and hearts of humanity could unite and act coherently, which created the significant, unified spike of energy. This means that a thought or an emotion can impact the entire planet (and ultimately the universe) when the mass consciousness or population comes together in a unified thought.[908]

Think of the power behind collective thought and how we would be positively impacted as a whole, if people worldwide held the frequency of peace and harmony for an extended period of time or better yet, ALL the time.

The Global Consciousness Project has continued to monitor global consciousness and worldwide events with their many expanded technologies, such as, global Brain-Painting and Global Harmony Replication.

On a smaller scale, I was playing a crystal bowl onstage at the 2014 American Society of Dowsers Conference with friends Jeff and Kris Gregory. I was connected to Divine Source and had moved into a state of bliss. I was doing the Spiral Breath as I played the crystal bowl. I sensed that the Divine Love, which had filled my heart, was flowing into the crystal bowl. I began to share the energy with the audience by turning the crystal bowl towards them as it rang out its tone - bathing them in the energy.

I could see the people in the audience sway back in their chairs as they received and integrated the energy. Then I noticed in my awareness that several people had come to stand in the aisles facing the stage. They began walking backwards away from the stage as they were dowsing with pendulums. I realized that my personal Merkaba was activated and they were measuring my energetic aura field. They all came to a stop approximately 40 feet out from the stage. All nodding in agreement with each other that they had the same measurement.

Then one gentleman flashed a very broad smile and gave me a 'thumbs up.' Without speaking a word, the audience felt the energy coming through me -through us and we became a unified field of love that was measurable.

13.2 Orbs in the Unified Field of Love - ASD 2014 (American Society of Dowsers) Gayle Mack (center) with Jeffery & Kris Gregory. Picture by Gary Allen

This picture is from that event. Above my head you can see a rainbow colored Orb with a beautiful geometric pattern within it. When the photo is increased in size, you can see several orbs above me and around Jeff and Kris, as well. Orbs have a tendency to appear in the presence of Unconditional Love. They too, can be considered Merkaba's.

You may also notice, when you are practicing spinning your Merkaba with the Spiral Breath and holding the resonance of Divine Love that nice things begin to happen to you without asking. Blessings just begin to unfold in a Graceful, Joyous way and specific intentions manifest into our lives.

Also, when you hold the frequency of Unconditional Love, whether by doing the Spiral Breath, raising up your Merkaba or implementing any of the modalities that I have mentioned on a regular basis, your circle of friends and acquaintances may shift. Those who do not believe in what you are doing or those that are unable to hold the high frequency that you are emanating will tend to move out of your immediate circle. This allows people who can and want to hold the higher resonance to move *into* your immediate circle.

Remember the definition of alchemy? When you change the energy, you change the manifestation of mass (matter).

When regularly doing the Spiral Breath and activating your Merkaba, do not be surprised if you pop into another dimension or see your body begin to shimmer in mother of pearl colors.

People have felt like they dropped off to sleep or 'blipped out' for a few minutes, only to find they have been sleeping for hours. Others have moved into a higher realm and have had experiences as if they had been gone for hours, to find that they were only gone for a few minutes. If you are on a schedule, you may want to set a soothing alarm clock to gently bring you back into your waking consciousness.

Sometimes when you access a higher realm, you will consciously be aware of where you have been and what you have learned. Other times you will not. When you do not remember, it can be that your conscious mind is not ready for the "Knowing" and it will filter into your waking consciousness when you are.

The more you practice the Spiral Breath and activate your Merkaba, the easier it will be to hold the higher resonance; the stronger your Light will be and the faster you will achieve this wonderful way to access your Light Body and the Perfect Freedom to travel the Higher Realms of the Universe.

Activating your Merkaba takes a conscious commitment in order to achieve this level of enlightenment. Most likely, it will not be achieved in a day, although it has been done. The more you practice, the higher your resonance and Light will become.

Experiment with this technique. Try programming your Merkaba to take you to a sacred site, such as Stonehenge or connect with a spiritual guide, like Archangel Michael. Spin your Merkaba with a friend and see how your experiences compare. The possibilities are endless. Enjoy!

13.3 Merkaba graphic by Steve Valdeck

Just for knowing… with today's technology, powerful auric fields can be tracked by the military through satellites and computers. If you choose, you can practice to cloak your Merkaba or make it invisible. Within the center of a balanced electromagnetic, counter-spinning Merkaba lies the Zero-Point-Energy frequency. The frequency of Zero-Point-Energy is cloaking. Expand your 'inner' frequency to encompass your 'outer' frequency.

Oftentimes, when I raise my resonance to channel, do energy work or activate my Merkaba, helicopters will hover above my location within a few minutes of starting. This is because the energy field that I emit when I connect to Divine Source blows a hole through the monitored manmade electromagnetic grid created by technology, such as, HAARP, ELF, Radio Wave and Cell towers that overlay and blanket the Earth. "They" (the powers that want to be in control) have to come check out the source of the above normal energy.

[897] *The Ancient Secret of the Flower of Life* (Volume 1) by Drunvalo Melchizedek page 5
[898] *The Book of Knowledge: The Keys of Enoch* by J.J. Hurtak pages 339-349
[899] *The Ancient Secret of the Flower of Life* (Volume 2) by Drunvalo Melchizedek page 309
[900] *The Ancient Secret of the Flower of Life* (Volume 1) by Drunvalo Melchizedek page 1-4
[901] *The Ancient Secret of the Flower of Life* (Volume 1) by Drunvalo Melchizedek page 4
[902] *Pisitis Sophia: A Coptic Text with Commentary* by J.J. Hurtak and Desiree Hurtak Volume Four - Book Four: 134 page 760
[903] *Pisitis Sophia: A Coptic Text with Commentary* by J.J. Hurtak and Desiree Hurtak 1:10 pages 78-91
[904] *The Book of Knowledge: The Keys of Enoch* by J.J. Hurtak pages 339-349
[905] *Sisterhood of the Emerald d Fire Handbook* written by Mary Hardy www.templeofsakkara.com
[906] *The Ancient Secret of the Flower of Life* (Volume 1) by Drunvalo Melchizedek page 5
[907] *The Ancient Secret of the Flower of Life* (Volume 2) by Drunvalo Melchizedek pages 361-365
[908] *Coherent Consciousness and Reduced Randomness: Correlations on September 11, 2001*, by Roger Nelson published in the Journal of Scientific Exploration in 2002.

Chapter 14:
There Where is the Nous, Lies the Treasure

There where is the Nous, lies the treasure.
When someone meets you in a moment of vision,
Is it through the Soul [Psyche] that one sees
or is it through the Spirit [Pneuma]?
Jesus replies,
… It is neither through the Soul nor the Spirit,
but the Nous between the two which sees the vision.

"He is calling upon us to be fully human [Anthropos]"
THE GOSPEL OF MARY MAGDALENE [909]

I believe that the 'Nous' activates our Glia Brain and connects our heart and our higher mind. Activating our pineal, amygdala and frontal lobes through Divine Unconditional Love allows us to access the 'Treasure' of the Higher Realms.

The 'Treasure' is consciously waking up to our full potential – waking up our Light Body and living in a state of Blissful Higher Consciousness through Divine Love!

We have the ability, as well as, everything we require to be 'Fully Realized' - 'Fully Integrated' Human Beings - to be Anthropos.

We are created in the image of God - Divine All That Is. We already possess within us 'God given' gifts that are real and achievable! We have been conditioned to believe that these gifts are outside of us, unobtainable and are things that they make movies about.

Truth is, we are wired for Faith, multidimensionality and Ascension! It is in our DNA and the very essence of our soul. When we begin to utilize teachings and techniques that can raise our frequency and resonance, we find results. With results, regardless of size, results generate belief. With Belief comes Faith and Faith generates Belief. And yes, there are pure essential oil blends to help us 'Believe™' and energetically support us as we journey back into Faith.

It was Faith that led me to ask God for a 'way' to heal my head and brain injury. *"Like an arrow to its mark…, you will be given!"* In expectation of my Faith, I received the Spiral Breath technique. In Faith, I utilized this 'gift' and each time I did the Spiral Breath, I came closer to *my* mark - which was "being better than I was before the injury." It was Faith and Expectation of its deliverance that allowed me to Believe.

I AM *"Surrounded by my Answer."* I AM *"Enveloped by what I desired" and my Gladness be full."*

From my 'Fullness,' I share, so that others may find the *"Joy of goals Met"* and *"continue (or begin) their story to perfection in Unity."*

It is time that we, both as individuals and as conscious humanity, return to Anthropos!

In the Pistis Sophia V:141, Jesus said to his disciples,

"…Remember that even before I was crucified I said to you: I will give you the keys of the kingdom of Heaven. Now again I am saying to you: I will give them to you." And as Jesus said this, he intoned a song of praise to the Great Name. The regions of the ways of the midst concealed themselves and Jesus and his disciples were sustained upon an air of exceedingly strong Light."

We have the "Keys!" We have the "Keys to Ascension!"

We have been Graced with the teachings that we require in order to achieve this 'Light state of Being.' Wisdom has been preserved and passed on to us through the words and actions of Jesus, Mary Magdalene and The Mary's, as well as, Ancient Sages from many cultures. ALL the Wisdom that the 'Wise Ones of the Ages' share with those who search and those who listen came through Divine ALL That Is!

> *"For those who have ears, let them hear."*
> THE GOSPEL OF MARY

> *"and it Shall be given you; Seek and ye shall find; knock and it Shall be opened unto you. For every one that Asketh Receiveth and he that Seeketh Findeth and to him that knocketh it Shall be opened."*
>
> *"… when you Search for me with All your heart."*
> MATHEW 7:7-8, LUKE 11:9 AND JEREMIAH 29:13

Consciously or unconsciously, We chose to be present at this time in history. We are blessed beyond words to witness and experience firsthand the magnitude of the higher frequencies of Light and celestial cosmic alignments at this time!

Yes, humanity seems trying at times, but it is up to us, as individuals and as community, to create Peace within ourselves in order to share it with others. Having tools, Knowledge and Wisdom to assist us through this transition of remembering our divinity and self-empowerment is a blessing!

We have the knowledge of the glia brain, the frontal lobes; the pineal, the limbic system and the Thousand Petal Lotus, along with the wisdom of energy and alchemy. We have tools and techniques, like the gift of the Spiral Breath, to help activate the parts of our 'being' that can facilitate our desired Return to Light.

The Spiral Breath can be viewed as a form of Alchemy. It has the ability to quickly and easily, change the energy of blocked or stagnant emotions. Out of a painful, unfortunate incident that altered my life as I had known it, the Grace of the Spiral Breath became my blessing. May the Spiral Breath bless you as it has me!

We can enhance the Spiral Breath process with the use of pure essential oils, brain wave entrainment, color, sound and frequency modalities, as well as, utilizing the power of Forgiveness, Grace, Compassion and Divine Love. All of these support our Return to Light!

Having achieved my Light Body multiple times and having experienced the Realm of Unperishable Stars, I can honestly and whole heartedly say that it is worth it!

The levels of Joy, Love and Inner Peace that I have experienced are so blissful that I have dedicated my life to helping others experience these energies and vibrational realms. If every being experienced this level of Divine Bliss, there would be no room for hate, fear or war.

My divine purpose is to share the techniques that helped me return to health, along with the wisdom that raised me to higher levels of Unconditional Love and Divine Light.

When I stray from walking this path of Wisdom and the Principles of Truth, life gets complicated and chaotic. It really is so much easier and much more fun to stay in the daily practice of Grace, Love and Wisdom.

I have shared a lot of information in this book and on many topics. As you can see, from breath to sound, to light, color, vibration, resonance and frequency, they all are interconnected and part of the Whole. We are woven together with Vital Life Force energy that spans from the core of the Earth through the cosmos, from the unmanifested into the manifested.

The ALL is woven together to create a magnificent tapestry of Light – a cloak of God's Glory! It is *our* cloak! It is *our Light!*

The time that you put into your journey of achieving your 'Fully Realized state of Being' will greatly be rewarded! The techniques and information shared in this book are simple and achievable. They will help you activate your Glia Brain, Pineal, Amygdala and Frontal Lobes in order to achieve Higher Consciousness and move you closer to the *'Treasury of Light.'*

The more Divine Love you hold in your heart, the higher you can raise your vibration. Higher vibration and resonance increases the production of glia cells in your frontal lobes and activates the anterior lobes of your amygdala, which in turn, increases activity to produce new neural pathways to enhance and support more positive thoughts, actions and reactions. The increase of positive bio-chemical memory and neurotransmitters will result in more Joy in your life, which brings more to be Grateful for!

The only thing that gets in your way is you and the lack of tools and/or discipline. You have been presented with the Spiral Breath technique and several additional modalities to assist you. Now it's up to you to hold your Divine Light. Heal what requires healing and forgive what requires forgiving. Give yourself permission to be the very best you can be. Take action and hold yourself accountable.

Remember the definition of alchemy? When you change the energy, you change the energy of mass. When you change your energy, you change the energy of your life! It begins with you. Be an alchemist!

When you place your Attention on the Aspect of BECOMING the best you can be, you will find along your Journey, that you moved into the Aspect of BEING. When you reflect on the Aspect of Becoming and the Aspect of Being, you will also come to the Realization that they are ONE in the SAME.[910]

---

[909] *The Gospel of Mary Magdalene* translated by Jean-Yves Leloup page 9
[910] *The Kybalion: A Study of The Hermetic Philosophy of Ancient Egypt and Greece* by Three Initiates page 52-53

Link to Spiral Breath Visual Meditation
https://youtu.be/346Ocj40aGA
Link to Spiral Breath Visual Meditation Tutorial:
https://youtu.be/ruS-a7gq3M8

Summary:

1. Begin each morning giving Thanks and having Gratitude for being 'Graced' with another day to share and receive Love and Light.
2. Activate your glia brain, pineal and frontal lobes with the Spiral Breath and hold the frequency of Divine Love within your heart.
3. Set the course of your day to unfold your blessings before you step out of bed. Allow your first step into your new day to be centered in Love and Divine Joy!
4. If you mis-step; then re-step. Re-center yourself with the Spiral Breath, as often as you require until holding the vibration of Divine Love BECOMES your 'normal' way of BEING.
5. Practice Forgiveness and Compassion and exercise your Courage.
6. Remember to take time throughout your day to acknowledge the Blessings that have unfolded, great and small.
7. Use the Spiral Breath to help clear any negatively charged issues or emotions before you slumber. Allow your Inner Peace and Joy to radiate through your heart and be 'Full' before you drift to sleep.
8. Repeat numbers 1 through 8.

✡ ✡ ✡

As Jean-Yves Leloup put it so appropriately in his commentary in *The Gospel of Mary Magdalene*:

"We are this Anthropos – both "Already" and "Not yet" – just as the acorn is both already and not yet the oak tree in all its' splendor."

Walk forth! With every step, with every breath, with every thought, action and reaction - 'Be' a Fully Integrated;

Fully Realized Human!

Be the Immaculate Mirror of God's Energy!

Many Blessings!

GRAS List:

Here is the link for the FDA approved list of essential oils 'Generally Recognized As Safe' (GRAS). The Essential oils referenced in this list are those that are oleoresins (**solvent-free**) and **natural extractives** (including distillates). These SOLVENT-FREE and NATURAL EXTRACTIVES are generally recognized as safe for their intended use, consumption in historical and commonly used amounts within the meaning of section 409 of the Act. Keep in mind that VERY FEW companies follow these pure guidelines. Do your homework before consumption or applying topically!

A company that you can TRUST is Young Living Essential Oils.
(See reference page)

- https://www.fda.gov/food/ingredientspackaginglabeling/gras/
- http://www.accessdata.fda.gov/scripts/cdrh/cfdocs/cfcfr/CFRSearch.cfm?fr=182.20

Glossary:

Alchemy: 1) an ancient pre-chemistry practice that transforms, creates and/or combines matter from one form into another 2) the ability to transform base metals into gold and into essential minerals known as the Universal Elixir of Life. 3) the ability to transform old thought patterns and emotions into positive, constructive and beneficial patterns.

Alchemist: one who practices the art of alchemy.

Amplitude: 1) refers to the length, height and width of a wave, such as ocean, sound, radio waves or light waves, as they move or vibrate. 2) the measured angular distance of a star from the true east or west point of the horizon, at the moment of rising or setting.

Amygdala: is an almond shaped gland in the limbic system found inside of the brain approximately one inch from each temple. The amygdala gland has two parts: the anterior lobe and the posterior lobe. The anterior amygdala is where positive and pleasurable emotions reside. The posterior lobe is where negative and not-so-pleasurable emotions reside, such as, fear, anxiety, anger, rage, depression, etc. Activating the anterior lobe of your amygdala stimulates the frontal lobe of your brain and elevates our mood. Amygdalae is the plural form, although the singular form amygdala is acceptable as both.

Anthropos: Holding the frequency of Unconditional Love of Christ Consciousness to the degree that your frequency and cellular structures become Divine superluminal Light and fully accessing the multidimensional realms before physical form.

Ascension: 1) the act of transforming the physical body into the higher vibrational and multidimensional realms 2) the act of moving into a higher or more powerful position.

Astrocytes: One of four major types of glial cells. Astrocytes are found only in the central nervous system and not in the peripheral nervous system. Astrocytes are involved in multiple functions in disease and normal brain function.

Canonical Gospels: there are more than fifty gospels written in antiquity, but only four were canonized. They are Matthew, Mark, Luke and John. Irenaeus of Lyons, c. 185 declared in his "Against the Heresies" 3, 11, 8-9 that these four gospels would be the "Pillars of the Church" and no others. His reasoning was based on Eziekiel 1 or Revelation 4:6-10, which references to the four corners of the Earth, the four winds and of God's throne borne by four creatures with four faces… (the face of a man, a lion, an ox and an eagle).[9][12]

Canonical hours: The Apostles celebrated the Divine seven times a day in prayer at the third, sixth and ninth hours, as well as, midday and midnight. That would be 6 am, 9 am, Noon, 3 pm, 6 pm, 9 pm and Midnight. They are also referred to as the Book of Hours and the Liturgy of Hours.

CERN: French Conseil Européen pour la Recherche Nucléaire or European Nuclear Research. It uses the world's largest and most powerful particle generator called a Large Hadron Collider

Chakra: a Sanskrit word which means "spinning wheel of energy." Each chakra is a wheel of energy or vortex made of subtle electromagnetic energy that is connected to our central nervous system. Vital life force energy comes up from the Earth into the soles of our feet and moves up our legs. At the base of the spine, the two paths of energy come together and cross, forming an alternating standing columnar wave current of energy that moves up the spine and out through the top of the head.

Channeling: the ability to tap into and communicate wisdom, information, energy and light from a higher vibrational and divine source. There are several forms of channeling, as in: Trance (mentally unconscious of the message shared), Conscious (being aware of the shared message), Relay (hearing with your inner voice and then repeating it), Visionary (seeing the message, event and/or the messenger), Dream State (receiving message during your dreams), Hands On or Distance Healing (channeling Divine energy through your body to share with another being), Automatic Writing (receives message through handwriting), Inspiration and Praying.

Chi (Qi): means 'breath' or 'air.' Figuratively, Qi (Chi) is the Universal Life Force that animates all form and sets the world into motion.

Clairaudience: the ability to hear something outside the normal range of perception, as in spiritual guidance or wisdom.

Clairsentience: clair means "clear" suffix sentience means "feeling." One who perceives or processes the ability to know, see or feel past, present or future of personal information and events from the energy of an object that is invisible or out of site; by touching or having knowledge about an object; having a sixth sense. Clairsentience can sense spirits/guardians/guides, sense auras and loved ones who are no longer living.

Clairvoyance: meaning clear vision; the ability to gain information from an object, location, person or physical.

Dowsing: the practice of obtaining information beyond the physical senses using various mechanisms, such as a pendulum for yes/no answers, "L" rods or a forked branch used to find water for wells, Ley Lines, minerals, etc.

Dowser: one who practices the art of dowsing.

Elements: Elements are simple substances that cannot be broken down by chemical means into any other substance. Each atom of an element contains a specific number of protons designated by its atomic number. There are 92 natural elements, 22 synthetic elements created in laboratories and 4 theoretical ones yet to be made or discovered.[913]

ELF: (Extremely Low Frequency) ELF (pronounced as individual letters) is a high tech weapon that uses extremely low radio frequencies which mimics natural brain waves. There are two main types of ELF bombardment: implanted chips through vaccinations and GPS instrumentation, as well as, RMN (remote neural monitoring) for general broadcasting. These frequencies in excess, can lower immune systems cause brain fog, depression and nervous disorders, loss of memory, stress, inability to cope, manic behavior, dehydration, heart attacks, headaches, migraines and render the public dossal. When used in conjunction with HAARP (extremely high frequencies) manipulate weather patterns can happen.

EMP: Electro Magnetic Pulse is an intense burst of electromagnetic (EM) energy caused by an abrupt, rapid acceleration of charged particles, usually electrons; often used as weaponry. An EMP can contain energy components from very-low-frequencies radio (VLF) to Ultraviolet wavelengths (UV). Short bursts of charged particles are sometimes called a transient electromagnetic disturbance.

Enlightened Consciousness: achieving a fully awakened consciousness of perfect knowledge, wisdom and infinite compassion that intuits, senses insights and/or wisdom enabling one to live a more harmonious life.

Enlightenment: achieving a state of a higher vibrational and fully awakened consciousness.

Entrainment: a synchronization of two or more rhythmic cycles. When two or more interacting oscillating vibrations lock into phase and assume the same rate so that they can vibrate in harmony.

Esoteric: hidden wisdom or inner wisdom of a spiritual nature, originally taught in the ancient mystery schools and temples.

Essene: The word Essene was derived from the Aramaic and Greek words asayya and essenoi, respectively, which mean healer, physician, alchemist or one on the path of the 'Way'.

Excitoxins: are a class of chemicals (usually amino acids) that overstimulate neuron receptors. Neuron receptors allow brain cells to communicate with each other. Excitotoxins fire impulses at extremely rapid rates that the neurons become exhausted and die. The most effected areas of the brain are the hypothalamus and temporal lobes, which regulate behavior, emotions, on-set of puberty, sleep cycles and immunity. Chemical excitotoxins also excite taste buds and are used as "flavor enhancers" in processed and packaged foods.[914]

Excototoxicity: is the pathological process by which nerve cells are damaged or killed by excessive stimulation by neurotransmitters, such as glutamate and aspartate, as well as substances, such as, MSG, aspartame (NutraSweet), hydrolyzed protein and "flavor enhancers"

Extrasensory Perception: ESP, also called 'sixth sense' is the ability to receive or sense information through the mind and the frontal lobe, such as precognition or retro-cognition. ESP encompasses clairaudience, clairsentience, clairvoyance, telepathy and 'knowing.'

Fellowship of Isis: Rediscovering the Love and Compassion of the Goddess: is a peaceful society that honors the good in all faiths and the Divine Feminine in all of Her forms. The priesthood of the F.O.I. is one of peace, tolerance and respect of all spiritual expression. F.O.I. has over 26,000 members worldwide from all cultures, races and religions. http://www.fellowshipofisis.com

Fibonacci Spiral: an approximation of the Golden Spiral created by drawing circular arcs connecting the opposite corners of squares in the Fibonacci tilling. A tilling with squares whose side lengths are successive Fibonacci sequence numbers.[915]

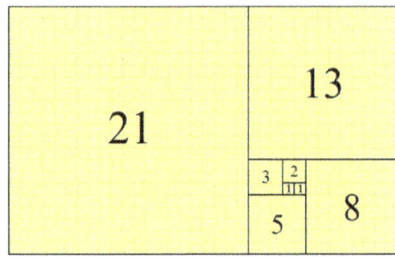

Glossary 1 By 克勞棣 - Ow n work, CC BY-SA 4.0, https://commons.wikimedia.org/w/index.php?curid=38708516

Fibonacci Sequence: 1, 1, 2, 3, 5, 8, 13, 21… Each number is the sum of the two preceding numbers. This sequence is found throughout nature including seashells, fruit, vegetables, plants,

Firewalk: a ceremony of walking barefoot through fire, over a bed of hot embers or hot stones. It is often used as a Rite of Passage, an initiation; as a test of one's individual strength, courage, faith and for healing. It has been practiced in cultures across the earth, from Greece to China to Native American Indians. It dates back to the Iron Age in India – c.1200 BCE

Gematria: was originally an Assyro-Babylonian system of numerology that was adopted by the Jewish and Greek cultures, which assigns a numerical value to the 22 letters of the Hebrew and Greek alphabets.

Glands: are organs or specialized groups of cells that separate certain elements from the blood and secrete them in a form the body can use or eliminate easily.

Glia Brain: is the white matter of our brain that addresses the subconscious, energetic, spiritual and emotional realms. It is the largest organ in the body and it operates from the heart. The glia brain and glia cells orchestrate *all* the cellular components of the nervous system through a massive communication network that organize, synchronize, manage and direct all forms of information, including glial, hormonal, immunological, vascular and neuronal.

Glia Cells: Glia is short for "neuroglia." Glial are nervous system cells that are not neurons or part of connective tissue or vascular cells. There are four main categories: Oligodendrocytes, Microglia, Astrocytes, and Schwann cells. The myelinating glia cells wrap the nerves, brain and organs in a seamless protective coating.

Gnosis: the Greek for 'knowing' as in, the spiritual and esoteric knowledge of mystical enlightenment or insights

Gridkeepers: those who work with the ley lines and natural electromagnetic energy grids that encompass the Earth to maintain balance.

HAARP: (High Frequency Active Auroral Research Program) is a United States military defense program for upper ionosphere and solar-terrestial research. HAARP technology is a massive high powered, high frequency phased array radio wave transmitter (IRI) that utilizes and heats the ionosphere with its focused beam capability, making it a directed-energy weapon. It can create nuclear scale explosions, modify weather patterns, with the capability to create tidal waves, tsunamis, earthquakes, tornados and hurricanes. The electromagnetic waves reflect back to Earth and penetrate every form of matter. The electromagnetic and radio waves alter the normal Schuman waves, as well as brain waves. It is proving extremely harmful to the ionosphere, atmospheric ozone, the physical human body/organs/immune system and all living life forms. The technology is also used to communicate with submarines and link satellites. HAARP technology incorporates ultra-high frequency (UHF) incoherent scatter radar (ISR), extremely low frequencies (ELF) and very low frequencies (VLF) receivers, magnetometers; optical, infrared and Light Detection and Ranging (LIDAR) spectrometers, field aligned ionospheric VHF reflectors, cameras and more.

Hermetic: of or relating to the ancient tradition encompassing mystical, alchemical, astrological, astronomy and theosophical writings or teachings, attributed to Hermes Trismegistus, in the first three centuries AD.

Hertz: (symbol Hz) is the unit of frequency measurement in the International System of Units (SI units) and is defined as one cycle or rotation of spin per second. 1 Hertz rotates one complete cycle. It is named after Heinrich Rudolf Hertz who proved the existence of electromagnetic waves.

Hierophants (hierodulai): Greek for 'Sacred' High Priestess/Priest who is initiated and trained to in the sacred mysteries and esoteric principles.

Hieros Gamos: Greek word means "Sacred Marriage." It is the absolute union of the Sacred Masculine and the Sacred Feminine co-existing as One.

Homeostasis: the state of or ability of the body, a living organism or cell to seek and maintain a condition of equilibrium or stability within its internal environment when dealing with external changes in the conditions around it.

Innervate: pronounced "inNERVate," with emphasis on the "nerve." To **innervate** is "to stimulate," "to supply with energy" or to "put the nerves into" something. When nerves go into muscle fiber, they **innervate** the muscle fiber.

Ionosphere: is the electrically charged air cavity that surrounds the Earth's upper atmosphere. It ranges between 40 to 600 miles above the Earth's surface.

In Phase: in electronic signaling, phase is a definition of the position of a point in time on a waveform cycle. Two waves of the same frequency are in phase if they cross the x axis at the same point in the same direction. See graphic 9.5 page 232.

Knights Templar: were originally, an order of priests skillfully trained to protect the lineage, teachings and followers of Jesus and Mary Magdalene. In 1118, the Poor Knights of Christ and the Temple of Solomon were founded. Priests and men of noble birth were members. The Knights Templar provided safe passage to travelers and their innovative ideas formed the first banking system. They quickly became the wealthiest and most powerful military orders. They were also known for their architectural skills and the building of magnificent Notre Dame Cathedrals, castles and strongholds. The Roman Catholic Church officially endorsed them around 1129. However, King Phillip IV of France, who was deeply in debt to the Order, pressured Pope Clement V to disband the Order in 1312. The cruel punishment for being a member forced them to become a secret Order. The Order of the Knights Templar still exists today, though their foundational mission has been altered with the times.

Kundalini: is the feminine form of the Sanskrit term meaning 'circular' or 'coiled.' Kundalini is used to refer to the primal, vital force of Feminine energy that is coiled at the base of the spine and the first or Root Chakra. Sometimes called the 'sleeping goddess.' When awakened, the Kundalini energy rises up through the six chakras, spiraling up the spine to open and activate the seventh Crown Chakra for access to Higher Consciousness.

Light Body: 1) the light that radiates out from our body, often referred to as our 'aura' 2) raising the frequency of our physical cells to match the frequency and speed of Light.

Lightworkers: those dedicated to achieving Ascension for Earth and humanity by assisting the process of raising the frequency through Christ Consciousness into our Divine Ineffable Light.

Limbic System: is located in the center of the brain. The main sections consist of the amygdalas, cingulate gyrus, fornix, pineal, pituitary, hippocampus, hypothalamus, thalamus, olfactory bulbs and limbic cortex. It is often referred to as our 'emotional brain.'

Megahertz: (symbol MHz) is the unit of frequency measurement in the International System of Units (SI). Hertz is defined as one cycle or rotation of spin per second. 1 Hertz rotates one complete cycle. One Megahertz (MHz) rotates one million cycles per second.

Merkaba (also spelled Merkabah): is a combination of electromagnetic energy, Tachyon Energy and the same higher dimensional Light energy that is found within the stars and the universe. It is an aspect of our Spiritual Light body in a fluid, rotating light. The Ancient Egyptians defined Mer as two counter-rotating fields of light spinning within itself, Ka as spirit and Ba as body. A Merkaba is a *self* generated, multidimensional, living field of Light energy that transports you through space, time (past, present, future, parallel realities) and dimensions like a vehicle. It is also known as a Vehicle of Ascension and a Chariot of Light.[916]

Messiah: literally means 'anointed one;" given to Jesus, a king or High Priestess/Priest anointed through sacred ceremonial tradition with 'holy oil.'

Messianic: Most often, but not always, referring to a member of the Abraham culture/religions or the descendents of the Davidic line through King David and King Solomon.

Metatron's Cube: is a sacred geometry figure comprised of 13 equal circles. Six circles of equal size surround a center circle with six more equal circles spaced at the points. Lines are drawn from the center of the first circle to the centers of each of the other 12 circles. This configuration contains every shape that exists in the universe. These sacred geometric shapes are also the building blocks of all physical matter and are known as the Platonic Solids.

Microglia: One of four major types of glia cells. Microglia are the smallest glial cells in the central nervous system. Their primary function is to protect the immune system of the brain and the central nervous system from infection and disease.

Nag Hammadi Scripture: is a collection of ancient Gnostic texts discovered in 1945 near the Upper Egyptian town of Nag Hammadi. Twelve leather bound papyrus codices, written in the Coptic language, containing fifty two mostly Gnostic Treatises were found in a sealed jar by a local farmer. The writings also included three works belonging to the Corpus Hermeticum and a partial translation of Plato's Republic. The Gospel of Thomas is the only complete text and the best known of the Nag Hammadi Scriptures. It is believed that the texts were buried in 367 AD by the priests of the nearby Pachomian monastery after Saint Athanasius condemned the use of non-canonical scriptures

Nazarene: 1) a title that was given to Jesus 2) a messianic title 3) a title given to messianic followers of Jesus

Neuroglia: The scientific name for 'glia' cells.

Neurohormones: are chemical messenger molecules that are released by neurons and enter the bloodstream ,whereupon they travel to distant target sites within the body. Neurohormones, such as oxytocin and vasopressin, share characteristics with both neurotransmitters and hormones. Similar to neurotransmitters, neurohormones are released by neurons. Similar to hormones, neurohormones travel in the bloodstream.[917]

Neuromodulators: any of various substances, as certain hormones and amino acids, that influence the function of neurons, but do not act as neurotransmitters.[918]

Neuropeptides: any of various short-chain peptides, as endorphins, that function as neuromodulators in the nervous system and as hormones in the endocrine system.[919]

Neurotransmitters: any of several chemical substances, as epinephrine or acetylcholine, that transmit nerve impulses across a synapse to a postsynaptic element, as another nerve, muscle or gland.[920]

Neuroplasticity: the capacity of the nervous system to develop new neuronal connections, strengthen existing neuronal connections or dissolve unused neuronal connections in the brain.

Nous: The Greek term *nous* (pronounced noose) means higher mind and is revered as the *'finest point of the soul.'* It connects the heart and the limbic system to higher consciousness.

Oligodendrocytes: One of the four major types of glia cells. Oligodendrocytes form the myelin electrical insulation that wraps the axons in the central nervous system. They are present in the brain and central nervous system, but not in the peripheral nervous system.

Ormus: also known as ORMES, are Orbitally Rearranged Monatomic Elements. ORMES are metallic microclusters in a high-spin, non-metallic state that promotes superconductivity, superfluidity, supercurrent frequency within living cells; enhances the energy flow and repairs damaged DNA. Alchemists refer to ORMES/ORMUS as the "noble metals," "food of the gods" and the "white powder of gold" that is referenced in the Old Testament Bible and the Egyptian Book of the Dead.

Oscillate: 1) to move or travel back and forth between two points. 2) to swing backward and forward like a pendulum. 3) a flow of electricity periodically changing intensity from a maximum to a minimum. 4) a periodical change in directional flow.

Out of Phase: Two waves of the same frequency are out of phase if they do not cross the x axis at different times in the same direction. The amount by which the waves are out of phase with each other can be expressed in degrees from 0° to 360°, or in radians from 0 to 2π. If the phase difference is 180 degrees (π radians), then the two waves are said to be in antiphase.

Pistis Sophia: is an ancient Gnostic text written in Greek. The translation means Wisdom (Sophia) in Faith or Faith in Wisdom. It gives the accounts of the separation from the 'Oneness' and the malintentions of the Archons, the Fall of Sophia/Wisdom/Mary Magdalene and the infusion of Christ Consciousness to help Sophia remember her ultimate journey to enlightenment.

Plasma: from Ancient Greek meaning 'moldable substance.' is a form of matter containing an approximately equal number of positive ions and electrons. Plasma has been called the fourth fundamental state of matter, with the other three being solid, liquid and gas.

Prana: Sanskrit term meaning 'Absolute Energy'. Prada is all pervading. It is found in all things having life. It is the Universal Energy or Vital Life Force that sustains all life.

Precognition: foreknowledge of an event through paranormal sensing.

Reticular Activating System: The reticular activating system (RAS) is a network of neurons located in the brain stem that project anteriorly to the hypothalamus to mediate behavior, as well as both posteriorly to the thalamus and directly to the cortex for activation of awake, desynchronized cortical EEG patterns.

Sacred Geometry: is a meta-science that reveals how shape and form are primary underlying principles of manifestation. It is based on the thirteen sacred shapes that are known as Platonic Solids. They are universal shapes that are the building blocks of all creation. The geometric proportions have been studied and incorporated into the design and construction of sacred spaces, such as religious and ceremonial structures, monuments, altars, statues, community parks, fountains and religious art, etc. Each shape has been given a divine symbolic meaning..

Sanskrit: an ancient Indo-European language of India since c. 1200 BC, in which Vedas and Hindu scriptures, religious texts and classical epic poems are written.

Schwann Cells: One of the four major types of glial cells. Schwann cells are the glial cells found in the peripheral nervous system and they are also myelin electrical insulation that wraps the axons forming cells. There are three classifications of Schwann cells: myelinating, nonmyelinating and terminal.

Sophia: the living reality of Divine wisdom – the Feminine Principle of God. "Jesus appears as the Revealer, the Savior who through the Sophia shows the many levels of salvation." Pistis Sophia.

Sphenoid Bone: a compound bone that forms the base of the cranium, behind the eye and below the front part of the brain. It is located in the middle of the skull towards the front, in front of the temporal bone and the basilar part of the occipital bone. The sphenoid bone is one of seven bones that articulate to form the orbit. It has two pairs of broad lateral "wings," along with several other projections and contains two airfilled sinuses. The Sphenoid bone resembles a butterfly with its wings extended. Most of the muscles of mastication are attached to the sphenoid bone. Many foramina and fissures are located in the sphenoid that carry nerves and blood vessels of the head and neck, such as the superior orbital fissure (with ophthalmic nerve), foramen rotundum (with maxillary nerve) and the foramen oval (with mandibular nerve).

Spiral Breath: a breath technique that activates the 'nous' for higher consciousness by connecting the heart, limbic system and frontal lobes.

Star Gate: is an energy vortex that enables nearly instantaneous interdimensional and interplanetary travel across the universe and cosmos. It has been suggested that this is the purpose of CERN.

Subtle Organizing Energy Field (SOEF): The Subtle Organizing Energy Field is the perfectly organized, non-manifested state of subtle vibrational energy that exists before it is manifested or condensed into matter or mass.

Superior Olivary Complex: (SOC or super olive) is a collection of brainstem nuclei that function in multiple aspects of hearing and is an important component of the ascending and descending auditory pathways of the auditory system. The SOC is the first major site of convergence of auditory information from the left and right ears. It is divided into three primary nuclei: Medial Superior Olive (MSO), Lateral Superior Olive and the Medial Nuclei of the trapezoid body. In humans, the SOC is located from the Rostral Medulla to the Mid-Pons and receives projections primarily from the anteroventral cochlear nucleus.

Sushumna Channel: the energy that flows in the core of the spine. Its channel is said to be the pathway to enlightenment, the passageway through which awakened energy rises from the first base chakra to the crown chakra.[921]

Swara Yoga: is a type of yoga that emphasizes the study, control an manipulation of breath as a means to achieve self-realization.

Tachyon: are electromagnetic energy particles that move faster than the speed of light. Tachyon Energy is also called Universal Life Force, Chi, Prana and Aura. Nikola Tesla reduced the auric field down to Tachyon Energy which is faster than the speed of light. This is the field of Light that Jesus refers to as the spiritual "White Light." Tachyon is from the Greek word 'tachytis' meaning swift, velocity. Tachyon particles change direction and refocus creating a spiral motion that uses three combinations of charged pairs: (+ +), (+ - or - +) and (- -). This spiral wave generates three electrical properties: resistance, capacitance and inductance. Tachyon energy is the first energy that comes from Zero-point energy. It is a standing columnar wave and tracks the same energy pattern of our DNA and all living matter.

Telekinesis: the ability to move objects at a distance with the power of the mind or other nonphysical means like 'throwing ones energy.'

Telepathy: from the ancient Greek (tele) meaning "distant" and pathos/patheia meaning "feeling, perception, experience," is the extrasensory transmission of information from one person to another without using sensory or physical interaction; communicating through thought.

Tetragrammaton: from Greek to tetragrammaton - 'word' of four letters. Tetra meaning four and gramma – letter or something written. In the original Hebrew, the proper or sacred name of God was transliterated in four letters to YHWH (sometimes written in the older style as YHVH) as Yahweh or JHVH as Jehovah. The four letters of the Tetragrammaton form the root meaning "to be" and some have understood the original meaning to be "He-Who-IS" or He-Who-Brings." The ancients believed that God's name was too sacred to speak aloud. There are 153 Tetragrammaton found in the Book of Genesis.

Tetrahedron: Geometry. A solid shape contained by four plane faces; a triangular pyramid.

Therapeutae: a priestess/priest trained in the Hermetic, esoteric, alchemical, astro-logical, and healing arts from the ancient temples, such as Alexandria, Ephesus and Sakkara temples.

Toroid: a spherical or toroidal object made up of electromagnetic waves that hold themselves together gravitationally, with the waves' gravitational binding produced by their energy.[922]

Torus: in physics, it is known as the "perfect" shape. It is a circular shape of the Flower of Life pattern that funnels a continuous flow of energy up and down through it; re-entering itself, while rotating around its central axis. This form creates energy vortexes, resulting in two connecting portals called a "white hole" and a "black hole." The white hole pushes energy out and the black hole brings it back in. There are three standard types of a Torus (Tori), depending upon the speed of rotation of the torus. They are a ring torus, horn torus and a spindle torus.

Transcend: to rise above or go beyond the range or limits, to triumph over the negative or restrictive aspects of thought, actions; to overcome; exceed

Transcendence: The existence or experience beyond the normal or physical laws or limitations, as in.

Transfigure: To transform into something more beautiful or elevated.

Vagus Nerve: also known as the pneumogastric nerve, is the tenth cranial nerve (CN X). It interfaces with the parasympathetic control of the heart, lungs, and digestive tract. In the human body, the vagus nerve is the longest nerve of the autonomic nervous system. the ending part of the vagus nerve is known as the spinal accessory nucleus.

Visionary: one who is able to relate or see visions in a dream or trance state or as a supernatural apparition; one who is thinking about, has original ideas about or is planning what the future will or could be.

Wisdom: Proverbs 8:22-23, "The Eternal Yahweh himself produced me [Wisdom] from the beginning before any other works… From time infinite I was installed, from the start, from times earlier than the earth." See also Sophia.

---

[912] https://opusdei.org/en-us/article/what-are-the-canonical-and-the-apocryphal-gospels-how-many-are-there/
[913] *The Chemistry of Essential Oils Made Simple* by David Stewart Ph.D, D.N.M. page 88
[914] https://experiencelife.com/article/excitotoxins/
[915] By 克勞棟 - Own work, CC BY-SA 4.0, https://commons.wikimedia.org/w/index.php?curid=38708516
[916] *The Book of Knowledge: The Keys of Enoch* by J.J. Hurtak pages 339-349
[917] https://www.physiologyweb.com/glossary/n/neurohormone.html
[918] https://www.dictionary.com/browse/neuromodulator
[919] https://www.dictionary.com/browse/neuropeptide?s=t
[920] https://www.dictionary.com/browse/neurotransmitter?s=t
[921] https://yogainternational.com/article/view/energy-rising-a-beginners-guide-to-sushumna
[922] John Wheeler, *Relativity and Quantum Information* by Charles W. Misner, Kip S. Thorne, and Wojciech H. Zurek, April 2009 Physics Today pages 40 - 46, American Institute of Physics, S-0031-9228-0904-030-7 https://www.its.caltech.edu/~kip/PubScans/VI-50.pdf

Gayle Mack's resources:

For Pure Essential Oils and the Essential Oil Blends:
Young Living Essential Oils - Independent Distributor # 23012
https://www.myyl.com/gaylemack

Referenced in the Schumann Resonance section - technology partnered with NASA, **Independent BEMER Distributor**, gaylemack.bemergroup.com

For DVD's, Articles, Sessions, Conferences, Public Engagements:
The Spiral Breath Technique Tutorial and Meditation DVD can be found on www.KeysToAscension.com and Amazon

Additional Video Featured in:

- *The Temple of Sakkara: Holding the Frequency of the Heart* with Mary Hardy featuring Gayle Mack
  (Note: contains another version of the Spiral Breath Technique)

- *Healing the Planet with Pyramid Energy, Crop Circles and Orbs* with Mary Hardy featuring Gayle Mack and Patty Greer

- Mary Hardy YouTube
  https://www.youtube.com/channel/UCSdfmSDOf5m4IuUhe0ed53Q/videos

Additional Resources:

- **Mary Hardy: Books, DVD's**
  The Temple of Sakkara / Sisterhood of the Emerald Fire / Brotherhood of the Emerald Fire
  www.templeofsakkara.com

- **David Young Music is featured on the Spiral Breath DVD**
  http://www.davidyoungmusic.com/

- **DeSpark - Vital Mineral formula**
  www.divinequantum.com

- **Zervana Holograms (7th Dimensional Labyrinth) and EMF (ElectroMagnetic Field) Protectors**
  www.sovereign-alliance.com

- *The Hindu-Yogi Science of Breath* by Yogi Ramacharaka
  https://holybooks-lichtenbergpress.netdna-ssl.com/wp-content/uploads/The-Science-of-Breath.pdf

- *The Complete Master Cleanse: A Step-by-Step Guide to Maximizing the Benefits of the Lemonade Diet* by Tom Woloshyn - VitaLight Color Therapy
  http://vitagem.com/products/the-master-cleanse/

- Liposomal Lecithin
  http://www.livingherbalfarmacy.com/

- The Lost Sea Caverns > Wild Cave Tour
  140 Lost Sea Rd.
  Sweetwater, Tennessee 37874
  (423) 337-6616
  http://thelostsea.com/wild-cave-tour/

- The Fellowship of Isis: Rediscovering the Love and Compassion of the Goddess:
  http://www.fellowshipofisis.com

- The Academy of BioEnergetics Zenia Richler DBE, NMD, FAAIM,
  http://academyofbioenergetics.com

- American Society of Dowsers (ASD)
  https://dowsers.org/

- United States Psychotronics Association
  http://www.psychotronics.org

- Enigma Tours - Tobi and Gerda Dobler
  www.enigmatours.com
  Tours of Rennes le Château, Cathar and Knights Templar Fortresses and Sacred Sites.

About the Author:

GAYLE MACK, NMD, DBE, Rev

I grew up on a farm in Ohio. My maternal grandparents were both from strong Hungarian gypsy lineage. Their parents and grandparents were hands-on and herbal healers.

I was graced that my grandparents informally schooled me in the wisdom of nature and the elements. They taught me through their words and actions to be respectful of nature and to honor all that God had created.

My grandparents taught me to be aware and to listen to the wind, the water; the plants and to animals. We would sit on the bank of the running creek on their farm and they would ask me, "Can you hear the water sprites? What are they saying?" "Was that a dragonfly or a fairy?"

We would stand before a tree or sit at its' roots and listen as the tree spoke its' wisdom. We could tell when the wind shifted and when it was going to rain. Sometimes, messages came on the wind. We knew when a neighbor needed help or when trouble of some kind was coming.

My grandparents also taught me to ask permission before picking a plants' bounty. I learned to ask permission before touching a butterfly or petting a bird or animal. Equally as important was to say *"thank you"* when I was done.

I had a way of communicating with animals. Deer and rabbits would come out of the woods and sit with me. I had a pet pig that would meet me at the bus stop, but that's another story. Humming birds would rest in my hand and I would pet them. On occasion, I would carry them around in my pocket.

If an animal, bird or person was injured I was innately guided to place my right hand over them or the injured area and send them energy so they would heal. My hands seem to have a mind of their own.

As I learned to pay attention to nature, I learned to *listen*.

As I practiced listening, I realized that I could hear a person or animals thoughts. Wisdom, warnings, knowing and simple understanding came through in non-verbal communication.

I became so open that I would hear people's thoughts. This became a problem as it could get overwhelming and very loud. At times, I would comment on what I heard but wasn't spoken. I had to learn to buffer. I asked God to just let me hear what I was intended to hear for the greatest good. And it was so.

As a child, I would pray to Mother/Father God. It was a natural assumption on my part. To me, it just made sense (though the nuns in catechism didn't think so).

As far back as I can remember, I saw Jesus and the Mary's. They would show themselves to me when I prayed, when I was to give someone a healing or a message; they would guide me through rough times and watch over me when I was pushing the envelope or being fearless. I thought it was funny, at my young age, that the three ladies who appeared with Jesus were all named 'Mary' like my grandmother. Mary Magdalene, Mary Jacobi and Mary Salome. Each Mary had a different energy about them. I knew which one was interacting with me by the way their energy 'felt.' Although they each had different energy, they all (including my grandmother) had the same amazing energy of Unconditional Love.

In the beginning, the Mary's and Jesus were just present – smiling and watchful over me. When they smiled, their eyes would say so much without even speaking a word.

Then they began to converse with me. I would ask a question and the appropriate one would answer. At times they would give me guidance and other times they would ask the questions and I would answer.

When my mother remarried and the abuse from my stepfather started, it was Jesus and the Mary's who gave me strength, advised me on how to handle situations and showed me who to trust.

Listening to Jesus and the Mary's was as natural for me as listening to my mother or grandparents. When they began giving me messages to share with others, without hesitation, I shared them. Wisdom, way beyond my years of age, flowed from my lips.

Throughout my life, I have shared Divine messages, witnessed amazing healings and had phenomenal experiences. I have had some experiences that one would see in a Spielberg or sci-fi movie.

Of all my experiences, I have only had a few that were scary. These experiences, however, enabled me to draw on my Divinely Given and life acquired wisdom, as well as, reflect the strength of my faith and personal courage. Most of the time, my experiences are extraordinary! And through it all, I learned to trust Divine explicitly. I know without doubt that God would not have me experience things or send me on quests and ask me to shift energy without a purpose or guidance, grace and protection. I learned to Listen and Trust!

In 1987, I went to a Goddess circle. As I sat in sacred space, I could feel my ancestors gathering behind me. I could see them behind me as I looked forward into the circle. I knew the woman that I saw directly behind me was my grandfather's grandmother. To her right and slightly behind was her daughter, (my grandfather's mother) and to her left were my grandmother's parents.

My ancestors continued to come forth and gather for my awakening. I only saw them in my minds' eye as I looked forward into the Sacred Space. When I looked behind me, I just saw the wall that I was sitting against. My friend Melissa kept asking "What are you looking at?"

It was a strange feeling, yet comforting at the same time. I had the sense that I was "home." That night I was initiated into the Sacred Mysteries. I was so moved from this experience that I joined the Fellowship of Isis and began apprenticing under a very wise and kind Priestess Hierophant named Marsharee.

The next day after the Goddess Circle, I describe the people that I saw in my mind's eye to my grandparents. Excitedly, my grandfather said, "You just described my grandmother and mother. Grandma confirmed that I described her parents. I later picked them out in pictures.

In 1989, I was ordained a Priestess and then Priestess Hierophant by Lady Olivia Robertson and her brother, Lord Durdin Strathloch, founders of the Fellowship of Isis in Ireland. This ordination set my dedication to bring forth the knowing of the Divine Feminine and it became my way of being.

In 1993, while participating in ceremony at the Temple of Isis in Egypt, I became my Light Body. I achieved this 'state of being' twice on that trip. The first time during ceremony at the main alter in the Temple of Isis on Philae and the second time while lying in the sarcophagus in the King's Chamber of the Great Pyramid.

Since then, I have become Light multiple times during various spiritual events and channelings. During a Melchizedek Initiation at the Conclave of Michael in Banff, Canada I became a column of light.

I have experienced multidimensionality and it has been witnessed by many people. Having accessed my Light Body numerous times, I became fully aware that there was much more to life than just existing in it.

It is truly difficult to put into words how amazing it feels when you are in your Light Body, because there really are no words that I have found to describe it. Amazing, wonderful and phenomenal are minuscule words in comparison. It is one of those glorious things that you just have to experience to know.

And if I can do it, anyone who wishes can.

My journey through life has taken me in several directions. I am a Master Cosmetologist, a Naturopath, a Minister, a Channeler and a Healer.

The journey to return to the "Me that I was before my head injury" brought me an unexpected Blessing - the Blessing of the Spiral Breath. This experience challenged and reinforced my Faith in myself and Divine Mother/Father God. It is from this foundation of Faith that I share my story, my journey and my Blessings.

As a child, I was taught that I am not special, I AM just open. Everything that I do, you can do when you open your heart and your mind and step fully into Divine Unconditional Love.

Jesus said, "Timeless truth, I tell you: 'whoever believes in me, those works which I have done you will also do, and you will do greater works than these, because I am going to the presence of my Father."

JOHN 14:12

Simply said,
"With endless truth,
All these things I do,
you can do and more."

Let's do more!

Index:

153: 96, 97
5G: 70, 71, 218, 273
5G RF-EMF (Radio Frequency-Electromagnetic Field): 71
5-MeO-DMT (Akashon): 58, 60-62

A

Absolute Zero Point: 251-252
Accessory Nerve (CN XI): 84
AC (Alternate Current): 66
Adenohypophysis (Anterior Pituitary Lobe): 54
Adrenocorticotropic Hormone (ACTH): 50, 54
Adrenal Gland: 50
Adrenaline: 50, 61, 242
Adrenocortex: 54
Akashic Records: 64, 65
Alchemy: 65, 256, 261, 306, 311, 313, 319
Alchemist: 33, 89, 214, 313
Alpha Brain Wave: 128, 228, 231-247
Alternating Current (AC): 66, 275
Amplitude: 214, 231, 242, 271-272, 319
Amygdala: 1, 4-9, 12-15, 37-42, 45, 47, 79, 88, 89, 93, 124, 164, 277, 280, 290-291, 300, 309, 312-313, 319
Anodea Judith: 182
Antenna: 42, 70, 121, 123, 127, 174, 290
Anthropos: 309, 316, 319
Aromatherapy: 43
Aromatic Benzene Rings: 266, 267
Ascension: ix, 310, 319
Astral Travel/Projection: 60, 64, 243, 285
Astrocytes: 43, 115, 118, 119, 120, 121, 125, 231, 319
ATP (Adenosine Triphosphate): 69
Auditory Cortex: 39
Aura: 12, 174, 200, 287, 305
Australian Blue Cypress™: 277
Autonomic Nervous System (ANS): 50, 84
Awaken™: 77
Axons: 43
Ayahuasca: 62

B

Barbara Ann Brennan: 174-177
Believe™: 310
Benzene Rings (see Aromatic Benzene Rings):
Beta Brain Wave: 228, 231-247
Binaural Beats: 15, 68, 76, 245
Bio-Acoustic: 218
Bio-chemical Memory: 26-28, 31-33, 43, 47, 51, 143, 144
Bioplasma: 252
Blavatsky, Master M. H.: 56
Blood Brain Barrier (BBB): 52, 59, 77, 117, 271
Brain Power™: 74
Brain Sand: 58
Brain Wave: 52, 59, 61, 76, 128, 228, 231-247
Brainstem: 1, 2, 4, 11, 12, 14, 36, 40, 49, 83 - 89, 91, 93, 286-289, 300
Bruce Tainio: 273-274

C

Calcite Crystals: 65, 66, 67, 68, 71, 73
Calcify (Calcification): 58, 73
Calcium Waves: 115, 121, 231
Canonical Gospels: 320
Canonical Hours: 320
Capacitor: 127
Cassia™: 76
Cedarwood™: 76, 280
Cellular Memory: 9
Central Nervous System (CNS): 7, 42, 44, 59, 86, 87, 114, 117, 118, 173, 180, 185
Cerebral Cortex: 45, 48, 61, 114, 122, 231
Cerebellum: 1, 11, 36, 87, 93
Cerebrospinal Fluid: 65, 79, 81, 184-187
CERN (Conseil European pour la Recherche Nucleaire or European Organization of Nuclear Research): 71, 273, 320
Chakras: 9, 55, 83, 130, 135, 173-205, 210, 293, 300, 302, 320
Channeling:
Chi (see Qi also): 32, 301, 320
Chocolate: 59
CHOSN Ones: 266
Christ Light: 77, 78

CICIL: 38
Cingulate Gyrus: 37, 93
Circadian Rhythm: 51, 69, 228
Clairaudience: 285, 320
Claircognazence: 285
Clairempathy: 285
Clairgustance: 285
Clairsalience: 285
Clarity™: 77
Clairsentience: 285, 320
Clairtangency: 285
Clairvoyance: 285, 320
Claustrum: 129
Coccyx /Tailbone: 185, 186
Coherence: 123
Color Therapy: 211
Compassion: 88, 130, 135, 146, 165-166, 315
Conscious: 36, 136, 142, 238
Contralateral Axonal Projections: 115
Corpus Callosum: 58, 93, 96, 115
Cortisol: 50, 61, 242
Corticotrophin Releasing Hormone (CRH): 50
Cosmic Consciousness: 40
Cosmic Gateway: 174
Courage: 146, 149-153, 315
Cranial Nerves: 84, 183
Crown Chakra (see Seventh Chakra): 8, 11, 12, 14, 78, 89, 94, 176, 182, 183, 195, 265, 286-289, 293-294, 300
Crown of Thorns: 129
Cypress™: 77, 280
Crystals: 15, 65, 66, 68, 76, 196, 200, 219

D

Darek Faidyka: 44
David Stewart, Ph. D., D.N.M.: 267, 279
DHEA: 242
Discernment: 165, 168, 265
Delta Brain Wave: 51, 59, 61, 228, 231-247
DeSpark: 74, 333
Dinshah P. Ghadiali: 211-213
Direct Current (DC): 275
Discernment: 168, 265
Divine Accordance: 156, 166, 168
Divine All That Is: 1, 309
Divine I AM: xi, 150

Divine Love: 312-315
Divine Light: 12, 80
Divine Mother: ix, 88, 169, 277, 289
Divine Wisdom: 81
DMT (N-dimethyltryptamine): 58, 60, 61, 62, 64, 67, 181, 242, 243
DNA (deoxyribonucleic Acid): 27, 40, 66-69, 75, 79, 88, 100, 122, 125-129, 131, 200, 217, 218, 222, 265-271, 275, 278, 280, 281, 297
Dopamine: 45
Dorado Azul™: 278
Dowsing: 196-200, 321
Dynamo Jack/John Chang: 37

E

Earth Gateway: 173
Earth Star: 173
ECG (Electrocardiogram): 123, 124
EEG (Electroencephalograph): 46, 52, 65, 124, 231, 304
EGG (ElectroGaia Gram): 304
Eighth Gate: 14, 78, 96, 291
Einstein, Albert: 125, 126, 178, 267
Electromagnetic: 66, 67, 68, 69, 70, 71, 95, 122,123, 173, 175, 214, 228, 254, 271-275, 297, 303-304
Elements: 214, 321
ELF (Extremely Low Frequency): 69, 71, 273, 321
EMF (ElectroMagnetic Field): 67, 68, 72, 122, 127, 228
EMP (ElectroMagnetic Pulse): 71, 72, 321
EMR (ElectroMagnetic Radiation): 127
Endocrine Disrupters (EDC's) 75
Endocrine Gland: 55
Endocrine System: 49, 53
Entrainment: 227, 321
Envision™: 77, 167
Essential Oils: 9, 29, 31, 42, 43, 166, 167, 188, 199, 200, 240, 265-282, 295-296, 333
Esoteric: 63, 64, 83, 89, 91, 321
Essene: 63, 281, 321
Eye of Horus: 93, 94
Extrasensory Perception: 20, 64, 121, 182, 322

F

Faith: 3, 4, 130, 154, 162, 309
Fibonacci Spiral: 1, 11, 99, 217, 286, 290, 322

Fifth Chakra (Throat Chakra): 176, 193

Fight or Flight: 35, 50, 51, 238
Firewalk: 152, 153, 323
First Chakra: 173, 176, 179, 189, 294
Fluoride: 72, 73
Flower of Life: 97, 98, 99, 100
Forgiveness: 88, 130, 146, 154-157, 312, 315
Forgiveness™: 29, 43, 88, 130, 154, 165, 166, 278
Fornix:, 37
Fourth Chakra (see Heart Chakra): 176, 192, 294
Fractal(s): 100, 125, 126
Frankincense: 77
Frequency: 9, 12, 75, 97, 135, 141, 209, 214, 217, 218, 219, 228, 231, 271-272
Frequency Following Response (FFR): 228, 246
Frequencies:176, 214, 217, 228, 255
Frontal Cortex: 120, 122
Frontal Lobe: xi, 11, 15, 58, 15, 20, 33, 38-41, 47, 51, 52, 56, 61, 65, 76, 79, 87, 90-93, 125, 129, 164, 227, 271, 280, 285, 286, 289-291, 299, 309, 311-313
FSH (Follicle-Stimulating Hormone): 54, 55
Fully Realized Human Being: xi, 125, 309, 316

G

Gamma Brain Wave :15, 231-247
Ganglia: 143
Gematria: 219-221, 323
GM/GMO (Genetically Modified Organism): 73, 74
GHIH (Growth Hormone-Inhibiting Hormone): 55
GHRH (Growth Hormone Releasing Hormone): 51
GigaHertz: 70, 72
Glia Brain: ix, x, xi, 5, 6, 7, 9, 15, 23, 33, 37, 39, 43, 47, 52, 65, 87, 90, 113-118, 122, 124, 125, 131, 135, 222, 227, 237, 271, 277, 280, 285, 290-291, 299, 309, 311-312, 323
Glia Cells: ix, 40, 43, 114-118, 121, 124, 125, 127, 129, 271, 277, 323
Global Consciousness Project: 303-304
Glucocorticoids: 50
Glutamate: 115, 119
Gnosis: 63, 129, 130, 182, 323
GnRH (Gonadotropic-releasing Hormone): 54

Golden Means: 217
Golden Ratio: 217
Gospels of Mary Magdalene: x, xi,139, 149, 150, 165, 169, 253, 311
Grace: 2, 6, 8, 88, 113, 143, 146, 149, 150, 152, 160, 165, 169, 170, 188, 265, 271, 285, 289, 311, 312, 315
GRAS (Generally Regarded As Safe): 271, 276, 317
Gratitude: 29, 88, 157-167, 262, 265, 278, 315
Gratitude™: 167, 265, 313
Gregorian Chants: 222
Grey Matter: 114, 119, 122, 128
Gustatory: 43

H

HAARP (High Frequency Active Auroral Research Program): 71, 273, 323
Harmony: 113, 121, 147, 166, 263, 298
Harmony™: 167, 265, 295
Heart Chakra: 11, 13,176, 192, 265, 294
Hermes Trimegistus: 165, 214, 215, 253, 272
Hermetic Law: 89, 231, 256-263, 272, 324
Hertz (Hz): 69, 75, 80, 210-214, 223-224, 231-233, 271-272, 324
Heterodyning: 69
hGH (human Growth Hormone): 54, 55, 242
Hieros Gamos: 77, 290-291, 302, 324
Higher Consciousness: ix, 17, 35, 40, 56, 60, 77, 96, 113, 121-222, 258-259, 263, 277, 282, 291, 303, 309, 312
Highest Potential™: 3, 77, 265
Hippocampus: 37, 45-48, 93
Hologram: 128
Homeostasis: 50, 51, 114
Hope: 85
HPA (Hypothalamus-Pituitary-Adrenal gland axis) 50, 55
Hypothalamus: 26, 37, 47-55, 58, 86, 87, 93, 123, 142, 144
HPT (Hypothalamus-Pituitary-Thyroid axis): 55
HU: 80
Hyssop™: 77, 280

I

Ida: 178-182
Idaho Blue Spruce™: 277
Immuno-excitotoxicity: 73

Infrared: 71
In Phase: 232, 324
Inner Peace: 29, 163-167, 312
Inspiration™: 77, 167
Interneurons: 43
Intestines: 59, 85, 173
Intrinsic Cardiac Nervous System (Heart-Brain): 122
Isaac Newton, Sir: 210, 211
Iso-Principle: 227

J

Jesus: 80, 89,126, 164, 253, 277, 281, 299, 310,339
John 16:23-24: 3, 4, 162
Joy: 29, 60, 85, 154, 166, 222, 298, 312, 315
Joy™: 31, 77, 295

K

Kenneth Killick: 254-256
Kidney: 58, 85
KiloHertz: 69
Kinesiology: 76
Krebs Cycle: 69,
Kundalini: 15, 64, 76, 78, 83, 91, 93, 94, 173, 178, 181-189 294, 302, 325

L

Large Irregular Activity (LIA): 46
Large Regular Activity (LRA): 46
Left Hemisphere: 38, 52, 129, 180, 290
Leukocytes: 59
Ley Lines: 67, 299
Light Body: ix, xi, 65, 80, 90, 96, 113, 126, 130, 258, 298, 306, 309, 325
Limbic Cortex: 37
Limbic System: x, xi, 1, 5, 6, 7, 9, 12-15, 20, 23, 26, 28, 33, 35-38, 42, 45, 52, 65, 74, 76, 81, 83, 87-91, 93-95, 113, 124, 131, 135, 142, 184, 187, 222, 227, 285-287, 290, 300, 311, 325
Liver: 54, 59, 69, 85, 178, 271, 274, 280
Long-Term Potentiation (LTP): 27, 45
Love: 136, 312, 315
Lungs: 178
Lutenizing Hormone (LH): 54, 55
Lymphatic System: 266
Lymphocytes: 59

M

Magnify Your Purpose™: 77, 166, 265
Mammary Glands: 54
Mary Magdalene: x, 65, 88, 89, 126, 165, 169, 220, 253, 277, 281, 299, 310
Medulla Oblongata: 86, 87, 93, 123
Megahertz: 69, 70, 72, 272, 325
Meg-MegaHertz: 272
Melanocyte-stimulating Hormone (MSH) 54
Melatonin 58-62, 242
Merkaba 13, 14, 89, 96, 296-307, 325
Metatron's Cube 98, 99
Micro-crystals 65, 67, 71
Micro-clusters 66, 68, 71
Microglia 118, 119, 326
Microwave 70
Midbrain (Mesencephalon) 35, 58, 85, 86, 87
MindWise™:74
Mitral Cells: 43
Monoterpenes: 271
Myelin: 120,121, 124
Myelin Sheath: 114, 115, 118, 119, 120, 124
Myelinated: 48, 125
Myelinating: 115, 119, 125, 271
Myrrh™: 77
Myrtle™: 77
Mystical Marriage: 77, 96, 182, 285, 290

N

Near-Death-Experience (NDE): 242
Nerve Axon Fibers: 114
Nerve Pairs: 182-184
Nervous System: 49
Neural Networks: 27, 33
Neurochemical: 26, 40
Neuroendocrine Hormones: 51
Neuroglia (see also Glia/Glial Cells): 114, 326
Neurohormones: 51, 326
Neurohypophysis (Posterior Pituitary Lobe): 54
Neuromodulators: 50, 326
Neurons: 26, 114-117, 120, 124-129, 269
Neuropeptides: 26, 50, 326
Neurotransmitter: 26, 33, 50, 58, 59, 114, 117, 119, 122, 124, 265, 313, 326

Neuroplasticity: 125, 327
Nikola Tesla: 56, 113, 217, 223, 254, 268, 274
Node of Ranvier: 125
Nonmyelinating: 118, 119
Norepinephrine: 45
Nous: x, 88-90, 309, 327

O

Occiput (Occipital): 2, 5, 11, 12, 13, 52, 237, 286-290
Octave(s): 217
Odor of Sanctity: 277
Oligodendrocytes: 118, 119, 120, 327
Olfactory Bulb: 37, 42, 49, 51, 124, 269
Olfactory Ensheathing Cells (OEC:) 44
Om (Great): 263
OmegaGize: 74
Onycha™: 77
Optic Nerve: 58
Orb: 305, 333
Ormus: 327
Oscillate: 227, 237, 242, 272, 327
Out-of-Body-Experience (O.O.B.E.): 243
Out of Phase: 327
Ovaries: 54, 59
Oxytocin: 51, 54

P

Packets of Possibilities: 279
Pancreas: 85
Parasympathetic Nervous System (PNS): 84, 173, 181, 238
Peace & Calming™: 29, 167
PEAR (Princeton Engineering Anomalies Research): 76
Pendulum: 196-200
Peptides: 50, 52
Peripheral Nerves: 118
Peripheral Nervous System: 114
Perisynaptic (see also Terminal Schwann Cells): 119
Pesher Technique: 327
Phenolic(s): 270-271
Phi: 217
Pi: 80, 222
Piezoelectric: 65, 66, 67, 68

Pineal: 7, 52, 56-83, 88, 93, 96, 216, 228, 277, 286, 290-291, 299, 311-312
Pingala: 178-182
Pinolin: 58, 60
Pituitary: 7, 49, 50, 51, 52, 53, 54, 55, 56, 77, 78, 93, 277, 286, 290-291
Pistis Sophia: 298, 310, 327
Plasma: 301, 327
Pons: 86, 87
Prana: 17, 76, 78, 178, 180, 297, 327
Pranayama: 289
Prana Tube: 180, 293-294
Precognition: 285, 328
Prolactin (PRL): 54
Psilocybin: 62
Psychoacoustic Heartbeat Synchronization: 67
Pythagorean: 95, 96, 218
Pythagorean Scale: 75, 80, 212, 216, 218, 222, 223
Pythagorus: 216

Q

Q Helical Antenna: 70
Quantum Jumping: 64, 243

R

Radar Waves: 70, 71
Radio Waves: 70
Random Number Generator: 303
Realm of Imperishable Stars: 129, 130, 312
Release™: 29
Receiver(s): 42, 67, 87, 114
Receptor Sites: 267
REM (Rapid Eye Movement): 46, 59, 60, 127, 237, 241, 244
Resonance: 12, 218, 219, 256, 280
Reticular Activating Formation: 40, 79, 86, 87, 88
Reticular Activating System (RAS): 87, 328
Retina: 59
RNA (Ribonucleic Acid): , 60, 218
Right Hemisphere: 38, 52, 129, 180
Robert Becker, Dr.: 69
Root Chakra (see also First Chakra: 176, 179, 183, 186, 189, 294
Root Lock (Moola, Bandha): 186-188, 293-294
Rose Essential Oil: 277

Rose of Sharon™: 77

Royal Raymond Rife, Dr.: 274

S

Sacred Geometry: xi, 9, 67, 100, 177, 220, 247, 328

Sacred Sandalwood™: 76

Sacred Space: 200-205

Sacral Chakra (Second Chakra): 190

Sacrum: 185

Saint John: 225

Samadhi: 182

Sandalwood: 75

Sanskrit: 17, 173, 178, 328

SARA™: 29, 43, 278

Scar Tissue: 121

Schumann (Resonance): 128, 333

Schwann Cells: 116, 118, 119, 328

Second Chakra (Sacral Chakra): 176, 183, 186, 190

Seed of Life: 97, 98

September 11: 304

Serotonin: 45, 58, 59, 61, 235, 242

Sesquiterpenes: 270-271

Seventh Chakra (Crown Chakra): 56, 77, 96, 176, 183, 184, 195, 294

SHF (Super High Frequencies): 72

Shungite: 76

Sixth Chakra (Third Eye): 55, 56, 77, 96, 176, 183, 184, 194, 294

Smudge: 201-204

Solar Plexus (Third Chakra): 176, 183, 191, 293

Solfeggio Tones: 15, 68, 75, 76, 135, 138, 218, 222-226, 245

Sophia: 328

Space/Time: 180, 251, 297

Speed of Light: 126, 216, 251-254

Sphenoid Bone: 53, 328

Spinal Canal: 187, 293-294

Spinal Column: 15, 123, 178, 181, 185

Spinal Cord: 44, 83, 87, 115, 120, 122, 143, 186

Spinal Cord Injury (SCI): 59

Spinothalamic Tract: 48, 49, 86

Spiral Breath: nearly every page

Spirit Molecule (see DMT): 61

Spleen: 59, 85

Standard Scale: 212, 216-223

Standing Columnar Wave: 67, 68, 180, 255

Standing Gravitational Wave (SGW): 225

Star Gate: 328

Stellar Gateway: 174

STEM-C : 40

Stem Cells: 121

Stress Away™: 29

Subconscious: 27, 36, 37, 140, 142, 232, 238, 289, 295

Subtle Organizing Energy Field (SOEF): 130, 251-254, 259, 329

Superconsciousness: 126, 182, 190

Superquantum Field: 252

Surrender™: 31

Sushumna: 178-185, 329

Sweat Glands: 71

Sympathetic Nervous System (SNS): 50, 84, 173, 178, 181, 186, 238

Synapse: 26, 27, 31, 33, 43, 117, 124, 143

Synaptic Connection: 115

T

Tachyon (Tachion): 122, 251-254, 257-263, 301-302, 329

Tailbone/Coccyx: 185-186

T.D.A. Lingo: 40, 41, 88

Telekinesis: 285, 329

Telepathy: 60, 285, 329

TeraHertz: 70

Terminal Schwann Cells (see also Perisynaptic cells): 118, 119

Tesla (see also Nikola Tesla): 113, 217, 223, 254, 268, 274

Testes: 54

Tetragrammaton: 221, 329

Tetrahedron: 330

Thalamic Bodies: 58

Thalamus: 45, 48, 49, 50, 81, 86, 87, 123, 231

Therapeutae: 63, 281-282, 330

Theta Brain Wave: 55, 59, 61, 76, 228, 231-247

Third Chakra (Solar Plexus): 186, 191

Third Eye: 1, 4, 5, 8, 11-14, 38, 67, 76-78, 80, 89, 176, 194, 265, 286, 287, 290, 294. 299

Thousand Petal Lotus: 5, 6, 9, 14, 15, 65, 67, 78, 89, 176, 181-184, 187, 195, 290-291, 311

Throat Chakra (see also Fifth Chakra): 183, 193, 294
Thyroid: 54
Thymus: 174
Torus: 100, 177, 330
Toroidal: 13, 100, 126, 174, 177, 214, 286, 299, 303, 330
Transcend: 330
Transformation™: 31, 77, 167
Transducer: 127
Transformer: 66
Transmitter: 66, 87, 114, 127
Traumatic Brain Injury (TBI): 59
Tryptophan: 58
TRH (Thyrotropin-Releasing Hormone): 54
TSH (Thyroid Stimulating Hormone): 54, 55
Transcendence: 39, 40
Transmitter(s): 42, 114
Tree of Life: 99
Treasury of Light: 312
Tube Torus: 177

U

UHF (Ultra High Frequency): 72
Unconditional Love: ix, 6, 65, 88, 130, 135, 169, 247, 298, 299, 300-305
Unconscious: 27, 36, 136, 139, 143,
Unified Field: 301, 305
Universal Code: 56
Universal Energy Field: 174, 197, 199
Universal Gateway: 174
Universal Law (of Harmony): 227
Universal Knowledge 64
Universal Omnipresence, 300
Unmyelinated Axons: 125
Unperishable Stars: 312
Upper Cervicals: 58

V

Vagus Nerve: 84 - 86, 123, 330
Valor™: 29, 295
Vasopressin (ADH Antidiuretic Hormone:) 51, 54
Vehicles of Living Energy: 267, 281
Vertebrae Nerve Pairs: 183
Vesica Piscis: 94-97, 220

Vibration: 5, 66
Visionary: 330

Vital Life (Vital Life Force): 5, 15, 17, 20, 21, 61, 100, 178, 18-183, 186, 187, 222, 273, 294, 297, 301
Vortex: 67, 100, 216, 299

W

Wave-Particles: 217
WiFi: 68, 70
White Angelica™: 295
White Hole:177
White Light: 242, 253
White Matter (see Glia Brain): 114, 115, 119, 122,125, 271, 277
Wisdom: 135, 256, 265, 312, 330

Y

Yin/Yang: 262

Z

Zero Point Energy (ZPE): 251-254, 259-262, 303, 307
Zervana Holograms: 76

www.ingramcontent.com/pod-product-compliance
Lightning Source LLC
Chambersburg PA
CBHW051349290426
44108CB00015B/1939